IET COMPUTING SERIES 32

Network Classification for Traffic Management

IET Book Series on Big Data—Call for Authors

Editor-in-Chief: Professor Albert Y. Zomaya, University of Sydney, Australia

The topic of Big Data has emerged as a revolutionary theme that cuts across many technologies and application domains. This new book series brings together topics within the myriad research activities in many areas that analyze, compute, store, manage, and transport a massive amount of data, such as algorithm design, data mining and search, processor architectures, databases, infrastructure development, service and data discovery, networking and mobile computing, cloud computing, high-performance computing, privacy and security, storage, and visualization.

Topics considered include (but not restricted to) IoT and Internet computing; cloud computing; peer-to-peer computing; autonomic computing; data center computing; multicore and many core computing; parallel, distributed, and high-performance computing; scalable databases; mobile computing and sensor networking; green computing; service computing; networking infrastructures; cyber infrastructures; e-Science; smart cities; analytics and data mining; Big Data applications; and more.

Proposals for coherently integrated international coedited or coauthored handbooks and research monographs will be considered for this book series. Each proposal will be reviewed by the editor-in-chief and some board members, with additional external reviews from independent reviewers. Please email your book proposal for the IET Book Series on Big Data to Professor Albert Y. Zomaya at albert.zomaya@sydney.edu.au or to the IET at author_support@theiet.org.

Other volumes in this series:

Network Classification for Traffic Management

Anomaly detection, feature selection, clustering and classification

Zahir Tari, Adil Fahad, Abdulmohsen Almalawi and Xun Yi

The Institution of Engineering and Technology

Published by The Institution of Engineering and Technology, London, United Kingdom

The Institution of Engineering and Technology is registered as a Charity in England & Wales (no. 211014) and Scotland (no. SC038698).

© The Institution of Engineering and Technology 2020

First published 2020

The Institution of Engineering and Technology
Michael Faraday House
Six Hills Way, Stevenage
Herts, SG1 2AY, United Kingdom

www.theiet.org

British Library Cataloguing in Publication Data
A catalogue record for this product is available from the British Library

ISBN 978-1-78561-921-2 (hardback)
ISBN 978-1-78561-922-9 (PDF)

Typeset in India by MPS Limited
Printed in the UK by CPI Group (UK) Ltd, Croydon

Contents

About the authors

Zahir Tari is a full professor and discipline head of the School of Computer Science, RMIT University, Australia. His expertise is in the areas of system performance (e.g., cloud, IoT) as well as system security (e.g., SCADA, cloud).

Adil Fahad is an assistant professor and head of the department of Computer Information Systems, University of Al Baha, Saudi Arabia. His research interests cover wireless sensor networks, mobile networks, SCADA security, ad-hoc networks, data mining, statistical analysis/modelling and machine learning.

Abdulmohsen Almalawi is an assistant professor in the Department of Computer Science at the University of King Abdulaziz, Saudi Arabia. His research interests are in the areas of machine learning.

Xun Yi is a professor at the School of Computer Science, RMIT University, Australia. His research interests include data privacy, cloud security, privacy-preserving data mining, network security protocols, applied cryptography, e-commerce security and mobile agent security.

Abstract

Traffic classification is the process of identifying various applications and protocols existing in a network, which is crucial to both network management and security. In particular, a well-architected network should ensure the presence of a traffic classification module to prioritize various applications over the limited bandwidth for an effective Quality of Service. It is also important for the network operator to properly understand applications and protocols regarding network traffic in order to appropriately develop and implement an effective security policy.

Over the past decade, as traffic capacity continues to increase rapidly, traffic classification has been regarded with much concern both industrially and academically. In particular, three types of traffic classification methods are used to identify network flows, including *port-based*, *payload-based*, and *flow statistics–based* methods. The port-based method depends on scrutinizing standard ports utilized by popular applications. However, such a method cannot be relied upon all the time as not all present applications utilize standard ports. A few applications even overshadow themselves by using definite ports of distinct applications. The payload-based method basically searches for the applications' signature in the payload of the IP packets. As a result, this method overcomes the problem of dynamic ports and hence is used widely in many industrial products. In spite of its popularity, this payload-based method does not work with encrypted traffic and requires a significant amount of processing and memory. In the recent academic research, the flow statistics–based method classifies traffic by creating additional new features from transport layer statistics (TLS) (e.g., packet length and packet arrival time) without necessitating deep packet inspection, and then applying either supervised or unsupervised machine-learning algorithms on the TLS data to categorize network traffic into predefined categories depending on identified applications.

This book aims to provide the readers with an understanding of new methods that can be used to improving the accuracy, as well as the efficiency of network traffic classification. Four research aspects are being looked at to achieve the main purpose of this book. The first research aspect is to optimize various feature selection methods for improving the quality of the TLS data. The second aspect is intended to identify the optimal and stable feature set in the temporal-domain and the spatial-domain networks. The third one is related to the development of preserving the privacy framework to help network collaborators in the spatial-domain network to publish their traffic data and making them publicly available. The final research aspect is related to automatically provide sufficient labeled traffic flows for constructing a traffic classification model with a good generalization ability and to evaluate the generated traffic classification.

Glossary

A

- *Analytics* refers to the course of depicting conclusions based on the raw data. It helps us sort out meaningful data from data mass.
- *Algorithm* refers to a mathematical formula placed in software that performs an analysis on a set of data.
- *Accuracy* is also used as a statistical measure of how well a binary classification test correctly identifies or excludes a condition. That is, the accuracy is the proportion of true results (both true positives and true negatives) among the total number of cases examined.
- *Artificial intelligence* refers to the process of developing intelligence machines and software that can perceive the environment and take the corresponding action as and when required and even learn from those actions.
- *Anomaly detection* (also known as *outlier detection*) refers to the identification of items, data, instances, events, or observations which raise suspicions by differing significantly from the majority of the data.
- *Anomaly* (or *outlier*) emerges as a result of fraudulent behavior, mechanical fault, or attack.
- *Adjusted Rand index* (ARI) is Rand index that is adjusted for the chance grouping of elements.
- *Anomaly-based intrusion detection system* refers to an IDS that detects both network and computer intrusions and misuse by monitoring system activity and classifying it as either

B

- *Big Data* is an umbrella term used for huge volumes of heterogeneous datasets that cannot be processed by traditional computers or tools due to their varying volume, velocity, and variety (3V).
- *Bayesian network*, Bayes network, belief network, decision network, Bayes(ian) model, or probabilistic directed acyclic graphical model, is a probabilistic.
- *BIRCH* (balanced iterative reducing and clustering using hierarchies) is an unsupervised data mining algorithm used to perform hierarchical clustering.
- *Bernoulli sampling* is a sampling process where each element of the population is subjected to an independent Bernoulli trial.

C

- *Classification accuracy* refers to the "percentage of correct predictions." That is the case regardless of the number of classes.
- *Clustering* refers to a method whereby data points are grouped into different groups (called clusters), so that points within a given cluster are very similar to each other and different from the data points of other clusters.
- *Class label* is usually used in the context of supervised machine learning, and in classification in particular, where one is given a set of examples of the form (attribute values, class label) and the goal is to learn a rule that computes the label from the attribute values.
- *Cluster centroid* is the middle of a cluster.
- *CPU* (central processor unit) is the electronic circuitry within a computer that carries out the instructions of a computer program by performing the basic arithmetic, logic, controlling, and input/output (I/O) operations specified by the instructions.
- *Chi-square* statistic is commonly used for testing relationships between categorical variables. The null hypothesis of the Chi-square test is that no relationship exists on the categorical variables in the population; they are independent.

D

- *Dataset* is a collection of data.
- *Data mining* refers to the process of discovering patterns in large datasets involving methods at the intersection of machine learning, statistics, and database systems.
- *Data stream* is a set of infinite data points that consist of attribute values along with an implicit or explicit timestamp.
- *Dimensionality* refers to how many attributes a dataset has.
- *Data summarization* aims to provide a "good" quality of summary from a (large) dataset in such a way that this is still informative version of the entire dataset.
- *Dimensionality reduction* (or dimension reduction) is the process of reducing the number of random variables.
- *Deep packet inspection* is an advanced method of examining and managing network traffic. It is a form of packet filtering that locates, identifies, classifies, reroutes, or blocks packets with specific data or code payloads that conventional packet filtering, which examines only packet headers, cannot detect.
- *Deep flow inspection* is a packet filtering technique that analyses statistical characteristics like packet lengths, ratio of large packets and small payload standard deviation, and connection behavior of flows, to determine the actions to be applied to application flow or session packets (e.g., classify, mark, redirect, block, and drop).
- *Density-based clustering* locates regions (neighborhoods) of high density that are separated from one another by regions of low density.
- *DBSCAN* is density-based clustering algorithm which groups together points that are closely packed together (points with many nearby neighbors), marking

as outliers points that lie alone in low-density regions (whose nearest neighbors are too far away).

- *DENCLUE* is an algorithm that employs a cluster method based on kernel density estimation. A cluster is defined by a local maximum of the estimated density function.
- *Denial of service* is a cyber-attack in which the perpetrator seeks to make a machine or network resource unavailable.
- *Decision tree* refers to an algorithm that only contains conditional control statements. Decision trees are commonly used in operations research, specifically in decision analysis.

E

- *Expectation maximization* (EM) refers to an algorithm that produces maximum-likelihood (ML) estimates of parameters when there is a many-to-one mapping from an underlying distribution to the distribution governing the observation.
- *Euclidean distance* or Euclidean metric is the "ordinary" straight-line distance between two points in Euclidean space (i.e., a space that encompasses the two-dimensional Euclidean plane, the three-dimensional space of Euclidean geometry, and similar spaces of higher dimension).
- *Ensemble clustering* aims to combine multiple clustering methods to produce a better result than that of the individual clustering algorithms in terms of consistency and quality.

F

- *Filter-based algorithm* refers to an algorithm that relies on the general characteristics of the data to evaluate the quality of the generated candidate features without involving any data mining algorithm.
- *Feature* is a machine-learning expression for a piece of measurable information about something. For example, height, length, and breadth of a solid object. Other terms like property, attribute, or characteristic are also used instead of a feature.
- *Feature reduction* refers to the process of reducing the number of features to work on a computation intensive task without losing much information. Principal component analysis (PCA) is one of the most popular feature reduction techniques.
- *Feature selection* refers to the process of selecting relevant features for explaining the predictive power of a statistical model.
- *False-positive rate* (FPR) is the probability of falsely rejecting the null hypothesis for a particular test.
- *F-measure* is a measure of a test's accuracy.

G

- *Gaussian mixture model based* (GMM) is a category of probabilistic method that states that all generated data points are derived from a mixture of a finite Gaussian distribution that has no known parameters.

- *Grid-based clustering* differs from the conventional clustering algorithms in that it is concerned not with the data points but with the value space that surrounds the data points, creating the grid structure, that is, partitioning the data space into a finite number of cells. It quantizes the object space into a finite number of cells that form a grid structure on which all of the operations for clustering are performed.
- *Graphics processing unit* (GPU) is a programmable logic chip (processor) specialized for display functions. The GPU renders images, animations, and video for the computer screen. GPUs are located on plug-in cards, in a chipset on the motherboard or in the same chip as the CPU.

H

- *High-dimensional data* means that the number of dimensions is staggeringly high—so high that calculations become extremely difficult. With high dimensional data, the number of features can exceed the number of observations.
- *Hierarchical-based clustering* relies using clustering methods to find a hierarchy of clusters, where this hierarchy resembles a tree structure, called a dendrogram.
- *Hidden Markov model* (HMM) is a statistical Markov model in which the system being modeled is assumed to be a Markov process with unobservable (i.e., hidden) states.

I

- *Internet traffic* is the flow of data across the Internet.
- *Intrusion detection system* (IDS) is a device or software application that monitors a network or systems for malicious activity or policy violations.
- *Internet service provider* (ISP) is an organization that provides services for accessing, using, or participating in the Internet.

K

- *K-means* clustering is a type of unsupervised learning, used for segregating unlabeled data (i.e., data without defined categories or groups). The purpose is to find groups in the data, with the number of groups represented by the variable K. The algorithm works iteratively to assign each data point to one of the K groups based on the features that are provided.
- *K-nearest neighbors* (also known as KNN) is a simple algorithm that stores all available cases and classifies new cases based on a similarity measure (e.g., distance functions). KNN has been used in statistical estimation and pattern recognition already at the beginning of 1970s as a nonparametric method.
- *KDD* is a training dataset consists of approximately 4,900,000 single connection vectors each of which contains 41 features and is labeled as either normal or an attack, with exactly one specific attack type.

L

- *Labeled data* is a group of samples that have been tagged with one or more labels.
- *Least square regression error* (LSRE) refers to a statistical procedure to find the best fit for a set of data points by minimizing the sum of the offsets or residuals of points from the plotted curve. Least squares regression is used to predict the behavior of dependent variables.
- *Laplacian score* is a popular feature ranking-based feature selection method both supervised and unsupervised.

M

- *Machine learning (ML)* is the study and practice of designing systems that can learn, adjust, and improve based on the data fed. This typically involves the implementation of predictive and statistical algorithms that can continually zero in on "correct" behavior and insights as more data flows through the system.
- *Maximal Information Compression Index* (MICI) is a measure of the strength of the linear or nonlinear association between two variables X and Y.
- *Markov model* is a stochastic model used to model randomly changing systems.

N

- *Network traffic classification* (TLS) is an automated process which categorizes computer network traffic according to various parameters (e.g., based on port number or protocol) into a number of traffic classes. TLS can be used to identify different applications and protocols that exist in a network.
- *Network traffic data* refers to the data moving across a network at a given point of time. This data is mostly encapsulated in network packets, which provide the load in the network.
- *NP-complete* (NP-hard) refers to a problem that can be solved by a restricted class of brute force search algorithms and it can be used to simulate any other problem with a similar algorithm.
- *Naive Bayes* are a family of simple "probabilistic classifiers" based on applying Bayes' theorem with strong (naive) independence assumptions between the features.
- *Neural network* is a network or circuit of neurons, or in a modern sense, an artificial neural network, composed of artificial neurons or nodes.
- *Network traffic* monitoring can be considered as a knowledge discovery process in which the data of network traffic is analyzed.
- *NetFlow* is a feature that provides the ability to collect IP network traffic as it enters or exits an interface. By analyzing the data provided by NetFlow, a network administrator can determine things such as the source and destination of traffic, class of service, and the causes of congestion.
- *Normalized mutual information* (NMI) is a normalization of the mutual information (MI) score to scale the results between 0 (no mutual information) and 1 (perfect correlation). MI of two random variables is a measure of the mutual dependence between the two variables.

P

- *Peer-to-peer* (P2P) computing or networking is a distributed application architecture that partitions tasks or workloads between peers. Peers are equally privileged, equipotent participants in the application. They are said to form a peer-to-peer network of nodes.
- *Privacy-preserving* aims to make private (and thus protect) personally identifiable information (or data).
- *Principal component analysis* (PCA) is a statistical method that uses an orthogonal transformation to convert a set of observations of possibly correlated variables (entities each of which takes on various numerical values) into a set of values of linearly uncorrelated variables called principal components.
- *Partitioning-based clustering* refers to a division of the set of data objects into nonoverlapping subsets (clusters) such that each data object is in exactly one subset.
- *Pearson correlation coefficient* (PCC) computes the correlation between two random variables, and it determines whether they would have a linear dependency relationship.

Q

- *Quality of service* (QoS) refers to the description or measurement of the overall performance of a service, such as a telephony or computer network or a cloud computing service, particularly the performance seen by the users of the network.

R

- *Random forest* (RF) (also known as random decision forests) is an ensemble learning method for classification, regression, and other tasks that operate by constructing a multitude of decision trees at training time and outputting the class that is the mode of the classes (classification) or mean prediction (regression) of the individual trees.
- *Rand index* (RI) (or Rand measure), which is named after William M. Rand in statistics, and in particular in data clustering, is a measure of the similarity between two data clusters. From a mathematical standpoint, Rand index is related to the *accuracy* but is applicable even when class labels are not used.

S

- *Supervisory control and data acquisition* (SCADA) is a control system architecture that uses computers, networked data communications, and graphical user interfaces for high-level process supervisory management but uses other peripheral devices such as programmable logic controller (PLC) and discrete PID controllers to interface with the process plant or machinery.
- *Supervised feature selection* refers to a method that assesses the significance of a feature by computing the correlation to its class label.
- *Signature-based IDS* refers to an algorithm that discovers suspicious behaviors by comparing them with predefined signatures.

- *Statistical method* refers to a method that observes the activity of the data so as to create profiles representing acceptable behavior.
- *Support vector machines* (SVMs) are supervised learning models with associated learning algorithms that analyze data used for classification and regression analysis.
- *Supervised learning* is the machine learning task of learning a function that maps an input to an output based on example input–output pairs. It infers a function from labeled training data consisting of a set of training examples.
- *Sampling method* refers to the selection of a subset (a statistical sample) of individuals from within a statistical population to estimate characteristics of the whole population. Statisticians attempt for the samples to represent the population in question.
- *Supervised anomaly detection* requires a dataset that has been labeled as "normal" and "abnormal" and involves training a classifier (the key difference to many other statistical classification problems is the inherent unbalanced nature of outlier detection).
- *Semi-supervised anomaly detection* constructs a model representing normal behavior from a given normal training dataset and then tests the likelihood of a test instance to be generated by the learnt model.

T

- *Traffic classification* refers to an automated process which categorizes computer network traffic according to various parameters (e.g., based on port number or protocol) into a number of traffic classes.
- *Traffic flows* refers the study of interactions between travelers (including pedestrians, cyclists, drivers, and their vehicles) and infrastructure (including highways, signage, and traffic control devices), with the aim of understanding and developing an optimal transport network with efficient movement of traffic and minimal traffic congestion problems.
- *TCP/IP* refers to an Internet protocol suite that provides end-to-end data communication specifying how data should be packetized, addressed, transmitted, routed, and received. This functionality is organized into four abstraction layers, which classify all related protocols according to the scope of networking involved.
- *Traffic dispersion graph* (TDG) refers to a graphical representation of the various interactions ("who talks to whom") of a group of nodes. In general, the directed edges in a TDG can be used to identify the initiator of the interaction between a pair of nodes.

U

- *Unsupervised feature selection* refers to a feature selection method that identifies and selects relevant features without needing class label information.
- *Unsupervised machine learning* refers to a type of self-organized Hebbian learning that helps find previously unknown patterns in dataset without preexisting labels. It is also known as self-organization and allows modeling probability densities of given inputs.

- *Unsupervised anomaly detection* refers to a method that detects anomalies in an unlabeled test dataset under the assumption that the majority of the instances in the dataset are normal by looking for instances that seem to fit least to the remainder of the dataset.

W

- Wrapper-based algorithms refer to those algorithms that require the use of specific data-mining algorithms, such as clustering, in the evaluation process of the generated candidate features.

Chapter 1

Introduction

In recent years, knowing what information is passing through the networks is rapidly becoming more and more complex due to the ever-growing list of applications shaping today's Internet traffic. Consequently, traffic monitoring and analysis have become crucial for tasks ranging from intrusion detection, traffic engineering to capacity planning. Network traffic classification is the process of analyzing the nature of the traffic flows on the networks, and it classifies these flows mainly on the basis of protocols (e.g., TCP, UDP, and IMAP) or by different classes of applications (e.g., HTTP, peer-to-peer (P2P), and Games). Network traffic classification has the capability to address fundamentals to numerous network-management activities for Internet Service Providers (ISPs) and their equipment vendors for better quality of service (QoS) treatment. In particular, network operators need an accurate and efficient classification of traffic for effective network planning and design, applications prioritization, traffic shaping/policing, and security control. It is essential that network operators understand the trends in their networks so that they can react quickly to support their business goals. Traffic classification can also be a part of intrusion detection systems (IDS), where the main goal of such systems is to detect a wide range of unusual or anomalous events and to block unwanted traffic.

1.1 Importance of network traffic classification

Accurate traffic classification is essential for addressing QoS issues (including provisioning, Internet pricing, and lawful interception [LI]) and for security monitoring tasks.

QoS issues

One of the major challenges in the development of appropriate and effective QoS is the lack of a proper pricing strategy. An effective pricing strategy is central to the classification of the QoS that customers receive. A pricing strategy is also important because it facilitates generation of resources for the ISPs. Traffic classification has the capacity to sustain a realistic pricing mechanism. In the last few years, several pricing mechanisms have been proposed to create a suitable pricing plan. Generally, a good pricing model should charge consumers for the resources they utilize. This ensures transparency by eliminating opportunities for overcharging customers.

ISPs can develop effective and profitable business models through traffic classification. Most of the recommended Internet pricing methods are effective because they ensure that consumers are charged fairly for the QoS. However, no QoS solution has been implemented extensively to satisfy customers' needs. Consequently, appropriate QoS solutions should be implemented by taking into account technical efficiency, financial efficiency, and social effects. Technical effectiveness refers to the costs associated with using the technology of a given pricing scheme. Economic effectiveness refers to the effects of a pricing model on utilization of a network. Hence, a good pricing model should be implemented consistently and transparently.

The cost of implementing QoS is important and should not exceed the revenue that is likely to be generated from it. Network stability and consistency should also be taken into consideration when implementing the new QoS. In addition, a programmed traffic classification should be incorporated into the QoS-based pricing model. Currently, ISP networks in most countries are required to provide lawful intercept abilities (L1). Traffic categorization is a major solution to this legal requirement. Governments execute LI at different levels of abstraction. In the communications industry, a law enforcement group can appoint an individual to gather intercepted information.

The traffic patterns in an ISP system can be detected through traffic classification. In addition, traffic classification can be used to identify the categories of applications that are being used by a client at a particular time. This information can be retrieved from the network without contravening privacy laws that regulate the use of the Internet. Hence, IP traffic classification is important in the following ways. First, it facilitates the use of a class-based pricing model, which is fair to the customer and ensures sustainability. In this pricing model, ISPs are able to recover the cost of delivering the QoS by charging customers with different needs based on the services that they receive, as suggested in [1,2]. Second, real-time IP traffic classification facilitates the development of automated QoS architectures. This leads to an effective transfer of information concerning QoS needs between Internet-based applications and the network. The resulting improvement in QoS signaling enhances the use of IntServ and DiffServ. Finally, the classification enables ISP providers to comply with the requirement that their networks must provide L1 capabilities.

Intrusion detection systems (IDSs)

Apart from resolving QoS issues for ISPs, the other primary task of network traffic classification is to help network operators to recognize and identify anomalous behavior. In particular, network operators have always been interested in keeping track of the anomalies occurring on their network in order to protect customers from external or internal threats. Over the past 10 years, the number of vulnerabilities and attacks over the Internet, not only potentially targeting individuals' security but also national security, has increased enormously. In particular, the increased connectivity to the Internet and corporate networks by SCADA (Supervisory Control and Data

Acquisition) systems for controlling the national critical infrastructures (e.g., electricity, gas, water, waste, and railway) has expanded the ability of outsiders to breach security.

Examples of threats to SCADA include an attack on a SCADA-run sewage plant in Maroochy Shire, Queensland (Australia), causing 800,000 litres of raw sewage to be released into local parks and rivers, causing the death of local marine life as well as discoloring the water and generating a noxious stench that permeated the atmosphere [3]; and the Davis–Besse nuclear power plant in Oak Harbor, Ohio, was attacked by the Slammer SQL server worm, which disabled a safety monitoring system of the nuclear power plant for nearly 5 h [4]. More recently, Stuxnet [5], a threat specifically written to target industrial control systems, was discovered. The threat was designed to damage nuclear power plants in Iran [6]. Hence, the threat posed to critical infrastructures is far greater in terms of impact and scale of attack than common computer vulnerabilities and has the potentially to cause financial disasters and/or loss of life.

To cope with an increasing number of attacks and threats, a network traffic classification has been formulated as IDSs and has become an important security tool for managing risk, and an indispensable part of the overall security architecture. In particular, an IDS is used as a second line of defense to identify suspicious and malicious activities in network traffic. It gathers and analyzes information from various sources within computers and networks, and once an attack has been detected, it informs the network administrator of the incident so that an appropriate response can be made. Therefore, an accurate network classification approach plays an important role in assisting network operators to protect their networks against possible threats and attacks.

1.2 Limitations of existing solutions

A number of network traffic classification schemes have been investigated, proposed, and developed by the research community and the networking industry over the past 10 years. To show the evolution of traffic classification approaches between 1992 and 2014, we used the search of Microsoft Academic to calculate the number of papers matching the phrase of "traffic classification," "traffic flows," or "traffic identification" in the area of computer science (see Figure 1.1). First, well-known port numbers have been used to identify Internet traffic [7,8]. Such an approach was successful because traditional applications used fixed port numbers; however, extant studies show that the current generation of P2P applications tries to hide their traffic by using dynamic port numbers. In addition, applications whose port numbers are unknown cannot be identified in advance. Another technique relies on the inspection of packet content [9–11], and it analyses packets' payload content to see if they contain signatures of well-known or anomalous applications. Features are extracted from the traffic data and later compared to well-known signatures of applications provided by human experts. These approaches work very well for Internet traffic; however, studies [12,13] show that these approaches have a number of drawback and

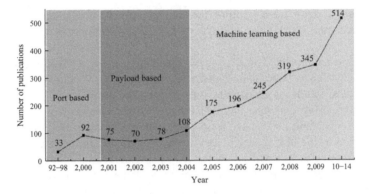

Figure 1.1   Evolution of network traffic classification approaches (1992–2014)

limitations. First, they cannot identify new or unknown attacks and applications for which signatures are not available, so these methods need to maintain an up-to-date list of signatures. This is a problem because new applications and attacks emerge every day; hence, it is not practical and sometimes impossible to keep up with the latest signatures. Second, deep packet inspection is a difficult task since it requires significant processing time and memory. Finally, if the application uses encryption, this approach no longer works.

Promising approaches [12–14] that have recently attracted some attention are based on transport layer statistics (TLS) data and efficient machine learning (ML). This assumes that applications typically send data in some sort of pattern, which can be used as a means of classification of connections by different traffic classes. To extract such patterns, only TCP/IP headers are needed to observe flow statistics, such as mean packet size, flow length, and the total number of packets. This allows the classification methods [12–14] to have sufficient information to work with.

As also depicted in Figure 1.1, research in ML-based network classification has been considered a substantial domain of knowledge for traffic classification tasks. However, there are still a number of fundamental issues which need to be taken into consideration and resolved in order to improve the accuracy and efficiency of network security and network traffic engineering. The remainder of this section briefly highlights the limitations of existing work.

- *Improve the quality of TLS data for accurate and effective network traffic classification.* Traditional methods [7,8], which mostly use IP headers for Internet traffic classification, do not provide high accuracy (more than 70%). This is because the knowledge available to the network is not sufficient. The research community dealt with the deficiency of such traditional methods by developing classification methods capable of inferring application-specific communication patterns without inspecting the packet payloads.

To classify Internet traffic data using TLS as a set of features, a dataset is prepared for analysis. In general, the size of Internet traffic data is very large, including thousands of traffic records with a number of various features (such as flow duration, TCP port, and packet inter-arrival time). Ideally, the use of a large number of features should increase the ability to distinguish network traffic applications [15]. However, this is not always true in practice, as not all the features of traffic data are relevant to the classification task. Among a large number of features present in TLS, some may not be relevant, and therefore could mislead the classifier, while some others may be redundant due to high inter-correlation with each other [16]. If irrelevant and redundant features are involved in the analysis, both the efficiency and the accuracy of the classification can be affected. Nevertheless, a number of research studies have applied ML algorithms to the TLS data to address the problem of network traffic analysis. However, the quality of TLS data can degrade the performance of these ML methods [12,17,18].

- *Identify the optimal and stable feature in the temporal-domain and the spatial-domain for accurate and effective network traffic classification.* The issue of improving the accuracy of network classification in both the temporal-domain (across different periods of time) and the spatial-domain (across different network locations) has been the subject of current studies [19,20]. However, many of these classical studies in this area neglect the insensitivity of feature selection (FS) methods, when selecting the representative set in the temporal-domain and the spatial-domain traffic data. For example, a given FS technique may select largely different subsets of features under small variations of the traffic training data. However, most of these selected features are as good as each other in terms of achieving high classification accuracy and better efficiency. Such an instability issue will make the network operators less confident about relying on any of the various subsets of selected features.

  To make the case worse, various FS methods [21,22] or different parameter settings of the same method may also result in largely different subsets of features for the same set of traffic data. Such an instability issue will make the network operators less confident about relying on any of the various subsets of selected features (that can change radically on datasets taken over a period of time).

- *Preserve the privacy for traffic data publishing for accurate network traffic classification.* A number of efficient and accurate network traffic classification and IDS using ML algorithms have been developed and attracted attention over the past 10 years [23–25]. This is due to the ability of ML algorithms (i) to learn without being explicitly programmed and (ii) to cope with a vast amount of historical data, making it difficult for human beings to infer underlying traffic patterns from such an enormous amount of data. However, a key problem in the research and development of such efficient and accurate network traffic classification and IDS (based on ML) is the lack of sufficient traffic data, especially for industrial network (SCADA) systems [25,26]. Unfortunately, such data are not so easy to obtain, because organizations do not want to reveal their private traffic data for various privacy, security, and legal reasons [25,27,28]. Therefore, network traffic data should be further protected before being published to prevent privacy leakage while still providing a maximal utility to data analysts using privacy preserving methods.

In fact, various privacy preserving methods [29–33] for different data publishing scenarios (e.g., marketing and biomedical data) have been proposed over the past few years. However, due to nature of the traffic data which contain different types of attributes, such methods are inappropriate for the privacy preservation of network traffic data.

- *Automatically labeling of raw traffic data for accurate and effective network traffic classification.* To overcome the problems of both supervised and unsupervised classification methods, a limited number of semi-supervised-classification models have been proposed [34,35]. These methods work by utilizing a small set of labeled data along with a larger amount of unlabeled data to improve the performance of the traffic classification. However, most of these models suffer from accuracy and efficiency problems. This is due to (i) the assumption that unlabeled flows must be classified or belong to fixed traffic classes (known as force assignments) and (ii) ignore to discover the emergence of new patterns and applications. As such, an automatically labeling process for efficient and accurate creation of ground truth to train and test the different ML algorithms is needed instead of the tedious and costly manual labeling procedure.

1.3 Research challenges

The aim of this book is to answer some of the important technical issues related to the selected topic. These will be presented as research challenges that we will be addressed in the various chapters of this book. This way would hopefully help the reader understand the importance of understanding the main focus of this book.

- *How various FS methods can be optimized and the quality of TLS data can be improved for accurate and effective network traffic classification?*
  This research challenge focuses mostly on improving the quality of the TLS data. In particular, the accuracy of the classification process will be affected by the large number of irrelevant features which provide no information about different classes of interest and worsen the accuracy. The efficiency of the classification process will also be poor due to highly correlated features (referred to redundant), which increases the number of features that need to be learnt and consequently increases the runtime of building and validating the classifier. Therefore, improving the quality of the TLS data is required in order to find representative features by optimizing various FS methods, which are used as a knowledge-discovery tool for identifying robust and truly relevant underlying characteristic features.
- *How to identify the optimal and stable feature set in the temporal-domain and the spatial-domain for accurate and effective network traffic classification?*
  Many FS methods have been proposed in the literature, e.g., [12,17,36,37] focused in improving accuracy and performance by discarding the relevant and/or redundant features. However, these studies neglected the insensitivity of the output of

FS methods to variations in the training dataset across different period of time (known as temporal-domain) and different network locations (known as spatial-domain). The instability issue of the FS raises serious doubts about the reliability of the selected features to validate the accuracy and efficiency of traffic classification in the temporal-domain and the spatial-domain network. As such, extensive analysis is desirable to provide insight into the main factors that affect the stability of the FS process, and the relationship between stability and predictive performance (known as optimality) of FS.

Nevertheless, it would be ideal to ensure the globally optimal feature subset and address the principal causes of stability we are concerned with. This is important to build traffic classification models that will remain accurate regardless of such time and location heterogeneity.

- *How to preserve the privacy for traffic data publishing for accurate IDS and network traffic classification?*

Preserving the privacy of network traffic data has specific and unique requirements that differ from other applications. In particular, network traffic data have various types of attributes: numerical attributes with real values, categorical attributes with un-ranked nominal values, and attributes with a hierarchical structure. Thus, the vast majority of current privacy-preserving approaches are not readily applicable to private data in traffic networks. This is because their design assumes that the data being protected have to be numeric. To help organizations to publish their traffic data and make them publicly available for the common good, a privacy-preserving approach must be devised to improve the anonymization schemes and preserve data utility for accurate data analysis by specifically dealing with the unique characteristics of network traffic data.

- *How to "automatically" label raw traffic data for evaluating and building an accurate network traffic classification?*

Any assessment of either the supervised or unsupervised traffic classification models requires labeled data. Nevertheless, in order to construct a traffic classification model with a good generalization ability, the availability of a large amount of labeled data is required. Unfortunately, labeled traffic data are scarce, time consuming, and expensive and require intensive human involvement. As such, it would be ideal to reduce the need and effort to label traffic flows by exploiting a small subset of labeled data along with a larger amount of unlabeled once. However, the subset of labeled data often can be limited to a fixed number, which can diminish the accuracy of the labeling process, especially with the emergence of new classes at any time in the network traffic flows. Thus, the goal of this research challenge is to address such an issue and improve the accuracy of the labeling process by making it more adaptive to the presence of new classes.

1.4   Suggested solutions

The following is a summary of the solutions for the research challenges discussed in the previous section.

- *Improve the efficiency and accuracy of FS methods to deal with high-dimensionality issue of data by selecting a reduced set of representative and nonredundant features without the need for data class labels.* Most of the existing FS methods have limitations when dealing with high-dimensional data, as they search different subsets of features to find accurate representations of all features. Obviously, searching for different combinations of features is computationally very expensive, which makes existing work not efficient for high-dimensional data. A new method is proposed, called AUFS (an efficient and accurate similarity-based unsupervised FS), that extends the k-mean clustering algorithm to partition the features into k clusters based on three similarity measures (i.e., PCC—Pearson correlation coefficient, LSRE—least square regression error, and MICI—maximal information compression index) in order to accurately partition the features.

- *Improve the quality of TLS data for accurate and effective network traffic classification.* A key issue with many FS methods [21,22,38,39] used to select a small subset from the original features of the TLS is that they are designed with different evaluation criteria (e.g., information-based measure and dependence-based measure). To address this challenge, new metrics are presented to extensively evaluate and compare such methods based on different criteria and from different perspectives. Additionally, a local optimization approach (LOA) [20] is described here to address the limitations of existing FS methods and to generate a highly discriminant set of features.

- *Identify optimal and stable features in the temporal-domain and the spatial-domain for accurate network traffic classification.* A global optimization approach (GOA) [40] is described with respect to both stability and optimality criteria, relying on multi-criterion fusion-based FS methods and an information theoretic method. Moreover, a new strategy based on a discretization method is presented to significantly improve the accuracy of different ML algorithms which suffer from the presence of continuous-valued features in the temporal-domain and the spatial-domain traffic data.

- *Preserve the privacy for traffic data publishing for accurate network traffic classification.* A privacy-preserving framework [41] is described in this book for publishing network traffic data in an efficient manner while preserving privacy of data providers. Unlike traditional privacy-preserving approaches that are still frequently used in many real-world applications, the privacy framework is designed specifically to deal with various types of attributes present in the traffic data, including numerical, categorical, and hierarchical attributes.

- *Automatically label raw traffic data for accurate network traffic classification.* A novel semi-supervised method is described for automatically traffic flows labeling, called *SemTra*. This method alleviates the shortage of labeled data by incorporating the predictions of multiple unsupervised and supervised models. In particular, the prediction information for unlabeled instances is derived from diversified and heterogeneous models, the strength of one usually complements the weakness of the other, thereby maximizing the agreement between them can boost the performance of the labeling process.

1.5 Book organization

The main objectives of the research on the specific topics of the book are addressed in seven chapters, with the current chapter presenting an introduction to the book. The remaining chapters of the book are structured as follows:

- Chapter 2 provides background for readers to understand the concepts and the models of the remaining chapters of this book. It briefly reviews the progress that has been made in three fields, namely *dimensionality reduction, clustering-based methods,* and IDS.
- Today, myriads of different methods are used to attain the network classification. The simplest of these would be to correlate parts of data patterns with the popular protocols. A rather advanced method statistically analyzes the packet inter-arrival times, byte frequencies, as well as packet sizes in order. Chapter 3 reviews and analyzes each method, with its advantages and disadvantages, from the following four methods of network traffic classification available: port-based classification, deep-packet inspection, connection pattern-based classification, and finally statistics-based classification.
- Chapter 4 surveys major clustering algorithms for traffic classification. As clustering algorithms are important alternative powerful meta-learning tools to accurately analyze the massive volume of data generated by modern applications, providing readers with some technical inside of their strength and weaknesses is critical. A concise survey existing (clustering) algorithms as well as a comparison both from a theoretical and empirical perspective are given in this last chapter. Empirically, extensive experiments are carried out, where the most representative algorithms are compared from each other using a large number of real (big) datasets, and this is based on three main metrics, namely stability, runtime, and scalability. We hope that this benchmark will provide readers with useful information and knowledge to be able to select specific clustering algorithms.
- Chapter 5 relates to the design of an efficient FS method, as most of the existing FS methods have limitations when dealing with high-dimensional data. It describes an *efficient and accurate similarity-based unsupervised FS* (AUFS) method that tackles mainly the high-dimensionality issue of data by selecting a reduced set of representative and nonredundant features without the need for data class labels. The AUFS method extends the k-mean clustering algorithm to partition the features into k clusters based on three similarity measures (i.e., PCC, LSRE, and MICI) in order to accurately partition the features.
- Chapter 6 describes the LOA to improve the quality of TLS data and find representative features for accuracy and the efficiency network classifier. In particular, LOA optimizes various FS methods and uses the concept of *support* to filter out irrelevant and redundant features, which provide no information about different classes of interest.
- Chapter 7 deals with the limitations of the LOA approach. The instability issue of this approach and other existing FS methods raise serious doubts about the reliability of the selected features. Thus, with the aim of enhancing the confidence

of network operators, a GOA is described to select not only an optimal but also a stable feature set to validate the accuracy and efficiency of traffic classification in the temporal-domain and the spatial-domain networks. In particular, GOA selects optimal features set from a global prospective to avoid a situation where the dependence between a pair of features is weak, but the total inter-correlation of one feature to the others is strong. Then, multi-criterion fusion-based FS technique, information theoretic method, and then a random forest framework with a new *goodness* measure are proposed to estimate the final optimum and stable feature subset.

- The sharing of traffic data among organizations is important, to create a collaborative, an accurate, and a global predictive traffic classification model across the spatial-domain networks. However, the chance that such traffic data may be misused can threaten the privacy and security of data providers. Thus, in Chapter 8, a novel privacy-preserving framework is described here for publishing traffic data and make them publicly available for the common good. In particular, the new privacy-preserving framework is designed to satisfy the privacy requirements of traffic data in an efficient manner by dealing with various types of features, including numerical attributes with real values, categorical attributes with un-ranked nominal values, and attributes with a hierarchical structure.

- In order to identify both the optimal and stable features, and also to build a traffic classification model with a good generalization ability using the supervised or unsupervised techniques, the traffic flows must be labeled in advance. Thus, in Chapter 9, a novel semi-supervised is proposed to reduce the effort of labeling traffic flows by exploiting a small subset of labeled data along with a larger amount of unlabeled once. Also, in the proposed semi-supervised approach, both supervised and unsupervised learning concepts are incorporated from local and global perspectives to improve the accuracy of the labeling process and adaptively handle the presence of the new traffic applications.

- Recent statistics-based methods to address the unsatisfactory results of traditional port-based and payload-based methods have attracted attention. However, the presence of non-informative attributes and noise instances degrades the performance of this method. Thus, to address this problem, in Chapter 10, a hybrid clustering classification method (called *CluClas*) is described to improve the accuracy and efficiency of network traffic classification by selecting informative attributes and representative instances. An extensive empirical study on four traffic datasets shows the effectiveness of the CluClas method.

- We conclude in Chapter 11 with a summary of what was covered in this book as well as the future direction of the various aspects discussed in the various chapters of this book.

Chapter 2
Background

This chapter provides the necessary background that will enable a reader to better understand the remaining chapters of this book. It briefly describes and reviews the progress that has been made in three fields, namely dimensionality reduction, clustering-based methods, and data-driven intrusion detection systems (IDSs). These three areas will hopefully provide a reader with a comprehensive background that will facilitate an understanding of the work carried out in this book.

2.1 Dimensionality reduction

In the era of big data, the dimensions of data increase significantly. In particular, the number of features increases such that not all features are *representative* for the learning machines. In addition, feature *redundancy* is more likely to occur. There are various challenges resulting from the existence of nonrepresentative and redundant features in the data. First, they reduce the accuracy of the data-mining algorithms by misdirecting the classification and clustering tasks [42]. Also, the existence of the redundant and nonrepresentative features would negatively affect the performance of the algorithms due to the large volume of data [43]. Moreover, they increase the processing time of the data-mining algorithms, which would result in very expensive complexity [44]. Furthermore, a large storage capacity is required to store the large volume of data [45]. Finally, the curse of dimensionality is a challenge to feature selection (FS) algorithms due to the sparseness of the data, which would deceive the mining algorithms by appearing to be equal in terms of the distance between them [46]. Consequently, various researchers proposed FS methods as efficient approaches, which would help to address the aforementioned challenges.

The FS process comprises (i) subset generation, (ii) subset evaluation, (iii) stopping criterion, and (iv) result validation [47]. This process is illustrated in Figure 2.1. The subset generation searches for a set of features based on a particular strategy in readiness for the evaluation at the next step. The three main types of search strategy, in addition to their strengths and weaknesses, are illustrated in Table 2.1.

Subset evaluation is the second step of the FS process, where every generated candidate feature is evaluated for its quality based on a specific evaluation criterion [54]. Evaluation criteria are broadly classified into *filter* and *wrapper* approaches whether or not the data-mining algorithms are to be applied in the evaluation of the selected

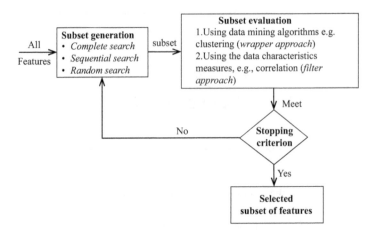

Figure 2.1   An overview of the feature-selection process

Table 2.1   Search strategies for subset generation

Complete search [48,49]	Sequential search [50,51]	Random search [52,53]
• Starts with an empty feature set and adds the features for the purpose of the evaluation and vice versa • **Pros**: Guarantees the search for the optimal result based on the adopted evaluation criteria • **Cons**: Exhaustive search, which induces performance overheads	• Starts with an empty feature set and adds one feature at a time until it reaches the stage when the features no longer enhance the quality of the subset features • **Pros**: It is simple to implement and obtains results quickly • **Cons**: It does not produce optimal features set	• Starts the search by selecting random subsets to be produced for the evaluation • **Pros**: Ensures the global optimization of the selected subset

features [55]. The filter approach [56,57] relies on the general characteristics of the data to evaluate the quality of the generated candidate features without involving any data-mining algorithm. This includes, but is not limited to, distance, information, correlation, and consistency measures. Filter-based algorithms have faster processing time than wrapper-based algorithms, as they do not include any data-mining algorithm [58]. Conversely, the wrapper-based algorithms [59,60] require the use of specific data-mining algorithms, such as clustering in the evaluation process of the generated candidate features [61]. Despite the fact that the wrapper approach can discover better quality candidate features than does the filter approach, this incurs high computational overheads [45].

Subset generation and evaluation of the FS process is iteratively repeated until they meet the requirement of the stopping criterion. The stopping criterion is activated by the completeness of the search, a preset maximum iteration times, or when the classification error rate is less than the preset threshold [62]. Then, the selected best candidate features are validated by conducting before and after experiment testing of different aspects, such as classification error rate, number of selected features, the existence of redundant/nonrepresentative features, and the time complexity [47].

Based on the availability of the class labels, the FS methods fall into two categories: *supervised* and *unsupervised*. The former, e.g., [20,47,63,377], assesses the significance of a feature by computing the correlation to its class label. It is often difficult to have the data class labels, especially for high-dimensional datasets, as it would take experts a long time to test and label the data. Therefore, unsupervised FS methods, e.g., [64–68], have been introduced as a solution to this problem. Such methods are much harder to design due to the absence of data class labels, which guide them in the process of searching for finding the representative features. Initially, traditional unsupervised FS methods addressed the problem (of the absence of class labels) by ranking features independently based on certain scores. However, they are not able to generate the best features set, as they do not compute the correlation between features [67]. The second of the unsupervised FS methods, e.g., [65,69], generally uses clustering to partition the features set into distinct clusters, where features in every cluster are similar to each other and dissimilar to the features of other clusters.

FS methods, which are designed for static data, cannot be efficiently used for data streams. This is because data streams have specific properties that do not exist in static data. An FS method should take into account the following properties in order to work efficiently in data streams. It should be restricted to read the data only once as it is impossible to store the entire stream. Also, it should take into account that many stream applications stream the features one-by-one and do not assume the existence of the entire feature space in advance (called dynamic feature space or streaming features). An FS method has to incrementally measure and update the representativeness of the features, as one feature might be representative in a time t but not in $t+1$ (concept drift) [70,71]. Furthermore, it is not enough to reduce the feature space from the stream; the instances must be reduced as well, because they usually contain great amounts of noise, redundancy, and nonrepresentativeness. Finally, an FS method should not be limited to data class labels; instead, it should be (unsupervised), as the data class labels are not available for most applications.

There are very few FS methods that work in data-stream applications. Every method contains some properties but not all of them. The online streaming feature selection (OSFS) [72] handles a stream of features one-by-one as they arrive. However, it requires the data to be labeled; it removes irrelevant/redundant features but not instances and only works for a single data stream. By contrast, Kankanhalli *et al.* [73] select a subset of relevant features from multiple streams based on the Markovian decision problem. However, this requires the full feature space to be known in advance and the data to be labeled and removes irrelevant/redundant features but not instances. Toshniwal *et al.* [74] developed an unsupervised FS method that does not require the data labels in order to select the nonrepresentative features. It is designed primarily for the purpose of outlier detection. However, it does not handle stream features one-by-one as they arrive; it removes irrelevant/redundant features but not instances and works only for a single data stream. Finally, the method proposed in [75] incrementally measures and updates the relevance of the features in order to accurately evaluate their relevance. On the other hand, it requires the full feature space to be known in advance and is designed to work only for a single data stream.

2.2   Clustering-based methods

This section provides a brief description and categorization of clustering methods. Clustering is a method whereby data points are grouped into different clusters, so that points within a cluster are very similar to each other and different from the data points of other clusters. Clustering methods do not require data class labels in order to partition the feature space and therefore they are widely used for unsupervised FS [70,76]. As later chapters are intended for unsupervised learning, clustering methods are used to select representative features without the need for data class labels. Clustering methods can be broadly categorized into partitioning methods where data is portioned into groups based on similarity or distance, density-based methods where data is partitioned into groups based on the density of the data, hierarchical methods where groups data based on either agglomerative or divisive strategy, and grid-based methods where data is assigned to cells and clustering is performed on each cell. Table 2.2 provides categorizations of these methods as well as their characteristics.

2.3   Data-driven IDSs

An IDS is a security mechanism that is intended to dynamically inspect traffic in order to detect any suspicious behavior or launched attacks. However, it is a challenging task to apply IDS for large and high-dimensional data streams. Data streams have characteristics that are quite distinct from those of statistical databases, which greatly impact on the performance of the anomaly-based ID algorithms used in the detection process. These characteristics include, but are not limited to, the processing of large data as they arrive (real-time), the dynamic nature of data streams, the curse of dimensionality, limited memory capacity, and high complexity. Therefore, the main challenge is to design efficient data-driven ID systems that are capable of efficiently dealing with data streams by considering these specific traffic characteristics. This section provides background information about some of the relevant work carried out in three major fields related to the topic, namely, *FSs, IDSs,* and *anomaly detection* in multi-data streams. This overview is intended to provide the reader with a better understanding of the major recent works in the area. By critically investigating and combining those three fields, researchers and practitioners will be better able to develop efficient and robust IDS for data streams.

Table 2.2   Characteristics of clustering methods

Methods	Characteristics
Partitioning [47,77,78]	• Uses mostly a distance based, where the dataset is partitioned into n parts, each representing a cluster with minimum data points • Each object is allocated to only one cluster • Does not maintain any hierarchical structure • Adopts iterative relocation mechanism in the partitioning to produce "optimal" results • Works efficiently with small-to-medium size datasets • k-Means is an example clustering algorithm used as a partitioning method
Hierarchical [79–82]	• Clustering is maintained based on hierarchical decomposition of the dataset • It is either agglomerative or divisive decomposition • Uses either distance or density based • Clusters cannot be corrected when they have been merged or split
Density based [83–85]	• Has been defined under proximity-based methods • Has good accuracy in detecting outliers • Capable of discovering clusters with arbitrary shape as it is based on density, not distance • DBSCAN clustering algorithm used as density-based algorithm
Grid based [86–88]	• The feature space is divided into a limited number of cells to form the grid • Clustering operations are performed inside the cells • Has fast processing time, as complexity depends on the number of grid cells and not the number of instances

FS is a preprocessing step that helps to optimize the performance of machine-learning algorithms in achieving their tasks. For example, when grouping the data into normal and outlier groups as in intrusion detection applications, the existence of redundant and nonrepresentative features would reduce the accuracy of classifying the data points and would also increase the processing time. Therefore, FS is applied as a preprocessing step for IDS in order to increase the classification accuracy and reduce the running time.

There are various security mechanisms (e.g., firewalls, cryptography, or access controls), which have been designed mainly to protect computer or information systems from malicious attacks. In addition to those security mechanisms, IDS has been developed as a second-line defense to discover attacks after they have been successfully launched [89]. IDS can be *host based* (e.g., to monitor the logs), *network based* (e.g., to monitor the networks traffic flow), or *data driven* (e.g., to detect any deviations from the normal pattern of the data), which is the focus of our interest.

Broadly, IDS is classified in terms of detecting intrusions into signature based and anomaly based [90]. The signature-based ID approach [91,92] discovers suspicious behaviors by comparing them with predefined signatures. Signatures are patterns

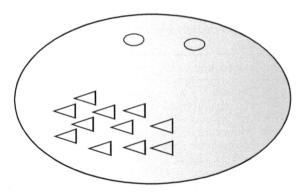

*Figure 2.2   Deviation of circle points (anomalies/outliers) from the normal
triangle ones*

associated with attacks, which are verified in advance by the human experts and are
used to trace any suspicious patterns. If the suspicious patterns and the signatures
match, an alarm is activated to warn the administrators or to take a predefined action
in response to the alarm [86]. The algorithms that are signature-based ID are efficient
in detecting *known* attacks with low false alarms and are reasonably quick to do so.
Despite the fact that most existing commercial IDs are signature based, most of them
cannot detect new types of attacks (also called *unknown attacks*), as their signatures
are new and not known in advance [86].

Unlike the signature-based IDS algorithms, anomaly-based IDS algorithms [93,
94] can identify new attacks because they appropriately model the "normal" behavior
of a non-attacked system. They can therefore identify serious deviations from the
normal profile to be considered *anomalies* (also called *outliers*) [95]. Anomalies
can emerge as a result of fraudulent behavior, mechanical faults, or attacks [96].
Figure 2.2 illustrates how the majority of the data points (triangle points) have a
particular distribution, while the circle points have a significant deviation from the
rest. The circle points are considered *outliers*.

Anomaly-based IDS algorithms can be categorized under three approaches
based on the form of the input data they use: *supervised* [97,98], *semi-supervised*
[99,100], and *unsupervised anomaly detection* [101,102]. Supervised anomaly detection approaches require training data in advance along with their class labels for
both normal and abnormal data, so as to accurately detect anomalies. The model is
then trained with both classes and applied to unlabeled data to determine the class to
which it belongs. Although there are plenty of classification methods that could be
applied in this category, the classes of the data are unbalanced because the "normal
class" is much bigger than the "anomaly class," which therefore negatively affects
the detection recall. Additionally, it is challenging to find accurate and representative
data class labels, particularly for the anomalies, as they emerge periodically and they
are uncountable [71]. On the other hand, semi-supervised anomaly-based detection

approaches require only one class label, which is either *normal* or *outlier*. The corresponding model is trained with the normal class only, and then any instance that does not belong to that class would be classified as an outlier. These approaches are much more applicable than supervised ones, because they do not require the specification of anomalous behavior. In addition, as the models for semi-supervised techniques could also be trained with anomaly class only, this provides substantial limitations because it is difficult to recognize all anomalies for the training of the data [103].

Both of the aforementioned approaches are limited as they rely on the availability of labeled data. Hence, they are restricted for specific applications, such as spacecraft fault detection, and therefore they are not generic. On the other hand, the unsupervised anomaly detection approach is generic and widely applicable as it does not need the data to be labeled [104]. This approach assumes that the normal data has a pattern that is significantly different from the pattern of the outliers. For instance, the normal data should form groups with instances that are very similar to each other and different from the outliers. Although this approach is widely applicable, the related techniques experience a high rate of false alarms [105].

Anomaly-based ID can mainly be categorized into classification, statistical, proximity based, and clustering methods. Classification methods [106,107] are supervised by nature, and they are applicable only if there are class labels in the training data. The classifier is trained with the labeled data and then applied for the testing of unlabeled data. The test data is then classified as an outlier if it is not classified as normal by the classifier. Classification methods seem to provide good accuracy in distinguishing between data and their related classes. Although such methods demonstrate good performance during the testing phase in comparison to the other methods, their detection accuracy depends on the accuracy of the labeled data [90].

Statistical methods [108,109] are another type of approach, which observe the activity of the data so as to create profiles representing acceptable behavior. There are two kinds of profiles: current and stored. The former regularly logs and updates the distribution of the data as long as the data is processed. Additionally, the data is assigned with an anomaly score by comparing them with the stored profile. If any anomaly score exceeds a predefined threshold, it is labeled as an outlier. Statistical methods do not need knowledge about labeled data or attack patterns in advance. Hence, they seem to be efficient in detecting recent attacks. On the other hand, it is difficult to establish a threshold that balances the occurrence of false positives and false negatives [110].

Proximity-based methods use distance metrics to calculate the similarity between data. It assumes that the proximity between an outlier and its nearest neighbor is different from its proximity to the remaining data. Such methods can be either distance or density based. Distance-based methods [111,112] search for a minimum predefined number of neighbors of a data point within a specific range in order to decide its normality. The point is labeled as an outlier if the neighbors within the range are less than the predefined threshold. On the other hand, density-based methods [113,114] compare the density of data with its neighbor densities so to decide its normality. The point is labeled as an outlier if its density is considerably less than the density of its neighbors. Generally, the effectiveness of proximity-based methods varies depending on the adopted measure as it is challenging to ensure effectiveness in particular situations. Furthermore, proximity-based methods seem to be inefficient in detecting outliers that form groups and are close to each other.

Lastly, clustering methods [115,116] work in unsupervised mode to recognize patterns of unlabeled data by grouping similar instances into groups. They cluster data by examining their relationships with other clusters. Indeed, normal data are those data, which belong to clusters that are dense and large. On the other hand, outliers can be identified based on the following three assumptions [96]: (i) outliers are objects, which have not been allocated to any cluster. In fact, the initial goal of clustering is to find clusters in particular, not the outliers; (ii) outliers are objects that are far, in terms of measured distance, from their closest cluster centroids. Indeed, every object is given a score based on its distance to its closest cluster centroid, and it should not exceed a predefined distance in order to be considered normal. The limitation of this assumption is that outliers cannot be found if they have already formed a cluster. The aforementioned assumptions have a common limitation in that they seem to detect only individual outliers but not groups of outliers, which form clusters by themselves [71]. To overcome this limitation, (iii) the last assumption defines the outliers as objects, which have been allocated to sparse or small clusters.

Generally, clustering methods do not require the data to be labeled so it can handle zero-day attacks. Also, it can adapt to cluster "complex objects" by adopting existing clustering algorithms, which can handle those particular types of objects. Furthermore, clustering methods are fast in the testing phase because every object is compared with the clusters only, which are relatively small in comparison with all the objects. On the other hand, the efficiency of clustering methods depends on the clustering algorithms in establishing the normal behavior of the objects. Also, clustering methods work efficiently when the outliers are individuals but not when they form groups of clusters. Finally, clustering methods are still computationally expensive even with some recent work attempting to resolve the performance problem [117].

Anomaly detection for multiple data streams

Anomaly detection is no longer limited to statistical databases due to the emergence of very large data (big data) with specific characteristics: volume, variety, and velocity (3V). Volume relates to the huge amount of data generated. Such data can be found in different formats, such as videos, music, and large images. Velocity refers to the high speed at which data is generated, captured, and shared. Variety refers to the proliferation of new data types. The real world has produced big data in many different formats, posing a challenge that needs to be addressed. A data stream is an ideal example of big data because: (i) a huge (volume) of data is gathered from different sources (i.e., sensors) to extract knowledge by mining and analyzing the collected big data; (ii) a data stream arrives in a timely manner at different speed rates (velocity); and (iii) sensors can stream different data types (variety).

Although anomaly detection for data streams has been investigated intensively, most of the recent research has focused only on *single data stream*. Therefore, we believe it is crucial to investigate how to detect anomalies or launched attacks arriving from *multiple data streams*. In fact, attacks like denial of service might cause severe damage to the systems if they have been flooded through multiple streams. Therefore, anomaly detection algorithms need to be improved and adapted to multiple data streams. A *data stream* is defined in [118] as a set of infinite data points that consist of attribute values along with an implicit or explicit time stamp. Anomaly-based ID methods are applied to detect outliers from not only a single stream but also from various data streams. This is often carried out by mining the relationships between those multiple streams, by (i) computing the correlations between multiple data streams and identifying points that have a high correlation; or (ii) computing the similarity by querying multiple data streams to determine high similarity points; or (iii) utilizing clustering methods to discover the relationship between the streams in order to filter the outliers [119].

Traditional anomaly-based algorithms, which are not designed for data stream applications, might not be able to mine the data points in data streams for the following reasons [120]. *First*, data arrives in the form of streams and should be tested for outlierness as long as they arrive, which could result in wrong decisions due to the dynamic nature of the data streams [121]. *Second*, data streams produce a very high volume of data, which would be too expensive to store. In fact, it has been suggested in [122] that data stream algorithms should be executed in the main memory and not requisite secondary storage. *Third*, unlike traditional methods for anomaly detection that assume the existence of the entire datasets in advance, the mining of data streams requires the consumption of a minimum amount of memory [123]. Therefore, the model should have only a single scan to access the data points in the storage for the purpose of detection.

In addition to the abovementioned characteristics, it is challenging to determine whether or not the data streaming points are outliers as the characteristics of the data streams may change over time. This phenomenon is known as *concept evolution* [124], and it takes place when a new class emerges from streaming data over time. Therefore, clustering techniques in particular should adapt to the concept evolution in order to reflect the real characteristics of data points. Additionally, data streams do not form a unified distribution of the data points, which seems to increase the complexity of detecting outliers [125]. High-dimensionality is also a characteristic of data streams due to the sparseness of the data, which could degrade the efficiency of detecting outliers, as high-dimensional data appear to be equal in terms of distance between the data points due to the sparse data [126]. Moreover, in some situations, different data streams with different data types, such as categorical or numerical, need to be mined; hence, it becomes challenging to finding the relationship between them [127]. Finally, most data-mining algorithms have high computational complexity when applied to data streams [128]. As a result, new algorithms should be designed, or improved from existing algorithms, to meet the requirements as well as the characteristics of multi-data streams so they can mine patterns efficiently and accurately.

There are a few existing solutions that specifically apply to anomaly detection in multi-data streams. The algorithm proposed in [129] attempts to solve the problem of judging the stream data points for outlierness as soon as they arrive due to limited memory capacity, which could result in wrong decisions. This is carried out by partitioning the data streams into chunks and later clustering each one by applying the k-means algorithm. Then, every point that deviates significantly from its cluster's centroid would be saved temporarily as a candidate outliers, and the normal points are discarded after computing their mean values in order to free the memory. To decide whether or not they are outliers, the mean value of the candidate clusters is then compared with that of a preset L number of previous chunks. Although this algorithm seems to be computationally efficient because it does not rely on distance measures, it has low detection accuracy. Additionally, several parameters need to be properly defined (e.g., number of clusters and L number of chunks to compare the mean value and the chunk size as well), which makes the algorithm less attractive for multi-stream data.

Another clustering-based approach is proposed in [130] to detect anomalies for multi-data streams. It partitions a stream into windows or chunks, each of which is clustered and associated with a reference. Then, the numbers of adjacent clusters, along with representation degree references, are computed to find outlier references that contain potential anomalies. This model is believed to have better scalability and accuracy.

Moradi Koupaie *et al.* [96] proposed an incremental clustering algorithm that has two main phases to detect outliers in multi-data streams. In the online phase, the data in the windows is clustered using the k-mean algorithm, where clusters that are relatively small or quite far from other clusters are considered to be online outliers and therefore need further investigation. During the off-line phase, the outlier from previous windows is added to the current window to be re-clustered by the k-mean algorithm. With higher confidence, it guarantees that any small or far clusters are real outliers as they have been given a survival chance. The work claims that the proposed algorithm is more accurate than existing techniques in discovering outliers; however, no evaluation results have been provided. Similar to other algorithms, many of its parameters need to be adjusted.

2.4   Conclusion

High-dimensional data is a big challenge for the machine-learning algorithms due to the existence of redundant and nonrepresentative features. FS is an efficient dimension-reduction technique used to reduce data dimensions by removing those redundant and nonrepresentative features. In real applications, most data do not have class labels (i.e., unsupervised) and therefore clustering techniques are used to select features, as they do not require data class labels. An example of this application is a data-driven IDS. This chapter briefly described and reviewed the progress that has been made in three fields, namely dimensionality reduction, clustering-based methods, and data-driven IDSs. These three areas will hopefully provide the reader with a comprehensive background enabling a better understanding of the work carried out in this book.

Chapter 3
Related work

The main purpose of a network scheduler is to classify differently processed packets. Today, myriads of different methods are used to attain the network classification. The simplest of these would be to correlate parts of data patterns with the popular protocols. A rather advanced method statistically analyzes the packet inter-arrival times, byte frequencies, as well as packet sizes in order. After the traffic flow classification has been done through a certain protocol, a preset policy is used for the traffic flow, including the other flows. This process is conducted in order to achieve a particular quality, i.e., quality of service. This application should be conducted at the exact point when traffic accesses the network. It should also be carried out in a manner that allows the traffic management to take place, isolating the individual flows and queue from the traffic. These individual flows and queue will be shaped differently as well. The next network traffic classification approaches [7,9,17] are considered the most reliable, as they involve a full analysis of the protocol. However, these approaches have certain disadvantages, the first being the encrypted and proprietary protocols. As they do not have a public description, they cannot be classified. Although the implementation of every single protocol possible in the network is a thorough approach, in reality, this is extremely difficult. A single-state tracking protocol might demand quite a lot of resources. Consequently, the method loses its meaning and becomes impractical and unattainable.

This work focuses on analyzing each method, with its advantages and disadvantages. The following are the four methods of network traffic classification available:

- Port-based classification
- Deep-packet inspection (DPI)
- Connection pattern-based classification
- Statistics-based classification

3.1 Port-based classification

One of the most popular methods used to classify the traffic on the Internet involves analyzing the packet's content found at a certain point in the network. These packets typically contain source and destination ports, i.e., their addresses. Although ports represent the endpoints of the logical connections, their purpose does not end there.

They also represent the means by which the program of the client determines the computer's server program in the network. This method relies on the concept that port numbers [7,8,131] in TCP or UDP packets are constantly used by the applications. TCP SYN packets are analyzed by the middle network classifier. The port number of TCP SYN packet is then referenced with the Internet Assigned Numbers Authority (IANA)'s list [132], which has all the registered ports. TCP SYN packets need to know the server side, which belongs to the TCP connection of the new client-server, in order for the classification to take place. UDP packets follow the similar process as the TCP SYN packets. Ranging from 0-65536, port numbers can be classified into three types. The first type belongs to the ports that are set for the privileged services (0-1024), i.e., the popular ports. The second type belongs to the ports known as registered (1024-49151). The third type are the private ports (above 49151), including the dynamic ones.

The port-based classification of the traffic is determined by associating one popular port number with a provided traffic type, i.e., of correlating the transport layer's port number with its application(s). For example, the port number 80 of the TCP correlates with the traffic of the http, whereas 6346 represents traffic of Gnutella, etc. This is why the port-based method is seen as the easiest. It just requires insight into the packets' header. And this is where its strength lies, in its simplicity and low cost. However, there are several disadvantages of using this method as well, the first being that it cannot be applied to the allocations of the dynamic ports [133]. For instance, web-classified traffic might be a different traffic that is using http. Hence, there is no method for matching a certain application to its port number, which is dynamically allocated [9].

Furthermore, a certain number of applications use port numbers which are assigned to different applications by IANA. In this way, they avoid detection and blocking from the access control operating systems. Many peer-to-peer (P2P) applications will often use other applications' port numbers [7,8], simply because they have not registered their port numbers with the IANA [134,135]. And finally, there is a certain number of IP layer encryption which hide the header (TCP or UDP), subsequently preventing the port numbers from being seen. All these disadvantages make the port-based classification method insufficient for all the applications. Subsequently, the idea of using more complex network classification methods has been suggested in the recent literature.

3.2   Deep packet inspection (signature-based classification)

As the recent literature has noted, the port-based method often leads to traffic estimates that are not correct. This causes problems with the quality of the network management as well as with the wrongly identified intrusions, i.e., viruses. Many have turned toward the intrusion detection systems (IDS). The need for the IDS appeared when the Internet suffered a number of virus outbreaks back in 2004. As the packet header inspection was not enough for the detection of the virus, the IDS vendors began conducting a deep analysis of the packet. Hence, the term "DPI" as well as efficient and accurate methods [9–11] has been formed. Many applications can be classified using the information L3 and L4. However, this does not apply to all of them. Some applications have to use a certain message type, such as IM streams voice, or an additional subclassification, such as URL, in order to be classified. The DPI will provide all of the above, doing both classification and subclassification. Predefined byte patterns are examined within the packets in a stateful or stateless manner to enable the protocol recognition. For example, the P2P traffic from the eDonkey has the string "e3 38," whereas the traffic from the web has the "GET" string. This is possible only if both the packet header and payload are accessible. DPI methods apply signature analysis to identify unique features, i.e., signatures of each application. These signatures are then combined into a reference database, which is used for comparing the particular traffic. This is conducted so that the classification engine will identify that particular application. Subsequently, reference updates must be conducted often so that recent developments, together with the applications, are combined with the existing protocols.

There are different signature analysis methods [9–11,136], and the most popular methods include the followings:

- Protocol/State analysis
- Behavioral and heuristic analysis
- Pattern analysis
- Numerical analysis

(A) Protocol/State analysis

A certain sequence of steps should be followed by certain applications. For example, when the client requests the normal FTP GET, the server should provide a proper response to it. When the communication protocols have already been defined and identified, then the application that incorporates a certain communication mode will be identified. P2P applications can be identified by using the application level signatures, according to Sen *et al.* [137]. To support the book, there has been an examination of BitTorrent, DirectConnet, Kazaa, eDonkey, and Gnutella, all of them being P2P protocols. The examination included different protocol stages: from the signaling and download, to the keep-alive messages and synchronization. On the other hand, the analysis conducted by Dreger *et al.* [138] included the application-layer protocols as a means of detecting different network intrusions, such as SMTP, FTP, HTTP, and IRC, whereas the analysis conducted by Ma *et al.* [139] concentrated entirely on the flow content by using the structural and statistical features so that the traffic can be identified. The traffic utilizes the same application-layer protocol.

The analysis of the Fast Track, WNP, and OpentNap P2P protocols was conducted by Spognardi *et al.* [140] so that the payload signatures could be identified. These signatures acted as a reference for Snort NIDS in order to monitor the network traffic. Dewes *et al.* [141] conducted the analysis on a number of chat protocols in order to accurately identify different payload signatures. Their results showed the rate of 91.7% for the recall regarding every chat connection. The precision of their method was at 93.13%. The protocol-based method fails with some applications simply because they might use protocols that are private and are not defined by traffic classification engine. Furthermore, there are applications which have communication orders that are almost identical, which impede this method. This paper [141] indicated that using one analysis method is not enough for complete network traffic classification. In order for the network traffic to be classified completely, different approaches should be used.

(B) Behavior and heuristic analysis

Communication behavior of an application differs when in the running mode, subsequently affecting network traffic differently. For instance, for each application, there are two modes: interactive and sleep. They both differ according to the volume of the network traffic. When in the interactive mode, the date exchanged between the server and client is extensive, thereby sharply increasing the network traffic. When in the sleep mode, there will be a period communication with light packet that the server sends to determine whether the client is alive. This is done periodically, whereas the interactive mode involves constant communication. Subsequently, the analysis of the traffic behavior should be done, as it will provide insights into the applications which are running. This analysis will provide the basis for the classification of the applications. Furthermore, the underlying protocol might be classified using a statistical (heuristic) analysis of the packets that have already been inspected. These two analyses, behavior and heuristic, usually, complement each other perfectly. This is why Karagiannis *et al.* [8] and Iliofotou *et al.* [142] suggested methods where host behavior patterns are analyzed and identified on the transport layer. In order to observe the traffic flow, the application, functional, and social levels of the patterns should be analyzed. Furthermore, this method is used by different antiviral programs in order to detect viruses and worms.

(C) Pattern analysis

The classification engine can use a certain pattern (string/bytes/characters) [143,144], which is incorporated into the packet's payload, in order to identify the protocols. Depending on the application, the pattern can be observed at different packet's positions, not just at off-set. However, this does not create an issue for the classification engine to identify the packets. What does create an issue is that certain protocols do not contain these patterns, string, and characters according to which the classification can be conducted. Therefore, this approach cannot be applied to all the protocols.

(D) Numerical analysis

Numerical characteristics, including the offsets, payload size, and response packets, are a part of the numerical analysis [145,146]. An excellent subject for this analysis is the Older Skype version (pre-2.0), where the client's request is 18 bytes, whereas the message that the client sends is 11 bytes. As there are many packets that need to be analyzed, the classification based on this analysis will take longer than the other ones. As there are a number of communications that are encrypted nowadays, one classification method is not sufficient for classifying all the applications. For instance, if the communication is encrypted, DPI cannot inspect the information found in the upper layers. Hence, many classification methods have begun employing the behavior/heuristic analysis, together with intelligent and clustering algorithms, which can help identify certain encrypted traffic. However, the issue of not being able to identify all the traffic still remains. This issue cannot be resolved by a single communication method, but rather a combination of methods.

The advantage of DPI methods [9–11] is that such methods can work well in the case of well-documented open protocols. Thus, with well-defined signatures, a correct and accurate decision can be guaranteed. However, the DPI method required the availability of the real traces to give a good and sufficient feedback for choosing the perfect and best performing byte signatures. Some applications can be missed, or the method can produce false positives if the signatures are not kept up to date. Moreover, this DPI method is based on a strong assumption that any packet payload could be inspected. However, the encryption of packet contents prevents the classification engine from extracting signatures or ports information.

3.3   Connection pattern-based classification

The communication pattern of a certain host is compared with the behavior pattern of different activities, i.e., applications in the connection pattern-based classification. Reference [10] utilizes this idea, using the classification algorithm on P2P traffic. BLINC [8] expanded the idea, thereby providing a general method applicable to a number of different applications. This general method used the source of destination ports, sets cardinality of unique destination ports, IPs, and the sets of the magnitude in order to describe characteristics of the network flow, which match different applications. Thus, the entire network traffic was observed prior to constructing the nodes' graphs, i.e., communicating hosts. Using filters, such as an edge on the packet, on SYN packet, etc., the edges are constructed. After the graph has been constructed, it is analyzed, using the properties of quantitative graph description, including node degree distribution, joint degree distribution, connectivity metrics, etc.

This method does not employ the packet payload in order to do the traffic classification [8], which enables the encrypted content to be identified. However, some behavior patterns of the application cannot always be found easily, especially in cases where several different applications are being deployed simultaneously and using one host. There are some other disadvantages of the method, including the longer start-up time, lack of local decision, the need for many flows so that the communication pattern can be identified. Finding the hosts takes time, and it cannot be conducted before the communication flows have been collected. Additionally, this connection pattern-based method requires a large amount of memory since all hosts are collected. Certain problems might arise while conducting some graph metrics calculation, as the CPU load might be high as well.

3.4   Statistics-based classification

Machine Learning (ML) has been extensively used in many fields, such as load prediction, medical diagnosis, and search engines. In last decades, many algorithms based
on statistical ML have been proposed [12–14,66] in flow classification or bandwidth
management. These approaches were able to achieve over 80% flow accuracy on average on their data sets. However, many open challenges still exist, such as imbalance
characteristics of training data sets and concept drifting of data distribution. In this
section, we focus on presenting a detailed review of previous works on this topic.

3.4.1   Feature selection

A feature is a computed statistic from one or several packets, such as a standard
deviation of inter-arrival times or mean packet length. A flow is described using
a set of statistical features as well as related feature values. The set of statistical
features is the same for every traffic flow, whereas the feature values depend on
the network traffic class and thus differ from flow to flow. In [147,148], different
datasets are used to define as many as 249 features, such as features of the flow
duration, flow activity, and packets' inter-arrival time. Even though there are many
available features, the curse of dimensionality still remains a problematic issue for
learning the data distribution in high-dimensional datasets. As redundant features
negatively influence the performance of algorithms, there are better options than
training a classifier by utilizing the maximum number of features obtainable. One
of the options requires the features to be divided into further sub-features based on
their usefulness. However, how this is done is still one of the central problems of
ML. Recently, there have been several attempts to address this problem by using the
reduction feature, which utilizes different requirements in order to define a feature
as the most useful, based on the working constraints in the practical network traffic
classification. The representative quality of a feature set considerably influences the
level of effectiveness of ML algorithms.

By using feature selection algorithms, the process of carefully selecting the number and types of features used to train the ML algorithm can be automated. A feature
selection algorithm [149] is broadly categorized based on the *filter*, *wrapper* [150],
or *hybrid* method. The filter method scores and ranks the features relying on certain
statistical metrics and chooses the features with the highest ranking values. Typically used statistical criteria include *t*-test, chi-square test, mutual information, and
principal component analysis (PCA). Even though filter approaches have low computation expense, they lack robustness against feature interaction. The wrapper method
evaluates the performance of different features using specific ML algorithms, thereby
producing feature subsets "tailored" to the algorithm used [151]. It searches the whole
feature space to find the features to improve classification or clustering performance,
but it also tends to be more computationally expensive than the filter model [62]. It
is well known that searching for optimal features from a high-dimensional feature
space is an NP-complete problem. The hybrid method attempts to take advantage

of the filter and wrapper models by exploiting their different evaluation criteria in different search stages [62]. For example, the hybrid methods of *t*-test and genetic algorithm, PCA and ant colony optimization, and the mutual information and genetic algorithm have been proposed.

Van Der Putten *et al.* [152] found that the choice of feature selection is more important for obtaining high performance than the choice of traffic classification methods. Dunnigan and Ostrouchov use PCA to choose the most important features which contribute to the covariance matrix of observation data. In [153], Zander *et al.* used the feature selection to find an optimal feature set and determine the influence of different features. In [144], Roughan *et al.* used up to four features to train the classifiers and achieved high traffic classification accuracy. Lei *et al.* in [154] for the first time proposed a hybrid feature selection method combined with chi-squared and C4.5 decision tree algorithm. This method also gives superior performance compared with the original C4.5 decision tree algorithm without selecting useful features. Valenti and Rossi in [155] considered both the nature of the input data and of the target traffic. The behavior features for P2P traffic flow are selected using two statistical metrics.

Because most feature selection algorithms are not effective for online traffic classification, Zhao *et al.* in [156] proposed a real-time feature selection method for traffic classification. The underlying idea is that the selected feature subset is calculated based on the first several packets in the flow. To evaluate the performance, the feature selection method is combined with a decision tree classification method. Experimental results show that the proposed method can achieve good performance for online traffic flow classification. In [157], Jamil *et al.* studied the online feature selection methods for P2P traffic. They discovered that the methods of chi-squared, fuzzy-rough, and consistency-based feature selection algorithms were the three best for P2P feature selection out of more than ten feature selection algorithms. They extended their previous works in [158] to determine the optimal online feature selection algorithms for P2P traffic classification using J48 algorithm. In particular, J48 is a ML algorithm which makes a decision tree from a set of training data examples, with the help of information entropy idea. They also showed that it can obtain high accuracy of 99.23% with low running time with the proposed feature selection method.

While most of the current feature selection methods have been used for balanced traffic data, in the case of imbalanced data, the feature selection is skewed and many irrelevant features are used. In [159], a new filter feature selection method, called "balanced feature selection," was proposed. The certainty coefficient is built in a local way guided by entropy theory, and the symmetric uncertainty is used in a global way. The search method selects an optimal feature for each class.

Even though many feature selection algorithms in ML have been used for the challenge of imbalanced data distribution and concept drift, more recently, however, Zhang *et al.* in [160] suggested a method of weighted symmetrical uncertainty with the metric of area under ROC curve, called WSU_AUC, to optimize flow classification when both the issues of imbalanced learning and concept drifting exist.

3.4.2   *Classification methods*

Based on the usage, ML methods [12–14,66,161] can be classified into four different categories: numerical prediction, association mining, clustering, and classification. Numerical prediction is a part of the supervised ML. It utilizes the models formed by the instances that were selected earlier in order to classify the unlabeled instances. Clustering is a part of the unsupervised ML as it combines similar instances into a particular cluster. Association mining searches for interaction between a subset of features. Classification and numerical prediction are almost identical, except for the difference in the output, which belongs to the continuous values category, not to the discrete one. Of these four, clustering and classification are considered the most important methods. Based on the ML, flow classification methods can be classified into supervised, unsupervised, and semi-supervised categories. Thus, the ML algorithms, utilized for the network traffic classification, can belong to one of the three categories next:

- Supervised ML algorithms
- Unsupervised ML algorithms
- Semi-supervised ML algorithms

(A) Supervised machine-learning algorithms

Classification models [17,153,161–164] are built by utilizing a training set of instances, which corresponds to a particular class. The class needs to be known prior to learning, as supervised algorithms do not utilize the unknown classes. Subsequently, the classification model predicts the class memberships for the new instances. This prediction is conducted based on the examination of the unknown flows' feature values. The supervised learning establishes the knowledge which helps classify new instances into predefined classes. The learning machine is then provided with example instances which have already been pre-classified into classes. Previous instances are analyzed and generalized in order to construct the classification model, i.e., learning process's output. Hence, the main emphasis of the supervised learning focuses on modeling the input/output relationships. Hence, the aim of the supervised learning is to identify the mapping of the input features into an output class. The knowledge learned is presented in the form of classification rules, a flowchart, decision tree, etc. Also, it is utilized for the classification of the new unseen instances in the later stages. Supervised learning involves two stages: testing and training. In the learning stage, the training is used to analyze the given data, i.e., the training dataset, and construct a classification model. The testing stage, or classifying stage, utilizes the model from the training stage so that the new, unseen instances are classified.

   In a supervised method, the learning algorithms could be grouped into two categories: parametric and nonparametric classifiers. For the parametric classifiers, the data distribution for each class is assumed to be known except for its distribution parameters. The class-conditional distribution can be obtained by estimating the parameters with training data. Some typical parametric classifiers include Naïve Bayesian, Gaussian mixture, and so on. For the nonparametric classifiers, the posterior probability is estimated directly from the data without any assumption about data distribution form. The common nonparametric classifiers are nearest neighbors, neural network, support vector machine (SVM), Gaussian process, etc. Researchers found that the application of these supervised ML algorithms to the traffic classification problem is able to achieve great performance. Moore and Zuev in [17] introduced the correlation-based feature method to eliminate irrelevant and redundant features from traffic data and then built an efficient Naïve Bayes classifier in combination with a kernel estimation method to classify the traffic into different types of services and applications. The classification performance is very promising, up to 96%, for their collected datasets with the choice of ten flow-behavior features. It is worth noting that the concept of the Naïve Bayes classifier assumes that the relation between features of a particular object is independent. However, in their recent work in [12], they pointed out that the traffic data, which is extracted from the header of packets and manually labeled using packet content, exhibits redundancy and interdependence among features describing each flow. Auld *et al.* in [12] proposed a Bayesian neural network which can incorporate the dependence among features, and thus more robust results are obtained.

In [165], a decision tree classifier is trained with the probabilistic features of average packet size, Round Trip Time of a flow, and FIN and PUSH in packets for accurately classifying http, ftp, smtp, and telnet applications. They also reported that an accuracy of 93% in the flow classification was obtained. In [144], the nearest neighbor method in combination with linear discriminant analysis is applied and built using only the features of average packet size and duration time of a flow to classify Internet traffic. For real-time classification of network traffic flows, Roughan *et al.* also used the SVM method to generate a network classifier to aid network operators to classify the real-time traffic flows into seven classes of predefined applications [144]. In particular, they considered the coarse classes of flows, including interactive, bulk data transfer, streaming and transactional, etc. Also, to identify the best combination of the features for better classification performance, they developed a feature selection method.

Williams *et al.* in [37] investigated the elimination of non-informative features on five popular ML algorithms for Internet traffic classification, including Naïve Bayes, C4.5, Bayesian Network, and Naïve Bayes Tree algorithms. In particular, only the features of packet lengths, total packets, total bytes, flow duration, inter-arrival times, and protocol are used for training these classifiers. Meanwhile, empirical studies were conducted with little training data to show the computational performance of these algorithms. They show that similar classification accuracy can be obtained by these algorithms, and the computational performance of C4.5 has the fastest classification speed in comparison with the remaining algorithms.

Using supervised algorithms, the performance of the CorelReef approach which is port-based, the BLINC approach which is host behavior-based, and also seven common statistical feature-based methods have been evaluated extensively on seven different traces by Lim *et al.* in [166]. Because the traffic flows would dynamically change and the concept of flow would not be constant, the resulting trained classifiers have limited ability to adapt seamlessly. Instead of trying to differentiate one traffic application from another, Xie *et al.* [167] proposed a bootstrapping approach where the classifier learns to classify the types of traffic applications in isolation. They demonstrated that the proposed method is robust against any change to traffic flows, such as the emergence of new applications.

More recently, a network traffic classification benchmark, called as NetraMark., was presented in [18]. They considered six design guidelines comprising comparability, reproducibility, efficiency, extensibility, synergy, and flexibility and integrated seven different state-of-the-art traffic classifiers. These seven ML algorithms include C4.5 decision tree, Naïve Bayes, Naïve Bayes kernel estimation, Bayesian network, k-nearest neighbors (kNN), neural networks, and SVM. The final decision hypothesis is derived with a weighted voting process to obtain single best classification results. Chen *et al.* [161] have proposed an efficient Malware Evaluator tool to categorize malwares into species and detect zero-day attacks. In particular, the tool defines its taxonomic features based on the behavior of species throughout their life cycle to build efficient learning models using both SVMs and decision trees. In [168], Zhang *et al.* proposed a new learning framework to address the issue of very few training samples for traffic classification using correlation information. The correlation of traffic flow is incorporated into a nonparametric approach to improve the classification accuracy. The performance of the proposed approach was evaluated in terms of average overall accuracy against different size of training dataset varying from 10 to 50 per class. The experimental results show that the accuracy of the proposed approach outperformed the existing classifications approaches when only small size of traffic samples is available.

The main task of a network traffic classifier involves identifying the traffic of the known applications inside the network packets of unseen streams. However, the challenge of correlating classes of network traffic, separated by the ML, to the applications that cause the network traffic is one that should be dealt with. Hence, supervised ML requires the training stage, in order to provide the necessary link between the classes and applications. A priori flow classification is needed within the training datasets during the training stage, which makes supervised ML attractive for identifying a particular pattern/patterns as well as application/applications, which are of interest. Training of the supervised ML classifier, by using the examples of every possible class to be seen in practice, is the most efficient method. In spite of that, the performance of the supervised ML classifier might deteriorate if the classifier is not trained using a mix of traffic or if the network links which are monitored begin noticing traffic of the applications that were previously not known. When the evaluation of the supervised ML scheme within an operational context is conducted, it is important to take into account: (i) how the new applications will be detected by the user, (ii) how supervised training examples will be provided to the classifier, and (iii) when the retraining will occur.

(B) Unsupervised machine-learning algorithms

Unsupervised ML algorithms [169] are also known as "clustering algorithms." In unsupervised ML scenarios, no labeled data are available, and the clustering algorithms attempt to group traffic flows into different clusters according to similarities in the feature values. Because the clusters are not predefined, the algorithm itself determines class distributions in a statistical manner. This is useful for cases where several network traffics are unknown.

Clustering methods do not utilize the training instances that are predefined, as the supervised ML algorithms do. Instead, they utilize internalized heuristics in order to identify natural clusters [170]. These natural clusters are formed when the same-property instances are grouped together. Thus, by utilizing clustering methods that are different, different categories of clusters can be formed. For instance, when there is an instance that can be a part of several clusters, then it belongs to the overlapping group. If an instance belongs to one group, then it is a part of the exclusive cluster group. If, on the other hand, it is a part of the group that has a particular probability, then it belongs to the probabilistic cluster category. If instances are divided into groups at the top level and are then divided further all the way to the individual instances, then these types of instances belong to the hierarchical category [170]. Three clustering methods can be identified: incremental clustering (where instances are grouped according to the hierarchy), the probability-based clustering method (where instances are grouped into classes probabilistically [64]), and the K-means algorithm (where instances are grouped in separate clusters in domains that are numeric).

McGregor *et al.* in [164] was one of the earliest works to use the concept of the unsupervised ML method to cluster and group network traffic flows using transport layer features with expectation maximization (EM) algorithm. This approach specifically partitions traffic flows into different groups of applications based on similar observable properties of flows. However, the authors do not evaluate the accuracy of the clustering as well as identify the optimal features of traffic flows that help the EM clustering to produce the best outputs. In [153], Zander *et al.* proposed AutoClass approach which uses Bayesian clustering methods and an extension of EM algorithm to address the limitations McGregor *et al.* [164] work by guaranteeing the converge of a global maximum and also define the best set of features for better clustering performance. To find the global maximum rather than the local maximum, AutoClass repeats EM searches starting from pseudo-random points in parameter space, and thus it performs much better than the original EM algorithm.

Both the early works in [163] and [153] have shown that building a network classifiers using the clustering algorithms and the transport layer characteristics has the ability to improve the identification of Internet traffic applications. Erman *et al.* in [34] proposed to use the K-means clustering algorithm which is a partition-based algorithm and the DBSCAN algorithm which is a density-based algorithm to evaluate the predicating performance instead of the AutoClass algorithm which is a probabilistic model-based algorithm. Similar to other clustering approaches, the K-means and DBSCAN clustering algorithms used Euclidean distance to measure the similarity between two flow instances. While the K-means algorithm produces clusters that are spherical in shape, the DBSCAN algorithm is able to produce arbitrary-shaped clusters, which enable a network classifier to find an accurate set of clusters with minimum amount of analysis. They also demonstrated that both K-means and DBSCAN perform better and work more quickly than the clustering method of AutoClass used in [153]. The K-means and DBSCAN clustering algorithms are tested on a real dataset and can achieve a recall of 80%. In [13], the same clustering algorithms were applied to the transport layer characteristics of Internet traffic to build accurate network classifiers that can differentiate between Web and P2P applications, the resultant classifier models have obtained an accuracy of between 80% and 95%, precision of between 71.42% and 97.84%, and recall of between 62.10% and 97.32%.

To extract sets of traffic flows that have common communication patterns, Bernaille *et al.* in [162] generated natural clusters of traffic applications by using only the first few packets of a TCP flow. In contrast to the previously published works, this method is the first to use the size of the first few packets of a TCP flow as the features rather than extracting the features based on the whole packets of a flow to accurately classify the traffic application at early stage. The underlying intuition is that the first few packets give sufficient information as they carry the negotiation phase of an application, which is a predefined sequence of messages proceeding through distinct phases. The traffic classification mechanism includes two phases. First, learning phase is performed offline to cluster TCP flows into distinct groups using a set of training data. In their experiments, 1-h packet trace of TCP flows from a mix of applications was fed to the K-means clustering algorithm as a training set. In particular, the K-means clustering algorithm used the Euclidean distance to measure the similarity between flows resulting in forms of natural clusters that are used to define a set of rules. Second, classification phase is performed online to identify the accurate application type by using the previously generated rules to assign a new flow to an appropriate and corresponding cluster.

Yuan *et al.* in [171] came up with a new unsupervised ML approach for network traffic flow classification based on the concept of information entropy. First, in order to partition the traffic flows into different levels, a clustering algorithm based on the concept of the information entropy method is sequentially applied on traffic data collected from different active hosts. Second, during the clustering process, the parameters of the clusters and the dynamic properties of the clusters are adapted to categorize traffic flows into broad-based application types. The experimental results show that the classification accuracy of the entropy-based clustering is significantly better than existing clustering approaches. However, to further improve the accuracy of such approach, a combination of the unsupervised learning method with a supervising learning method-based SVM algorithm is proposed.

More recently, a graph-based framework for clustering P2P traffic classification has been proposed by Iliofotou *et al.* in [172]. In particular, the authors used the traffic dispersion graphs (TDGs) to capture network-wide interaction. For a graph, each node is an IP address, and the edge between two nodes indicates some type of interaction between those two nodes. This graph is able to detect network-wide behavior which is common among P2P applications and different from other traffic. In their work, graph-based classification first clusters traffic flows into natural groups using flow-level features in an unsupervised way without using prior application-specific knowledge. Then, the generated TDGs are used to classify new coming flows into their corresponding clusters. Two bidirectional flows are considered in this method. The advantage of this method is not only its high predicative capacity but also its visualization ability.

Zhang *et al.* in [173] proposed a novel approach to tackle the issue of unknown applications in the extreme difficult circumstance of small supervised training samples. The superior capability of the proposed approach to detect unknown flows originating from unknown applications is relying on the sufficient utilization of correlation information among real-world network traffic flows. To do so, two methods have been introduced to first enhance the capability of the nearest cluster-based classifiers and then combine the flow predictions to further boost the classification performance. Wang *et al.* in [174] proposed a novel approach for clustering the traffic flow, which is based on random forest (RF) proximities instead of Euclidean distances. The approach first measures the proximity of each pair of data points by performing a RF classification on the original data and a set of synthetic data. After that, a K-Medoids clustering is employed to partition the data points into K groups based on the proximity matrix. Compared with the classic clustering algorithms, the results show that this method performs much better for traffic clustering in terms of both overall accuracy and per-class performance.

The major advantage of the unsupervised ML lies in the automatic discovery of classes which recognizes natural patterns, i.e., clusters in the datasets. However, these clusters need to be labeled so that the new instances are mapped to applications in an appropriate manner. The issue of mapping clusters one-on-one to the applications still remains in the unsupervised ML schemes. Theoretically, the number of clusters would be equal to the number of application classes, with every application dominating just one cluster group. However, in practice, there is discrepancy between the number of clusters and the number of application classes. In reality, there are always a larger number of clusters than there are application classes. Furthermore, there is the possibility that an application can spread over several clusters and even dominate them. Hence, the issue will arise when mapping from one cluster to the application that is the source. When conducting the assessment of the unsupervised ML within the operational context, it is important to take into account the way the clusters are labeled, i.e., the way they are mapped to certain applications. It is also important to consider how the labeling can be updated with every new application detected as well as the optimal amount of clusters (computational complexity, labeling, and label lookup costs as well as accuracy balancing) [66].

(C) Semi-supervised machine-learning algorithms

A semi-supervised ML algorithm falls between supervised ML and unsupervised ML. Semi-supervised learning is able to make use of a small amount of labeled training data and a large amount of unlabeled data and is widely used in the Big Data era because labeling the data is always an expensive task and unlabeled data is always easy to obtain.

In contrast to supervised ML, an accurate representation of data distribution is difficult to obtain in semi-supervised ML with a small amount of training data, so that supervised learning is not possible in this scenario. Also, instead of simply using the knowledge of clusters grouped with the limited training data for the external validation, semi-supervised ML tries to use the limited knowledge to guide the further learning process. There are two major methods in semi-supervised ML: by adapting the similarity measure or modifying the search for better clusters. In similarity measure-based methods, a similarity measure has already been applied to the limited training data to obtain the initial clusters, but the similarity measure is adopted to satisfy the available constraints. Several semi-supervised methods fall into this category, including Euclidean distance with a shortest path algorithm, Mahalanobis distance with a convex optimization, hierarchical single or complete link, and K-means. In search-based methods, the algorithm of searching clusters is adapted to assist the clusters to fit the new constraints or labels. In terms of statistical learning, the semi-supervised learning methods include the methods of generative models, graph-based methods, and low-density separation. The semi-supervised learning is similar to the process of concept learning for humans, where a small amount of instruction is provided before the self-learning and the experience or knowledge is accumulated during his/her future learning with a large amount of unlabeled input data. Because of this self-learning characteristic, the methods of semi-supervised ML are also introduced for the Internet traffic classification and achieved promising learning performance.

Erman *et al.* introduced in [34] a robust semi-supervised ML method relying on K-means for an accurate offline and online traffic classification. First, K-means clustering is employed to partition a small amount of training data. Second, a mapping from the clusters to the various known classes is obtained according to the available labeled flows. The introduced mapping is adapted with the unlabeled data, and thus the clusters are learnt by mapping to the different flow types. The self-learning performance is promising as reported in [175]; high flow and byte classification accuracy ($\geq 90\%$) are obtained over a 6-month period with a small number of labeled and a large number of unlabeled flows.

A graphical model is a common framework to incrementally learn domain-specific knowledge. Rotsos *et al.* suggested in [35] a probabilistic graphical model for semi-supervised traffic classification. They assumed that the data samples satisfy the Gaussian distribution and extend the Naïve Bayesian classifier to learn the unlabeled data. Unlike methods, such as SVM, the model suggested in [35] can obtain a set of well-defined parameters which easily adapts the model to the requirements of the classification process and achieves very good results with a significantly reduced training dataset. However, their works depend on the accuracy of IP address detection; the performance would be poorer when training and testing environments are different.

A Gaussian mixture model based was proposed in [176] as a new semi-supervised classification method to accurately categorize different Internet flows. To achieve an optimum configuration, a wrapper-based feature subset selection method and CEM cluster algorithm are combined. More recently, Zhang *et al.* [173] introduced a semi-supervised clustering method based on the extended K-means clustering algorithm. In particular, as the quality of K-means clustering outputs is affected by the random selection of the clusters' centers in the initialization phase, Zhang *et al.* used the variance of the traffic flows to initialize cluster centers instead to boost the clustering performance. Meanwhile, they selected the few labeled instances to perform a mapping from the clusters to the predefined traffic class sets.

Instead of focusing only on the data instances, Wang *et al.* [177] considered the other available background information in the network domain to detect unknown applications. They described this available information in the form of pair-wise must-link constraints and incorporated them in the process of clustering. In particular, the three available constraints in the Internet traffic were used along with variants of the K-means algorithm to perform hard or soft constraint satisfaction and metric learning. A collection of real-world traffic traces from various locations of the Internet has been used to show the benefit of the widely available flow constraints in improving the accuracy and purity of the cluster.

Li *et al.* proposed in [178] a semi-supervised network traffic classification method based on incremental learning to improve accuracy, time consumption, and limited application range in traditional network traffic classification. The proposed method takes full advantage of a large number of unlabeled samples and a small amount of labeled samples to modify the SVM classifiers. The utilization of incremental learning technology can avoid unnecessary repetition training and improve the situation of low accuracy and inefficiency in original classifiers when new samples are added. Wong *et al.* in [179] examined the P2P sharing protocols of BitTorrent. They proposed a new detection method that is based on an intelligent combination of DPI and deep flow inspection with semi-supervised learning.

A semi-supervised approach, proposed by Shrivastav and Tiwari in [180], incorporates clustering and classification as two main stages. The training dataset is partitioned into several separate groups, i.e., clusters during the clustering stage. After the clusters have been formed, the classification, i.e., assigning class labels to the clusters, takes place by utilizing labeled data. In order to test the approach, the KDD Cup 1999 data set, which includes both attack and normal data, has been used. The results from the testing are compared to the SVM-based classifier. A self-training architecture was suggested in [181], which incorporates a few base classifiers which allow for the traffic database to be automatically built up without prior knowledge about data. Furthermore, this database is based on raw *tcpdump* traces. The results of the real and emulated traffic traces show that IDS trained on the given dataset has the same performance level as the systems trained on the hand-labeled data.

A combination of the unsupervised and semi-supervised ML methods, called MINETRAC, was suggested by Casas *et al.* in [182]. This combination allows for different IP flow classes with the similar characteristics to be identified and classified. MINETRAC employs clustering methods, utilizing subspace clustering, evidence accumulation as well as hierarchical clustering algorithms to inspect the inter-flow structures. It also allows for the traffic flows to be categorized according to natural groupings by connecting the data structure evidence. The evidence is provided by the same set of traffic flows. Semi-supervised learning is utilized by the automatic classification. A small part of the ground truth flows is used for the mapping of the known clusters into their applications, or network services. These applications/network services are probably the source of the known clusters.

Zhang *et al.* in [183] came up with a semi-supervised learning method to target the problem of new network traffic generated by previously unknown applications in a traffic classification system, called a zero-day traffic problem. By incorporating a generic unknown class into conventional multi-class classification framework, this problem becomes how to obtain the training samples of zero-day traffic. After that, they extracted the zero-day traffic information from a set of unlabeled traffic which are randomly collected from the target network.

There are two main reasons why semi-supervised ML is very useful in traffic flow classification. First, fast and accurate classifiers can be trained with a small number of labeled flows with a large number of unlabeled flows which are easily obtained. Second, the semi-supervised ML is robust and can handle previously unseen applications and the variation of existing concepts. However, the semi-supervised ML approaches would be misleading in their learning process, specifically when there are few labeled training data. Hence, the assumed model has to be accurate at the beginning of the learning process.

3.4.3   Ensemble learning

To date, much work has been done in order to obtain a good classification or clustering performance using ML. Ensemble methods have many advantages in comparison with single learner methods that were previously discussed for traffic classification. In ensemble learning methods, weak learners work together and build final decision considering the result of each learner. Many different methods such as bagging and boosting have been proposed in classical ML for making the final decision

In [184], Yan *et al.* proposed a weighted combination method for traffic classification. This approach first takes advantage of the confidence values inferred by each individual classifier, then assigns a weight to each classifier according to its prediction accuracy on a validation traffic dataset. In [185], Reddy and Hota proposed to use *stacking* and *voting* ensemble learning methods to improve prediction accuracy. Several base classifiers were used in their method, including Naïve Bayes classifier, Bayesian network, and decision trees. Before training the classifiers, feature selection methods were applied to reduce the number of features, thereby reducing the training time. They showed that a high classification accuracy of up to 99.9% is obtained in their experiments. Meanwhile, their experimental results also showed that *stacking* performs better over *voting* in identifying P2P traffic.

He *et al.* [186,187] combined an ensemble learning paradigm with semi-supervised co-training methods for network traffic classification. Co-training semi-supervised learning utilizes both labeled and unlabeled samples. Because unlabeled samples are used to refine the classifiers, a high accuracy can be obtained by training with a small number of labeled samples mixed with a large number of unlabeled samples.

Aliakbarian and Fanian proposed in [188] a new ensemble method for network traffic classification. First, they choose the best subset of features using a multi-objective evolutionary algorithm so a new dataset is produced with them. As comparative algorithms, two ensemble methods, bagging and boosting, are used in this chapter. In the bagging method, the feature vector is chosen randomly; then, each feature subset inputs some weak learners. The final decision is obtained by using majority voting of these learners based on each learner's accuracy. In their boosting algorithm, the difference is that if a weak learner classifies a sample incorrectly, the probability of choosing this sample will increase in the next weak learner. Results show that the proposed ensemble method has better classification performance in comparison with other methods, specifically for P2P traffic.

Govindarajan [24] designed a hybrid ensemble approach for network intrusion detection. The ensemble classifier was designed using a radial basis function (RBF) and SVM as base classifiers. It was constructed by voting with the modified training sets which are obtained by resampling the original training set. They showed that this proposed RBF-SVM hybrid system is superior to the individual approach in terms of classification accuracy.

Both empirical results and theoretical analysis show that the ensemble method tends to yield better results compared to a single base classifier. The advantage of the ensemble method comes from the diversity amongst the models used. Moreover, the lower computation cost of weak classifiers makes them easier to apply network traffic analysis.

3.5 Network traffic classification issues

This section presents a comprehensive study of other relevant areas of network classification, including summarization, sampling, ground truth, and privacy-preserving for traffic data. This is an important task to discuss the open issues and challenges in the field that would help in improving the classification accuracy and efficiency.

3.5.1 Summarization

Network traffic monitoring can be considered a knowledge discovery process in which the data of network traffic is analyzed. In a data mining scenario, data summarization is a useful tool to discover underlying knowledge in the data. Recently, many researchers have introduced the data summarization method for network traffic monitoring and intrusion detection [81,189–192]. Currently, there are many existing data summarization methods for different applications, such as frequent itemset mining [193] and clustering [81,190,191,194].

Xu *et al.* [189] considered that compact summaries of cluster information to provide interpretive report help network operators achieve security and management by narrowing down the scope of a deeper investigation into specific clusters and explain the observed behavior. To do so, an information-theoretic and data mining approach are used to extract clusters of significance on the basis of the underlying feature value distribution (or entropy) in the fixed dimension. Given the extracted clusters along each dimension of the feature space, the compact summarization method is used to discover "structures" among the clusters and build common behavior models for traffic profiling. Hence, the essential information about the cluster such as substance feature values and interaction among the free dimensions is revealed in the structural behavior model of a cluster with a compact summary of its constituent flows.

Cohen *et al.* [190] developed algorithms that collect more informative summaries through an efficient use of available resources. Unbiased estimators that use these more informative counts were derived. The superior of these estimators are those with smaller variance on all packet streams and subpopulations. The proposed summarization algorithm generates a sketch of the packet streams, which allows us to process approximate subpopulation-size queries and other aggregates.

Mahmood *et al.* [81] proposed a summarization framework based on the concept of clustering to provide network operators with a concise report. They investigated the use of BIRCH which is hierarchical-based clustering algorithm to efficiently discover the interesting traffic patterns. Their framework was designed to deal with mixed types of attributes including numerical, categorical, and hierarchical attributes. In order to find multidimensional clusters and to deal with multivariate attributes in the network traffic records, they introduced three new distance functions within the BIRCH clustering algorithm. Then, these three distance functions are used to calculate the various types of traffic attributes and accurately describe the relationships among different records and clusters. The index nodes for the BIRCH can be considered holding summaries for each cluster and then used to form the final summary report.

In [191], Mahmood *et al.* proposed a three-level method to summarize network traffic. They generated a reasonably compact and accurate summary report from a given network traffic trace. They first applied hierarchical cluster formation to a traffic trace to identify a detailed set of aggregate traffic flows and then extract a compact summary report by applying a summarization algorithm to the clusters. Similar to their previous work, each node corresponds to a cluster C, and the CF-entries in the node correspond to the subclusters $C_1, \ldots, C_l$ of C. Two summarization methods were proposed using the size and homogeneity of clusters.

3.5.2   Privacy preserving

Network customers have become increasingly concerned about their personal data, especially with the great development in communication and IT systems. Thus, to protect the right to privacy, numerous statutes, directives, and regulations have been developed in recent decades [195]. The "right to privacy" is defined as "the right to be let alone" in Warren and Brandeis' report [196]. The current regulations in many countries enforce strict policies for storing and processing the personal data, which aim to guarantee people control of the flow of their personal data. The service suppliers in their IT systems are trained to implement these privacy regulations when handling personal data.

Guarda and Zannone in [195] helped researchers by providing them with referenced work for clear definition of privacy and data protection policies when developing privacy-aware systems, including the languages and methodologies. They also analyzed the current proposals in the corresponding research area for explicitly addressing privacy concerns. They reviewed the state-of-the-art in privacy requirements engineering, privacy policy specification, and privacy-aware access control and the relationships among these research areas in different countries to guarantee the consistency of enterprise goals, data protection, and privacy policies.

Park Yong in [197] undertook an empirical study to examine the relationship between online market structure and the provision of privacy protection in a composite sample of 398 heavily trafficked and randomly selected US commercial sites to answer the following question: How do online market conditions and website business characteristics affect the level of privacy protection? Their analysis shows that most corporate awareness does not readily translate into specific provisions of privacy protection, even though other scholars have found that managerial attention to privacy concerns in fact has increased recently, indicating a possible role of the markets in regulating privacy in different ways.

However, it is remarkably hard to keep Internet communication private. General privacy-preservation methods are committed to data protection at a lower privacy level, and the research into privacy protection methods is focused on data distortion, data encryption, and so on. One method of protecting the privacy of a network connection is to use an encrypted link to a proxy or server. Bissias *et al.* in [198] presented a straightforward traffic analysis attack against this kind of encrypted HTTP stream. Surprisingly, the source of the traffic can be effectively identified in their proposed attack. A designed attacker first creates a profile of the statistical characteristics of web requests from interesting sites, including distributions of packet sizes and inter-arrival times. After that, they compare the candidate-encrypted streams with these profiles. They show that the attacker achieves 40% when 25 candidate sites are considered and achieves 100% accuracy for 3 candidate sites. However, the accuracy would be decreased when there are longer delays after training.

The work of Bissias demonstrated that the supposedly secure channels on the Internet are prone to privacy infringement due to packet traffic features leaking information about the user activity and traffic content such as packet lengths, directions, and times. Iacovazzi and Baiocchi [199] called this method "traffic masking." In [199], they defined a security model that indicates what the best target of masking is and then proposed the optimized traffic masking algorithm that removes any leaking (full masking). After that, the trade-off between traffic privacy protection and masking cost, namely the required amount of overhead and realization complexity feasibility, can be determined.

3.5.3 Discretization

We have to note that the network traffic flow data is continuous. Most of the current ML methods, such as decision tree-based learning and Naïve Bayes methods, cannot be applied directly to the continuous features. To make those ML methods work, discretization is one of the methods used to cut the data into ranges and apply a variable number of cuts to the continuous attributes. Mazumder *et al.* [200] considered a discretization solution which partitions numeric variables into a number of subranges and treats each such subrange as a category. We measured the contribution of a given interval corresponding to a particular decision (normal or anomaly). An ideal discretization method which minimizes the number of intervals without significant loss of class-attribute mutual dependence was proposed by maximizing the interdependence between class labels and attribute values. There are three sub-modules to divide the task of discretization prior to the learning process. They first determine the number of discrete intervals, find the width or the boundaries of the intervals depending on the range of values of each continuous attribute, and map the attribute values from the continuous domain to the discrete domain.

As the Naïve Bayes classifier suffers from continuous attributes, Liu *et al.* [201] applied the discretization method on traffic data for accurate Internet identification. The underlying idea of this method is that the discretization provides an alternative to probability density estimation when Naïve Bayes learning involves continuous and quantitative attributes. The efficiency of the Naïve Bayes and the discretization method has been demonstrated with AUCKLAND VI and entry traffic datasets.

In [166], Lim *et al.* investigated the performance of the C4.5 decision tree algorithm when used with ports and the sizes of the first five consecutive packets. The performance results showed that the C4.5 decision tree algorithm was able to achieve the highest accuracy on every trace and application, with 96.7% accuracy on average, due to its own entropy-based discretization capability. Based on this observation, they proposed an entropy-based discretization method to discretize the input flow features and to improve the classification tasks of other ML algorithms as well (e.g., Naïve Bayes and kNN). The experimental study showed that the entropy-based minimum description length algorithm can significantly improve the performance of the candidate ML algorithms by as much as 59.8%, making all of them achieve more than 93% accuracy on average without considering the tuning processes of any algorithm. The authors have compared the performance of the entropy-based discretization against one of the simplest discretization method, namely the equal-interval-width, and they found the proposed method can significantly improve the classification accuracy by about 13%.

3.5.4   Sampling

A typical network traffic flow monitoring involves a collection of flow records at various intermediate network nodes/points, such as routers. While the monitoring of a fundamental task of network traffic flow seems to be easy, collecting and observing the traffic flows at high speeds are extremely challenging tasks especially under excessively resource-constrained environments. It is impractical to record all the traffic flow data and learn the patterns of these traffic flows because the resource requirements (e.g., memory and CPU) in routers are mostly used for number of vital functions such as route computation, forwarding, scheduling, protocol processing, and so on. Therefore, in network traffic flow monitoring, routers randomly select a subset of packets using sampling methods to meet this challenge.

The high demands of flow measurement as a fundamental ingredient in most network management tasks have attracted the attention of router vendors, including Cisco and Juniper, and motivated them to solve a basic flow measurement problem. The NetFlow [202] in routers was designed under this situation. NetFlow records and maintains the statistics features of traffic flow, including packet and byte counters and information about TCP flags (e.g., Urgent, Ack, Syn, and Fin), timestamps of the first and last packets among other information [202]. It observes each packet which enters or exits a router interface and checks to see if there is already a flow record for that packet. In the case where the flow record has been previously observed, the information from incoming packet is fused into the existing flow record. Otherwise, it creates a new flow record according to this new packet. The NetFlow also helps to sample the coming packets according to a configurable sampling ratio. Several variation methods have been proposed on the basis of this idea. While Flow sampling uses hash-based flow selection for flow sampling, rather than the traditional random packet sampling, FlowSlices [203] combines both hash-based flow selection and the random sampling method together. In particular, it uses different types of sampling for the resources of the routers, including memory, CPU. For instance, it uses packet sampling for regulating the CPU usage and flow sampling to regulate the memory usage.

Hohn and Veitch [204] used the results of sampling from a theoretical perspective for recovering traffic statistics. They applied their proposed approach, namely Inverted Sampling, to both packet and flow filtering. Three statistical information recovery layers were defined in their approach, including the packet layer which observes the spectral density for packet arrival, the flow layer which deals with the distribution for flow packet, and finally an internal flows layer which investigates the average rate of the packet arrival per flow packet. Extensive experimental analysis shows that the proposed inverted sampling approach could even retrieve exact characteristics and attributes, such as its spectrum or the distribution of flow size, from the raw traffic data.

Kumar and Xu [205] proposed a "sketch-guided sampling" method that relies on a probability function to estimate the flow size. This method is intended to decrease the sampling rate for large flows, while increasing the sampling rate for smaller flows. Consequently, using this method for sampling, the accuracy of small flows can improve significantly, while the accuracy of large flows can marginally deteriorate.

For the application of traffic flow size estimation, Ramachandran *et al.* proposed the FlexSample [206] method to explicitly improve the flow coverage by advocating the use of an online sketch to obtain flow size estimates. Using FlexSample, both the volume of the flow and the flow coverage can be accurately estimated.

Saxena and Kompella [207] improved the flexibility of flow monitoring by introducing a novel class-based sampling framework, namely CLAMP. This CLAMP framework increases the fidelity of flow measurements for a certain class of flows based on the interest of the network operators. In particular, the core idea of CLAMP is to encapsulate various class definitions using the composite Bloom filter to work together and also maximizing the objectives of flow coverage and the accuracy of certain class of flows during the implementation of the CLAMP framework.

He and Hou [208] studied three self-similarity sampling methods for Internet traffic: static systematic sampling, stratified random sampling, and simple random sampling. Three of the most important parameters for a self-similarity process have been taken also into account and investigated in their studies. These parameters include the mean (first-order statistics), the Hurst parameter (second-order statistics), and the average variance of the sampling results. Their work has made several major observations: first, they showed that all three sampling methods fail to identify the mean (first-order statistics) precisely, this is due to the natural characteristics of the Internet traffic; second, they also demonstrated that the Hurst parameter (second-order statistics) of Internet traffic can be captured accurately on the three sampling methods; third, they showed that static systematic sampling can cope with the smallest variation of sampling results across different sampling methods; and fourth, an important observation of a self-similarity process showed that the sampled mean is usually far less than the real mean because a sufficiently high sampling rate requires large values of samples to be available in advance which is less likely. To address this limitation, they proposed a biased systematic sampling method to provide much more accurate mean estimations and keep the overhead of sampling low.

Another important aspect of the sampling method is the resampling of the multi-class data for traffic flow classification. The resample of a multi-class is important to address the issue of imbalance of the Internet flows which occurs when some applications, known as "majority classes," generate much more traffic flows than other applications, known as "minority classes." For this imbalance scenario, the majority classes always have much better classification performance than the minority classes. However, the minority classes are also important to network traffic management. Similar to the imbalance learning problem in classic ML [209], many solutions have been proposed for network traffic flow classification. Zhen and Qiong [210] investigated the use of flow-rate-based cost matrix (FCM) which is cost-sensitive learning to improve the minority classes with a few bytes in Internet traffic classification, and then they proposed a new cost matrix known as weighted cost matrix to calculate the optimal weight for each cost of FCM. They also consider the data imbalance degree of each class to further boost the performance of network classifier on the issue of minority classes.

Yang and Michailidis [211] examined the problem of nonparametric estimation of network flow characteristics, namely packet lengths and byte sizes, based on sampled flow data. Two approaches were proposed: the first one is based on a single-stage Bernoulli sampling of packets and their corresponding byte sizes. Subsequently, the flow length distribution is estimated by an adaptive EM algorithm that in addition provides an estimate for the number of active flows. The flow sizes (in bytes) are estimated by using a random effects regression model that utilizes the flow length information previously obtained. The second one combines a two-stage sampling procedure in which the first stage samples flow amongst the active ones, while the second stage samples packet from the sampled flows. Subsequently, the flow length distribution is estimated using another EM algorithm and the flow byte sizes based on a regression model. In [212], Fernandes *et al.* explored the use of a stratified sampling method to select adequate samples. After the evaluation with two partitioning clustering methods, namely clustering large applications and K-means, the superiority of the stratified sampling method on both size and flow duration estimate is validated.

More recently, Zander *et al.* [213] proposed the method of subflow packet sampling to reduce ML sub-flow classifier's resource requirements with minimal compromise of accuracy. Two different classifiers, C4.5 decision trees and Naïve Bayes, were used to evaluate the classification performance.

3.5.5 Ground truth

The evaluation of the learning approaches for network traffic flow classification requires the availability of accurate ground truth. This is necessary to compare the results of such learning approaches with the right answer. However, it is impossible to obtain publicly available ground truth traffic packets included with known payload data; this is due to the privacy matter. Meanwhile, it is also usually inefficient and hard to generate ground truth data by manually triggering applications on different machines and labeling the corresponding generated flows.

In [214], Gringoli *et al.* presented a distributed system, named GT, for capturing Internet traffic in a computer network. They designed a special software agent, named "client daemon" which is deployed on each monitored machine in the network. The agent retrieves from the kernel the name of the application that generated each flow and sends this information to a remote back-end. The agent periodically scans a list of opened network sockets and searches the names of applications that own them. For each socket, the information is stored, including current time-stamp, local and remote IP address and port number, transport protocol, and application name. At the same time, a packet capture engine runs on the gateway router so that all the traffic coming from and into the local network is captured, while a database server collects the labels assigned by client daemons. Finally, a post-processing tool, called ipclass, is run to process the gathered information and packet. The tool connects the agent gt which collects socket information with the packet capture engine on routers. The ground truth is produced by labeling each flow with an application and pinpointing the flow's characteristics. The authors validated their method on a 218-GB dataset and showed more than 99% of bytes and 95% of flows.

Dusi *et al.* in [215] qualified the error that the classical approaches, such as port-based and DPI-based, make when establishing ground truth related to application-layer protocols. They also compared their developed "gt" tool [214] to these traditional approaches. The data they analyzed demonstrated that port numbers can still be a good source of ground truth information for web and email traffic, specifically in non-firewalled networks. Their analysis from experiments also showed that there is poor accuracy of ground truth with transport ports for P2P, Streaming or Skype traffic, as well as with DPI in which no more than 14% of bytes from P2P traffic, but almost 100% of Skype on TCP and Streaming can be achieved.

Gargiulo *et al.* in [181] developed a self-training system to build a dataset of labeled network traffic based on raw *tcpdump* traces without prior knowledge of data. Each packet is labeled either as normal or as belonging to an attack pattern, based on Dempster–Shafer theory. Results for both emulated and real traffic traces have shown that IDS trained on such a dataset perform as well as the same systems trained on correctly hand-labeled data.

A novel architecture, called Flowsing, was suggested by Lu *et al.* in [216]. This architecture concentrates on generating the correct ground truth, such as payload data, automatically. As a multi-agent-based offline ground truth generator, Flowsing's main aim is to generate correct full-scale ground. Ground truth database that the Flowsing generated includes the traffic traces and the flow statistical information that corresponds with them. A network traffic collection, traffic split, and traffic aggregation are three models that are a part of the Flowsing. The network traffic packets together with their process information are collected in the traffic collection part. These packets are then separated and categorized into pure flows offline, which are then assembled in the traffic aggregation part. Here, statistical information is calculated as well. After all three steps have been completed, full-scale ground truth is produced.

3.6 Conclusion

Accurate network traffic classification has been the basis of many network management activities. Many of these activities involve flow prioritization, diagnostic monitoring as well as traffic policing and shaping. The main goal of network traffic classification is to find the network traffic mixture. Even though a number of classification methods have been recently proposed, none of them have been validated entirely, as most validations were poor and ad hoc. There are many reasons for such poor validations, including unavailability of dependable validation methods. Furthermore, there are no reference packet traces that use well defined and clear content. All the methods used for the network classification have shown one consistency and that is that they cannot be used for a broad range of application traffic on the Internet.

Chapter 4

A taxonomy and empirical analysis of clustering algorithms for traffic classification

Clustering algorithms have emerged as an alternative powerful meta-learning tool to accurately analyze the massive volume of data generated by modern applications. In particular, their main goal is to categorize data into clusters such that objects are grouped in the same cluster when they are "similar" according to specific metrics. There is a vast body of knowledge in the area of clustering and there have been attempts to analyze and categorize them for a larger number of applications. However, one of the major issues in using clustering algorithms for big data that created a confusion amongst the practitioners is the lack of consensus in the definition of their properties as well as a lack of formal categorization. With the intention of alleviating these problems, this chapter introduces concepts and algorithms related to clustering, a concise survey existing (clustering) algorithms as well as providing a comparison both from a theoretical and empirical perspective. From a theoretical perspective, we come up with a categorizing framework based on the main properties pointed out in previous study. Empirically, extensive experiments are carried out where we compared the most representative algorithm from each of the categories using a large number of real (big) data sets. The effectiveness of the candidate clustering algorithms is measured through a number of internal and external validity metrics, stability, runtime, and scalability tests. Additionally, we highlighted the set of clustering algorithms that are the best performing for big data.

4.1 Introduction

In current digital era according to (as far) massive progress and development of internet and online world technologies, such as big and powerful data servers, we face huge volume of information and data day by day from many different resources and services, which were not available to human kind just a few decades ago. Massive quantities of data are produced by and about people, things, and their interactions. Diverse groups argue about the potential benefits and costs of analyzing information from Twitter, Google, Verizon, 23andMe, Facebook, Wikipedia, and every space, where large groups of people leave digital traces and deposit data. These data come from available different online resources and services, which are established to serve the customers. Services and resources, like sensor networks, cloud storages, and social networks, produce big volume of data and also need to manage and reuse that data or some analytical aspects of the data. Although this massive volume of data can be really useful for people and corporates, it could be problematic as well. Therefore, big volume of data or big data has its own deficiencies as well. They need big storages and this volume makes operations, such as analytical operations, process operations, and retrieval operations, really difficult and hugely time consuming. One resolution to overcome these difficult problems is to have big data clustered in "compact format" and still informative version of the entire data. Such clustering methods aim then to produce a "good" quality of clusters/summaries. Therefore, they would hugely benefit everyone from ordinary users to researches and corporate world, as it can provide an efficient tool to deal with large data, such as critical systems (to detect cyberattacks).

The main goal of this chapter is to provide readers with a proper analysis of the different classes of available clustering methods for big data by experimentally comparing them with real big data. The chapter does not refer to simulation tools but specifically implementing an efficient algorithm from each class and provide the experimental results on a variety of big data sets. Some aspects then need a careful attention when dealing with big data, therefore, helping to select those methods that are suitable for big data. *V*olume of the data is the first and obvious important characteristic to deal with when clustering big data comparing to conventional data clustering, as this requires substantial changes in the architecture of storage systems. The other important characteristic of big data is *V*elocity. This requirement leads to highly demand for online processing of data, where processing speed is required to deal with data flows. *V*ariety is the third characteristic, where different data types, such as text, image, and video, are produced from various sources, such as sensors and mobile phones. These three "Vs" (Volume, Velocity, and Variety) are the core characteristics of big data, which must be taken into account when selecting clustering methods.

Despite a vast number of surveys for clustering algorithms have been developed in literature [217–220] (in various application domains, such as machine learning, data mining, information retrieval, pattern recognition, bioinformatics, and semantic ontology); it is extremely difficult for users to decide a priori, which algorithm would be the *most appropriate* for a given big data set. This is because some of the limitations in existing reviews: (i) the characteristics of the algorithms are not well studied; (ii) the field has produced many new algorithms, which were not considered in these surveys; and (iii) no rigorous empirical analysis has been carried out to ascertain the benefit of one algorithm over another. Motivated by these reasons, this chapter attempts to review the field of clustering algorithms and achieve the following objectives:

- Propose a categorizing framework that systematically groups a collection of existing clustering algorithms into categories and compares their advantages and drawbacks from a theoretical point of view.
- Present a complete taxonomy of the clustering evaluation measurements to be used for empirical study.
- Make an empirical study analyzing the most representative algorithm of each category with respect to both theoretical and empirical perspectives.

Therefore, the proposed survey presents a complete taxonomy of clustering algorithms and proposes a categorizing framework that covers major factors in the selection of a suitable algorithms for big data. It further conducts experiments involving the most representative clustering algorithm of each category, large number of evaluation metrics, and ten traffic data sets.

The rest of this chapter is organized as follows. Section 4.2 provides a review of clustering algorithm categories. Section 4.3 describes the proposed criteria and properties for the categorizing framework. In Section 4.4, we group and compare different clustering algorithms based on the proposed categorizing framework. Section 4.5 introduces the taxonomy of clustering evaluation measurements, describes the experimental framework, and summarizes the experimental results. Section 4.6 concludes the chapter.

4.2 Clustering algorithm categories

As there are so many clustering algorithms, this section introduces a categorizing framework that groups the various clustering algorithms found in the literature into distinct categories. The categorizing framework is developed from an algorithm designer's perspective that focuses on the technical details about the general procedures of clustering process. Accordingly, the process of different clustering algorithms can be broadly categorized into the following classes:

- **Partitioning based**: In such algorithms, all clusters are determined promptly. Initial groups are specified and reallocated toward a union. In other words, partitioning algorithms divide data objects into number of partitions, where each partition represents a cluster. These clusters should fulfill the following requirements: (i) each group must contain at least one object, and (ii) each object must belong to exactly one group. For example, in K-means algorithm, a center is the average of all points and coordinates representing the arithmetic mean. In K-medoids algorithm, objects that are near the center represent the clusters. There are many other partitioning algorithms, such as K-modes, PAM, CLARA, CLARANS, and Fuzzy c-means (FCM).
- **Hierarchical based**: Data are organized in a hierarchical manner depending on medium of proximity. Proximities are obtained by the intermediate nodes. A dendrogram represents the data sets, where individual datum is presented by leaf nodes. The initial cluster gradually divides into several clusters as the hierarchy continues. Hierarchical clustering methods can be agglomerative (bottom-up) or divisive (top-down). An agglomerative clustering starts with one object for each cluster and recursively merges two or more most appropriate clusters. A divisive clustering starts with the data set as one cluster and recursively splits the most appropriate cluster. The process continues until a stopping criterion (frequently, the requested number k of clusters) is reached. The hierarchical method has a major drawback though, which relates to the fact that once a step (merge or split) is done, it can never be undone. BIRCH, CURE, ROCK, and Chameleon are some of the well-known algorithms of this category.

- **Density based**: Here, data objects are separated based on their regions of density, connectivity, and boundary. They are closely related to a point's nearest neighbors. A cluster, defined as a connected dense component, grows in any direction that density leads. Therefore, density-based algorithms are capable of discovering clusters of arbitrary shapes. Also, this provides a natural protection against outliers. Thus, the overall density of a point is analyzed to determine the functions of data sets that influence a particular data point. DBSCAN, OPTICS, DBCLASD, and DENCLUE are algorithms that use such a method to filter out noise (outliers) and discover clusters of arbitrary shape.

- **Grid based**: The space of the data objects is divided into grids. The main advantage of the approach is its fast processing time, because it goes through the data set once to compute the statistical values for the grids. The accumulated grid-data make grid-based clustering methods independent of the number of data objects that employ a uniform grid to collect the regional statistic data and, then, perform the clustering on the grid, instead of the database directly. The performance of grid-based method depends on the size of the grid, which is usually much less than the size of the database. However, for highly irregular data distributions, using a single uniform grid may not be sufficient to obtain a required clustering quality or fulfill the time requirement. Wave-Cluster and STING are typical examples of this category.

- **Model based**: Such a method optimizes the fit between a given data and some (predefined) mathematical model. It is based on the assumption that the data are generated by a mixture of underlying probability distributions. Also, it leads to a way of automatically determining the number of clusters based on standard statistics, taking noise (outliers) into account and thus, yielding a robust clustering method. There are two major approaches that are based on the model-based method: *statistical* and *neural network*. MCLUST is probably the most well-known model-based algorithm, but there are other good algorithms, such as expectation maximization (EM) algorithm (which uses a mixture density model), conceptual clustering (such as COBWEB), and neural network approaches (such as self-organizing feature maps). The *statistical* approach uses probability measurements in determining the concepts or clusters. Probabilistic descriptions are typically used to represent each derived concept. The *neural network* approach uses a set of connected input/output units, where each connection has a weight associated with it. Neural networks have several properties that make them popular for clustering. First, neural networks are inherently parallel and distributed processing architectures. Second, neural networks learn by adjusting their interconnection weights so as to best fit the data. This allows them to normalize or prototype. Patterns act as features (or attributes) extractors for the various clusters. Third, neural networks process numerical vectors and require object patterns to be represented by quantitative features only. Many clustering tasks handle only numerical data or can transform their data into quantitative features if needed. The neural network approach to clustering tends to represent each cluster as an exemplar. An exemplar acts as a prototype of the cluster and does not necessarily have to correspond to a particular object. New objects can be distributed

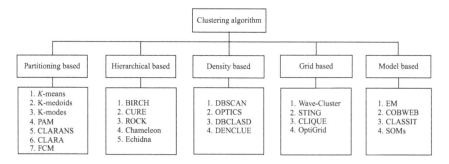

Figure 4.1   Overview of clustering taxonomy

to the cluster, whose exemplar is the most similar, based on some distance measure.

Figure 4.1 provides an overview of the clustering algorithms taxonomy following the five classes of categorization studied previously.

4.3   Criteria to compare clustering methods

When evaluating clustering methods for big data, specific criterion needs to be used to evaluate the relative strengths and weaknesses of every algorithm with respect to the three-dimensional properties of big data, including Volume, Velocity, and Variety. This section defines such properties and compiled the key criterion of each property.

- *Volume* refers to the ability of clustering algorithm to deal with large amount of data. To guide the selection of a suitable clustering algorithm with respect to the *Volume* property, the following criteria are considered: (i) size of data set, (ii) handling high dimensionality, and (iii) handling outliers/noisy data.
- *Variety* refers to ability of clustering algorithm to handle different types of data (numerical, categorical, and hierarchical). To guide the selection of a suitable clustering algorithm with respect to the *Variety* property, the following criteria are considered: (i) type of data set and (ii) cluster's shape.
- *Velocity* refers to the speed of clustering algorithm on big data. To guide the selection of a suitable clustering algorithm with respect to the *Velocity* property, the following criteria are considered: (i) complexity of algorithm and (ii) the runtime performance.

In what follows, we explain in detail the corresponding criterion of each property of big data:

1. *Type of data set:* Most of the traditional clustering algorithms are designed to focus either on numeric data or on categorical data. The collected data in real world often contain both numeric and categorical attributes. It is difficult for

applying traditional clustering algorithm directly into these kinds of data. Clustering algorithms work effectively either on pure numeric data or on pure categorical data, most of them perform poorly on mixed categorical and numerical data types.

2. *Size of data set:* The size of data set has a major effect on the clustering quality. Some clustering methods are more efficient than the other clustering methods, when the data size is small and vice versa.

3. *Input parameter:* A desirable feature for "practical" clustering is the one that has fewer parameters, since a large number of parameters may affect cluster quality because they will depend on the values of the parameters.

4. *Handling outliers/noisy data:* A successful algorithm will often be able to handle outlier/noisy data because of the fact that the data in most of the real applications are not pure. Also, noise makes it difficult for an algorithm to cluster an object into a suitable cluster. This therefore affects the results of the algorithm.

5. *Time complexity:* Most of the clustering methods required to be used several times to increase the clustering quality. Therefore, if the process takes too long, then it can become impractical for applications that handle big data.

6. *Stability:* One of the important features for any clustering algorithm is the ability to generate the same partition of the data irrespective of the order, in which the patterns are presented to the algorithm.

7. *Handling high dimensionality:* It is particularly an important feature in cluster analysis because many applications require the analysis of objects containing a large number of features (dimensions). For example, text documents may contain thousands of terms or keywords as features. It is challenging due to the curse of dimensionality. Many dimensions may not be relevant. As the number of dimensions increases, the data become increasingly sparse so that the distance measurement between pairs of points becomes meaningless and the average density of points anywhere in the data is likely to be low.

8. *Cluster shape:* A good clustering algorithm should consider the real data and be able to handle its wide variety of data types, all these different data types will take an arbitrary shape as a result of the clustering algorithm, which should be handled by the clustering algorithms.

4.4   Candidate clustering algorithms

This section aims to find the *good* candidate clustering algorithms for big data. By *good* we refer to those algorithms that satisfy most of the criteria listed in Section 4.3. Table 4.1 provides a summary of the evaluation we performed on the various methods described in Section 4.2 based on these criteria. After this evaluation, the next step is to select the most appropriate clustering algorithm from each category based on the proposed criteria, so to benchmark them for big data. In this way, the best algorithm is selected from each method, and these (selected algorithms) will be properly evaluated. This process produced the following selection: FCM [221], BIRCH [222], DENCLUE [84], OptiGird [87], and EM [223].

This section discusses each of the selected algorithms in details and shows how it works, its strengths and weakness, as well as the input parameters it takes.

Table 4.1 Categorization of clustering algorithms with respect to big data proprieties and other criteria described in Section 4.3

Categories	Abb. name	Volume		Handling noisy data	Variety	Cluster's shape	Velocity	Other criteria
		Size of data set	Handling high dimensionality		Type of data set		Complexity of algorithm	Input parameter
Partitional algorithms	K-means [224]	Large	No	No	Numerical	Non-convex	$O(nkd)$	1
	K-modes [225]	Large	Yes	No	Categorical	Non-convex	$O(n)$	1
	K-medoids [226]	Small	Yes	Yes	Categorical	Non-convex	$O(n^2dt)$	1
	PAM [227]	Small	No	No	Numerical	Non-convex	$O(k(n-k)^2)$	1
	CLARA [228]	Large	No	No	Numerical	Non-convex	$O(k(40+k)^2+k(n-k))$	1
	CLARANS [78]	Large	No	No	Numerical	Non-convex	$O(kn^2)$	2
	FCM [221]	Large	No	No	Numerical	Non-convex	$O(n)$	1
Hierarchical algorithms	BIRCH [222]	Large	No	No	Numerical	Non-convex	$O(n)$	2
	CURE [229]	Large	Yes	Yes	Numerical	Arbitrary	$O(n^2 \log n)$	2
	ROCK [230]	Large	No	No	Categorical and numerical	Arbitrary	$O(n^2 + nmmma + n^2\log n)$	1
Density-based algorithms	Chameleon [82]	Large	Yes	No	All type of data	Arbitrary	$O(n^2)$	3
	ECHIDNA [231]	Large	No	No	Multivariate data	Non-convex	$O(N \times B(1 + \log_B m))$	2
	DBSCAN [83]	Large	No	No	Numerical	Arbitrary	$O(n \log n)$ If a spatial index is used Otherwise, it is $O(n^2)$.	2
	OPTICS [85]	Large	No	Yes	Numerical	Arbitrary	$O(n \log n)$	2
	DBCLASD [232]	Large	No	Yes	Numerical	Arbitrary	$O(3n^2)$	No
	DENCLUE [84]	Large	Yes	Yes	Numerical	Arbitrary	$O(\log |D|)$	2
Grid-based algorithms	Wave-Cluster [233]	Large	No	Yes	Special data	Arbitrary	$O(n)$	3
	STING [88]	Large	No	Yes	Special data	Arbitrary	$O(k)$	1
	CLIQUE [234]	Large	Yes	No	Numerical	Arbitrary	$O(Ck + mk)$	2
	OptiGrid [87]	Large	Yes	Yes	Special data	Arbitrary	Between $O(nd)$ and $O(nd \log n)$	3
Model-based algorithms	EM [223]	Large	Yes	No	Special data	Non-convex	$O(knp)$	3
	COBWEB [235]	Small	No	No	Numerical	Non-convex	$O(n^2)$	1
	CLASSIT [236]	Small	No	No	Numerical	Non-convex	$O(n^2)$	1
	SOMs [237]	Small	Yes	No	Multivariate Data	Non-convex	$O(n^2m)$	2

Fuzzy c-means

FCM [221] is a representative algorithm of fuzzy clustering, which is based on K-means concepts to partition data set into clusters. The FCM algorithm is a "soft" clustering method, in which the objects are assigned to the clusters with a degree of belief. Hence, an object may belong to more than one cluster with different degree of belief. It attempts to find the most characteristic point in each cluster named the *center* of one cluster; then it computes the membership degree for each object in the clusters. The FCM algorithm minimizes intra-cluster variance as well; however, it inherits the problems of K-means, as the minimum is just a local one and the final clusters depend on the initial choice of weights.

FCM algorithm follows the same principle of K-means algorithm, i.e., it iteratively searches the cluster centers and updates the membership of objects. The main difference is that, instead of making a hard decision about which cluster the pixel should belong to, it assigns an object a value ranging from 0 to 1 to measure the *likelihood* with which the object belongs to that cluster. A fuzzy rule states that the sum of the membership value of a pixel to all clusters must be 1. The higher the membership value, the more likely a pixel will belong to that cluster. The FCM clustering is obtained by minimizing an objective function shown in the following equation:

$$J = \sum_{i=1}^{n} \sum_{k=1}^{c} \mu_{ik}^{m} |p_i - v_k|^2 \tag{4.1}$$

where J is the objective function, n is the number of objects, c is the number of defined clusters, μ_{ik} is the likelihood value by assigning the object i to the cluster k, m is a fuzziness factor (a value of > 1), and $|p_i - v_k|$ is the Euclidean distance between the ith object p_i and the kth cluster center v_k defined by the following equation:

$$|p_i - v_k| = \sqrt{\sum_{i=1}^{n} (p_i - v_k)} \tag{4.2}$$

The centroid of the kth cluster is updated using the next equation:

$$v_k = \frac{\sum_{i=1}^{n} \mu_{ik}^{m} p_i}{\sum_{i=1}^{n} \mu_{ik}^{m}} \tag{4.3}$$

The fuzzy membership table is computed using the previous equation:

$$\mu_{ik} = \frac{1}{\sum_{l=1}^{c} (|p_i - v_k| / |p_i - v_l|)^{2/m-1}} \tag{4.4}$$

This algorithm has been extended for clustering an RGB color image, where distance computation given in (4.2) is modified as follows:

$$|p_i - v_k| = \sqrt{\sum_{i=1}^{n} (p_{iR} - v_{kR})^2 + (p_{iG} - v_{kG})^2 + (p_{iB} - v_{kB})^2} \tag{4.5}$$

As mentioned earlier, this has an iterative process:

FCM pseudo-code:

Input: Given the data set, set the desire number of clusters c, the fuzzy parameter m (a constant > 1), and the stopping condition, initialize the fuzzy partition matrix, and set $stop = false$.

Step 1. Do:

Step 2. Calculate the cluster centroids, calculate the objective value J.

Step 3. Compute the membership values stored in the matrix.

Step 4. If the value of J between consecutive iterations is less than the stopping condition, then $stop = true$.

Step 5. While ($!stop$)

Output: A list of c cluster centers and a partition matrix are produced.

BIRCH

The BIRCH algorithm [222] builds a dendrogram known as clustering feature (CF) tree. The CF tree can be built by scanning the data set in an incremental and dynamic way, and thus it does not need the whole data set in advance. It has two main phases: the database is first scanned to build an in-memory tree and then the algorithm is applied to cluster the leaf nodes. CF tree is a height-balanced tree, which is based on two parameters: branching factor B and threshold T. A CF tree is built while scanning the data. When a data point is encountered, the CF tree is traversed, starting from the root and choosing the closest node at each level. If the closest leaf cluster for the current data point is finally identified, a test is performed to see whether the data point belongs to the candidate cluster or not. If not, a new cluster is created with a diameter greater than the given T. BIRCH can typically find a good clustering with a single scan of the data set and improve the quality further with a few additional scans. It can also handle noise effectively. However, BIRCH may not work well when clusters are not spherical, because it uses the concept of radius or diameter to control the boundary of a cluster. In addition, it is order sensitive and may generate different clusters for different orders of the same input data. The details of the algorithm are given in the following:

BIRCH pseudo-code:

Input: The data set, threshold T, the maximum diameter (or radius) of a cluster T, and the branching factor B

Step 1. (Loading data into memory) an initial in-memory CF tree with the data (one scan) is built. Subsequent phases become fast, accurate, and less order sensitive.

Step 2. (Condense data) rebuild the CF tree with a larger T.

Step 3. (Global clustering) use existing clustering algorithm on CF leafs.

Step 4. (Cluster refining) do additional passes over the data set and reassign data points to the closest centroid from phase #3.

Output:. Compute CF points, where $CF = $ (number of points in a cluster N, linear sum of the points in the cluster LS, the square sum of N data SS).

DENCLUE

This basic idea of the DENCLUE algorithm [84] is to analytically model the cluster distribution according to the sum of influence functions of the all data points. The influence function can be seen as a function that describes the impact of a data point within its neighborhood. Then, density attractors can be identified as clusters. Density attractors are local maximum of the overall density function. In this algorithm, clusters of arbitrary shape can be easily described by a simple equation with kernel density functions. Even though DENCLUE requires a careful selection of its input parameters (i.e., σ and ξ), since such parameters may influence the quality of the clustering results, it has the following several advantages in comparison with other clustering algorithms [238]: (i) it has a solid mathematical foundation and generalized other clustering methods, such as partitional and hierarchical; (ii) it has good clustering properties for data sets with large amount of noise; (iii) it allows a compact mathematical description of arbitrary-shaped clusters in high-dimensional data sets; and (iv) it uses grid cells and only keeps information about the cells that actually contain points. It manages these cells in a tree-based access structure and thus, it is significant faster than some influential algorithms, such as DBSCAN. All these properties make DENCLUE able to produce good clusters in data sets with a large amount of noise. The details of this algorithm are given in the following:

DENCLUE pseudo-code:

Input: The data set, cluster radius, and minimum number of object

Step 1. Take data set in the grid whose each side is of 2σ.

Step 2. Find highly dense cells, i.e., find out the mean of highly populated cells.

Step 3. If d (mean(c_1), mean(c_2)) $< 4a$, then two cubes are connected.

Step 4. Now, highly populated or cubes that are connected to highly populated cells will be considered in determining clusters.

Step 5. Find density attractors using a hill-climbing procedure.

Step 6. Randomly pick point r.

Step 7. Compute local 4σ density.

Step 8. Pick another point (r+1) close to previous computed density.

Step 9. If den(r) $<$ den(r+1) climb, then put points within (σ /2) of path into cluster.

Step 10. Connect the density attractor-based cluster.

Output: Assignment of data values to clusters.

OptiGrid pseudo-code:

Input: The data set (x), a set of contracting projections $P = \{P_0, P_1, \ldots, P_k\}$, a list of cutting planes BEST CUT $\Leftarrow \Phi$, and CUT $\Leftarrow \Phi$;

Step 1. For $i=0, \ldots, k$, do
Step 2. CUT best local cuts $P_i(D)$, CUT SCORE $\Leftarrow$ Score best local cuts $P_i(D)$
Step 3. Insert all the cutting planes with a score $\geq$ min cut score into BEST CUT;
Step 4. Select the q cutting planes of the highest score from BEST CUT and construct a multidimensional grid G using the q cutting planes;
Step 5. Insert all data points in D into G and determine the highly populated grid cells in G; add these cells to the set of clusters C;
Refine C: For all clusters C_i in C, do the same process with data set C_i;

Output: Assignment of data values to clusters.

Optimal grid

Optimal grid (OptiGrid) algorithm [87] is designed to obtain an optimal grid partitioning. This is achieved by constructing the best cutting hyperplanes through a set of selected projections. These projections are then used to find the optimal cutting planes. Each cutting plane is selected to have minimal point density and to separate the dense into two half spaces. After each step of a multidimensional grid construction defined by the best cutting planes, OptiGrid finds the clusters using the density function. The algorithm is then applied recursively to the clusters. In each round of recursion, OptiGrid only maintains data objects in the dense grids from the previous round of recursion. This method is very efficient for clustering large high-dimensional databases. However, it may perform poorly in locating clusters embedded in a low-dimensional subspace of a very high-dimensional database, because its recursive method only reduces the dimensions by one at every step. In addition, it suffers sensitivity to parameter choice and does not efficiently handle grid sizes that exceed available memory [235]. Moreover, OptiGrid requires very careful selection of the projections, density estimation, and determination of what constitutes the best or optimal cutting plane from users. The difficulty of this is only determined on a case-by-case basis on the data being studied.

Expectation maximization

EM algorithm [223] is designed to estimate the maximum likelihood parameters of a statistical model in many situations, such as the one where the equations cannot be solved directly. EM algorithm iteratively approximates the unknown model parameters with two steps: the E step and the M step. In the E step (expectation), the current model parameter values are used to evaluate the posterior distribution of the latent variables. Then the objects are fractionally assigned to each cluster based on this posterior distribution. In the M step (maximization), the fractional assignment is given by reestimating the model parameters with maximum likelihood rule. The EM algorithm is guaranteed to find a local maximum for the model parameters estimate. The major disadvantages for EM algorithm are the requirement of non-singular covariance matrix, the sensitivity to the selection of initial parameters, the possibility of convergence to a local optimum, and the slow convergence rate. Moreover, there would be a decreased precision of EM algorithm within a finite number of steps [239]. The details of the EM algorithm are given later.

EM pseudo-code:

Input: The data set (x), the total number of clusters (M), the accepted error to converge (e) and the maximum number of iterations

E-step: Compute the expectation of the complete data log-likelihood.

$$Q(\theta, \theta^T) = E\left[\log p\left(x^g, x^m | \theta\right) x^g, \theta^T\right] \tag{4.6}$$

M-step: Select a new parameter estimate that maximizes the Q-function,

$$\theta^{t+1} = \arg\max_\theta Q(\theta, \theta^T) \tag{4.7}$$

Iteration: Increase $t = t + 1$; repeat steps 2 and 3 until the convergence condition is satisfied.

Output: A series of parameter estimates $\{\theta^0, \theta^1, ..., \theta^T\}$, where represents the reaching of the convergence criterion.

4.5   Experimental evaluation on real data

In some cases, it is not sufficient to decide the most suitable clustering algorithm for big data based only on the theoretical point of view. Thus, the main focus of this section is to investigate the behavior of the algorithms selected in Section 4.4 from empirical perspective.

In what follows, the traffic data sets used for this experimental study in Section 4.5.1 are described. Section 4.5.2 provides the details of the experimental setup, whereas Section 4.5.3 presents a complete survey for performance matrices that proposed experimental metrics to be used experimentally to investigate the relative strength and the weakness of each algorithm. Finally, the collected results and comprehensive analysis study are given in Section 4.5.4.

4.5.1   The data sets

To compare the advantages of the candidate clustering algorithms, eight simulated data sets are used in the experiments, including multi-hop outdoor real data (MHORD) [240], multi-hop indoor real data (MHIRD) [240], single-hop outdoor real data (SHORD) [240], single-hop indoor real data (SHIRD) [240], simulated *spoofing* attack for SCADA system (detonated as SPFDS) [241,242], simulated denial of service attack *DOS* for SCADA system (detonated as DOSDS) [241,242], simulated of both *spoofing* and attacks for SCADA system (detonated as SPDOS) [241,242], and the operational state *water treatment plant* (WTP). We experimented also with two other publicly available data sets, namely DARPA [243] and *internet traffic data* (ITD) [244]. These two data sets have become a benchmark for many studies since the work of Andrew *et al.* [245]. Table 4.2 summarizes the proportion of normal and anomaly flows, the number of attributes, and the number of classes for each data set. This chapter does not collect the descriptions of the data sets due to space restrictions. Thus, we recommend that readers consult the original references [20,41,240–242] for more complete details about characteristics of the data sets.

4.5.2   Experimental set up

Algorithm 1 shows the experimental procedures to evaluate the five candidate clustering algorithms. In particular, cross-validation strategy is used to make the best use of the traffic data and to obtain accurate and stable results. For each data, all instances are randomized and divided into two subsets as training and testing sets. Consequently, we evaluate the performance of each clustering algorithm by building a model on training set and measuring and using the testing set to evolute the constructed model. To assure that the five candidate clustering algorithms are not exhibiting order effect, the result of each clustering is averaged over ten runs on each data set. The five candidate clustering algorithms studied here have different parameters, however, the experimental evaluation does not correspond to an exhaustive search for the best parameters setting of each algorithm. Given the data sets at hand, then the main objective is to use general

Table 4.2   Data sets used in the experiments

Data	No. of instances	No. of attributes	No. of classes
MHIRD	699	10	2
MHORD	2,500	3	2
SPFDS	100,500	15	2
DOSDS	400,350	15	2
SPDOS	290,007	15	3
SHIRD	1,800	4	2
SHORD	400	4	2
ITD	377,526	149	12
WTP	512	39	2
DARPA	1,000,000	42	5

configuration to set the parameters of the clustering algorithms. In general, finding an optimal number of clusters is an ill-posed problem of crucial relevance in clustering analysis [246]. Thus, we have chosen the number of clustering with respect to the number of unique labels in each data set. However, the true number of clusters may not be the optimal number for which particular clustering algorithm will disclose, to its best potential, the structure in the data.

Algorithm 1: Experimental procedure

---

1 **Input:**

2 Parameter $N := 10$; $M := 100$;
3 Clustering algorithms Cls := $\{cl_1, cl_2, \ldots, cl_m\}$;
4 DATA = $\{D_1, D_2, \ldots, D_n\}$;
5 **Output:**

6 *Validity and stability*;
7 **foreach** *Clustering$_i$* $\in [1, Cls]$ **do**
8   **foreach** *$D_i \in DATA$* **do**
9   **foreach** *times* $\in [1, M]$ **do**
10   *randomize instance-order for D_i*;
11   *generate N bins from the randomized D_i*;
12   **foreach** *fold* $\in [1, N]$ **do**
13   *Test$_{Data}$ = bin[fold]*;
14   *Train$_{Data}$ = data − Test$_{Data}$*;
15   *Train'$_{Data}$ = select Subset from Train$_{Data}$*;
16   *Test'$_{Data}$ = select Subset from Test$_{Data}$*;
17   *Cls$_{ASGN}$ = TestModel(Test'$_{Data}$)*;
18   *Validity* = CompuValidaty *(Cls$_{ASGN}$, Test$_{lbs}$)*;
19   *Assignment$_i^{cls}$ = assignment$_i^{cls}$ ∪ Cls$_{ASGN}$*;

20   *Stability* = ComputeStability $\left(Assignment_i^{cls}\right)$;

Following the procedure and the pseudo-code of each clustering algorithm discussed in Section 4.4, the candidate clustering algorithms were implemented in MATLAB® 2013a. The experiments were carried out on a 64-bit Windows-based system with Intel core (i7), 2.80 GHz processor machine with 8 gigabytes of RAM.

4.5.3 Validity metrics

In response to the growing necessity for an objective method of comparing clustering algorithms, a complete survey of performance metrics, which covers all the properties and issues related to the experimental study of clustering, is presented. In particular, this survey of performance metrics will allow researchers to compare different algorithms in an objective way, to characterize their advantages and drawbacks in order to choose a clustering from an empirical point of view. The survey covers three measurements, including validity evaluation, stability of the results, and runtime performance.

1. *Validity evaluation:* Unsupervised learning methods required different evaluation criteria than supervised learning methods in this section, we briefly summarize the criteria used for performance evaluation according to *internal* and *external* validate indices. The former evaluation criteria evaluate the goodness of a data partition using quantities and feature inherited from the data sets, this includes *Compactness* (CP) and *Dunn validity index* (DVI). The latter evaluation criterion is similar to the process of *cross validation* that is used in evaluating supervised learning methods, such evaluation criteria include *classification accuracy* (CA), *adjusted rand index* (ARI), and *normalized mutual information* (NMI). Given a data set whose class labels are known, it is possible to assess how accurately a clustering technique partition the data relative to their correct class label. Note, some of clustering algorithms do not have centroid and therefore the *internal* indices are not applicable to such algorithms (e.g., OptiGrid and DENCLUE). To address such issue, we get the centroid of a cluster by using the measure in [231,247] and euclidean distance metric.

In this section, the following notation is used: X is the data set formed by x_i flows; Ω is the set of flows that have been grouped in a cluster; and W is the set of w_j centroids of the clusters in Ω. We will call node to each of the k elements of the clustering method.

   i. **CP:** It is one of the commonly used measurements to validity clusters by employing only the information inherent to the data set. Thus, a good clustering will create clusters with instances that are similar or closest to one another. More precisely, CP measures the average distance between every pair of data point as follows:

$$\overline{CP}_i = \frac{1}{|\Omega_i|} \sum_{x_i \in \Omega_i} \|x_i - w_i\| \tag{4.8}$$

   where Ω is the set of instances (x_i) that have been grouped in a cluster and W is the set of w_i centroids of clusters in Ω. As a global measure of compactness, the average of all clusters is calculated as follows:

$$\overline{CP} = \frac{1}{K} \sum_{k=1}^{K} \overline{CP}_k, \tag{4.9}$$

   where K denotes the number of clusters in the clustering result. Ideally, the members of each cluster should be as close to each other as possible. Therefore, the lower value of CP indicates better and more compact clusters.

   ii. **Separation (SP):** This measure quantifies the degree of separation between individual clusters. It measures the mean *Euclidean* distance among cluster centroid as follows:

$$\overline{SP} = \frac{2}{k^2 - k} \sum_{i=1}^{k} \sum_{j=i+1}^{k} \|w_i - w_j\|_2 \tag{4.10}$$

where $\overline{SP}$ close to 0 is indication of closer clusters.

iii.   **Davies–Bouldin (DB) index:** This index can identify cluster overlap by measuring the ratio of the sum within cluster scatter to between-cluster separation. It is defined as

$$DB = \frac{1}{k} \sum_{i=1}^{k} \max_{j \neq i} \left(\frac{\overline{C_i} + \overline{C_j}}{\left\| w_i - w_j \right\|_2} \right) \tag{4.11}$$

where the DB close to 0 indicates that the clusters are compact and far from each other.

iv.   **DVI:** The DVI quantifies not only the degree of compactness but also the degree of separation between individual clusters. DVI measures intercluster distances (separation) over intracluster distances (compactness). For a given number of clusters K, the definition of such index is given by the following equation:

$$DVI = \frac{\min\limits_{0 < m \neq n < K} \left\{ \min\limits_{\substack{\forall x_i \in \Omega_m \\ \forall x_j \in \Omega_n}} \left\{ \left\| x_i - x_j \right\| \right\} \right\}}{\max\limits_{0 < m \leq K \forall x_i, x_j \in \Omega_m} \left\{ \left\| x_i - x_j \right\| \right\}} \tag{4.12}$$

If a data set containing compact and well-separated clusters, the distance between the clusters are usually large and their diameter is expected to be small. Thus, a larger DVI value indicates compact and well-separated clusters.

v.   **Cluster accuracy (CA):** CA measures the percentage of correctly classified data point of clustering solution compared with predefined class labels. The CA is defined as

$$CA = \sum_{i=1}^{K} \frac{\max(C_i | L_i)}{|\Omega|} \tag{4.13}$$

where C_i is the set of instances in the ith cluster, L_i is the class labels for all instances in the ith cluster, and $\max(C_i | L_i)$ is the number of instances with the majority label in the ith cluster (e.g., if label l appeared in the ith cluster more often than any other label, then $\max(C_i | L_i)$ is the number of instances in C_i with the label l).

vi.   **ARI:** ARI takes into account the number of instances that exists in the same cluster and different clusters. Such validate measure expected value is not zero when comparing partitions.

$$ARI = \frac{n_{11} + n_{00}}{n_{00} + n_{01} + n_{10} + n_{11}} = \frac{n_{11} + n_{00}}{\binom{n}{2}} \tag{4.14}$$

where n_{11} is the number of pairs of instances that are in the same cluster in both, n_{00} is the number of pairs of instances that are in different clusters,

n_{10} is the number of pairs of instances that are in the same cluster in A but in different clusters in B, and n_{01} is the number of pairs of instances that are in different clusters in A but in the same cluster in B.

The value of ARI lies between 0 and 1 and higher value indicates that all data instances are clustered correctly and the cluster contains only pure instances.

vii. **NMI:** This is one of the common external clustering validation metrics that estimates the quality of the clustering with respect to a given class labeling of the data. More formally, NMI can effectively measure the amount of statistical information shared random variables representing the cluster assignments and the predefined labels assignments of the instances. Thus, NMI is estimated as follows:

$$NMI = \frac{\sum d_{h,l} \log\left(|\Omega|.d_{h,l}/d_h c_l\right)}{\sqrt{\left(\sum_h d_h \log\left(d_h/d\right)\right)\left(\sum_l c_l \log\left(c_l/d\right)\right)}} \tag{4.15}$$

where d_h is the number of flows in class h, c_l is the number of flows in cluster l, and $d_{h,l}$ is the number of flows in class h as well as in cluster l. The NMI value is 1 when the clustering solution perfectly matches the predefined label assignments and close to 0 for a low matching.

2. *Stability of the results:* Since most clustering algorithms rely on a random component, stability of the results across different runs is considered to be an asset of the algorithm. This chapter carries out an experimental study to examine the stability of the candidate clustering algorithms. In doing so, we consider a pairwise approach to measuring the stability of the candidate clusterers. In particular, the match between each of the $n(n-1)/2$ runs of single cluster is calculated and the stability index is obtained as the averaged degree of match across different runs. Let $S_r(R_i, R_j)$ be the degree of match between runs R_i and R_j. The cluster pairwise stability index S_k is

$$S_k = \frac{2}{n(n-1)} \sum_{i=1}^{n-1} \sum_{j=i+1}^{n} S_r(R_i, R_j). \tag{4.16}$$

where

$$S_r(R_i, R_j) = \begin{cases} 1 & \text{if } R_i(x_i) = R_j(x_j) \\ 0 & \text{otherwise} \end{cases} \tag{4.17}$$

Clearly, it can be seen that the $S_k(C)$ is the average stability measure over all pairs of clustering across different runs. It takes values from $[0, 1]$, with 0 indicating the results between all pairs of R_i, R_j totally different and 1 indicating that the results of all pairs across different runs are identical.

3. *Time requirements:* A key motivation for selecting the candidate clustering algorithms is to deal with big data. Therefore, if a clustering algorithm takes too long, it can became impractical for big data.

4.5.4 *Experimental results and comparison*

First of all, this section presents a comparison of the clustering outputs with respect to both the external and internal validity measurements. After that, the candidate clustering algorithms are analyzed from stability, a runtime performance, and scalability perspective.

Evaluating validity

The aim of this test is to determine how accurately a clustering algorithm can group traffic records from two different populations. Assessing the validity of clustering algorithms based on a single measure only can lead to misleading conclusions. Thus, we have conducted four type of external tests: Cluster Accuracy (CA), ARI, Rand index (RI), and NMI. Such measurements would allow us to exploit a prior knowledge of known data partitions and cluster labels of the data. Note, the class labels of instances (e.g., attack/normal) are used for evaluation purpose only and are not used in the cluster formation process.

Table 4.3 shows results of the candidate clustering with respect to the external validity measurements. It can be seen from Table 4.3 that EM algorithm provides the best clustering output based on all external measurements in comparison to the remaining clustering algorithms. The second best clustering algorithm in terms of external validity is FCM algorithm. The analysis reveals that BIRCH, OptiGrid, and DENCLUE respectively yield the lowest quality of clustering output in comparison to EM algorithm and FCM algorithm.

Table 4.4 reports the results of clustering algorithms according to the internal validity measurements. This is very important especially when there is no prior knowledge about the correct class labels of the data sets. Each of the validation measure evaluates different aspects of a clustering output separately, and based just on the raw data. None of them uses explicit information from the domain of application to evaluate the obtained cluster, in particular, to be able to apply internal measurements on all clusters. Note that the best value for each measure in each of the clustering algorithm is shown in bold. There are several observations from Table 4.4. First, it can seen that the DENCLUE algorithm often produces compact clusters in comparison to other clustering algorithms. The compactness of the DENCLUE is only 37.26% of that of OptiGrid, 47.27% of that of EM, 47.48% of that FCM, and 75.74% of that of BIRCH. Second, for separation measure, we observe that EM algorithm often yields cluster with higher mean separation among the considered clustering algorithms. The separation results of EM algorithm is 42.27% of that of DENCLUE, 50.52% of that of OptiGrid, 52.98% of that of FCM, and 80.60% of that of BIRCH. Third, according to the Davies–Bouldin index (DB), it can be seen that EM, DENCLUE, and Opti-Grid, respectively, were often able to produce not only compact clusters but also well-separated clusters.

Evaluating stability

The main focus of this section is to compare the stability of the candidate clustering algorithms outputs for 10-fold on all data sets. The stability would measure a

Table 4.3 *External validity results for the candidate clustering algorithms*

Measures	Cls. algorithms	MHIRD	MHORD	SPFDS	DOSDS	SPDOS	SHIRD	SHORD	ITD	WTP	DARPA
CA	**DENCLUE**	67.904	69.729	68.042	61.864	66.731	63.149	71.265	51.909	64.350	70.460
	OptiGrid	71.914	71.105	72.045	72.191	70.632	72.234	37.216	40.953	51.953	62.215
	FCM	75.387	73.271	74.682	74.222	72.873	74.723	75.553	59.974	66.435	73.114
	EM	82.512	81.940	82.786	82.919	82.114	79.450	82.023	65.035	72.085	80.685
	BIRCH	71.310	69.763	69.553	69.930	69.716	68.351	70.365	24.510	59.343	77.343
ARI	**DENCLUE**	57.772	45.248	41.535	39.822	44.510	35.081	46.267	35.663	47.665	60.665
	OptiGrid	35.894	30.297	32.140	29.402	29.970	32.598	29.956	55.824	32.137	52.137
	FCM	58.439	53.418	61.489	64.181	57.038	58.776	59.168	38.567	49.926	58.534
	EM	70.047	69.481	73.914	70.655	79.205	67.864	66.731	44.403	55.343	65.725
	BIRCH	52.424	44.011	52.470	41.662	39.627	40.377	56.462	19.260	51.260	61.483
RI	**DENCLUE**	74.988	73.527	71.217	68.384	70.043	69.115	75.024	44.164	57.460	75.477
	OptiGrid	76.909	75.404	75.963	75.448	75.631	76.550	75.359	49.252	59.201	66.201
	FCM	64.876	81.210	75.118	77.645	74.855	66.113	88.302	53.160	62.694	78.981
	EM	87.873	83.664	84.858	65.113	88.302	81.210	84.499	68.081	74.808	84.395
	BIRCH	73.099	65.823	77.521	71.422	73.069	70.589	74.156	33.184	62.357	79.890
MI	**DENCLUE**	59.853	48.916	39.949	49.533	46.986	37.158	47.439	36.561	49.762	65.762
	OptiGrid	34.966	38.308	36.906	39.429	37.328	34.029	47.197	54.081	33.411	53.411
	FCM	64.256	65.680	76.428	69.129	69.708	72.129	73.242	39.242	50.589	59.257
	EM	74.925	85.077	82.405	86.374	85.550	81.742	85.572	64.029	58.871	67.142
	BIRCH	58.450	58.780	56.230	57.930	57.376	55.750	57.979	25.980	52.764	64.994

Table 4.4 Internal validity results for the candidate clustering algorithms

Measures	Cls. algorithms	MHIRD	MHORD	SPFDS	DOSDS	SPDOS	SHIRD	SHORD	ITD	WTP	DARPA
CP	DENCLUE	1.986	1.207	1.886	1.104	1.300	1.391	1.357	1.014	1.485	0.832
	OptiGrid	1.629	1.678	1.643	1.232	1.271	2.505	2.330	2.454	1.189	1.973
	FCM	3.243	1.523	3.014	2.540	2.961	3.504	2.548	3.945	2.555	2.727
	EM	3.849	2.163	4.683	2.405	2.255	4.354	3.198	1.537	2.874	1.367
	BIRCH	3.186	3.466	3.310	5.164	1.692	2.793	5.292	5.529	1.834	4.131
SP	DENCLUE	2.973	1.450	2.776	1.247	1.632	1.810	1.742	1.073	1.993	0.716
	OptiGrid	1.914	1.990	1.936	1.311	1.370	3.247	2.981	3.170	1.245	2.437
	FCM	3.972	1.636	3.660	3.017	3.588	4.326	3.028	4.926	3.038	3.271
	EM	4.535	2.389	5.597	2.696	2.505	5.178	3.706	1.592	3.294	1.375
	BIRCH	3.566	3.907	3.717	5.979	1.742	3.086	6.136	6.425	1.916	4.719
DB	DENCLUE	1.788	2.467	4.273	3.524	4.551	0.821	4.990	6.870	7.702	5.987
	OptiGrid	3.798	5.582	3.085	1.703	2.655	5.573	2.128	4.673	5.078	8.502
	FCM	3.972	2.315	4.036	4.104	3.586	6.964	5.760	10.824	10.239	9.238
	EM	8.164	2.065	4.672	4.989	3.198	2.645	4.776	10.882	10.013	2.320
	BIRCH	4.943	6.471	3.234	2.512	2.600	5.002	5.272	11.882	9.336	6.641
DVI	DENCLUE	0.343	0.508	0.354	0.560	0.472	0.444	0.454	0.620	0.420	0.837
	OptiGrid	0.526	0.518	0.524	0.615	0.603	0.446	0.457	0.449	0.630	0.484
	FCM	0.491	0.606	0.498	0.517	0.500	0.485	0.516	0.476	0.516	0.509
	EM	0.524	0.580	0.512	0.567	0.575	0.516	0.538	0.640	0.548	0.669
	BIRCH	0.568	0.562	0.565	0.539	0.646	0.580	0.537	0.536	0.632	0.550

Table 4.5 Stability of the candidate clustering algorithms

Data sets	Clustering algorithms				
	EM	OptiGrid	BIRCH	FCM	DENCLUE
MHIRD	0.495	0.532	0.567	0.596	0.415
MHORD	0.408	0.528	0.537	0.589	0.487
SPFDS	0.478	0.518	0.544	0.599	0.451
DOSDS	0.481	0.593	0.561	0.608	0.467
SPDOS	0.479	0.531	0.556	0.591	0.441
SHIRD	0.476	0.513	0.504	0.559	0.492
SHORD	0.486	0.532	0.562	0.519	0.492
ITD	0.473	0.215	0.372	0.272	0.292
WTP	0.436	0.357	0.307	0.278	0.311
DARPA	0.459	0.481	0.397	0.284	0.359

particular clustering algorithm rather than a general property of the data set, thus higher values indicate lower output changes and it is always preferable. For comparison, Table 4.5 displays the stability results obtained for each clustering algorithm on all data sets. Note that the sequence roughly orders the candidate clustering algorithms according to growing stability values. Let us point out some of the most notable phenomena that can be observed regarding the presented stability results. First, the stability level in most cases only rarely approaches 0.599, indicating that clustering algorithms often suffer from stability issue and almost fail to produce stable output. Second, it can be seen that in most cases, the EM algorithm achieves the highest stability value (in comparison with the other clustering algorithms) on all data sets, except for ITD, WTR, and DARPA data sets. Third, it can be seen that the OptiGrid and DENCLUE algorithms often yield the highest stability values for ITD, WTR, and DARPA data sets among all considered clustering algorithms. This confirms their suitability to deal with high-dimensional data sets. Final, Table 4.5 shows that FCM scores the lowest stability values on all data sets and becomes more notable on data sets with high problem dimensionality. Future work would investigate that the stability of clustering algorithms depends on different parameter settings.

Evaluating runtime and scalability

A key motivation for this section to evaluate the runtime of the candidate clustering algorithms is their ability to group similar objects efficiently. This is particularly important when the size of the collected data is very large. In order to compare the effectiveness of the candidate clustering algorithms, we applied each clustering algorithm to the ten data sets. We then measure the execution time required by each algorithm on Intel core i7 2.80 GHz processor machine with 8 gigabytes of RAM. Table 4.6 records the runtime of the five candidate clustering algorithms. First, we observe that the DENCLUE is significantly faster than all other clustering algorithms.

Table 4.6   Runtime of the candidate clustering algorithms

Data sets	Clustering algorithms				
	DENCLUE	**OptiGrid**	**BIRCH**	**FCM**	**EM**
MHIRD	0.336	0.081	1.103	0.109	3.676
MHORD	0.290	0.290	2.253	7.511	60.689
SPFDS	2.5095	8.365	67.401	139.03	830.55
DOSDS	1.73229	5.7743	86.031	126.471	581.59
SPDOS	6.5178	32.6625	208.875	226.55	1,543.4
SHIRD	0.011	0.038	0.811	0.603	3.140
SHORD	0.017	0.058	0.780	0.824	4.929
ITD	7.107	23.689	241.074	262.353	1,982.790
WTP	0.230	0.388	1.246	1.768	6.429
DARPA	17.347	56.716	364.592	401.795	20,429.281
Average	3.610	12.806	97.416	124.701	2,544.647

The runtime of DENCLUE is 0.1% of that of EM, 2.89% of that of FCM, 3.71% of that of BIRCH, and 28.19% of that of OptiGrid. This indicates that DENCLUE algorithm is more efficient than others when choosing clustering to deal with big data. Second, the EM algorithm is scored the slowest runtime among all other algorithms and its runtime is slower than FCM, BIRCH, OptiGrid, and DENCLUE algorithms by 20.40%, 26.12%, 198.70%, and 704.94%, respectively. This indicates that EM algorithm is less efficient in term of time complexity than others and it is not recommended for big data.

4.6   Conclusion

This survey provided a comprehensive study of the clustering algorithms proposed in the literature. In order to reveal future directions for developing new algorithms and to guide the selection of algorithms for big data, a categorizing framework is provided to classify a range number of clustering algorithms. The categorizing framework is developed from a theoretical viewpoint that would automatically recommend the most suitable algorithm(s) to the network experts while hiding all technical details irrelevant to an application. Thus, even future clustering algorithms can be incorporated into the framework according to the proposed criteria and properties. Furthermore, the most representative clustering algorithms of each category have been empirically analyzed over a vast number of evaluation metrics and traffic data sets. In order to support the conclusion drawn, we have added Table 4.7 which provided a summary of the evaluation. In general, the empirical study allows to make the following conclusions for big data:

- No clustering algorithm performs well on all the evaluation criterion, and the future work should be defecated to accordingly improve the drawbacks of each clustering algorithm for handling big data.

Table 4.7   Compliance summary of the clustering algorithms based on empirical evaluation metrics

Cls. algorithms	External validity	Internal validity	Stability	Efficiency problem	Scalability
EM	Yes	Partially	Suffer from	Suffer from	Low
FCM	Yes	Partially	Suffer from	Suffer from	Low
DENCLUE	No	Yes	Suffer from	Yes	High
OptiGrid	No	Yes	Suffer from	Yes	High
BIRCH	No	Suffer from	Suffer from	Yes	High

- EM and FCM clustering algorithms show excellent performance with respect to the quality of the clustering outputs, except for high-dimensional data. However, these algorithms suffer from high-computational time requirements. Hence, the possible solution is to rely on programming language and hardware technology which may allow such algorithms to be executed more efficiently.
- All clustering algorithms suffer from stability problem and to mitigate such an issue ensemble clustering should be considered.
- DENCLUE, OptiGrid, and BIRCH are suitable clustering algorithms for dealing with large data sets, and especially DENCLUE and OptiGrid algorithm which can deal also with high-dimensional data.

Chapter 5
Toward an efficient and accurate unsupervised feature selection

Both redundant and nonrepresentative features result in large-volume and high-dimensional data, which degrade the accuracy and performance of classification as well as clustering algorithms. Most of the existing feature selection (FS) methods have limitations when dealing with high-dimensional data, as they search different subsets of features to find accurate representations of all features. Obviously, searching for different combinations of features is computationally very expensive, which makes existing work not efficient for high-dimensional data. The work carried out in this chapter, which relates to the design of an *efficient and accurate similarity-based unsupervised feature selection* (AUFS) method, tackles mainly the high-dimensionality issue of data by selecting a reduced set of representative and nonredundant features without the need for data class labels.

The AUFS method extends the k-mean clustering algorithm to partition the features into k clusters based on three similarity measures (i.e., PCC—Pearson correlation coefficient, LSRE—least square regression error, and MICI—Maximal Information Compression Index) in order to accurately partition the features. Then, the proposed centroid-based FS method is used, where the feature with the closest similarity to its cluster centroid is selected as the representative feature, while others are discarded. Experiments have shown that AUFS can generate a reduced representative and nonredundant feature set that achieves good classification accuracy in comparison with well-known unsupervised FS methods.

5.1 Introduction

There has been extensive research in the field of FS because of the need to reduce the high dimensionality of data. High-dimensional data suffers from redundant and nonrepresentative features that result in the following challenges. First, these features reduce the accuracy of the data-mining algorithms by misdirecting the classification (supervised) and the clustering (unsupervised) processes [42]. Figure 5.1 illustrates the impact of nonrepresentative features when they are used to classify the data. Figure 5.1(a) shows that there are two clusters when all used features are representative, which is correct. On the other hand, Figure 5.1(b) shows a "bad" data classification accuracy due to the use of the nonrepresentative feature F3. This clearly

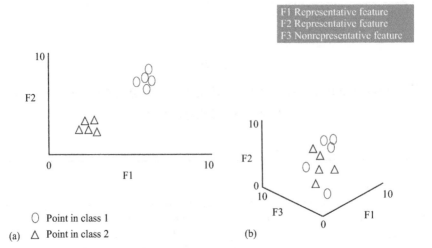

*Figure 5.1   Impact of nonrepresentative features in classification accuracy: (a) bad
classification and (b) good classification*

shows that the features used in the classification cannot distinguish data after the inclusion of F3. Additionally, the existence of redundant and nonrepresentative features
negatively affects the processing time of the algorithms due to the large volume of
data, which requires substantial storage space [163].

Despite the fact that many approaches [248,249,380] have attempted to address
the FS challenges, most of them are not efficient to be applied on high-dimensional
data and they require labeled data. These are called *supervised approaches*. Most of the
high-dimensional and big data are not labeled, this makes existing approaches unsuitable. The methods proposed in [250] and spectral feature selection (SPEC) [251] are
probably the two most well-known *unsupervised approaches* used to select the representative features: [250] selects the reduced set of representative features by using
k-nearest neighbor (NN) (*k*NN) to cluster the feature space using MICI similarity
measure. On the other hand, SPEC [251] extends the Laplacian score to weight all
the features and to select the top *n* features as the subset of representative features.
However, these two methods are computationally expensive, which makes them inappropriate to be applied in high-dimensional and big data. Additionally, SPEC has not
addressed the issue of feature redundancy because it evaluates features individually.
Even though these two approaches are unsupervised approaches, they are not efficient
to select representative features with high-dimensional data.

Many FS methods [20,47,63,377] have attempted to address the FS challenges.
However, most of them are not efficient when applied to high-dimensional data,
because they require labeled data. These are called *supervised methods*. Therefore,
they are outside the scope of this chapter. Most of the high-dimensional data are not
labeled, making existing methods unsuitable. The methods proposed in [250] and
SPEC [251] are probably the two most well-known *unsupervised methods* (i.e., they
do not require data class labels) used to select the representative features. However,

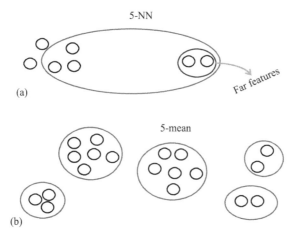

Figure 5.2   Comparison of clusters produced by the method in [250] and AUFS:
(a) clusters with non-representative features and (b) clusters with
representative features

they have limitations in terms of accuracy and performance. In regard to accuracy, the method proposed by Mitra *et al.* [250] partitions the feature space using kNN clustering. However, kNN is inefficient when data are not dense as it produces low-quality clusters [252]. Therefore, it is not suitable for high-dimensional data because, mostly, it is not dense. According to the method proposed in [250], and as illustrated in Figure 5.2(a), one of the three nearest features may be selected to represent the far features (i.e., features that are distant from others), which have different characteristics. Consequently, the classification accuracy will be low because of the badly selected representative features. On the other hand, SPEC [251] has not addressed the issue of feature redundancy because it individually evaluates features, which would negatively affect the classification accuracy.

In terms of performance, both of the methods proposed in [250] and SPEC [251] experience high computational complexity. Because the method proposed in [250] uses kNN, it inherits the computational issues of such an approach because it calculates the distance between k and all its neighbors. On the other hand, SPEC [251] also suffers from high time-computational complexity as it is based on spectral graph theory, which is computationally expensive [253]. Although these two methods can be applied to high-dimensional data, they experience computational complexity.

The AUFS method overcomes the limitations of existing solutions with the following features: (i) it addresses the problem of high-dimensional data by designing an accurate method for selecting a reduced set of representative features, (ii) it has an efficient computational time by not requiring any search strategy for testing different subsets of features, and (iii) it works with unsupervised data (i.e., unlabeled data), which has more challenges than supervised data because of the absence of class labels. AUFS adapts the k-mean algorithm to cluster the feature space as it is more powerful in clustering the features of high-dimensional data. The reason is that distant far features as in Figure 5.2(b) will form clusters and representative features will be selected from them. This results in more accurate feature clustering. In detail, AUFS partitions the feature space into k clusters based on computing different similarity measures to assign the features into clusters. Then, from every cluster, only the feature that has the minimum dissimilarity to its cluster centroid is selected, and this ensures that the selected feature represents all features within the cluster. This is done to enable the inclusion of only the representative features, and to remove redundant features.

Experimental results show that AUFS generates a reduced representative feature set that, when used by classifiers/evaluation models, achieves the best accuracy according to the evaluation metrics for the used datasets: it has the lowest FPR (false positive rate), the highest precision, and F-measure in comparison with SPEC [251] and the method proposed in [250], whether the evaluation model is Naive Bayes, lazy NN, or J48 decision tree. In addition, when compared with the benchmark methods, AUFS had the lowest running time when selecting the features.

5.2   Related work

Based on the availability of the data class labels, FS methods fall into two categories: *supervised* and *unsupervised*. Later, we briefly describe the representative methods of both categories.

5.2.1   Supervised feature selection methods

We start by introducing supervised FS methods.

- *Information gain [71].* This is a supervised FS method that requires data class labels to select a set of representative features. It builds a decision tree to measure the information in class prediction. This is done by observing the value of features. Any feature with high value of information is established as a splitting point. On the other hand, the features with low value of information indicate that the points are not ready to be partitioned. Generally, information gain can be defined as the difference between the original information obtained from the proportion of the class labels and the new information obtained after partitioning.
- *Fisher score [254].* This is a supervised FS method that requires data class labels in order to select a reduced set of representative features. The selected features have to meet a specific criterion that the feature values of samples in the same class are similar. Conversely, feature values of samples belonging to different classes are dissimilar. The n number of features with the highest fisher score are selected as the representative features.
- *Chi-square [255].* This is a statistical-based supervised FS method. It statistically measures the relevance of each feature to the class label individually. Specifically, it measures the association of each feature with the class label in order to evaluate its relevance. As it evaluates each feature individually, it is unable to discover and remove redundant features. Let us say that we have a set of features with a

range of continuous values. Chi-square first transfers the continuous values into discrete intervals. The values of each feature are assigned to their own interval. Then, a merging step is applied to maintain the validity of the original feature space.

Supervised FS methods [20,47,63,377], including the abovementioned representative ones, share a common limitation, in which they are limited to the existence of data class labels. In other words, they evaluate the relevance/correlation of the features to the class labels. However, it is often difficult to have the data class labels, especially for high-dimensional datasets because, in real applications, most data do not have class labels, thereby making existing methods unsuitable. Although manual labeling can be a solution, it would take experts a long time to test and label the data, which is infeasible.

5.2.2   Unsupervised feature selection methods

Unsupervised FS methods [64,67,68,250,251] have been proposed to overcome the need for data class labels. Such methods are much harder to design due to the absence of data class labels, which guide them in the process of searching for the representative features. Initially, traditional unsupervised FS methods addressed the problem (of the absence of class labels) by ranking features independently based on certain scores. However, they are not able to generate the best features set, as they do not compute the correlation between features [67]. The second of the unsupervised FS methods e.g., [69,250], generally uses clustering to partition the feature space into distinct clusters, where features in every cluster are similar to each other and different from the features of other clusters. Later, we describe two well-known and representative unsupervised FS methods, which are selected for benchmarking.

Spectral feature selection

SPEC [251] is an unsupervised FS method that does not require data class labels in order to select representative features. It extends the Laplacian score [256] both to weight all the features and to select the top n features as the subset of representative features. It finds the representativeness of a feature by estimating its consistency with the spectrum of a matrix that is derived from radial-base function (RBF) similarity matrix. In particular, a specific graph is built based on the similarity matrix, which SPEC uses to weight features.

Given a dataset D, evaluation functions and number of samples, the following steps are taken by SPEC to weight the features:

- The similarity matrix S is constructed from the dataset.
- A graph G is constructed based on S.
- An adjacency matrix W and diagonal matrix D will be built from G.
- It evaluates each feature individually using the given evaluation functions.

Because SPEC evaluates the representativeness of different features individually, it does not handle any feature redundancy.

Mitra's method

Mitra *et al.* [250] proposed an unsupervised FS method that does not require data class labels to select representative features. It selects a reduced set of representative features from high-dimensional data using different similarity measures. They proposed a new similarity measure called MICI (see Section 5.3) in order to compute the similarity between the features. Mitra *et al.* [250] use kNN clustering algorithm to cluster the feature space with an MICI similarity measure so that the features within a cluster are highly similar, while those in different clusters are dissimilar. Then, from every cluster, they use the compactness methodology to select the features. The only feature that is selected is the one that has the minimum dissimilarity to its NN.

The methods proposed in [250] and SPEC [251] are probably the two most well-known *unsupervised approaches* used to select the representative features from high-dimensional homogeneous data. Even though these two methods are unsupervised, they have classification accuracy and computational time-complexity limitations when selecting representative features from high-dimensional data, as explained in Section 5.1.

5.3   Similarity measures

Here, we introduce the similarity measures used to measure the dependency of the features to (i) allocate the feature to a relevant cluster and (ii) decide which feature of a cluster to be selected as a representative feature. The reason for adopting these linearly dependent measures is their effectiveness for the purpose of FS as they are not sensitive to the location along with the scatters of the distribution of the features data [250]. Therefore, they are promising when working with high-dimensional data. These linearly dependent measures are illustrated later. For all similarity measures, x will denote a cluster centroid, whereas y denotes a feature.

- **PCC [257].** PCC is a measure that computes the correlation between two random variables, and it determines whether they would have a linear dependency relationship. It can be computed by calculating either the correlation between a feature and a predicted class label or between a feature and a feature. Unlike the former, which measures the extent to which features are correlated to their class labels, the latter is adopted in our method to measure the correlation between the features and the cluster centroids to assign features to clusters. In fact, a feature and a feature correlation are better suited to our method as we are concerned with unsupervised learning, which does not assume the existence of the data class labels. Generally, correlation coefficient is fast and capable of identifying representative features without the need for pairwise correlation computation. Formally, it is computed as follows:

$$PCC(x,y) = \frac{n\left(\sum xy\right) - \left(\sum x\right)\left(\sum y\right)}{\sqrt{\left[n\sum x^2 - \left(\sum x\right)^2\right]\left[n\sum y^2 - \left(\sum y\right)^2\right]}} \tag{5.1}$$

The result of the correlation between x and y is between 0, which indicates that the feature and the cluster centroid are completely uncorrelated, and 1 that indicates their complete correlation.

- **LSRE [258]**. LSRE computes and analyses the degree of the correlation between a feature and a cluster centroid by drawing a line that is best fitted to the data. It is computed based on linear model $y = ax + b$, where a and b are given by minimizing the mean square error and n denotes the number of features, which is always 1, as we process one feature at a time. The error is the distance between the actual data and the model data and is calculated based on the following equations:

$$LSRE(x,y) = y_n - (ax_n + b) \tag{5.2}$$

a is the slope of the x and is calculated by

$$a = \frac{\sum xy - \left(\sum x \sum y/n\right)}{\sum x^2 - \left(\left(\sum x\right)^2/n\right)} \tag{5.3}$$

b is the y-intercept and is calculated by

$$b = \frac{\sum y - (a \sum x)}{n} \tag{5.4}$$

The final result of the former equations shows the degree of the linear dependency correlation of a feature and a cluster centroid based on given value of (5.2). They are completely correlated when $LSRE = 0$.

- **MICI [250]**. MICI is an index technique for measuring the similarity between a feature and a cluster centroid. Let $\sum$ be the covariance matrix of the random features. MICI is defined as $MICI(x,y) =$ the smallest eigenvalue of $\sum$, i.e.,

$$MICI(x,y) = (var(x) + var(y)) - \sqrt{(var(x) + var(y))^2 - 4var(x)var(y)(1 - \rho(x,y)^2)} \tag{5.5}$$

A feature and a cluster centroid are linearly dependent when the value of *MICI* is zero and the value increases as much as the amount of dependency decreases.

5.4 The proposed feature selection method

AUFS is primarily designed to select a reduced set of representative and nonredundant features from high-dimensional data without the need of the data class labels. The accurate selection of representative features would result in high classification accuracy. AUFS uses the three linearly dependent similarity measures PCC [257], LSRE [258], and MICI [250] to partition the feature space. Linearly dependent measures are chosen because they are not sensitive to the order along with the distribution of features. Also, a single similarity measure might favor a specific model, and, therefore, will produce better selection of representative features for that model over other models. Finally, the three measures proved their effectiveness for FS experimentally as shown in [250]. Therefore, PCC, LSRE, and MICI are used in the k-mean algorithm to compute the dependency between features and cluster centroids. Before giving the details of the proposed method, we first define what we mean by *representative features* and *redundant features*.

For the next definitions, let us assume that we have the following sets:

- $F=\{f_1, f_2, \ldots, f_n\}$: the set of all features in column vectors.
- $C=\{c_1, c_2, \ldots, c_n\}$: the set of all cluster centroids.
- ε is a subset of features (i.e., $\varepsilon \subset F$) in a cluster with centroid $c_r \in C$.

Definition 5.1 (Definition: Representative feature). $f_i \in \varepsilon$ *is a representative feature in c_r if and only if*

$$PCC\ (f_i, c_r) > PCC\ (\varepsilon, c_r) \tag{5.6}$$

$$LSRE\ (f_i, c_r) < LSRE\ (\varepsilon, c_r) \tag{5.7}$$

$$MICI\ (f_i, c_r) < MICI\ (\varepsilon, c_r) \tag{5.8}$$

Any feature f_i that is not representative is said to be *nonrepresentative*.

Definition 5.2 (Definition: Redundant feature). *A feature f_i is redundant in a given cluster if it exists another feature f_j in the same cluster such that*

$$PCC\ (f_i, f_j) = 1 \tag{5.9}$$

$$LSRE\ (f_i, f_j) = 0 \tag{5.10}$$

$$MICI\ (f_i, f_j) = 0 \tag{5.11}$$

5.4.1 *More details about the AUFS method*

After defining the various concepts, we now provide details of the various steps of the proposed AUFS. Unlike the wrapper approach, where related algorithms [59,60,259] experience performance degradation due to the use of complex data-mining algorithms, the filter approach is used in AUFS as it has better performance (i.e., processing time) because it does not use any data-mining algorithm to evaluate the generated set of features.

In addition to adopting the filter approach, AUFS is categorized as an unsupervised method as it does not depend on the availability of the data class labels. It is therefore based on various existing clustering techniques that process data without requiring their class labels, such as k-mean [260]. However, the k-mean algorithm needs to be extended to integrate the three abovementioned similarity measures (i.e., PCC, LSRE, and MICI) in order to properly cluster the features, as the use of a single similarity measure will be biased toward specific models and therefore will not produce accurate classification. The three similarity measures will cover most of the possible linear-dependent correlations between features and therefore will reflect the real accuracy of AUFS as well as other methods used in the benchmark.

Algorithm 1 shows that AUFS has two main stages: (i) the original feature space is partitioned into a predefined number of clusters using the extended k-mean algorithm (with three similarity measures); (ii) using each similarity measure during the clustering stage, AUFS computes the similarity between the centroid vector of each

---

Algorithm 1: The AUFS method

---

1 **Input:**

2 F: $\{f_1, f_1, \ldots, f_n\}$, is a set of features;

3 SM_j: $\{1 = PCC, 2 = LSRE, 3 = MICI\}$, is the similarity measure;

4 k: the number of clusters, $n - 1 > k > 1$;

5 **Output:**

6 R: the representative and nonredundant feature set;

7 **foreach** $j \in [SM_j]$ **do**
   ```
   // F is partitioned into k clusters based on j
      measure
   ```
8      $[idxbest, Cbest] \longleftarrow$ kmean (F,k,SM_j);
   ```
   // get a list of clusters' ids
   ```
9   clusIds=unique(idxbest);
   ```
   // get the index for each feature
   ```
10   featuresIndex=[1:size(F,2)];
   ```
   // go through each cluster and find the
      representative features
   ```
11   **for** $i = 1 : size(clusIds, 1)$ **do**
12   clusterFeatures= featuresIndex(1,[idxbest(:,1)==clusIds(i)]');
13   clusterData=data(:,clusterFeatures);
14   clusterMean=Cbest(:,i);
15   distances=zeros(size(clusterFeatures,2),1);
16   **for** $k = 1:size(clusterData,2)$ **do**
17   distances(k,1)= calcDistance(clusterMean,clusterData(:,k),SM_j);
18   [dis,indx]=min(distances);
19   FeatureSelected= [FeatureSelected,clusterFeatures(1,indx)];
20   R =[FeatureSelected, size(F,2)];
21   **return** R;

---

cluster and all features in that cluster to find the representative features and removes the rest (i.e., nonrepresentative and redundant features). Then, the representative features from every cluster will form the reduced feature set. Following are the details of the various steps carried out by AUFS to select a reduced set of representative features:

- First, AUFS partitions the feature space by applying the k-mean into k clusters using every similarity measure, namely, PCC, LSRE, and MICI. Each similarity measure is computed individually.
- Second, the centroids are initialized to be the first feature vectors from the feature space based on the k value. For example, if $k=10$ then the first ten features vectors

are the initial clusters centroids. k value is determined based on the required reduction of the feature space.

- Third, AUFS assigns every feature to a cluster (i.e., hard clustering). To do so, the similarity between every centroid and all the features in the feature space are computed. Every feature is therefore assigned to its relevant cluster. This process is repeated until the reassigning of features no longer changes the centroids, meaning that the set of centroids is stable (i.e., does not change).
- Fourth, AUFS finds the representative feature of every cluster. The feature of a cluster that has the highest similarity (i.e., the highest PCC or the lowest LSRE and MICI) to its centroid (mean) is selected as the representative feature for the cluster.
- Lastly, AUFS ignores all the remaining features of every cluster (and therefore retains only the representative features). This guarantees the removal of redundant as well as nonrepresentative features and produces the set of all representative features.

The AUFS is a novel method because (i) the way it selects representative features ensures that the selected feature accurately represents all the features of a cluster, as the feature with the closest similarity to its cluster centroid is going to be selected; (ii) it uses only one parameter and is not overwhelmed by having to find the best parameters, since AUFS, namely, has k (the number of clusters) which is the number of features to be selected, as one feature is selected to represent every cluster; (iii) AUFS has low computational time complexity as it does not require the search as well as the evaluation of different subsets of features to find representative features, thereby, reducing the computational complexity of AUFS. In addition, by removing all features other than representative ones, redundant features will be definitely removed because they will be a part of the nonrepresentative features, which would reduce computational time.

5.4.2   An illustrative example

A simple example is given here to illustrate the way that AUFS algorithm works to select representative features from the feature space and removes redundant ones. This example covers one measure, as the example is also applicable with the two others. Let us make up the feature set, such as $F = \{F_1, F_2, F_3, ..., F_9\}$ be the feature vectors, $k = 3$ be the number of clusters, and $j = $ PCC be the similarity measure. First, the feature set is partitioned into three clusters based on computing PCC between every feature from the feature set and every centroid c_1, c_2, and c_3 so every feature is assigned to its relevant cluster centroid (see Table 5.1(a)).

Table 5.1(b) provides an allocation of every feature from the feature set to its cluster based on PCC. Then from every cluster, a feature that has the highest similarity to its centroid is selected to be the relevant feature for the cluster and discards the rest features. For example, in Table 5.1(b), cluster #1 has three features assigned to it, namely, F_1, F_3, and F_5. F_5 is only selected from cluster #1 as representative feature, because it has higher PCC to c_1 than F_1 and F_3. On the other hand, F_1 and F_3 are discarded. Consequently, the reduced, representative, and nonredundant subset of features from the three clusters is $\{F_5, F_2, F_4\}$.

Table 5.1   (a) PCC between the centroids and all the feature vectors in the feature set. (b) Allocation of a feature to its most similar cluster centroid

PCC	c_1	c_2	c_3	Feature no.	Cluster no.
F_1	0.85	0.32	0.2	F_1	1
F_2	0.28	0.98	0.4	F_3	1
F_3	0.88	0.44	0.15	F_5	1
F_4	0.15	0.37	0.97	F_2	2
F_5	0.96	0.42	0.31	F_8	2
F_6	0.65	0.60	0.93	F_9	2
F_7	0.26	0.58	0.95	F_4	3
F_8	0.56	0.93	0.33	F_6	3
F_9	0.33	0.75	0.42	F_7	3

5.5   Experimental setup

This section describes the performance of the AUFS method with different datasets. In order to properly investigate the accuracy and the time complexity of AUFS, two well-known algorithms were used for the comparison: Mitra's method [250] and SPEC [251]. These two methods were selected as they are well-known unsupervised FS methods that do not require the data class labels for selecting features. These two algorithms and AUFS were evaluated using three different families of classifiers, namely, Naive Bayes [261], J48 decision tree [262], and the lazy NN [263] (also called IB1). In addition to the classifiers, k-fold-cross validation was applied on all datasets to efficiently evaluate the accuracy of the benchmark methods. The entire dataset was first divided into subsets of equal size depending on the selected k folds. Then, only one k was used as the testing subset and the rest ones were the training subsets. Finally, the average value of all folds was set as the average result. In the evaluation, k was set to 10 as suggested in [264] to demonstrate the efficiency of our proposed method along with the benchmark methods. All the three algorithms were implemented in MATLAB® programming language. They were executed under Mac operating system OS X Yosemite with 2.4 GHz Intel Core 2 Duo and 8 GB RAM.

5.5.1   Datasets

Three datasets were used in the experiments, namely, spambase, water treatment plant, and physical activity monitoring (PAMAP2). The preference of the selection of those datasets is because they are commonly used for the aim of data-mining algorithms as well as they are from diverse domains. They are found in UCI Machine Learning Repository website. The three datasets were mainly collected for the purpose of classification and clustering as clustering is a part of the proposed method to filter out redundant and nonrepresentative features. Here is a brief description of each dataset:

- *Spambase:* It is a multivariate dataset that contains spam and non-spam email classes, where each email is described by 57 real data type features. The total number of emails (records) is 4,601. https://archive.ics.uci.edu/ml/datasets/ Spambase

- *Water treatment plant:* The collected multivariate data are the measures of the daily sensor readings in urban wastewater treatment plant. The goal of this data is to train any learning model to classify the operational state of the plant to predict the occurrence of faults at any stage of the treatment process. It has 527 objects, where each object is described by 38 real data type features. https://archive.ics.uci.edu/ml/datasets/Water+Treatment+Plant.

- *PAMAP2 data set:* It is a multivariate time-series data set that is collected by monitoring 18 different physical activities of 9 people, such as walking, lying, and cycling. PAMAP2 consists of 3,850,505 objects that are described by 54 features, including the class label of the activities ID. http://archive.ics.uci.edu/ml/datasets/pamap2+physical+activity+monitoring.

5.5.2   Evaluation metrics

The major concern of the FS method is to select a reduced set of features. The accurate selection of representative features should increase the classification accuracy of the classifiers as the redundant and nonrepresentative features should be removed. The selection of representative features should be done within an acceptable running time. Therefore, two groups of evaluation metrics were selected, namely, classification accuracy and running time as shown later.

Classification accuracy

The primary aim of this experiment was to investigate whether the reduced representative set of features competitively improved the accuracy of the classifiers in terms of data classification. We first applied AUFS on three given datasets; then the results (representative features set) were provided to the data-mining classifiers (i.e., Naive Bayes, J48, and IB1) to test the efficiency of the reduced features in terms of classification accuracy. The evaluation metrics used for classification accuracy were FPR, *Precision*, and *F-measure*. These metrics were appropriate given the main aim of the AUFS method, which is the accurate selection of representative features to increase the classification accuracy of the data. They are calculated based on Table 5.2 and are provided later.

- FPR: The percentage of normal instances that are detected as anomalies over all normal instances, which is defined as follows in terms of the metrics defined in Table 5.2:

$$FPR = \frac{FP}{FP + TN} \tag{5.12}$$

- Precision: The percentage of correctly detected anomaly instances over all the detected anomaly instances. This is defined as follows in terms of the metrics defined in Table 5.2:

$$Precision = \frac{TP}{TP + FP} \tag{5.13}$$

Table 5.2   Standard confusion metrics for evaluation of
normal/anomaly classification

Actual label of flows	Predicted label of flows	
	Normal	Anomaly
Normal	True negative (TN)	False positive (FP)
Anomaly	False negative (FN)	True positive (TP)

- *F*-measure is the equally weighted (harmonic) mean of precision and recall. This is defined as follows:

$$F\text{--}measure = \frac{Recall \times Precision}{Recall + Precision}. \tag{5.14}$$

Running time

High-dimensional data require more processing time particularly when there are redundant and nonrepresentative features. Therefore, the major purpose of AUFS is to remove those redundant and nonrepresentative features in order to improve the accuracy of the classification task within a short running time.

5.6 Experimental results

This section presents and analyses the experimental results. For every FS method, Naive Bayes, IB1, and J48 decision tree classifiers were used to evaluate the classification accuracy of the generated representative feature sets with different similarity measures. All the experiments were carried out on three datasets. For every data set, every method was run with all possible similarity measures developed for that method. The method proposed in [250] already includes the three similarity measures (i.e., PCC, LSRE, and MICI), while SPEC works with the RBF kernel similarity measure. To investigate their classification accuracy, we compared these methods by considering all of their similarity measures individually. The experimental results are presented in Tables 5.3–5.11, and they clearly show that AUFS has consistently the lowest FPR as well as the highest precision and *F*-measure for the three similarity measures.

For example, the water treatment plant dataset shows that the proposed AUFS method achieved a higher accuracy result compared to the two other methods based on the *F*-measure. The accuracy range varies between 5%–94% and 15%–29% compared with [250] and SPEC, respectively, when using the Naive Bayes classifier as shown in Table 5.3. Moreover, the spambase dataset shows that AUFS also achieves a higher

Table 5.3   Classification accuracy using water treatment plant dataset with Naive Bayes

Feature selection method	Similarity measure	FPR	Precision	F-measure
[250]	PCC	0.021	0.45	0.5294
	LSRE	0.039	0.2593	0.3415
	MICI	0.012	0.6471	0.7097
AUFS	PCC	0.018	0.55	0.6471
	LSRE	0.02	0.5455	0.6667
	MICI	0.006	0.7692	0.7407
SPEC [251]	RBF kernel	0.031	0.4286	0.5714

Table 5.4   Classification accuracy using water treatment plant dataset with IB1

Feature selection method	Similarity measure	FPR	Precision	F-measure
[250]	PCC	0.0058	0.625	0.4545
	LSRE	0.0039	0.7778	0.6087
	MICI	0.0039	0.7143	0.4762
AUFS	PCC	0.0019	0.8889	0.6957
	LSRE	0.0019	0.875	0.6764
	MICI	0.0019	0.8899	0.6957
SPEC [251]	RBF kernel	0.0058	0.7273	0.64

Table 5.5   Classification accuracy using water treatment plant dataset with J48 decision tree

Feature selection method	Similarity measure	FPR	Precision	F-measure
[250]	PCC	0.0117	0.6	0.6207
	LSRE	0.0078	0.6923	0.6667
	MICI	0.0058	0.7692	0.7407
AUFS	PCC	0.0019	0.9	0.75
	LSRE	0.0039	0.8333	0.7692
	MICI	0.0039	0.8462	0.8148
SPEC [251]	RBF kernel	0.0078	0.7143	0.7143

Table 5.6 *Classification accuracy using spambase dataset with Naive Bayes*

Feature selection method	Similarity measure	FPR	Precision	F-measure
Method in [250]	PCC	0.4258	0.5915	0.7285
	LSRE	0.3917	0.6135	0.7473
	MICI	0.4659	0.5758	0.7233
UFSDA	PCC	0.1191	0.8146	0.8097
	LSRE	0.1202	0.8268	0.8535
	MICI	0.425	0.5986	0.7328
SPEC [251]	RBF kernel	0.4283	0.5921	0.7312

Table 5.7 *Classification accuracy using spambase dataset with IB1*

Feature selection method	Similarity measure	FPR	Precision	F-measure
[250]	PCC	0.1313	0.8002	0.8044
	LSRE	0.1065	0.8382	0.8435
	MICI	0.0911	0.8495	0.8129
UFSDA	PCC	0.08	0.8721	0.8549
	LSRE	0.0789	0.8777	0.8743
	MICI	0.0721	0.8836	0.8621
SPEC [251]	RBF kernel	0.4763	0.5688	0.7161

Table 5.8 *Classification accuracy using spambase dataset with J48 decision tree*

Feature selection method	Similarity measure	FPR	Precision	F-measure
[250]	PCC	0.1022	0.8341	0.8117
	LSRE	0.0681	0.8887	0.8619
	MICI	0.0886	0.8476	0.8002
AUFS	PCC	0.0552	0.9	0.883
	LSRE	0.0567	0.9122	0.9086
	MICI	0.0624	0.9003	0.8831
SPEC [251]	RBF kernel	0.4788	0.5678	0.7156

Table 5.9   *Classification accuracy using PAMAP2 dataset with Naive Bayes*

Feature selection method	Similarity measure	FPR	Precision	F-measure
[250]	PCC	0.0801	0.5241	0.5314
	LSRE	0.0421	0.8494	0.8467
	MICI	0.0394	0.8015	0.7913
AUFS	PCC	0.0601	0.5461	0.5501
	LSRE	0.0306	0.8763	0.8705
	MICI	0.0366	0.8325	0.8217
SPEC [251]	RBF kernel	0.0721	0.5172	0.5284

Table 5.10   *Classification accuracy using PAMAP2 dataset with IB1*

Feature selection method	Similarity measure	FPR	Precision	F-measure
[250]	PCC	0.0681	0.6889	0.686
	LSRE	0.0015	0.9935	0.9935
	MICI	0.003	0.9901	0.9901
AUFS	PCC	0.0652	0.6985	0.6957
	LSRE	0.0002	0.9992	0.9992
	MICI	0.0027	0.9908	0.9908
SPEC [251]	RBF kernel	0.0821	0.6678	0.6597

Table 5.11   *Classification accuracy using PAMAP2 dataset with J48 decision tree*

Feature selection method	Similarity measure	FPR	Precision	F-measure
[250]	PCC	0.0711	0.7185	0.7159
	LSRE	0.0017	0.9937	0.9937
	MICI	0.0034	0.9883	0.9883
AUFS	PCC	0.069	0.7291	0.7258
	LSRE	0.0009	0.9967	0.9967
	MICI	0.0032	0.9934	0.9934
SPEC [251]	RBF kernel	0.0874	0.6974	0.6833

accuracy result compared to the two other methods based on the F-measure. The accuracy range varies from 4%–9% to 23%–26% compared to [250] and SPEC, respectively, when using the J48 decision tree classifier as shown in Table 5.8.

The advantage of the AUFS method over existing FS methods is clearly the accurate selection of representative features and therefore the improvement of the classification accuracy, and this for the following reasons. This can be explained by the following. First, K-mean works best in clustering the features with high-dimensional data as it is not sensitive to the non-dense data. Therefore, this would result in better partitioning of the features and consequently an accurate selection of representative features. Second, the way in which representative features are selected contributes to improving the classification accuracy by guaranteeing the representativeness of the selected features. Actually, it is not enough to assume that all features grouped in a given cluster are representative; this is not an adequate method of properly measuring the representativeness of features. Conversely, AUFS strictly limits the representativeness of features to only those features that have the highest similarity to the cluster centroids, and this applies to every similarity measure. This way of selecting representative features helps AUFS to obtaining better classification accuracy by guaranteeing that the selected features will represent all the features in the clusters. Third, all the features in a cluster other than representative features are discarded to ensure the removal of any redundant features. As a result, this method ensures the generation of a reduced representative feature set that helps the classifiers to accurately classify the data.

As SPEC uses one similarity measure, the average of the similarity measures of every method is then computed for every dataset with the three evaluation classifiers in order to further investigate their classification accuracy, as shown in Table 5.12. After computing the average of the similarity measures of every method, AUFS continues to achieve the best results for all the accuracy metrics as well as for all datasets, whether the evaluation model is Naive Bayes, IB1, or J48 decision tree.

Further experiments were also carried out to investigate which one of the similarity measures works the best for the proposed method for all the tested datasets in terms of the classification accuracy. The average classification accuracy of the three evaluation models was computed. The results are presented in Table 5.13, which indicates that AUFS achieved the best results with the LSRE similarity measure for all tested metrics. AUFS has the lowest FPR, the highest precision, and F-measure compared to the other similarity measures. Actually, regression similarity measures are very efficient for classification and prediction tasks [396].

In addition to considering the classification accuracy, we also investigated the computational time complexity of AUFS in producing the representative feature set. The three methods were tested on three datasets and their average time complexity was determined, as shown in Figure 5.3. AUFS has the lowest time complexity followed by the method proposed by Mitra *et al.* [250] and SPEC, respectively. The reason that AUFS has lower computational time complexity than SPEC and Mitra's method [250] is that it does not require any search strategy to examine different subsets of features in order to find the representative feature set. Instead, AUFS selects

Table 5.12   The average accuracy of different similarity measures used for every method

Dataset	Method	Evaluation model	FPR	Precision	*F*-measure
Spambase	Method in [250]	Naive Bayes	0.4278	0.5936	0.73303
		IB1	0.1096	0.8293	0.8223
		J48 decision tree	0.0863	0.8568	0.8246
	AUFS	Naive Bayes	0.2214	0.7466	0.7986
		IB1	0.077	0.8778	0.8637
		J48 decision tree	0.0581	0.9041	0.8915
	SPEC	Naive Bayes	0.4283	0.5921	0.7312
		IB1	0.4763	0.5688	0.7161
		J48 decision tree	0.4788	0.5678	0.7156
Water treatment plant	Method in [250]	Naive Bayes	0.024	0.4521	0.5268
		IB1	0.0045	0.7057	0.5131
		J48 decision tree	0.0084	0.6871	0.676
	AUFS	Naive Bayes	0.0142	0.6215	0.6848
		IB1	0.0019	0.8846	0.6892
		J48 decision tree	0.0032	0.8598	0.778
	SPEC	Naive Bayes	0.0312	0.4286	0.5714
		IB1	0.0058	0.7273	0.64
		J48 decision tree	0.0078	0.7143	0.7143
PAMAP2	Method in [250]	Naive Bayes	0.0538	0.731	0.7225
		IB1	0.0242	0.8908	0.8898
		J48 decision tree	0.0254	0.9001	0.8993
	AUFS	Naive Bayes	0.04243	0.7516	0.7474
		IB1	0.0227	0.8961	0.8952
		J48 decision tree	0.0243	0.9064	0.9053
	SPEC	Naive Bayes	0.0721	0.5172	0.5284
		IB1	0.0821	0.6678	0.6597
		J48 decision tree	0.0874	0.6974	0.6833

Table 5.13   The average classification accuracy of different similarity measures

Similarity measure	Evaluation model	FPR	Precision	*F*-Measure
PCC	Naive Bayes	0.0655	0.6369	0.6689
	IB1	0.049	0.8198	0.7487
	J48 decision tree	0.042	0.843	0.7862
LSRE	Naive Bayes	0.0567	0.7495	0.7969
	IB1	0.027	0.9173	0.8499
	J48 decision tree	0.0205	0.914	0.8915
MICI	Naive Bayes	0.1558	0.7334	0.765
	IB1	0.0255	0.9214	0.8495
	J48 decision tree	0.0231	0.9133	0.8971

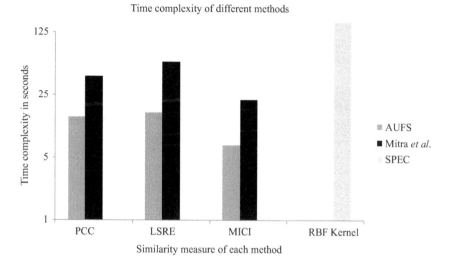

Figure 5.3 Average time complexity of different methods

the feature that has the highest similarity to its cluster centroid as the representative feature of that cluster. Furthermore, AUFS has a smart process of selecting representative features and removing redundant ones, which results in reducing the time complexity. Indeed, AUFS removes all features other than representative ones from clusters; and therefore, redundant features will definitely be removed, as they will be considered being nonrepresentative. Finally, Mitra's method [250] has higher running time due to the complexity of kNN unlike the adapted k-mean proposed in the AUFS method.

5.7 Conclusion

Redundant and nonrepresentative features, which result from high-dimensional data, have negative consequences on any applied classification algorithms essentially in terms of high computational time complexity and low classification accuracy. Selecting a reduced feature set, which only has representative and nonredundant features, is critical, particularly when targeting high-dimensional datasets. A filter-based approach unsupervised FS method is described in this chapter, and the challenge is to accurately select a reduced feature set that represents the majority of features in a cluster with high-dimensional data. The selection of a reduced feature set would definitely enhance the classifiers to accurately classify the data. Also, the features are selected without applying any search strategy for selecting the best subset of features.

In the described experiments using three datasets, the AUFS method is compared with two unsupervised FS methods. We clearly showed that AUFS outperforms the benchedmarked methods in selecting a reduced feature set that helps the selected evaluation classifiers to accurately classify the data with the lowest computational time complexity.

Future work will focus on improving AUFS so to produce the representative feature set in the online mode. UFSAD will later be extended to consider the specific characteristics of data streams (and could be called UFSAD-MS). As illustrated in Figures 5.4 and 5.5, this work could be followed by two versions for multiple streams: the centralized and distributed versions of UFSAD-MS. These two versions are evaluated so as to select the best approach in terms of performance. Figure 5.4 shows the centralized version, where UFSAD-MS waits for windows of features from every

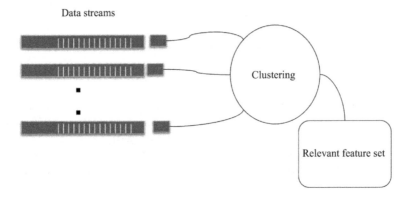

Figure 5.4   UFSAD-MS centralized version

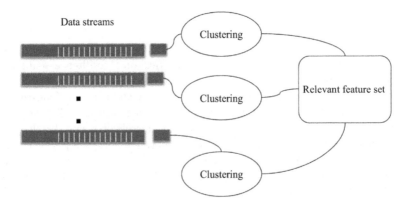

Figure 5.5   UFSAD-MS distributed version

stream and later clusters them to find the relevant features. Conversely, Figure 5.5 depicts the distributed version, where UFSAD-MS clusters every stream individually and then aggregates their selected relevant features. Experimental results are not shown as the two versions of UFSAD-MS are currently being implemented. The implementation will cover all the required properties for FS schemes to work in multi-data streams.

Chapter 6

Optimizing feature selection to improve transport layer statistics quality

There is significant interest in the network management and industrial security community about the need to improve the quality of transport layer statistics (TLS) and to identify the "best" and most relevant features. The ability to eliminate redundant and irrelevant features is important in order to improve the classification accuracy and to reduce the computational complexity related to the construction of the classifier. In practice, several feature selection (FS) methods can be used as a preprocessing step to eliminate redundant and irrelevant features and as a knowledge discovery tool to reveal the "best" features in many soft computing applications. This chapter investigates the advantages and disadvantages of such FS methods with new proposed metrics, namely *goodness*, *stability*, and *similarity*. The aim here is to come up with an integrated FS method that is built on the key strengths of existing FS methods. A novel way is described to identify efficiently and accurately the "best" features by first combining the results of some well-known FS methods to find consistent features and then use the proposed concept of *support* to select the smallest set of features and cover data optimality. The empirical study over ten high-dimensional network traffic datasets demonstrates significant gain in accuracy and improved runtime performance of a classifier compared to individual results of well-known FS methods.

6.1 Introduction

Network traffic classification has attracted a lot of interest in various areas, including supervisory control and data acquisition (industrial network) security monitoring, Internet user accounting, quality of service, and user behavior. Classification-based methods [12,17] rely on a set of "good" features (that can provide a better class separability) in order to develop accurate and realistic traffic models. The identification of good features for classification is a challenging task because (i) this requires expert knowledge of the domain to understand which features are important, (ii) datasets may contain redundant and irrelevant features that greatly reduce the accuracy of the classification process, and (iii) the efficiency of the classifiers (e.g., based on machine-learning (ML) methods) is reduced when analyzing a large number of features. Indeed, a number of studies, e.g., [151,265], have shown that irrelevant/redundant features can degrade the predictive accuracy and intelligibility of the classification model, maximize training and testing processing time of the classification model, and increase storage requirements. This chapter addresses these issues and describes a new method that identifies a small set of "good" features that can increase the accuracy and efficiency of network traffic classification.

Previous classification approaches that used the basic information from IP headers and payload (such as the packet content) for classification did not work well. IP headers contained a few features (such as IP addresses, port numbers, and protocols) that cannot accurately distinguish between applications. Payload-based methods relied on deep inspection of packet content which resulted in significant processing and memory constraints on the bandwidth management tool. Recent approaches [12–14,18] have addressed the abovementioned limitations by (i) avoiding deep packet inspection by creating additional new features from TLS, e.g., statistical information in features of the traffic such as packet length and packet arrival time (see Section 6.4) and (ii) applying ML methods to learn from the data. Even though these approaches provide a promising alternative, they suffer from the presence of a large number of irrelevant/redundant TLS-based features. To improve such approaches, we need to properly eliminate redundant features and identify the most relevant features (which we refer to as *best* features).

Existing ML-based approaches [12,13,17,18,266] focus on achievable classification accuracy through the use of various ML methods such as classification and clustering; however, they suffer from irrelevant and redundant features. On the other hand, FS methods [151,265] can be used for identifying the best features by eliminating irrelevant features. FS methods can be divided into two main categories: the *wrapper method* and the *filter method* [151,265]. The former [151] employs an existing ML method (e.g., support vector machine [36] and Bayesian neural network [12]) as a classifier and uses the classifier's accuracy as the evaluation measure to select the best possible features. Such a method tends to be not only computationally expensive but also inherits *bias* toward the predetermined learning algorithm. The latter method [265] relies on the natural characteristics of the data (e.g., correlation) and does not require a predetermined mining algorithm to select feature subsets. As a result, this method does not inherit the *bias* [62] of any mining algorithm and it is also computationally effective. However, different filter-based methods use different evaluation criteria (e.g., information based, dependence based, consistency based, and distance based). Therefore, one of the key challenges (in selecting a filter method) is to define appropriate *metrics* that can be used to properly compare existing FS methods to classify traffic. This chapter proposes new metrics, called *goodness* (to measure the quality of the generated feature set by each FS method), *stability* (to measure the sensitivity of a FS method under variations to the training traffic data), and *similarity* (to measure the diversity and disagreement between FS methods). These three metrics enable us to compare and understand the inner instruments of each FS method and the common differences between them. As shown in the proposed experiments (in Section 6.4), each FS method has its own advantages and no single method performs equally well on all three metrics.

The other key challenge (for traffic classification) is to preserve the maximum number of relevant features for traffic classification. It is found that classification accuracy is related to the number of relevant features used in the classification process.

However, different FS methods choose different sets of relevant features. Even worse, they do not always choose the same number of relevant features. This is problematic for the following reasons: (i) different FS methods may yield feature subsets that can be considered local optima in the space of feature subsets, (ii) the representative power of particular FS methods may constrain its search space such that the optimal subset cannot be reached, and (iii) a "combined" approach can give a better approximation to the optimal subset or ranking of features (which is often not applicable with a single FS method). In addition to the new metrics, the second contribution of this chapter is an algorithm that combines the benefits of several well-known FS methods, which is inspired by similar work in sensor fusion [267], classifier combination [268,269], and clustering ensemble algorithms [270,271].

To the best of our knowledge, this is the first ensemble-based method to be used for FS. In this approach, a FS method is considered a domain expert. Features that were supported by many domain experts are considered important in contributing to high classification accuracy and more efficient computation. Our proposed approach presents an efficient way of selecting the "best" features for network traffic classi-fication by introducing the concept of *support* as an optimality criterion to keep the size of the feature set small. Figure 6.1* provides an overview of the implementation of the FS methods and ML algorithms for traffic classification in practice.

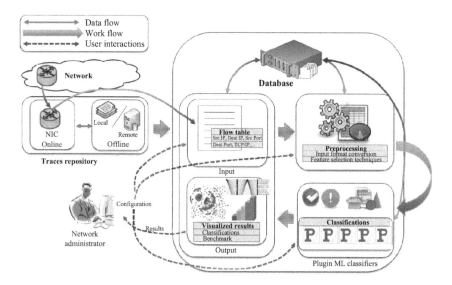

Figure 6.1 *The process of network traffic classification consists of four parts: (1) traffic data repository (from/to which traffic data is retrieved and stored), (2) data preprocessing (for traffic flow feature selection), (3) classification engine (which comprises various types of classification methods), and (4) dispersion graph (for traffic visualization) [18]*

---

*The limitations of data repository in terms of space required and recycling of storage are out of scope for this book.

The proposed metrics and approach are evaluated using four publicly available benchmark traffic datasets. The extensive experiments carried out here show that the proposed approach indeed provides a robust and meaningful way of identifying "best" features for traffic classification by exploiting the advantages of each FS method (see Section 6.6.3 for details).

This chapter is organized as follows. Section 6.2 describes the steps of the general FS process. Section 6.3 introduces the three new metrics in details. Section 6.4 describes the experimental methodology, including benchmark traffic datasets. Section 6.5 presents the initial investigation based on the proposed metrics, followed by a discussion of the experimental results. Section 6.6 summarizes the main important details of the local optimization approach (LOA).

6.2   FS methods for benchmarking

There is a wide variety of FS methods in the literature. However, with high-dimensional network traffic data, neither the wrapper method nor complex search algorithms are applicable. In this chapter, we resorted to the use of filter methods [249,272–276], since they do not rely on the use of any data mining algorithm. They are simpler to implement and have fewer parameters to be tuned. However, filter methods are designed with different evaluation criteria and a given method is often tailored to a specific domain, which therefore may not work well on other domains. To identify the *best* features for network traffic, we have analyzed some well-known FS methods, each being the best one for a specific criterion. In the end, we selected six FS methods, which cover the following evaluation criteria: information, dependence, consistency, distance, and transformation. These are information gain (IG) [272] and gain ratio (GR) [273] (for information-based criteria), principal component analysis (PCA) [274] (for transformation-based criteria), correlation-based feature selection (CBF) [275] (for dependence-based criteria), chi-square, [255] (for statistical criteria), and consistency-based search (CBS) [276] (for consistency-based criteria).

Before describing the specifics of each of the six FS methods, let us first look at their common characteristics. As shown in Figure 6.2, all these methods share a similar process for selecting a *best* subset [277], in which the selection process of the *best* subset (by each FS method) has four steps which include subset generation, subset evaluation, stopping criterion, and final subset validation. Consequently, a feature is selected if additional information is obtained when it is added to the previously selected feature set and discarded in the opposite case since the information obtained is already contained (redundant) in the previous set.

Here are the specifics of the six selected FS methods.

- **IG [273]:** This is one of the approaches used for decision tree construction of the *ID3*[†] (Iterative Dichotomizer 3 algorithm) [262]. It measures the number of bits of

---

[†]It uses the information theory to determine the most informative attributes and to have tree with minimal branching.

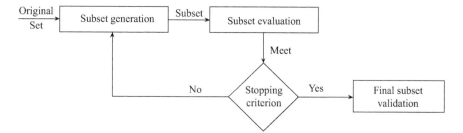

Figure 6.2   Feature selection process [62]

information provided in class prediction by knowing the value of features [278]. The feature with the highest value of IG is considered the *splitting point*, while a feature with the minimum value reflects the *impurity* in data partitions. IG is defined as the difference between the original information (which is based on the proportion of the class) and the new information (which is obtained after partitioning). A variety of FS methods based on information criterion have been proposed including mutual information and term strength. However, Yang [279] reported that IG performed much better on their multi-class benchmarks due to its ability to aggressively reduce non-informative features. Therefore, IG has been chosen in our approach as a generalized form for the information-based criterion.

- **Gain ratio [273]:** This approach incorporates "split information" of the feature into the IG measure. Gain ratio attempts to overcome the bias of IG toward the feature with a large number of distinct values by applying normalization to IG using a split information measure (which represents the potential information generated by splitting the training dataset into partitions). The features are ranked based on the value of gain ratio. Therefore, the ratio becomes unstable if the value of the splitting point reaches zero. In general, gain ratio is an information theoretic measure that selects features with an average-or-better gain and its advantage over IG is that it does not consider features with a large number of distinct values.

- **PCA [274]:** This approach searches for k-based vectors used to represent the original traffic data. Such data is projected onto a much smaller space. PCA combines the essence of attributes by creating a small set of variables. The input data is a linear combination of principal components and explains the entire changes with several components. The purpose is to provide an effective explanation through dimension reduction using linear equations. Although the p components are required to reproduce the total system variability, often much of this variability can be accounted for by a small number, say k, of the principal components. If so, there is almost as much information in the k components as there is in the original p variables. The k principal components can then replace the initial p variables, and the original dataset, consisting of n measurements on p variables, is reduced to one consisting of n measurements on k principal components. PCA and linear discriminant analysis (LDA) approaches transform the data in the high-dimensional space to a space of fewer dimensions, and they are considered to be the only two FS methods available for this criterion [280]. However, Yan *et al.* [281] report that LDA suffers from two intrinsic problems: (i) singularity of within-class scatter matrices and (ii) limited available projection directions. Therefore, we have chosen PCA (in our approach to represent the transformation-based criterion) since it outperforms LDA [282].

- **Correlation-based feature selection (CBF) [275]:** CBF is a widely used filtering algorithm. For a given traffic dataset, the algorithm tries to find an optimal subset which is best related to the predicted class and does not contain any redundant features. Two aspects are noteworthy: feature–class correlation and feature–feature correlation. The former indicates how much a feature is correlated to a specific class while the latter represents the correlation between two features. Fayyad and Irani [283] used an information theory method to discretize numeric features and then used *symmetrical uncertainty* to measure feature–feature correlation where there is no notion of one feature being a class [275]. The advantage of such a method is that it is fast and can identify relevant features as well as redundancy among relevant features without pairwise correlation analysis [275].

- **Chi-square [255]:** This approach uses a discretization method based on a statistical measure and evaluates flows individually with respect to the classes. It measures the association between the class and input feature F. The range of continuous valued features needs to be discretized into intervals. A numeric feature is initially stored by placing each observed value into its own interval. The next step, chi-square X^2 measurement, determines whether the relative frequencies of the classes in adjacent intervals are similar enough to justify merging. The merging process is controlled by a predetermined threshold, which is determined by attempting to maintain the validity of the original data. Reference [279] reported that chi-square performs well due to its ability to potentially perform as a FS and discretize numeric and ordinal features at the same time. In other words, it works as a combined discretization and FS method [255].

- **Consistency-based search (CBS) [276]:** This method uses a consistency measure that does not attempt to maximize the class separability but tries to retain the discriminating power of data defined by original features. In other words, using this measure, FS is formalized as finding the smallest set of features that can identify flows of a class as consistently as the complete feature set. Therefore, the consistency measure is capable of handling irrelevant features in the original space reflected as a percentage of inconsistencies. For instance, if two instances of the pattern represent different classes, then that pattern is considered to be inconsistent. The consistency measure can help remove both redundant and irrelevant features. This type of evaluation measure is characteristically different from other measures because of its heavy reliance on the training dataset and use of min-features bias in selecting a subset of features [276].

The aforementioned FS methods involve relevant feature adding and redundant feature removal to identify *best* subset. Here, we first provide some basic definitions of relevant and redundant, and then we introduce these mechanisms.

Definition 6.1 (irrelevant feature). *A feature is said to be irrelevant if it carries no information about the different classes of interest. Such features have no discriminative power.*

Definition 6.2 (redundant feature). *A feature is said to be redundant if it has a high correlation with another feature. This feature can either decrease the accuracy or increase over-fitting.*

Let us introduce the mechanism of relevant feature adding and redundant feature removal

Definition 6.3 (adding). *For a given feature set S_i, let f^+ be the feature such that*

$$f^+ = \arg{}^{\ddagger}\max\ M_i(S_i) \tag{6.1}$$

where M_i denotes the criterion used by the FS methods to generate the best feature subset. ADD(S_i) is the operation that adds a feature f^+ to the current set S_i to obtain the set S_{i+1} if

$$ADD(S_i) = S_i \cup f^+ = \{S_{i+1}, S_i, S_{i+1}\} \tag{6.2}$$

Definition 6.4 (removing). *For a given feature set S_i, let f^- be the feature such that*

$$f^- = \arg\max\ M_i(S_i)^{\S}, \tag{6.3}$$

where M_i denotes the criterion used by the FS methods to generate the best feature subset. Thus, REM(S_i) is the operation of removing a feature f^- to the current set S_i to obtain set S_{i-1} if

$$REM(S_i) \equiv S_i \setminus \{f^+\} = S_{i-1}, \ \ S_i, S_{i-1} \subset X \tag{6.4}$$

6.3   The new metrics

Section 6.2 described six well-known FS approaches covering various criteria. However, one of the major problems is the lack of metrics to properly compare such methods in order to reveal the best features in network traffic. Here, we suggest three new metrics to address such a problem:

- *Goodness* refers to how well a generated subset can accurately classify the traffic flows.
- *Stability* refers to the property of selecting the same set of features irrespective of variations in the traffic data that has been collected over a period of time.
- *Similarity* compares the behavior of multiple FS methods on the same data and also evaluates how different criteria differ in generating an optimal set for a given dataset.

Evaluating goodness

The aim here is to evaluate the accuracy of the final output of the selected FS methods (described in Section 6.2). In practice, a straightforward way is to measure the results directly using prior knowledge about the data. In network traffic data, however, we often do not have such prior knowledge. Therefore, we need to rely on indirect methods [277] (e.g., error rate), such as the one that monitors the change in classification performance caused by the change of features. On extremely imbalanced dataset, the error rates cannot provide the information on minority class (e.g., attack), thus the goodness rate (GR) is used as a performance metric. For a selected feature subset, we simply conduct the before-and-after experiment to compare the goodness rate (GR) of the classifier learned on the full set of features and that learned on the final selected subsets.

The goal is to explain how to evaluate the *goodness* of the final set, since varying an independent measure (denoted as M_i) will produce different sets of features. The following steps are used to validate (the goodness of) the output set generated by an independent measure:

- Apply a Naive Bayes classifier to the data with only the optimal subset produced by independent measure M_i. Naive Bayes is chosen because it does not require feature weighting [284]; therefore, its performance depends solely on the number of features selected. Moreover, Naive Bayes has been shown to work better than more complex methods [285]. Hence, we emphasize the advantages of using the simplest of the computational methods to ensure that the process is tractable in time.
- Validate the goodness of the results using the fitness function, which is defined as follows:

$$Goodness(S_i) = \frac{1}{Y} \sum_{i=1}^{Y} \frac{N_i^{tp}}{N_i} \tag{6.5}$$

where Y is the number of classes in the dataset, N_i^{tp} denotes the number of true positive of each class, and N_i is the total number of instances for class i.

Evaluating stability

The aim here is to measure the *stability* of the selected FS methods, motivated by the need to provide network experts with quantified evidence that the selected features are relatively robust to variations in the traffic data. In practice, network operators tend to have less confidence in FS methods that produce a different set of features on datasets taken over a period of time. Therefore, a candidate set of features that not only yields high prediction but also has a relatively stability is preferable [286]. Let $S = \{S_1, S_2, \ldots, S_{|D|}\}$ be a collection of feature subsets obtained by running a single FS method $t \in T$, each time with the same configuration, on different traffic datasets (say D, where $|D|$ is the total number of datasets used). Let X be a subset representing all the features that occur anywhere in S:

$$X = \{f_i | f_i \in S, F_{f_i} > 0\} = \bigcup_{i=1}^{|D|} S_i, X \neq 0 \tag{6.6}$$

where F_{f_i} is the frequency of the feature f_i. In a situation when the confidence of a feature needs to be measured, then the following formula is used:

$$stab(f_i) = \frac{F_{f_i} - 1}{|D| - 1} \tag{6.7}$$

where F_{f_i} is the frequency of feature $f_i \in X$ in the collection S, and $|D|$ denotes the total number of generated subsets. Thus, all confidence values are normalized between [0,1]. The measure of stability of the feature $f_i \in X$ in collection S takes the following properties:

- $\text{stab}\,(f_i) = 0$: f_i does not appear anywhere in the observed subsets.
- $\text{stab}\,(f_i) = 1$: f_i appears in each subsets of the system.

To evaluate the average confidence of all features in the collection S, we need to extend (6.7). Let N be the total number of frequencies of any feature f_i that appears in collection $S \cdot N$ will then be

$$N = \sum_{i \in X} F_i = \sum_{i=1}^{|D|} |S_i|, \{N \in IN, N \geq n\} \tag{6.8}$$

Therefore, the stability over all features $f_i \in X$ in collection S is defined as

$$stab(S) = \sum_{f_i \in X} \frac{F_{f_i}}{N} \times \frac{F_{f_i} - 1}{|D| - 1} \tag{6.9}$$

F_{f_i}/N represents the relative frequency of the features $f_i \in X$ in a subset. If $\text{stab}\,(\text{S})$ value is close to 1, this indicates that all subsets are identical, in particular, only if $N = |D| \times |X|$. In contrast, suppose $\text{stab}\,(\text{S})$ value is close to 0 (if $N = |X|$), then this implies a low level of stability in overall subsets.

Evaluating similarity

The stability measure can only evaluate the stability of an FS method on different traffic datasets [286]. However, it is important to compare the behavior of different FS methods on the same traffic dataset or evaluate how, for a given dataset, the candidate FS methods differ in their preference for particular features. Therefore, we propose a similarity measure to allow a comparison of multiple FS methods results. This will, in turn, enable the evaluation of how an optimal subset generated (using one criterion) can differ according to another criterion.

Given F_{f_i} is the number of frequency of features f_i in a collection S, the computation of the desirable properties of the proposed similarity measure is done as follows. If the value of $\text{Sim}\,(|\text{T}|)$ is close to 1, this will indicate high similarity; and any value close to 0 will indicate low similarity. Similarity is defined as follows:

$$Sim(T) = \sum_{f_i \in X} \frac{F_{f_i}}{N} \times \frac{F_{f_i} - 1}{|T| - 1} \tag{6.10}$$

where $|T|$ denotes the total number of FS methods that have been applied on a single dataset.

Let $|D|$ be the number of used traffic datasets. The similarity between two candidate FS methods, say t_1 and t_2, (across different datasets), is defined as

$$Sim(t_1, t_2) = 1 - \frac{1}{2} \sum \left| \frac{F_{f_i}^{t_1}}{N^{t_1}} - \frac{F_{f_i}^{t_2}}{N^{t_2}} \right| \tag{6.11}$$

where $F_{f_i}^{t_1}$ denotes the number of occurrences (frequencies) of feature f_i in t_1 and $F_{f_i}^{t_2}$ is the frequency of the same feature in t_2.

Both $Sim(T)$ and $Sim(t_1, t_2)$ take value from [0,1], with 0 indicating that there is no similarity between the candidate FS methods' outputs, and 1 indicating that such methods are generating identical subsets.

6.4   Experimental methodology

The main focus of this section is to demonstrate the benefits of the proposed metrics as an evaluation framework (to find an appropriate FS method that improves the performance of the classification process). In what follows, we describe the network traffic trace data collected over different periods of time. We also show the performance results of the different FS methods for the network traffic classification.

Datasets

We compare the candidate FS methods on labeled Internet traffic data [148]. The TCP traffic flows in such data have been manually classified and collected by monitoring a high-performance network. We limit ourselves to the available traffic data. This data consists of ten datasets of flows taken from 2 days of network activity. Each dataset consists of flows (objects), and each flow is described by a set of features and its membership class. Each set covers randomly the same length of time throughout the 24-h period.

Data collection

Publicly available labeled traffic datasets are very rare due to security and privacy concerns [287]. The traffic datasets collected by the high-performance network monitor (described in [245]) are one of the largest publicly available network traffic traces that have been used in our experiment. These datasets are based on traces captured using its loss-limited, full-payload capture to disk where timestamps with resolution of better than 35 ns are provided. The data was taken for several different periods of time from one site on the Internet. This site is a research facility which hosts up to 1,000 users connected to the Internet via a full-duplex Gigabit Ethernet link. Full-duplex traffic on this connection was monitored for each traffic set. The site hosts several biology-related facilities, collectively referred to as the Genome Campus (Cambridge Lab).

Traffic categories

Classes of traffic are common groups of applications. Some approaches have simpler definitions of classes (e.g., normal versus attack), but others have more complex

Table 6.1   *An example of network applications*

Classification	Application
BULK	FTP
DATABASE	Postgres, Sqlnet Oracle, Ingres
INTERACTIVE	SSH, klogin, rlogin, telnet
MAIL	imap, pop2, SMTP
SERVICES	X11, DNS, ident, ldap, NTP
WWW	http
P2P	KazaA, Bittorrent, GnuTella
ATTACK	Internet worm and virus attacks
GAMES	Microsoft Direct Play
MULTIMEDIA	Windows Media Player, Real

Table 6.2   *An example of features used as input for traffic classification [147]*

Features
Flow metrics (duration, total packets)
Packet inter arrival time (mean, variance)
Size of TCP/IP control fields
Total packets (in each direction of flow)
Payload size (mean, variance)
Effective bandwidth based
Fourier-transform of packet
TCP-specific values derived from tcptrace (e.g., total of pushed packets)

definitions (e.g., the classification of specific applications) [288]. We have used the class descriptions provided in [148], which can be used as the basis for evaluating the candidate FS methods to identify important features for traffic classification. Table 6.1 shows the classes for the corresponding applications. The complete description can be found in [148].

Flow features

Each flow is characterized by a set of unique features that correspond to a specific class. Such features allow for discrimination between various traffic classes. Table 6.2 provides a few examples drawn from the 249 per-flow features that are available from the dataset. A full description of these features can be found in [148]. The aim is to identify the best features that are independent of a particular network configuration.

Classification flows

The application of a classification scheme requires the features of the objects to be classified. By using these features, the classifier allocates an object (flow) to a specific class. In this dataset, the object classified is a TCP/IP traffic flow, which is represented as a flow of single or multiple packets between a given pair of hosts. The flow is defined by n-tuple consisting of the IP addresses of the pair of hosts and the TCP port numbers used by the server and client. In this work, we are limited to the training and testing sets available (ten datasets), which consist only of TCP and semantically complete TCP connections. Semantically complete flows are flow events for which a complete connection *setup* and *tear-down* was observed.

Experimental setup

To evaluate the effectiveness of the selected FS methods (to compute the "best" features for network traffic), we have used various sizes of datasets. Table 6.3 shows information about the structure of datasets for evaluation. It is clear from the numbers that there are a different number of flows in each dataset. This is due to a higher density of traffic during each block of 28 min. In these sets, each record comprises a set of features and a class label of the flow. The features are either continuous or discrete. The former is quantitative and the latter is on a qualitative scale. The goodness of each FS method is evaluated by applying K-fold cross validation on each traffic dataset. In this process, the dataset is divided into K subsets. Each time, one of the K subsets is used for testing while the remaining $K - 1$ subsets form the training set. Performance statistics are calculated across all K trials. In these experiments, the value of K is set to 10, since this was suggested by Kohavi [289] as the best empirical number for accuracy estimation and model selection. Therefore, we also expect that this K value will provide a good indication of how well the classifier performs and classifies unseen data based on all features (of the original datasets).

Figure 6.3 shows the different steps involved in evaluating the goodness of the candidate FS methods. The first step provides the FS methods with the required information (i.e., IP traffic generated by different applications). In practice, such methods identify the smallest set of features that can be used to differentiate between applications. In the second step, the filtered traffic data is used to train a supervised ML algorithm (e.g., Naive Bayes) and to create the classifier model. This process of using a cross validation to generate goodness results is repeated for each dataset. The statistics of goodness are accumulated for all ten datasets.

Table 6.3   Flow statistics (percentages of flows) according to applications

Total flows 378,101	WWW 86.77%	MAIL 7.56%	BULK 3.05%	SERV 0.56%	DB 0.70%
	INT 0.03%	P2P 0.55%	ATTACK 0.47%	MMEDIA 0.28%	GAMES 0.02%

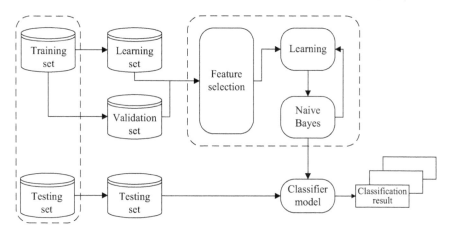

Figure 6.3 Final subset validation process

In this chapter, these FS methods were the implemented using version 3.7.7 of the WEKA software suite (readers are referred to [290] for more details).

6.5 Preliminary experiments

The six selected FS methods are compared using the new metrics (see Section 6.3). For a given selected subset, an experiment is conducted using a Naive Bayes classifier to compare the goodness of the optimal subsets generated by different FS methods.

6.5.1 Experimental results

This section discusses the various experimental results.

Classification of the traffic based on all the features

The Naive Bayes classifier is used to characterize the network traffic flows using the original full dataset without applying any FS method. From the results shown in Figure 6.4, the classifier achieved goodness on average of 67.94%, which means that on average, only 67.94% of flows have been correctly classified according to their target classes using all the features. As expected, this result is not satisfactory because of the presence of irrelevant and redundant features in the datasets. However, it can also be seen in Figure 6.4 that the model trained on some datasets (e.g., datasets #3, #4, #5, and #6) outperforms the remaining sets. This suggests that there is a low similarity between the corresponding flows of the datasets. The results also suggest good class separability, and this is why there is a significant increase in the number of correctly classified flows. Therefore, in the remainder of this chapter, we will use different FS methods to discard the irrelevant and redundant features.

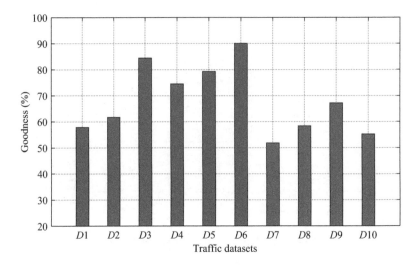

Figure 6.4   Classification of the traffic based on all features

Evaluation of "goodness"

Both Table 6.4 and Figures 6.5 and 6.6 compare the classification goodness rate (GR) of the six FS methods on the ten datasets. For the classification task, the applications of network traffic are expected to be correctly classified. Therefore, an FS method with high GR is desired. Note that the sequence CBF, chi-square, InfoGain, PCA, CBS, and GainRatio roughly order the FS methods according to increasing GR. This ordering is notable in Figures 6.5 and 6.6 and Table 6.4 on the achieved criterion values. From the results, the FS methods achieve a higher classification of goodness in comparison with the outcomes of using a full features set. Overall, the goodness rate (GR) of the classification model has been substantially improved (mainly by removing these irrelevant and redundant features from network traffic data), except for GainRatio. The average GR using GainRatio is 61.73%, which is much lower than for Naive Bayes with all features. This indicates that the optimal subset selected by GainRatio may include some features that provide *poor* class separability. As a result, such features would reduce the accuracy of the (Naive Bayes) classifier.

Temporal variation of FS goodness

Figure 6.6 shows that most FS methods (except for GainRatio) enable the classification scheme to perform better than the base case (i.e., complete feature set). It is also shown in Table 6.4 and Figure 6.6 that no FS performs well on all datasets. Figure 6.5 shows a comparison of the performance of six widely used FS methods on ten different datasets. Overall, CBF has the best performance on all of the datasets, except for the dataset #9. Chi-square achieves the best performance on the datasets #2, #3, and #7 but has the worst performance on datasets #1, #5, and #8. IG peaked

Table 6.4   The goodness rate (GR) of FS methods on the ten datasets

FS methods	D_1	D_2	D_3	D_4	D_5	D_6	D_7	D_8	D_9	D_{10}
CBF (%)	96.98	94.60	93.65	95.47	94.91	87.29	94.60	92.69	44.19	93.8
InfoGain (%)	87.78	88.96	95.95	83.06	50.36	86.75	94.99	89.70	87.71	48.40
Chi-square (%)	67.36	92.68	95.94	85.55	48.12	84.92	95.51	76.50	90.99	89.32
PCA (%)	78.89	65.23	79.57	82.41	90.76	90.57	71.38	81.99	84.35	86.93
CBS (%)	21.58	93.58	76.92	27.79	96.40	92.80	67.06	93.38	42.57	69.02
Original (%)	57.89	61.70	84.45	74.51	79.29	90.07	51.86	58.35	67.12	54.20
GainRatio (%)	9.48	12.28	96.27	89.72	88.11	88.64	94.52	93.91	29.77	14.63

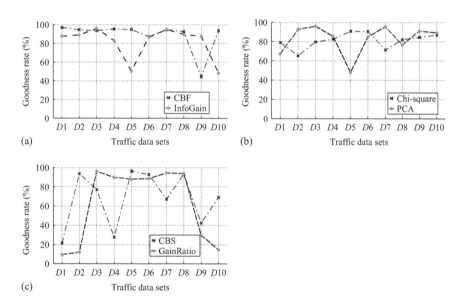

Figure 6.5   Classification of the traffic based on features of the candidate FS methods: (a) goodness of CBF and InfoGain, (b) goodness of PCA and chi-square, (c) goodness of CBS and GainRatio

on datasets #3, #7, and #8 but has the worst performance on datasets #4, #5, and #10. PCA achieves the best performance on datasets #5 and #6 but has the worst performance on the datasets #1, #2, #3, #4, and #7. CBS achieves the best performance on the datasets #2, #5, and #6 but has the worst performance on the other datasets (i.e., #1, #4, #7, #9, and #10). Gain ratio peaked on the datasets #3, #7, and #8 but performed significantly worse than the other methods on datasets #1, #2, #9, and #10. We therefore conclude that we cannot rely on a single method, and this is our main reason for developing a *hybrid approach* to identify a reliable (best) set of features that help classifiers to perform well on all datasets.

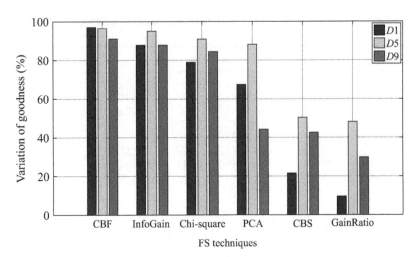

Figure 6.6   Comparison of effectiveness of existing FS methods on three randomly chosen datasets (D1, D5, D9)

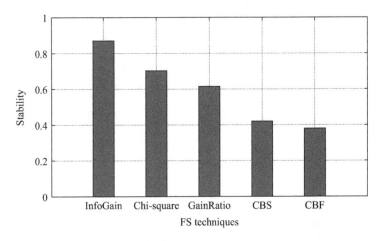

Figure 6.7   Comparing feature selection stability on traffic data

Evaluating stability of candidate feature selections

Figure 6.7 shows the stability results obtained from each FS method. First, it can be seen that the clear winner is InfoGain, as this achieves the highest stability value of 0.87 for the ten traffic datasets under consideration. Second, chi-square appears to have a better stability result than GainRatio, CBF, and CBS, respectively, with a value of 0.70. Interestingly, GainRatio has a better stability score with 0.60. Notably better (higher) values in terms of method stability can be observed amongst InfoGain, chi-square, and GainRatio, with InfoGain being the most different from the other

Table 6.5   Comparing feature selection similarity on traffic data

Datasets	D_1	D_2	D_3	D_4	D_5	D_6	D_7	D_8	D_9	D_{10}
Similarity	0.28	0.27	0.29	0.26	0.29	0.27	0.28	0.25	0.24	0.27

two methods. However, these three methods yield more stable results than CBF and CBS, which can be explained by the fact that they provide feature preference in a global respective. Finally, the stability of CBF and CBS is quite similar in terms of stability evaluation, but they achieved the worst stability scores with 0.42 and 0.39, respectively. The main reason for this is that the features provided by CBF and CBS focus on the top ranked or selected subsets. Consequently, they account poorly for feature interdependencies.

Evaluating similarity of candidate feature selections

Table 6.5 shows the similarity results obtained by performing n runs of FS methods. This information given by the proposed similarity measure reveals the behavior of n FS methods on the same dataset. It can be seen from the figure that there is low similarity between feature subsets (produced by InfoGain, chi-square, CBF, CBS, GainRatio) on each traffic dataset, with similarity values between 0.24 and 0.30. As suggested in Section 6.2, each FS method produces an optimal set considerably different from those produced by other methods. This outcome leads us to conclude that an optimal subset selected using one criterion may not be the optimal subset when using another criterion.

6.5.2   Discussion

As can been seen from the previous section, the results are not conclusive for any single FS method. As such, the more FS methods available, the more challenging it is to find a suitable one which will identify the best features for network traffic data.

This section provides a simple tabular approach to categorize the different FS methods based on the proposed metrics. This way of comparing can serve two purposes: (i) grouping FS methods with similar characteristics as well providing a way to compare such methods on the same framework, and (ii) providing an intermediate step toward building an integrated FS method to choose the best set of features for network traffic data. We categorize the normalized values of the proposed *evaluation metric* (EM) into three categories: *low*, *medium*, and *high* using the following criteria:

$$\begin{cases} 0 \ Low & \text{if } 0 \le EM \le \sigma \\ 1 \ Med & \text{if } \sigma < EM < \frac{H-(M-\sigma)}{2} \\ 2 \ High & \text{if } \frac{H-(M-\sigma)}{2} \le EM \le 1 \end{cases} \tag{6.12}$$

Table 6.6   *Evaluation of FS methods on the categorization framework*

FS tech	Goodness	Stability	Similarity
CBF	High	Low	Low
InfoGain	Medium	High	Low
Chi-square	Medium	High	Low
PCA	Medium	Low	Low
CBS	Medium	Low	Low
GainRatio	Low	Medium	Low

where M and H denote medium and high, respectively. The value of σ is set according to the various experimental results (presented in Section 6.5). In particular, the value of σ is set to 0.60 for evaluating *goodness* as this is the lowest goodness rate among the candidate FS methods. The value of σ is set to 0.4 to evaluate *stability* as this is lowest score for stability among the candidate FS methods. The same applies to *similarity* as this value indicates that most selected features were supported by less than two methods.

Table 6.6 summarizes the values for each method with regard to *goodness*, *stability*, and *similarity*. We use these comparisons to help illustrate the appropriateness of each FS method using (6.12).

1. For the *goodness* metric, prevailing ordering can be recognized among FS methods: all FS methods have an average value, except for CBF, whose value depends on the good quality of its output compared to the other methods. This suggests that CBF is recommended for cases when FS methods fail to produce good-quality output.
2. In terms of stability, all FS methods are almost unstable, with the exception of IG and chi-square.
3. From Table 6.6, one can notice constant low similarity between values yielded by the candidate FS methods on the same dataset. This suggests that a large number of features are consistently excluded while the rest appear in the selected subsets with low similarity. Also, it suggests that an optimal subset selected using one criterion is almost not optimal according to another criterion [62].

Based on the developed categorization approach, it can be seen that in most cases, there is no visible "winner" among the FS methods. As a result, there is no FS method that satisfies all evaluation criteria. Hence, we cannot rely on a single FS method to select the best set of features.

6.6   The local optimization approach (LOA)

The previous section showed that any single FS method cannot perform well on all datasets and that different FS methods generally produce different results. Given a

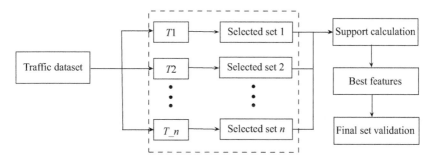

Figure 6.8 The LOA approach

traffic dataset, and without any a priori knowledge, the problem still *remains* regarding the selection of an FS method that will perform the best. Therefore, instead of choosing a particular FS method, we have looked at "combining" five FS methods so to "aggregate" their benefits in selecting the best features. This new approach is called the *LOA*. The reader may later notice that we have excluded *PCA*, as this method transforms the original features to new ones to produce the best approximation of the original features. Therefore, this does not strictly fall into the category of FS. Figure 6.8 depicts the overall idea of LOA: given a dataset, local optimization aims to select the most reliable subset of features based on feature subsets selected by FS methods. As different FS methods produce different subsets of features, we introduce the concept of *support* to indicate the importance of a specific feature. The idea behind this concept support is that the judgment of a group is superior to that of individuals. The underlying assumption is that an important feature for traffic analysis is very likely to be supported by most FS methods.

Definition 6.5. (support): *Let $F = \{f_i | 1 \leq i \leq m\}$ be a set of features in a given dataset, and $T = \{t_j | 1 \leq j \leq n\}$ be a set of existing FS methods. We then use a matrix A to record the occurrence of features for different methods, where $\alpha_{i,j}$ are binary values indicating whether the feature f_i is selected by a method t_j (1 for selected, 0 for not selected). Therefore, the support of feature $f_i \in F$ is defined as follows:*

$$support(f_i) = \frac{\sum_{j=1}^{n} \alpha_{i,j}}{|T|} \tag{6.13}$$

where $|T|$ is the number of methods that have been applied.

The following steps are taken by LOA to identify the most reliable subset of features to be used for a particular training set.

- Apply the five FS methods on a training dataset and keep all the selected features in an initial pool. As different FS methods use different ways to generate feature subsets, finding salient features is often hard. Therefore, to make the best of the different methods, LOA applies the five FS methods on a training set to generate an initial pool of five sets of features. Features that have not been selected by any of the five FS methods are discarded.

- Calculate the frequency of the observed features. Let S_{best} be the set of selected features, where $S_{best} = \{f_1, \ldots, f_n\}$. Then, the frequency of f_i is defined by $F(f_i) := m_i$, where m_i is the number of times F has the value f_i.
- Order the feature value of F based on their occurrences (frequency). Let us have $\hat{f}_1, \hat{f}_2, \ldots, \hat{f}_n$ such that $F(\hat{f}_1) \geq F(\hat{f}_2) \geq \cdots F(\hat{f}_n)$.
- Using (6.13), calculate the support of the features in the S_{best} by counting the number of times they are selected by FS methods divided by the cardinality of T, where $0 < F(f_i) \leq |T|$. This is based on our assumption that the importance of a feature is indicated by the number of occurrences in the "optimal" feature subsets generated by the different FS methods we applied. We hypothesize that a larger count of occurrences implies more distinct and reliable features.
- Examine the degree of support in the observed features. To do so, we apply an arbitrary threshold to retain only the top N features whose supports are above the threshold. The features in the S_{best} have been selected by at least one of the five FS methods; but to retrieve an optimal set of features, a threshold must be set to keep only those features that are sufficiently distinct and reliable. For instance, if a feature selected by at least three out of five FS methods is considered reliable enough, then we apply a threshold of $supp \geq 0.60$.

6.6.1　The algorithm

Algorithm 1 summarizes the various steps of LOA to compute the most informative features in a single dataset, which we denote as *DATA*. This algorithm is divided into two parts. In the first part (lines 1–17), the algorithm extracts an initial pool of five sets of features by applying the five FS methods and returns the corresponding generated feature subsets. In particular, the search starts with an initial set of features, say S_0, then this set S_0 is evaluated by an independent measurement, say t_i. Evaluate each newly generated subset S_i using t_i. Compare the current subset, S_i, with the previous optimal set $S_{optimal}$. As a result, if the current set is better than the previous set, then it is considered as the current optimal subset. Iterate the search until a sufficiently optimal set, $S_{optimal}$, found independent measurement t_i. Output $S_{optimal}$ as the *optimal* set. Then add the optimal set, $S_{optimal}$, of method t_i to the initial pool set S_{Sel}. The second part of the algorithm (lines 18–30) measures the support of each feature value in S_{freq} and includes those whose support exceeds the threshold into the set of reliable features, S_{best}. Finally, the selected features are significant features that contain indispensable information about the original features. The algorithm would need an $O(k)$, (where k is the number of FS methods) for identifying a pool of features, followed by $O(g)$ for the operation of calculating the support of features and selecting the most supportive set. Thus, the algorithm has a total complexity of $O(k + g)$ for choosing the final set of features (see Section 6.6.6).

6.6.2　An illustrative example

A simple example is given later to illustrate the use of the proposed LOA approach to select the *best* possible features. Figure 6.9(a) represents a unity of the sets of rows which correspond to the various FS methods T (where $t_i \in T$) and the columns

---

Algorithm 1: Local optimization algorithm

---

    input :
1 $DATA \longleftarrow \{f_1, f_2, \ldots, f_{n-1}\};$
2 $Feature\ Selectors(T) \longleftarrow \{CBF, Chi, \ldots, t_n\};$
    output:
3 S_{best}; // a best subset of features
4 Apply FS methods to obtain initial pool of features **for** $Selector_i^t \in [1, T]$ **do**
5 | $S_0 \longleftarrow$ initialize($DATA$);
6 | $\gamma_{optimal} \longleftarrow$ evaluate($S_0, DATA, t_i$);
7 | **repeat**
            // Evaluate S_0 by using independent FS method
8 | | $S \longleftarrow$ generate($DATA$);
            // Generate a subset S for evaluation
9 | | $\gamma \longleftarrow$ evaluate($S, DATA, t_i$);
            // Evaluate the current subset S by t_i
10 | | **if** γ *is better than* $\gamma_{optimal}$ **then**
11 | | | $\gamma_{optimal} \longleftarrow \gamma$;
12 | | | $S_{optimal} \longleftarrow S$;
13 | | **end**
14 | **until** *(reach δ)*;
        // Add the final $S_{optimal}$ of t_i to the initial pool
15 | $S_{Sel} \longleftarrow S_{sel} \cup S_{optimal}$;
16 | Return S_{Sel}; // Return the initial pool of features
17 **end**
18 Preserve the maximal of relevant feature
19 $\beta \longleftarrow 0.60$;
20 $S_{freq} \longleftarrow \emptyset$;
21 $S_{best} \longleftarrow \emptyset$;
22 FindBestSet(β, S_{sel}, S_{best});
23 $S_{freq} \longleftarrow$ ComputeFreq(S_{Sel});
24 $S_{Sort} \longleftarrow$ Sort(S_{freq});
25 **for** $f_i \in S_{Sort}$ **do**
26 | **if** $Support(f_i) \geq \beta$ **then**
27 | | $S_{best} \longleftarrow S_{best} \cup \{f_i\}$;
28 | **end**
29 **end**
30 Return S_{best};

---

represent the features themselves (where $f_i \in F$). The binary values of Figure 6.9(a) indicate whether or not a feature is selected by the corresponding FS method t_i, where 1 stands for *selected*, and 0 for *not selected*. For instance, FS method t_1 selects features $\{f_1, f_2, f_4, f_7, f_{10}\}$. In the last row of Figure 6.9(a), the frequency of a feature that has been selected is calculated by counting the number of times we observe f_i taking the binary value (1).

T	f_1	f_2	f_3	f_4	f_5	f_6	f_7	f_8	f_9	f_{10}
t_1	1	1	0	1	0	0	1	0	0	1
t_2	0	0	1	1	0	0	1	1	0	1
t_3	1	0	1	1	1	0	1	1	1	1
t_4	1	0	0	0	0	0	1	0	0	0
t_5	1	1	0	0	0	1	1	0	0	0
freq	4	2	2	3	1	1	5	2	1	3

(a)

Feature no.	Frequency	Support
f_7	5	1
f_1	4	0.80
f_4	3	0.60
f_{10}	3	0.60
f_2	2	0.40
f_3	2	0.40
f_8	2	0.40
f_5	1	0.20
f_6	1	0.20
f_9	1	0.20

(b)

*Figure 6.9   Procedure of local optimization approach (LOA): (a) applying a set of
T on a training set and (b) frequency*

Figure 6.9(b) shows a list of the features sorted by frequency. Then the support of a feature is calculated using (6.13). A predetermined threshold is applied to retrieve the *best* features. For example, if the predefined threshold of *support*(f_i) ≥ 0.60 is applied, then the features {f_7, f_1, f_4, f_{10}} are selected.

6.6.3   Result and analysis

The aim here is to evaluate the performance of the proposed LOA algorithm. We first compare the performance of LOA against the five FS methods (see Section 6.2). Then, we evaluate the effect of various parameter settings on the performance of LOA. For each FS method, Naive Bayes is used to evaluate the classification goodness rate on selected features, as we have no prior knowledge about the most reliable features for Internet traffic data.

Table 6.7 summarizes the goodness rate (GR) of LOA on ten datasets using the Naive Bayes algorithm. As can be seen from Table 6.7, LOA performs well and was stable on all datasets.

Table 6.7   The GR of LOA approach on ten different datasets

Dataset	D_1	D_2	D_3	D_4	D_5	D_6	D_7	D_8	D_9	D_{10}
Goodness rate	97.51	95.94	97.89	96.03	97.48	97.09	96.05	97.32	90.51	93.84

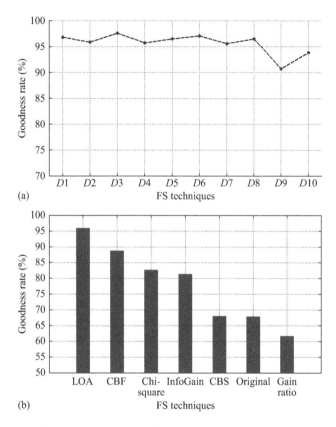

Figure 6.10   Evaluation LOA against the selected FS methods: (a) goodness of LOA on ten different datasets, (b) averaged goodness of FS methods including LOA

From the results shown in Figure 6.10, we observe that the LOA achieves an average goodness of 95.97%. Given the average goodness shown in Figure 6.10(a), it can be seen that we were able to achieve higher GR in comparison with the remaining FS methods. The experimental results shown in Figure 6.10(b) clearly demonstrate the performance of LOA across all the datasets. Notice, the GR on the datasets number #9 and #10 are not as good for either LOA or any other FS method. The reason is that the HTTP class in these two datasets includes 2,600 records, which are related to a

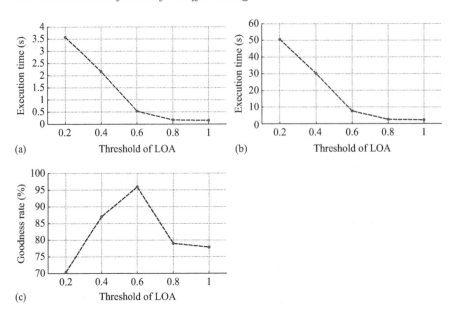

Figure 6.11　Influence of parameterizing LOA: (a) building the classifier model,
(b) testing the classifier model, and (c) the goodness rate

different class HTTPS. However, LOA has the best GR among all the methods on #9
and #10 datasets.

6.6.4　Choice of parameters

As discussed in the previous section, the main parameter in LOA is the *support* threshold, which we refer to as β, used for selecting the best feature set. The performance
of LOA critically depends on the value of β. Thus, the choice of the parameter β
not only affects the training and the testing time of classification but also influences
the goodness of the classification model. As discussed previously in Section 6.6, the
choice of β is a trade-off between lower GR and higher processing requirements due
to the increased number of features in the selected feature set. This section investigates
the effects of this parameter setting on the performance of LOA.

Runtime performance

We apply the proposed LOA approach to samples of traffic selected randomly from
the ten datasets, and the final result set is fed to the ML classifier (Naive Bayes) to
generate and test the classifier model. We then measure the execution time required
by Naive Bayes for different threshold settings.

　　Figure 6.11 and Table 6.8 show the runtime performance of the classifier with
the threshold varying between 0.2 and 1.0. For various threshold settings, the test
was repeated ten times to give the average execution time and the GR. As predicted
earlier, the complexity of the classifier is linear with respect to the number of input

Table 6.8 Influence of different setting of support threshold

Supp. threshold	Goodness		Set size	Runtime (s)	
	GD	St. dev		RT	TT
0.2	70.39	21.13	25	3.57	50.54
0.4	87.04	7.60	14	2.16	30.12
0.6	95.97	4.11	6	0.53	7.59
0.8	78.95	39.00	3	0.17	2.47
1	77.86	32.00	1	0.15	2.21

features. Furthermore, LOA shows a significant reduction in computation time for the classifier when compared to using the full set of features.

Figure 6.11(c) shows how classification goodness evolves with the value of the threshold, along with runtime performance. It can be shown that the maximum value of GR for the parameter β is achieved when the support is set to 0.60. This suggests that the goodness would not increase if β were to be achieved. On the other hand, it can be seen that the high runtime performance is achieved when β set to 1.0 and that the higher parameter of support decreases the accuracy. Therefore, we have found that $0.8 > \beta > 0.4$ provides the appropriate and stable region for the trade-off between increasing the goodness rate and lowering the processing time.

6.6.5 Impact of FS methods on runtime

One of the key motivations for using FS methods is to reduce the amount of time required by any ML algorithm (e.g., Naive Bayes) to build the model and evaluate new incoming flows. This is particularly important because the model-building phase is computationally time consuming. Therefore, we use the output of the LOA and the other candidate FS methods to measure the execution time required by Naive Bayes to build the classification model on a Core dual 2.2-GHz Intel processor machine with 2 gigabytes of RAM.

Figure 6.12(a) shows the normalized build time for Naive Bayes when using the output of the LOA approach in comparison to the candidate FS methods. The dataset comprises network traffic [245] from all days of week, and the number of instances in the dataset was varied between 1,000 and 10,000 (the size of the dataset is ultimately limited by the amount of memory since Naive Bayes needs to load the entire training data into the memory before building the model). For each of the feature sets, the test was repeated ten times to give the average execution time and to achieve greater confidence in the results. It can be seen that LOA shows a significant reduction of times in comparison to InfoGain, GainRatio, and chi-square. Note also that there is substantially smaller variance in computational performance for Naive Bayes when using LOA in comparison to CBF and CBS.

Figure 6.12(b) illustrates the classification speed to evaluate new flows based on selected features by LOA and the candidate FS methods. This is particularity important

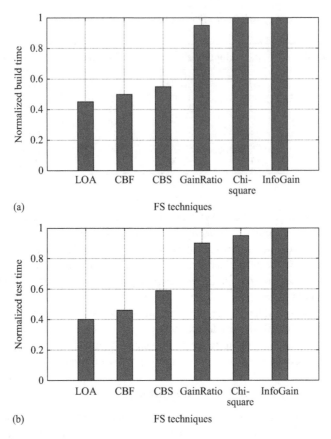

Figure 6.12   Evaluation LOA against the selected FS methods, where value 1
represents the lowest build and classification time: (a) normalized
build time of the model and (b) normalized classification time of the
model

when considering real-time classification of potentially thousands of simultaneous
network flows. The results show that we can successfully reduce the computation
time if our selected feature subset is used in comparison to InfoGain, GainRatio, and
chi-square. However, it is obvious that there is a smaller variance in computational
performance for Naive Bayes when using LOA in comparison to CBF and CBS.

6.6.6   Comparing FS methods computational performance

This section compares the execution time of LOA against the candidate FS methods to
generate optimal features. For the analysis, the performance of each method was tested
with traffic samples varying from approximately 1,000 to 10,000 traffic records, and
all operations were performed on a Toshiba Satellite with Intel Pentium Core dual
2.2 GHz processor and 2 gigabytes of RAM. Figure 6.13 shows that the time needed

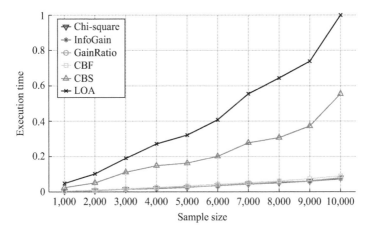

Figure 6.13   Comparison of runtime performance

by InfoGain, GainRatio, chi-square, and CBF methods is quite low. This is because these methods use a sequential search which is fast in producing results as the order of the search space is usually $O(m((n^2 - n)/2))$ or less (where m is the number of instances and n is the initial number of features). It is also notable that the cost of CBS is very high compared to the other FS methods, as it requires $O(mpn^p)$ (where p is the number of relevant features). On the other hand, the LOA execution time was significantly higher than other FS methods; this is because LOA relies on all FS methods to generate the initial feature set. A promising future research direction would be to reduce the execution time of LOA by using parallel computing such as multicore CPU or graphics processing units.

6.6.7   Summary of results with different datasets and limitations of LOA approach

In addition to the ten datasets collected by the high-performance network monitor [245] (discussed in Section 6.4), the capabilities of the proposed LOA have been further assessed against the baseline FS methods with two of the recent and most widely used datasets.

The first one is *wide2009* [291] dataset, where its flows are categorized into six classes: P2P, DNS, FTP, WWW, CHAT, and MAIL. The second dataset is KDD99 [292], which is the most widely used dataset for the evaluation of anomaly detection methods. The KDD99 dataset consists of 60,000 single connection vectors and labeled as either normal or an attack. Table 6.9 gives an overview of the datasets used along with their associated information.

Figure 6.14(a) compares the performance of LOA approach and the baseline FS methods by considering the three metrics *goodness, stability,* and *similarity.* The values of these three metrics are computed as explained in Section 6.5.2. It can be seen from Figure 6.14 that LOA has an advantage over the other related FS methods.

Table 6.9   Summary of the datasets used for performance evaluation

Datasets	No. of instances	No. of features	No. of classes
high-performance network [245]	377,526	249	13
wide2009 [291]	20,000	20	6
KDD99 [292]	60,000	41	5

FS Tech	Goodness	Stability	Similarity
LOA	High	Low	High
CBF	High	Low	Low
InfoGain	Medium	High	Low
Chi-square	Medium	High	Low
CBS	Medium	Low	Low
GainRatio	Low	Medium	Low

(a)

FS Tech	Goodness	Stability	Similarity
LOA	High	High	High
CBF	High	Medium	Medium
InfoGain	High	High	Medium
Chi-square	High	High	Medium
CBS	High	Medium	Medium
GainRatio	High	Medium	Medium

(b)

FS Tech	Goodness	Stability	Similarity
LOA	High	High	High
CBF	High	Medium	Medium
InfoGain	High	High	Medium
Chi-square	High	Medium	Medium
CBS	High	Low	Medium
GainRatio	High	Medium	Medium

(c)

Figure 6.14   Comparing the performance of FS methods on two more traffic datasets, namely: wide2009 [291] and KDD99 [292]: (a) on high-performance network dataset, (b) on wide2009 dataset, and (c) on DARPA (KDD99) dataset

First, the features obtained by LOA help the Naive Bayes classifier to achieve a higher goodness rate in comparison with the remaining FS methods on all the four datasets. Second, LOA preserves the maximum number of relevant features for traffic classification by considering only highly supported features.

In general, the experimental results shown in Figure 6.14 indicate that the three metrics are mostly satisfied by the proposed LOA approach (in comparison to the related approaches). However, it can be seen from Figure 6.14(c) that the LOA approach still suffers from the stability issue on traffic data of the high-performance network monitor. This is due to the high variations in these datasets, since these datasets are collected for different periods of times and from different locations. In Chapter 7, we will work on developing a new approach to address the sensitivity of the baseline methods and the LOA approach to variations in the traffic datasets.

6.7 Conclusion

Identifying the best and most robust (in terms of similarity) features from large datasets of Internet traffic is of critical importance in light of the emergence of new and distributed applications. This chapter made three contributions with regard to the problem of computing the best features (in network traffic). It introduced three new metrics, and their primary purpose of these metrics is to gain a deeper understanding of the properties of the FS methods as well as to compare the quality of their outputs (selected subsets). The experimental results showed that no existing FS method performs well on all three metrics. Motivated by this, the proposed method exploits the advantages of individual FS methods to obtain an optimal feature set that is better than any individual set. We also showed how to select the best subset based on the concept of *support* to extract the optimal set. The LOA method was analyzed in light of the optimality criteria. Results obtained on real network traffic data illustrate the ability of LOA to identify the best features for traffic classification. As expected, the joint contributions of the five well-known FS methods had a compensatory effect. Experimental results also showed that LOA performs significantly better than an individual method.

Integrated FS approaches are computationally more expensive than the single run; however, as demonstrated empirically, once computed, they provide increased robustness and performance, being able to identify the best features for traffic classification, not adequately handled by these methods. We have identified the need for developing an adaptive threshold instead of the fixed threshold beta used in LOA.

Chapter 7

Optimality and stability of feature set for traffic classification

Feature selection (FS) methods can be used as a preprocessing step to eliminate meaningless features, and also as a tool to reveal the set of optimal features. Unfortunately, as detailed in Chapter 6, such methods are often sensitive to a small variation in the traffic data collected over different periods of time. Thus, obtaining a stable feature set is crucial in enhancing the confidence of network operators. This chapter describes a robust approach, called global optimization approach (GOA), to identify both optimal and stable features, relying on a multi-criterion fusion-based FS method and an information-theoretic method. GOA first combines multiple well-known FS methods to yield possible optimal feature subsets across different traffic datasets and then uses the proposed adaptive threshold, which is based on entropy to extract the stable features. A new *goodness* measure is proposed within a random forest framework to estimate the final optimum feature subset. The effectiveness of GOA is demonstrated through several experiments on network traffic data in spatial and temporal domains. Experimental results show that GOA provides up to 98.5% accuracy, exhibits up to 50% reduction in the feature set size, and finally speeds up the runtime of a classifier by 50% compared with individual results produced by other well-known FS methods.

7.1 Introduction

Many factors can contribute to the usefulness of machine-learning (ML) algorithms for Internet traffic classification. The quality of network traffic data, e.g., transport layer statistics (TLS) [15], is one of these factors [12,17]. If the data contains irrelevant or redundant features, then the knowledge discovery process during the training becomes noisy and unreliable. In practice, FS methods play a fundamental role in the success of many classification tasks where data analysis is a challenge due to high dimensionality, e.g., *text classification* [284], *handwritten signature classification* [293], *bioinformatics* [294], and *intrusion detection system* [15,295]. Indeed, feature subset selection enables a classifier to selectively focus its attention on relevant features while ignoring the (possibly misleading) redundant features. The main advantage of an FS method is that by concentrating on predictive features only and not considering the irrelevant ones, the accuracy of the classifier may be higher and the association between features and the target class may be easier to learn. However, as explained in Chapter 6, most of the FS methods concentrate on feature relevance and neglect the stability issue. Such an issue is important in traffic analysis when high-dimensional data is used, and FS is used as a knowledge discovery tool for identifying characteristic discriminators. For example, in traffic data analysis, a given FS method may select largely different subsets of features, called *discriminators*, due to variations in the traffic training data. Such instability dampens the confidence of network operators in investigating any of the various subsets of selected features for network traffic identification (e.g., arbitrarily picking the same set of features under training data variation). It is important to note that the stability of FS results should be investigated together with classification accuracy since network operators tend to have less confidence in feature sets that change radically on datasets taken over a period of time. Moreover, unstable features in traffic application are problematic, as there is no prior knowledge about the data and, therefore, in most cases, these features are subsequently analyzed further, requiring much time and effort. Therefore, when using FS to identify the "best" discriminators for network classification, it is preferable to generate a candidate set of features that not only yields high prediction but also has a relative stability. However, for the purpose of network traffic classification, there has been very little attempt to identify such features.

Apart from identifying stable and optimal features for traffic classification, TLS involves several continuous-valued features. Examples of such features include the number of packets, number of bytes, and duration for each connection. As a consequence, these features can have a negative impact on some ML algorithms, in terms of both accuracy and/or training time [296]. Therefore, the main focus of this chapter is to address the issues of stability and the presence of continuous-valued features.

This chapter deals with the issues described earlier, and it describes a new FS method as well as a discretization algorithm to enhance the capabilities of the network classification task. The significant innovative ideas of this chapter are as follows:

- A general framework that not only provides the optimal features but also automatically discovers the stable features for network traffic. For this purpose, the proposed GOA method proceeds in *three* phases. The first phase combines multiple FS methods to yield the optimal feature subsets across different traffic datasets. In the second phase, instead of relying on a fixed threshold, GOA adapts the concept of *maximum entropy** [297] that culls stable features based on feature distribution. Intuitively, features with a distinct distribution are considered to be stable and are therefore extracted. This process automatically adapts to feature distribution (i) to yield feature subsets with a distinct distribution (with highest distribution) and (ii) to help narrow the scope for a deeper investigation into specific features set (Section 7.3.2 for details). In the third phase, the extracted features (obtained from the first and second phases) are passed to a more computationally intense procedure, called *random forest* filtering, to determine the most representative features that are strongly related to target classes (e.g., WWW,

*It is a general method for estimating probability distributions from the data.

FTP, Attack). The feature subset with the highest goodness is chosen as the final optimal set for network classification (Section 7.3.3).

- Optimal discretizations produced by *entropy minimization heuristics* method [283]. The necessity of using such a method on traffic data can have many reasons. Many ML algorithms primarily handle nominal features [298–300] or may even deal only with discrete features. Even though ML algorithms can deal with continuous features, learning is less efficient and effective [298]. Another advantage derived from discretization is the reduction and simplification of data which makes the learning faster and produces a more accurate, compact, and smaller output. Also, the noise present in the traffic data is reduced. In particular, feature discretization involves partitioning the range of continuous-valued features into a set of mutually exclusive intervals with interval boundaries so that the loss of class/attribute interdependence is minimized (Section 7.5.2).

- The proposed approach is evaluated using publicly available benchmark traffic datasets [148]. In particular, we compare the effectiveness and efficiency of the candidate features set against two well-known methods, namely, fast correlation-based feature selection (FCBF)-Naive Bayes (NB) [17] and Bayesian neural network (BNN) [12]. Also, we studied the robustness of the candidate features to classify a range of applications in both the temporal domain: comparing across different period of time, and the spatial-domain: comparing across different network-locations.

The rest of this chapter is organized as follows. Section 7.2 briefly reviews some well-known FS methods and also analyses their performance according to the new optimality versus stability metrics. Section 7.3 describes the GOA approach, and Section 7.4 shows the various performance results with the various benchmark datasets. Concluding remarks about this chapter are given in Section 7.6.

7.2 Optimality versus stability

The performance of ML algorithms degrades when there are many irrelevant and redundant features. To achieve the best possible performance with a particular ML algorithm, FS methods should remove such irrelevant and redundant features from the data. However, we are faced with two problems: (i) each FS method conducts a search for an optimal subset using its own independent criteria (e.g., distance, dependence); therefore, an optimal subset selected by one criterion may not be optimal according to other criteria; also (ii) to evaluate the output of a particular FS method, we need to use prior knowledge about the data. For dynamic network traffic data, we often do not have such prior knowledge. Therefore, we need to rely on some indirect methods [62,277], such as the one that monitors the change in classification performance caused by the change of features.

To simplify further discussion, in this section, we define the optimal subset selection with respect to the proposed *goodness* measure in Chapter 6.

Definition 7.1 (optimality). *Given a dataset, say D, with subset of features, say* S_D, *which is selected by a given FS method* $t_i \in T$, *with a particular classification algorithm, then* $S_D^{t_i}$ *is said to be an optimal feature subset if the goodness of the generated classifier is maximal.*

$$Goodness(S_D^{t_i}) = \arg\max \left[\frac{1}{Y} \sum_{i=1}^{Y} \frac{N_i^{tp}}{N_i} \right] \times 100 \qquad (7.1)$$

where Y is the number of classes in the dataset, N_i^{tp} *denotes the number of true positives of each class, and* N_i *is the total number of instances for class i. Note the goodness measure takes into account the bias of the majority of classes, which is important since the distribution of traffic applications is different.*

The other important metric used to evaluate FS methods is *stability*. This is motivated by the need to provide network experts with quantified evidences that guarantee that the selected features are relatively robust against variations in the traffic data. In a practical classification scenario, network operators tend to have less confidence in the use of FS methods (to produce different sets of features from samples of traffic data over a period of time). Thus, it is preferable to have a candidate set of features that not only yields high prediction accuracy but also has higher relative stability over different samples. Given an FS method, say t_i, the desirable properties of stability measures of t_i, denoted as $Stab(t_i)$, are

- $0 \leq Stab(t_i) \leq 1$.
- $Stab(t_i)$ close to 1 indicates *high* stability.
- $Stab(t_i)$ close to 0 indicates *low* stability.

Next, we define the stability of FS methods and outline a framework to measure the stability index based on entropy.

Definition 7.2 (stability). *Let* t_i, *where* $t_i \in T$, *be an FS method applied on two samples* D_1 *and* D_2 *of traffic dataset D, which generates two subsets of features* S_1 *and* S_2. *Then* t_i *is said to be stable if its stability index takes the value of one, meaning that* t_i *selects the same set of features for both data samples irrespective of minor variations in the traffic data. Therefore, the stability index of FS method* $t_i \in T$ *is defined as follows:*

$$Stab(t_i) = [1 - RU(X)] \times 100 \qquad (7.2)$$

where

$$RU(X) = \frac{H(X)}{\log(|N|)}$$

where

$$H(X) = \frac{1}{N} \sum_{i=1}^{N} -\frac{N_k^i}{S} \log\left(\frac{N_k^i}{S}\right)$$

where N is the total number of features, S is the number of runs, and N_k^i *is the frequency of specific feature* f_i *observed across different datasets* $|D|$.

The stability index of the FS method $t_i \in T$ has the following properties:

- $stab(t_i) = 0$, if t_i does not select the same features in each run.
- $stab(t_i) = 1$, if t_i selects identical subset of features in each run.

7.2.1 Selecting feature set from global perspective

Chapter 6 was dedicated to FS methods that eliminate both irrelevant and redundant attributes from a local perspective. Thus, they can be tricked in a situation where the dependence between a pair of features is weak, but the total intercorrelation of one feature to the others is strong. This chapter introduces a new method to select informative features from a global perspective. The process of discarding irrelevant and redundant features from a global perspective and only keeping the optimal features is depicted in Algorithm 1 (see below). In particular, the method of removing the irrelevant and redundant features is divided into two parts. In the first part, an evaluation criterion (e.g., information gain and consistency based) is used to evaluate the relevant degree and the reliability of each individual features for predicting the accurate class label. Therefore, features whose relevant value is zero are undesirable and thus removed from the feature space, which means that features do not have the power to distinguish between different types of traffic flows and applications. The remaining features are then ranked in descending order according to their relevant degrees, and the mean of the relevant degrees for features whose relevant degree greater than zero is computed, namely, μ_{rv}. In the second part, intercorrelations between previously selected features are computed, and the total values of the redundancy degree of the related to that features are added. The weight factor w is calculated (line 5.a) to be used for selecting informative features from a global perspective. Finally, features greater than zero are selected, meaning that they not only can accurately predict the class but also have a low correlation to other features.

7.2.2 An initial investigation

There is a wide variety of FS methods in the literature, which have been categorized into groups broadly based on the following [21,22,38,39]: information-based criterion, dependency-based criterion, consistency-based criterion, statistical-based criterion, and distance-based criterion. In this section, the selection of a feature set from a global perspective (as explained in Section 7.2.1), using the valuation criteria of these FS methods, is investigated with respect to the optimality and stability metrics. The aim is to identify an FS method that not only improves the model performance but also yields unambiguous outputs. Therefore, to make the best use of the traffic data and obtain stable results, a *cross-validation* strategy is used. For each dataset, the order of the flows is randomized because many ML methods exhibit order effects [301]. In the proposed experiments, we obtain N feature subsets and the corresponding goodness rate for each FS method on each dataset. We also obtain the stability for each FS method across different datasets. Algorithm 2 shows the various steps for measuring the *goodness* and the *stability* for each FS method on traffic data.

Figure 7.1 compares the candidate FS methods in terms of the proposed stability values and optimality scores. It can be seen that, in most cases, there is no clear

---

Algorithm 1: The process of globally selecting features

Input:
Given the input dataset D
Specify the number of optimal features K.

Remove irrelevant features
1. Compute the relevant score for each feature, x_i.

1.a $RS(x_i, Y)$= e.g., information gain = $2.0 \times \left[\frac{gain}{H(Y)+H(x_i)} \right]$.

2. Rank the features in descending order based on the value of $RS(x_i, Y)$.
3. Select x_i whose relevant score is greater than 0.

3.a If $RS(x_i, Y) > 0$ then $X_{rr} = X_{rr} \cup \{x_i\}$.

4. Compute the mean of relevant scores.

4.a $\mu_{rv} = \frac{\sum_{i=0}^{|X_{rr}|} RS(x_i,Y)}{|X_{rr}|}$.

Remove redundant features
5. For each $x_j \in X_{rr}$.

5.a Compute the inter-correlation score between features, as

$IS(x_i, x_j)$= e.g., information gain = $2.0 \times \left[\frac{gain}{H(Y)+H(x_i)} \right]$.

6. Compute the mean of the inter-correlation score as

6.a $\mu_{rd} = \frac{\sum_{i=0}^{|X_{rr}|} IS(x_i,x_j)}{|X_{rr}|}$.

7. Compute the weight value based on both the relevant and redundant scores.

7.a $w = \frac{\mu_{rd}}{\mu_{rr}}$.

8. For each $x_j \in X_{rr}$.

8.a Use the weight value to calculate the importance of features

$S(x_i) = w \cdot x_{rv}^i - x_{rd}^i$.

8.b Select the optimal features $S_{optimal}$.

If $S(x_i) > 0$, then $S_{optimal} = S_{optimal} \cup x_i$.

9. Return the final set of optimal features, $S_{optimal}$.

---

winner amongst the FS methods. As a result, there is no FS method that satisfies both the evaluation criteria. For example, Composite Bloom Filter (CBF) performs very well on the optimality metric but performs poorly on the stability metric. Gain Ratio (GR) performs equally poorly on both metrics. Therefore, the final conclusion is that each of these FS methods has its own advantages and also does identify features that

---

Algorithm 2: Experimental procedure

---

1 **Input:**
2 Parameter $N := 10$; $M := 10$;
3 Feature selector $T := \{t_1, t_2, \ldots, t_m\}$;
4 DATA $= \{D_1, D_2, \ldots, D_n\}$;
5 **Output:**
6 *Goodness & Stability*;
7 **foreach** *Selector*$_i^t \in [1, T]$ **do**
8   **foreach** $D_i \in DATA$ **do**
9   *Subset* = *Selector*$_i^t(D_i)$;
10   *Superset*$_i^t$ = *Superset*$_i^t \cup$ *Subset*;
11   **foreach** *times* $\in [1, M]$ **do**
12   *randomise instance-order for* D_i;
13   *generate N bins from the randomised* D_i;
14   **foreach** *fold* $\in [1, N]$ **do**
15   *Test*$_{Data}$ = *bin*[*fold*];
16   *Train*$_{Data}$ = *data* $-$ *Test*$_{Data}$;
17   *Train*$'_{Data}$ = *select Subset from Train*$_{Data}$;
18   *Test*$'_{Data}$ = *select Subset from Test*$_{Data}$;
19   *Classifier* = *learner*(*Train*$'_{Data}$);
20   *Result*=apply *Classifier* to (*Test*$'_{Data}$);
21   *Goodness*=ComputeGoodness (*Result*);

22   *Stability*=ComputeStability (*Superset*$_i^t$);

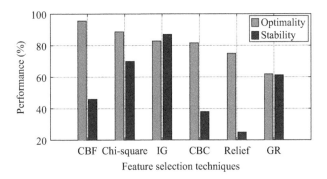

Figure 7.1   Stability and optimality of FS methods on real-traffic data

are both stable and accurate (i.e., with a high goodness value). This is our motivation for developing a *multi-criterion fusion-based approach* to identify an optimal and stable set of features that help classifiers to perform well and gain the confidence of network experts.

7.3   GOA—the global optimization approach

As explained earlier, existing traffic classification approach, e.g., [12,15,17,36,168], rely on a single FS method. However, a single FS method does not perform well for both evaluation criteria. Thus, the *GOA* is proposed here with the aim of discovering most-valuable features for the description of traffic flows with respect to both stability and optimality criteria. GOA is based on a hybrid FS method that can reflect the trade-off between optimal and stable features. The overall process and methodology of GOA is depicted in Figure 7.2, where the first phase combines several well-known FS methods (i) to provide an initial pool of feature subsets with good generality across different traffic datasets (Section 7.3.1), and (ii) to reduce the possibility of including the irrelevant features in the subsequent analysis. In the second phase, instead of relying on a fixed threshold, an *entropy-based* method is proposed to adaptively select only robust (i.e., both stable and accurate) features from the larger initial pool of features. Relying on the information-theoretic method, the algorithm effectively finds the optimal cutoff of the robust features based on the underlying distribution of the selected feature set, substantially reducing the number of features that are input to the third phase (Section 7.3.2). Finally, the third phase uses a more computationally intensive procedure of *random forest* filtering to choose the best candidate feature subset that is then passed to the classification algorithm (described in Section 7.3.3) for network traffic classification.

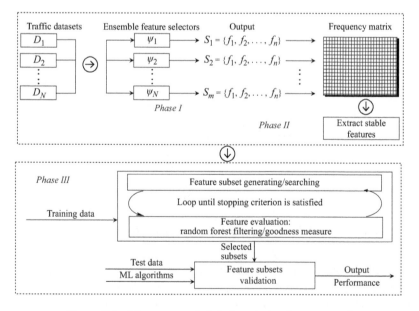

Figure 7.2   The proposed global optimization approach

7.3.1 Integration of feature selection

There are two essential steps in creating an FS integration. The first step involves running a set of different FS methods on traffic datasets. The second step aggregates the output features of the different FS methods. To make the best of the different FS methods, the first step of the integration approach combines five well-known FS methods that cover various independent criteria including information gain [273,283], gain ratio [262,273], chi-square [249], CBF [275,302], and CBC [276]. The reader may notice that we excluded *relief* [303], as this approach has several shortcomings. First, this method searches only for one nearest hit and one nearest miss. Noisy data could make this approximation inaccurate. Second, if there are missing values for features, the algorithm will crash because it cannot calculate the distance between those instances [304].

In general, the method of selecting informative features first is used for each FS method (explained in Table 7.1), and thus the output would be dependent on its evaluation criterion, e.g., information gain [273,283] and chi-square [249]. The second step aggregates the outputs of different FS methods as follows:

- Let $S^* = \{S_1^*, \ldots, S_n^*\}$, where $n > 1$, be an initial pool of feature subsets $S_i^* = \{f_k | k = 1 \cdots d, f_k \in S\}$, obtained from applying n FS methods on a given dataset D, where $D > 1$.
- Compute the frequency of features $f \in Y$ in the initial pool. Let X be a subset of Y representing all features that appear anywhere in the initial pool S^*:

$$X = \{f | f \in Y, F_f^* > 0\} = \bigcup_{i=1}^{n} S_i^*, \ X \neq 0 \tag{7.3}$$

- Order the features of X based on their frequency. Let $\hat{f}_1, \hat{f}_2, \ldots, \hat{f}_n$ be such as $F(\hat{f}_1) \geq F(\hat{f}_2) \geq \cdots F(\hat{f}_n)$. Then $S_{sorted} = \{\hat{f}_1, \hat{f}_2, \ldots, \hat{f}_n\}$.
- Pass the sorted set of features S_{sorted} to the second phase of GOA.

7.3.2 The adaptive threshold

This section introduces the concept of *maximum entropy* [297] to compute an optimal cutoff and to automatically cull robust features from largely (unstable) selected features. Maximum entropy has been shown to be a viable and competitive concept in many domains including language modeling [305] and part-of-speech tagging [306]. It is a general method for estimating probability distribution from data. One of its advantages is that when nothing is known, the distribution should be as uniform as possible; that is, it has maximal entropy. Another advantage is that maximum entropy can satisfy any given constraints to find the optimal solution.

The maximum entropy is used to find the optimal cutoff and automatically cull robust features by estimating the conditional distribution of given features obtained from the first stage. Therefore, the selected features should satisfy the given constraints before they are passed to the third stage. In addition to selecting stable features, the other motivation of this adaptive threshold is to reduce computational time required by the intensive search approach by selecting only a small set, since only $2^m - 1$ are needed to be checked compared to $2^n - 1$ (where $m \ll n$, m refers to number of features in S, where n the total number of features in the datasets).

The remaining parts of this section introduce the concept of the entropy-based adaptive threshold.

(A) Conceptual view of the adaptive threshold

Let X be a categorical random variable whose value is one of the N possible categories or values $c_1,\ldots,c_N$, where $N \geq 2$. We observe a sequence of m realizations of X, i.e., m independent draws $x_1,\ldots,x_m$ from X, where $m > 2$. Let m_i be the number of times the ith category appears in our sample. So $0 \leq m_i \leq m$ for all $i = \{1; 2; \ldots; N\}$. Then the relative frequency of each category in our sample gives us the empirical distribution of X, which induces an empirical probability distribution on X as follows

$$p_i = p(X = c_i) = \frac{m_i}{m}. \tag{7.4}$$

So if some category c_j does not appear in our sample, then $p_j = 0$. If all m draws come from only one category c_k, then $p_k = 1$ and $p_i = 0$ for $i \neq k$. Similarly, we define the empirical *entropy* of X with

$$H(X) = -\sum_{i=1}^{N} p(x_i) \, \log \, p(x_i) \tag{7.5}$$

where $0 \, \log \, 0 = 0$. Moreover, $H(X)$ is bounded above as follows. We assume $m < N$, then

$$H(X) = -\sum_{i=1}^{N} p_i \log(p_i)$$

$$= -\sum_{i=1}^{N} p_i \log\left(\frac{m_i}{m}\right)$$

$$= \sum_{i=1}^{N} p_i(\log(m) - \log(m_i))$$

$$\leq \sum_{i=1}^{N} p_i \log(m) = \log(m) \tag{7.6}$$

because $\sum_{i=1}^{N} p_i = 1$. If $m > N$, a similar logic as earlier would give us $H(X) \leq \log(N)$. So, in general, we have $0 \leq H(X) \leq H_{\max}(X) = \log(\min\{m; N\})$. The upper bound $H_{\max}(X)$ allows us to "standardize" $H(X)$ by putting it on a scale of 0 to 1, independent of m or N. In this chapter, we consider the standardized entropy as the relative uncertainty:

$$RU(X) = \frac{H(X)}{H_{max}(X)} \tag{7.7}$$

Let $A \subset \{c_1, \ldots, c_N\}$ be the set of observed values of X, i.e., the distinct draws that make up our random sample. Then

1. $RU(X) = 0$ implies that $H(X) = 0$, which only happens if $\log(p_i) = 0$ or $p_i = 0$. If $\log(p_i) = 0$ and $p_i \neq 0$, then $p_i=1$ for some i and $p_j = 0$ for all $j \neq i$. In other words, $H(X) = 0$ if and only if our random sample consists of m draws, all of which come from the same ith category. In this situation, we can say that there is no uncertainty, i.e., zero entropy.
2. If $m < N$, then some categories must be absent in our sample, i.e., A is a strict subset of X. In this situation, $RU(X) = 1$ implies that $H(X) = \log(m)$, which can happen only if $p_i = 1/m$ for all i such that $c_i \in A$ (and $p_j = 0$ for all c_j not in A). This is shown in the following:

$$H(X) = -\sum_{j=1}^{N} p_j \log(p_j)$$

$$= -\sum_{i=1}^{m} \frac{1}{m} \log\left(\frac{1}{m}\right)$$

$$= -\log\left(\frac{1}{m}\right)$$

$$= \log(m) \tag{7.8}$$

So when $m < N$, then $RU(X)$ is at its maximum of 1 if every category $c_i \in A$ occurs the same number of times as every other $c_j \in A$, which means that the empirical distribution is a uniform distribution over A and we have maximum unpredictability.
3. If $m > N$, then for $RU(X)$ to be equal to 1, we must have $H(X) = \log(N)$ which, using the same logic as earlier, can only happen if $p_i = 1/N$ for all i. In other words, the empirical distribution is a uniform distribution over X. This can only happen if all the categories in X are present in our sample an equal number of times. In this case, A and X represent the same set.
4. If $m = N$, then $p_i = 1/m$ and $p_i = 1/N$ give us the same result. In this situation, every category in X is represented in our random sample exactly once.

We can generalize the previous formulation by letting $H_{max}(X|A) = \log(|A|)$. When $m < N$, then $|A| = m$ and $H_{max}(X|A) = \log(m)$. When $m < N$, then $|A| = N$ and $H_{max}(X|A) = \log(N)$. So, either way, we have $RU(X) = 1$ if and only if $p_i = 1/|A|$. In this chapter, we refer to the *relative uncertainty* as the *confidence* measure.

(B) Extracting stable features

We identify stable features using the confidence measure defined in (7.7). Let N be the total number of frequency of any feature $f \in Y$ in set S_{sorted}. Then the (induced) probability distribution P_A on A is given by

$$P_A(\hat{f}_1) = \frac{f_i}{N} \tag{7.9}$$

where f_i is the frequency of a feature. Then the (conditional) relative uncertainty (referred to as a confidence measure) $C(P_A) = C(X|A)$ measures the degree of uniformity in the observed features in A. If $C(P_A)$ is close to 1, say $\beta = 0.9$, then the observed features are uniformly distributed, and thus the features are considered to be important. We say a subset S_{best} of A contains the best features if S_{best} is the smallest subset of A such that (i) the probability of any value in S is larger than the remaining values; (ii) $R = A - S$ is close to being uniformly distributed (e.g., $C(P_A) = C(X|R) > \beta$). Consequently, S contains the best features in A, while the remaining features are less frequently selected.

7.3.3 Intensive search approach

As stated previously in Section 7.2, high stability does not necessarily imply a high accuracy rate and vice versa. In this section, the goal is to select feature subsets from the candidate set (obtained from previous stages) that leads to good generalization. By using filters in the first stage, we intend to find a small and robust set of candidate features that pass the second stage (confidence measure), which are inputs into a more computationally intensive subset selection procedure referred to as *random forest filtering*. The strength of the intensive search approach is that it focuses directly on optimizing the performance of the prediction random forest filtering by maximizing the goodness measure presented in Section 7.2. Consequently, a feature is eliminated if it gives little or no additional information beyond that subsumed by the remaining features. In particular, this will be the case for both irrelevant and redundant features. Therefore, while this method has encountered some success in selecting optimal features, it is often prohibitively expensive to run and can break down when a large of number of features are present. Thus, to mitigate such a problem, we need to select only a small number of the original features. This is achieved in our approach via the adaptive threshold discussed in the previous section. However, the choice of a ML algorithm for the intensive search approach and a search strategy needed to be considered. This will be discussed in the following subsections.

Random forest

Ensemble algorithms have achieved success in ML by combining multiple weak learners to form a strong learner [307]. The random forest method [308] centers around this idea by adding n additional layers of randomness to *bagging* [307]. Such a method builds each tree using a different bootstrap sample of the data, and it can change how the classification or regression trees are built. While in traditional trees, each node is split using the best split among all variables, in random forest, each node is split using the best among a subset of predictors randomly chosen at that node. This method appears to give better performance than other ML algorithms (such as neural networks and support vector machines), and also it can be robust against over-fitting [308].

In what follows, we briefly discuss the steps of the random forest approach that is used for identifying the final optimal features for traffic classification:

- Split the data into training sets and testing sets.
- Learning sets used to train classifiers based on RF and determine the importance of features. This can be done by growing the regression tree with the following modification: rather than choosing the best split among all predictors, randomly sample m of the predictors and choose the best split from those features.
- At each bootstrap iteration, predict the data not in the training sets (referred to as "out-of-bag," OOB data) using the tree grown in the previous steps.
- Calculate the goodness rate by aggregating the OOB predictions.
- Estimate the importance of features by examining the extent to which the goodness rate increases when (OOB) data for that feature is permuted while all others are left unchanged. In this way, a set of features with a high goodness rate is selected.

Search strategy

Random forest filtering requires a larger number of training sets to search for the best performing features subset [309]. For instance, let us consider a traffic dataset with N features, there exist 2^N candidate subsets. This search space is exponentially prohibitive for an exhaustive search. Therefore, an important issue in identifying the "best" candidate features (for traffic classification) is the choice of a wrapper as an efficient search strategy. These strategies broadly fall into three categories: exponential, randomized, and sequential. In this chapter, we consider one of the well-known sequential search strategy, so-called SFS (sequential forward selection) [310], as the complexity of the search scheme for *random forest* is in the order of N^2.

SFS determines the "best" set of features for extraction by starting from an empty set and sequentially adding a single feature in the superset to the subset if it increases the value of the *goodness* (see Section 7.2). Table 7.1 shows how the forward selection search has been modified to produce a ranked list of features.

For example, if we provide a set of features (e.g., $f_1, \ldots, f_4$) to the search process, it starts by adding a single feature (e.g., f_1) to the empty set and evaluates its score. In iteration 1, the best single feature is f_2 with a score of 40; therefore, this will be added to the subset. In iteration 2, all two-feature subsets that include f_2 are evaluated. In this case, the addition of f_3 results in the best score, which is equal to 65. In iteration 3, f_1 will be added to the subset but the best score is only 60 (by adding f_1), which is worse than the previous score. The search terminates since no single feature addition can improve the best subset from the previous iteration. In this case, the search has been forced to stop after iteration 3. Therefore, the selected best features are $\{f_2, f_3\}$.

Table 7.1　*Procedure of sequential forward selection (SFS)*

Iteration no.	Feature set	Score	Best addition
Iteration 0	$[\ldots,\ldots,\ldots,\ldots]$	0.0	
	$[f_1,\ldots,\ldots,\ldots]$	20	
Iteration 1	$[\ldots,f_2,\ldots,\ldots]$	40	f_2
	$[\ldots,\ldots,f_3,\ldots]$	30	
	$[\ldots,\ldots,\ldots,f_4]$	15	
	$[f_1,f_2,\ldots,\ldots]$	30	
Iteration 2	$[\ldots,f_2,f_3,\ldots]$	65	f_3
	$[\ldots,f_2,\ldots,f_4]$	47	
Iteration 3	$[f_1,f_2,f_3,\cdots]$	60	
	$[\ldots,f_2,f_3,f_4]$	57	f_1
Iteration 4	$[f_1,f_2,f_3,f_4]$	62	f_4

The algorithm

Algorithm 3 has three parts and selects the best and stable features from the original space. In the first part (lines 1–12), the algorithm extracts an initial pool of features by applying the global selection procedures (see Section 7.2.1) on different traffic data taken over different periods of time and returns a consensus rank feature subset. In the second part (lines 13–28), an efficient approximation is performed to identify the most stable features in S from A. The algorithm starts with an appropriate initial value (e.g., β) and searches for the optimal cutoff threshold from earlier via "linear approximation" (increasing the threshold β by linear growth factor at the i steps). The algorithm iterates to find the most stable subset as long as the confidence measure of the (conditional) probability distributed P_R on the remaining features sets R is less than β. The algorithm examines each feature in R and includes it in S if its probability exceeds the threshold. The algorithm stops either if the probability of a feature exceeds the maximum probability value or if the probability distribution of the remaining feature value is close to being uniformly distributed.

However, the earlier step has a high probability of producing a subset of representatives and stable features. It may include some features that are most likely to be more strongly correlated, and this can degrade the performance traffic classification task. Thus, in the third part (lines 29–41), the algorithm uses an intensive search method based on the random forest learning approach to guarantee the quality of the final subset features.

It starts the search from initial subset S_0 and iterates to find the best subsets using sequential forward selection. Each generated set S is evaluated using the goodness measure (see Section 7.2) and compared with the previous best one; if S is better, it becomes the current best subset. The search iterates until the best subset of features is found and the goodness measure provides a natural stopping criterion. Thus, the respective algorithm tends to produce better feature subsets, since the mining algorithm uses the goodness measure as a dependent measure. Finally, the remaining

---

Algorithm 3: Global optimization approach

---

1 **Input:** Feature selectors $T := \{t_1, t_2, \ldots, t_m\}$;
2 DATA$= \{D_1, D_2, \ldots, D_n\}$;
3 Parameters $S_{Optimal} := \emptyset$ $S_{InitPool} := \emptyset$, $S_{frequency} := \emptyset$, $S_{Sorted} := \emptyset$;
4 **Output:** S_{final}; // Return the best features in terms of Optimality and
    Stability
5 **Obtaining Optimal Features** ApplyFS $(DATA, T, S_{initialPool}, S_{Optimal}, S_{frequency}, S_{Sorted})$;
6 **for** $D_i \in DATA$ **do**
7   **for** $t_j \in T$ **do**
8          $S_{Optimal} :=$ SelectGlobalFeatures (D_i, t_j, α); // select features as
                 explained in Section 7.2.1
9      $S_{initPool} := S_{initPool} \cup S_{best}$;

10 $S_{frequency}=$ CountFrequency $(S_{initPool})$;
11 $S_{Sorted}=$ SortFeatures $(S_{frequency})$;
12 Return S_{Sorted};
13 **Entropy-based Stable Features Extraction**

14 Parameters $\beta := 0.98, i = 1$; Initialization $S_{Stable} := \emptyset$, $R := S_{Sorted}$;
15 ExtractStableFeatures $(S_{Stable}, R, \beta, i)$

16 $P_R :=$ ComputeProb (R);
17 $\delta :=$ ComputeRU (P_R);
18 $\mu :=$ FindMax (P_R);
19 **while** ($\beta \leq \delta$) **do**
20      $\mu := \mu \times i$;
21      $i++$;
22   **for** $f_i \in R$ **do**
23          $P_{f_i} :=$ ComputeProb (f_i);
24   **if** $P_{f_i} \geq \mu$ **then**
25              $S_{Stable} := S_{Stable} \cup \{f_i\}$;
26              $R := R \setminus \{f_i\}$;
27      $P_R :=$ ComputeProb (R), $\delta :=$ ComputeRU (P_R);

28 Return S_{Stable};
29 **Intensive Search Approach**

30 Parameters $\gamma := 0, \theta_{goodness} := 0$; Initialization $S := \emptyset, S_0 := S_{Stable}$, $S_{final} := S_0$;
31 $D = \{f_1, f_2, \ldots, f_{n-1}\}$;
32 EvaluateFinalSet $(S_{final}, \theta_{goodness}, \gamma)$;
33 $\theta_{goodness} :=$ EvaluateFeatures (S_0, D, RF); // Evaluate S_0 by Random Forest
    RF
34 **repeat**
35      $S :=$ Generate (D); // Generate a subset for evaluation
36      $\gamma :=$ EvaluateFeatures (S, D, RF); // Evaluate the current a subset S
             by RF
37   **if** $\gamma \geq \theta_{goodness}$ **then**
38          $\theta_{goodness} := \gamma$;
39          $S_{final} := S$;
40 **until** *Maximized* $\{\theta_{goodness}\}$;
    // Loop until maximum *goodness* is reached
41 Return S_{final};

---

features are all significant features that contain indispensable information about the original features set.

7.4   Evaluation

This evaluation shows how the output features of GOA improve the performance and the accuracy of the classification. We have compared the performance of GOA with that of two well-known network traffic FS methods: FCBF-NB [17] and BNN [12]. These two approaches are inherently different. FCBF-NB selects the most valuable features derived using FCBF and threshold of NB [17], whereas BNN uses feature interdependent ranking described in [12]. In particular, the proposed GOA approach, and the baseline methods (FCBF-NB and BNN), would follow the same network environment of local optimization approach (LOA) approach presented in Figure 6.2.

To provide a quantitative comparison, we require test data containing network traffic with a range of application types. In the absence of such publicly available data with annotated labels (to indicate application type), we decided to use widely available and acceptable traffic datasets from Cambridge Lab [148]. This is one of the largest publicly available network traffic traces that were collected by a high-performance network monitor.

The collated data are based on traces captured using loss-limited, full-payload capture to disk where timestamps with resolution of better than 35 ns are provided. The data was acquired over several different periods of time from two different sites. These two sites are both research centers but conduct research in different departments and are located in different countries. These sites are referred to as sites A and B. Each site hosts up to 1,000 users connected to the Internet via a full-duplex gigabyte Ethernet link. Full-duplex traffic on this connection was monitored by a high-performance network for each traffic set. From site A, we use 3-day-long datasets taken over weekdays in 2003, 2004, and 2006 (for simplicity, we refer to these as Day1, Day2, and Day3). From site B, we use datasets collected on weekdays in late 2007 (referred to as site B). Table 7.2 lists the number of flows alongside the type of applications for each site and time period.

7.4.1   GOA evaluation based on the proposed metrics

This section compares the effectiveness of the GOA approach and the baseline FS methods for network traffic (namely, FCBF-NB [17] and BNN [12]) according to both proposed metrics, *optimality* and *stability*. In particular, we follow the same experimental procedures (see Section 7.2) to assess all FS methods.

Figure 7.3 shows a comparison of the stability and optimality of the GOA approach and the baseline FS methods (FCBF-NB [17] and BNN [12]) over the traffic datasets. From the estimated optimality rate in Figure 7.3, we can observe that the GOA approach and FCBF-NB have achieved slight improvement over BNN method. Also, when it comes to the stability comparison between all FS methods, we observe that GOA approach achieves substantial improvement in comparison to

Table 7.2   Data statistics number of the flows

Applications	Day1 (2003)	Day2 (2004)	Day3 (2006)	Site B	Random set
WWW	279,477	140,875	218,620	208,214	6,000
MAIL	28,124	16,487	3,978	10,598	543
BULK	12,151	10,793	5,351	545	264
ATTACK	1,751	987	35	3,932	600
CHAT	0	0	66	500	51
P2P	2,085	2,762	22,287	17,323	408
DATABASE	2,794	2,606	91,181	0	786
MULTIMEDIA	496	4	19	11	48
VOIP	0	0	93	1,025	102
SERVICES	1,808	1,111	70	455	316
INTERACTIVE	86	36	323	310	693
GAMES	5	0	0	147	139
GRID	2	1	0	93	50

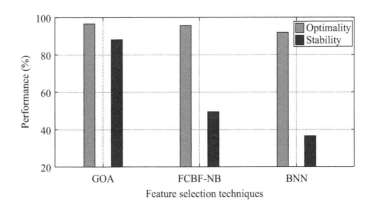

Figure 7.3   Stability and optimality of GOA approach and the baseline FS methods on real-traffic data

both FCBF-NB and BNN methods (refer to Figure 7.3). The good results of the GOA approach with respect to the proposed metrics prove the strength of multiple-criteria fusion to produce not only an optimal but also a stable features set for traffic classification task. Also, we used the simple tabular approach (see Chapter 6, Section 7.4.1) to categorize the different FS methods based on both proposed metrics, *optimality* and *stability*. This way of comparing can serve two purposes, including grouping FS methods with similar characteristics and also providing a better and fair way to compare such methods on the same framework. In particular, we compare the proposed GOA approach with the candidate FS methods (discussed in Section 7.2.1) as well as two well-known network traffic FS methods: FCBF-NB [17] and BNN [12].

Table 7.3   Evaluation of FS methods on the categorization framework

FS Tech	CBF	Chi-square	IG	CBC	CBC
Optimality	High	Medium	Medium	Medium	Medium
Stability	Low	High	High	Low	Low
FS Tech	**GR**	**LOA**	**FCBF-NB**	**BNN**	**GOA**
Optimality	Low	High	High	High	High
Stability	Medium	Low	Medium	Low	High

Table 7.4   Standard confusion metrics for evaluation accuracy

Actual connection label	**Predicted connection label**	
	E1	**E2**
E1	True positive (TP)	False positive (FP)
E2	False negative (FN)	True negative (TN)

Table 7.3 summarizes and categorizes the stability and optimality values of GOA approach and the baseline FS methods into three categories: *low*, *medium*, and *high* using (6.2), which was introduced in Chapter 6. Based on the developed categorization approach, it can be seen from Table 7.3 that the performance of the proposed GOA approach has satisfied both optimality and stability metrics compared to the well-known FS methods, including the previously proposed LOA, FCBF-NB, and BNN methods.

7.4.2   *Comparison between GOA, FCBF-NB, and BNN*

To avoid being biased toward our proposed metrics, the capabilities of the GOA approach and the baseline methods (i.e., FCBF-NB [17] and BNN [12]) have been further assessed with three commonly used types of tests including classification accuracy, subset size, and performance. To quantify the accuracy of classification models, we use standard measurements such as overall *classifier accuracy* (CR), *precision* (PR), and *recall* (RC), which are defined as follows in terms of metrics defined in Table 7.4.

- Overall accuracy: Percentage of correctly classified instances over the total instances.

$$CR = \frac{TP + TN}{TP + TN + FP + FN} \qquad (7.10)$$

- PR: Number# of class members classified correctly over the total number of instances classified as class members for a given class.

$$PR = \frac{TP}{TP + FP} \qquad (7.11)$$

- RC: The number of class members classified correctly over the total number of class members for given class.

$$RC = \frac{TP}{TP + FN} \qquad (7.12)$$

(A) Classification accuracy

The aim of this experiment is to check whether the output features are able to help classifiers to distinguish different types of network applications (e.g., WWW, P2P, and attack). We use three metrics to compare the three methods. Half of the traffic data has been used as training data and the remaining half has been used for testing.

Figure 7.4(a) and Table 7.5 show the classification accuracy for each method in terms of *CR*, *PR*, and *RC*. The results have been computed based on the classification

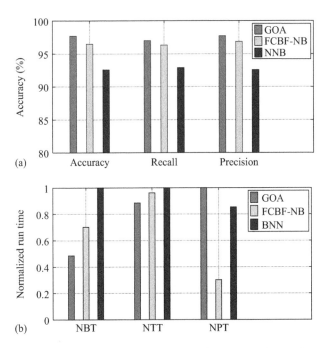

Figure 7.4   *Comparing the accuracy and the performance of classification using the output set of GOA, FCBF-NB, and BNN: (a) comparing the accuracy, recall, and precision of GOA, FCBF-NB [17], and BNN [12]; (b) normalized build time speed and classification speed for each feature set obtained by GOA, FCBF-NB [17], and BNN [12]*

*Table 7.5   Comparison of GOA against FCBF-NB and BNN in terms of
classification rate, subset size, and runtime*

Methods	Classif. rate			Subset size	Runtime (s)		
	CR	PR	RC		PPT	BT	TT
GOA	97.7	97.01	97.7	5	41.32	6.83	0.46
FCBF-NB [17]	96.5	96.33	96.86	12	16.59	9.87	0.50
BNN [12]	92.55	92.87	92.55	20	35.25	14.06	0.52

of the flows. For a traffic classification task, traffic applications are expected to be correctly classified. Therefore, achieving higher percentages of such metrics is desirable. Note, the proposed approach (GOA) consistently achieves higher average classification accuracies and produces a feature set that yields results comparable to, and in most cases better than, both FCBF-NB and BNN. These results support the stability of our approach in terms of classification accuracy.

(B) Runtime performance

A key motivation for using GOA is to reduce the size of the features set required to classify traffic data. First, we built a classification model using training data and measured the execution time needed to build the classifier. This is an important consideration because the model-building phase is computationally time consuming. Second, we measured the time required by the classification task. This is particularly important when considering real-time[†] classification of potentially thousands of simultaneous traffic flows. In order to test the computational performance of the output of the GOA in comparison with the other two approaches, we use data size of 10,000 flows. The size of the training set is ultimately limited by the amount of available memory because the classification algorithm must load the entire training set into memory before building the model. For the analysis, all operations are performed on an Intel Pentium Dual Core 3.4 GHz processor machine with 2 GB of RAM.

Figure 7.4(b) shows the runtime performance of the classification algorithm using the output of all methods. This test was repeated five times to give the average execution time required to build the classifier and to classify the traffic. Note that GOA shows a significant reduction in computation time in comparison with both BNN and FCBF-NB. However, from Figure 7.4(b), it can be observed that the preprocessing time of the proposed GOA is more computationally expensive than the other two approaches, BNN and FCBF-NB. This is because the GOA approach incorporates multiple FS evaluation criteria to produce the candidate set of features for traffic classification. Thus, future work will be devoted to improving the speed-up factor of the GOA approach by using (i) the GPU environment and/or (ii) parallel computing.

[†]GOA will not be applied for real time, but its candidate features set which is identified in this chapter.

(C) Subset size

FS methods aim to select a small subset of features that have the highest discriminating power. Therefore, the output feature subset size is used to compare the GOA approach and the other two FS methods. This is important since network classifiers need to analyze a large volume of traffic data; therefore, the smaller subset results in greater classifier efficiency and quicker classification task. One of the columns of Table 7.5 shows the size of the subset selected by each FS method. Results show that different approaches produce a different number of features. It is interesting to note that GOA produces a significantly smaller subset than both the approaches (50% smaller than FCBF-NB and 75% smaller than BNN). This suggests that the proposed adaptive threshold and the learning algorithm-based stopping criterion are effective in finding the optimal number of the candidate features.

7.4.3 *Relevance of selected features*

Previous sections showed a quantified evaluation, where GOA approach outperformed the benchmarks methods in both classification accuracy and performance. This section investigates whether features identified by GOA are indeed meaningful in networking terms when observed by someone without access to knowledge of the class values (i.e., type of application) associated with the flows.

Table 7.6 provides an insight into the ranking of the optimal features that have been identified by the GOA approach with the other two FS methods based on feature-independent selection (Naive Bayesian) and correlated-features (BNN). As mentioned earlier, the majority of these features are derived directly by observing one or more Transmission Control Protocol (TCP)/IP headers using a tool such as *tcptrace* or by performing simple time analysis of packet headers. Upon comparing each reduction, we note that the features selected by GOA are identified by previous studies and some of the prominent features are supported by FCBF-NB [17] and BNN [12]. On the other hand, we note a limited overlap in a number of significant differences between the other two feature-reduction methods. In addition to this, the values of features (selected by BNN [12]) are dependent upon the RTT which will be subject to change depending on the monitored site, which makes the features less stable than those features selected by GOA.

7.4.4 *Temporal decay and spatial robustness*

The temporal robustness of the candidate features that are selected by GOA is evaluated. This experiment illustrates the temporal stability of selected features when classifying new traffic. As a preliminary investigation, FS methods are performed on the four available traffic datasets. Three datasets are taken over different periods of time; for simplicity, these are as Day1 (2003), Day2 (2004), and Day3 (2006). First, the algorithm GOA is applied to construct the training model using filtered features from the Day1 datasets (2003). The generated model is tested for classification of datasets from Day2 (2004) and Day3 (2006). It is assumed that there will be some, if

Table 7.6   Comparative ranking of the most valuable features. FCBF-NB rank refers to [17]. BNN rank refers to [12]. GOA rank refers to the proposed approach described in Section 7.3

GOA rank	FCBF-NB rank	BNN rank	Feature # no.	Description
1	1	–	–	Port number *server → client*
–	2	–	–	Port number *client → server*
2	3	9	–	The count of all packets seen with the PUSH bit in the TCP header. *Server → client*
–	4	–	–	The total number of bytes sent in the initial window, i.e., bytes seen in the data before receiving the first ACK packet from endpoint. *Client → server*
4	5	–	–	The total number of bytes sent in the initial window. *Server → client*
–	6	–	–	The average segment size observed during the lifetime of the connection calculated as the value reported in the actual data bytes filed divided by the actual data packet reported
–	7	–	–	Median of the total bytes in IP packets *client → server*
–	8	–	–	The count of all the packets with at least one byte of TCP data payload. *Client → server*
–	9	–	–	Variance of bytes in (Ethernet) packet. *Server → client*
–	10	–	–	minimum segment size *Client → Server*
5	11	–	–	The total number of round-trip time (RTT) samples found
3	12	7	–	The count of all the packets seen with the PUSH bit set in the TCP header. *Client → server*
–	–	1	–	First quartile of size of packet in bytes (all packets)
–	–	2	–	Post-loss ACKs: the total number of ACK packets received after we observed a (perceived) loss event and are recovering from it. *Server → client*
–	–	3	–	The total number of ACK packets seen carrying TCP SACK BLOCK. *Client → server*
–	–	4	–	Maximum idle time, calculated as the maximum time between consecutive packets seen in the direction. *Client → server*
–	–	5	–	Third quartile of size of packets in bytes. *Client → server*
–	–	6	–	Third largest FFT component of packets IAT. *Server → client*
–	–	8	–	The total data transmit time, calculated as the difference between the times of capture of the first and last packets carrying nonzero TCP data payload. *Server → client*
–	–	19	–	The time spent idle (where idle time is the accumulation of all periods of 2 s or longer when no packet was seen in either direction)

Continued

Table 7.6 (Continued)

GOA	FCBF-NB	BNN	Feature #	Description
–	–	10	–	Minimum number of total bytes in IP packet. *Client → server*
–	–	11	–	The total number of ACK packet seen. *Server → client*
–	–	12	–	Maximum of bytes in (Ethernet) packets. *Client → server*
–	–	13	–	The standard deviation of full-size RTT samples, where full-size segments are identified as the segments of the largest size seen in the connection. *Client → server*
–	–	14	–	The standard deviation of full-size RTT samples. *Server → client*
–	–	15	–	The average throughput calculated as the unique bytes sent divided by the elapsed (e.g., the time deference between the capture of the first and the last packets). *Client → server*
–	–	16	–	The maximum window advertisement seen. *Client → server*
–	–	17	–	The number of transitions between transaction mode and bulk transfer mode
–	–	18	–	Median of bytes in (Ethernet) packet in both directions

not considerable, change in the variety of applications and the composition of traffic in the period 2003–06.

The objective of this experiment is to test whether candidate features of the proposed GOA are able to help a classifier to distinguish between traffic applications across different periods of time. It is evident from Figure 7.5(a) that the classification accuracy for GOA features remains stable at an average CR of 98.07%. This suggests that the candidate features result in high and stable classification results for traffic from the same site and across different periods.

To evaluate the effectiveness of the spatial independence of the candidate features, the model is trained using network data from one site and tested against data from a different site. Therefore, the model is built using a subset of each of the Day3 and site B datasets. Each model is then generated against the remaining dataset from that site. Note that there is no overlap between the training sets and testing sets, and we do not validate the accuracy of the model using the same datasets. Three experiments were performed to evaluate the ability of the candidate features to accurately classify the traffic from different sites. The first experiment uses Day3 (to represent site A) with filtered features to construct the model and uses the generated model to classify the traffic from site B. The second experiment used 50% of data from site B and the remaining 50% from Day3 to build the model.

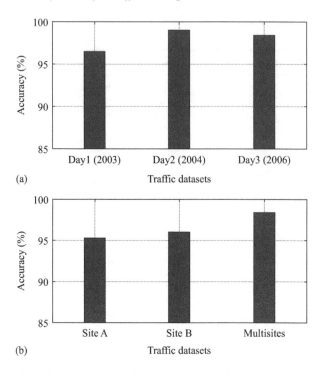

Figure 7.5   *Classification of the traffic using the candidate features (temporal stability and spatial accuracy): (a) overall accuracy of classification traffic over different period of time using the candidate features set (temporal stability), (b) accuracy of a model trained from one site and applied to each other site (spatial accuracy)*

The generated model is then used to measure the accuracy across different networks. Figure 7.5(b) shows the accuracy results for the model trained on Day3 and tested on site B, and vice versa. It is clear from this figure that the accuracy of the candidate features used to classify traffic on different sites is 95.02%. However, we notice that there are drops (in accuracy) in comparison to classifying the traffic on the same sites. The main reason for this happening is that there are some variations in the distribution of applications and the composition of the traffic has changed, since the collected traffic at site B is from a totally different network and almost 2 years later. To overcome this difficulty, combining decisions of several classifiers could lead to better classification results. A full investigation of such properties would be a valuable contribution by future work. In the second experiment, we evaluate the model built with multisite training datasets. Figure 7.5(b) shows that there is a substantial increase in overall accuracy at 99.1% in comparison with the model which is specifically built from a given site. This indicates that collaboration to share traffic data between multisite (spatial networks) and ISP organizations can generate a more efficient and representative classification model than just building the model from a single site. However, this collaboration is very beneficial, ISPs and websites are extremely reluctant to share their traffic data among them. The reason being they are competitors in business, and they are worried that the customers' privacy would be affected if they share data. To address such an issue, a new privacy-preserving framework for traffic data publishing is described in the next chapter.

7.5   Impact of the candidate features on different ML algorithms

This section examines the performance of the candidate feature set optimized by the GOA approach on different ML methods. This is an important task as the third stage of the proposed approach uses a predetermined learning algorithm to guide the search to determine the final set of best features. Such a method uses its predictive accuracy as the primary measure and, therefore, it may inherit bias toward the predetermined learning algorithm. To avoid such case, the GOA outputs are evaluated on five standard classification algorithms, namely K-nearest neighbors algorithm, NB [39,311], ID3 [312], support vector machine [313–315], and logistic regression (LR) [273,283]. These ML algorithms can achieve superior performance and they are the top five out of ten evaluated ML algorithms. In addition, these five ML algorithms work differently and represent an ideal cross section of learning algorithms to use for a test on learning bias.

7.5.1   The sensitivity of the candidate features on different ML algorithms

As mentioned in the previous section, one very important advantage of using GOA is the trust that a system administrator can have in the output of GOA to classify traffic data regardless of the ML algorithm that is used. To evaluate the sensitivity of GOA's output to different ML algorithms, the GOA approach was performed as described in Section 7.3. The performance of each ML algorithm is evaluated by applying K-fold cross validation to the three datasets. In this process, each dataset is divided into K subsets. Each time, one of the K subsets is used for testing while the remaining $K-1$ subsets form the training set. Performance statistics are calculated across all K trials. Throughout this experiment, the value of K is set to 10, a widely accepted empirical value [289] for accuracy estimation and model selection.

Figure 7.6 shows the accuracies achieved by NB, ID3, $7K$-NN, LR, and Support Vector Machine (SVM) using the candidate feature set (obtained by GOA). The results confirm our hypothesis that there is little difference between the accuracies induced by the five learning algorithms. It can be seen that the accuracies of all algorithms using such features are high and equivalent. The only case where there is a significant difference is the accuracy of NB and SVM, suggesting that these algorithms suffer from the presence of continuous-valued features in the traffic data. Throughout the remainder of this chapter, we examine various ways to improve the performances of such ML algorithms by discretizing the input features. In the following subsections,

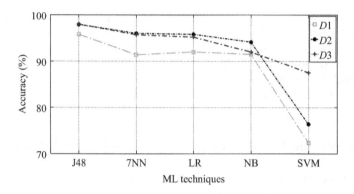

Figure 7.6   The average effect of discretization on the three traffic datasets

we first briefly describe the discretization method, then we present the experimental results of the ML algorithms after applying the discretization method.

7.5.2   Discretization to improve classification accuracy

The candidate features for the classification of traffic datasets involve continuous-valued features ("continuous" refers to features taking numerical values). As discussed in the previous section, the accuracy of some ML algorithms suffers from the presence of such features. To address this problem, we use the state-of-the-art supervised discretization method developed by Fayyad and Irani [283], due to its ability to improve performance compared to other methods (such as *equal width interval binning* and *Holte's 1R discretizer*) [300]. In general, this discretization method partitions the range of the features into subranges (at least two). Essentially, the method combines an entropy-based splitting criterion such as *information gain*, with a minimum description length stopping criterion. The best cut point is the one that makes the subintervals as pure as possible, i.e., where the information value is smallest. The method is then applied recursively to the two subintervals. For a set of instances S a feature f_i and a cut point T, the class information entropy of the partition obtained by T is given by

$$E(f_i; T; S) = \frac{S_1}{S} Ent(S_1) + \frac{S_2}{S} Ent(S_2) \tag{7.13}$$

where S_1 and S_2 are two intervals of S bounded by cut point T, and $Ent(S)$ is the class entropy of a subset S given by

$$Ent(S) = \sum_{i=1}^{C} p(C_i; S) \log (p(C_i; S)) \tag{7.14}$$

To determine the optimal stopping criteria, *minimal description length principle* is applied. This strategy is used to partition T if and only if the cost of encoding the partition and the classes of the instances in the intervals induced by T is less than the cost of encoding the classes of the instances before splitting. Therefore, the partition is accepted if and only if the cut point T is

$$Gain(f_i; T; S) > \frac{\log(N-1)}{N} + \frac{\Delta(f_i; T; S)}{N} \qquad (7.15)$$

where

$$Gain(f_i; T; S) = Ent(S) - E(f_i; T; S)$$

and

$$\Delta(f_i; T; S) = \log(3^c - 2) - [c \cdot Ent(S) \\ -c_1 \cdot Ent(S_1) - c_2 \cdot Ent(S_2)]$$

In (7.15), N represents the number of instances, c, c_1, and c_2 are the number of distinct classes present in S, S_1, and S_2, respectively. The first component is the information needed to specify the splitting point; the second is a correction due to the need to transmit which classes correspond to the upper and lower subintervals.

7.5.3 Impact of discretizing the candidate features

The comparison made here is related to the effectiveness of using the candidate feature subset and discretization method as a preprocessing step to improve the model performance of various ML methods. The discretization method was performed in the way described in Section 7.5.2. Throughout this experiment, the number of bins, K, is set to 10, since this was suggested by [300] as the best heuristics setting, based on S-Plus's histogram binning algorithm [300].

Figure 7.7(a) shows that the discretization method prior to the aforementioned ML methods can substantially improve accuracy. Specifically, we found that the performance of SVM and NB was significantly increased. This is because the entropy-based discretization (i) approximates the class distribution and thus helps to overcome the normality assumption used for continuous features and (ii) provides regularization to such ML methods.

The performance of the remaining ML methods on traffic data using the entropy discretization did not degrade but remained the same. The only slight decrease was in C4.5, one possible reason being that such ML method did not take full advantage of the local entropy discretization that could be performed on the traffic data. From Figure 7.7, it can be seen that the aim of the GOA approach and discretization method to improve the performance of the network traffic task has been fulfilled.

7.6 Conclusion

In light of the emergence of new services and distributed applications, it has become critically important to identify not only the best but also most robust (in terms of stability and optimality) features from large network traffic datasets. This chapter first introduced a novel approach, called GOA, to exploit the *optimality* and *stability*

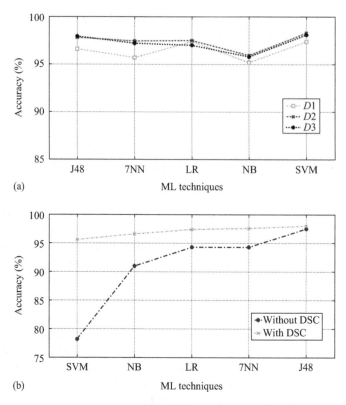

(a)

(b)

Figure 7.7   Impact of the output of GOA and the discretization method on different classification algorithm: (a) influence of discretization method on the three datasets, (b) comparing the average accuracy for each ML method with and without discretization method

metrics to address the limitation of existing FS methods and to produce representative features that satisfied both metrics from a global prospective. The GOA approach involved (i) combining well-known FS methods to filter out a mass of irrelevant features in the first step, (ii) adopting a threshold based on information theory to extract only stable features, and (iii) obtaining a more compact subset and avoiding over-fitting random forest filtering. Finally, this chapter presented a strategy based on a discretization method to enhance the performance of GOA approaches and to significantly improve the accuracy of different ML algorithms. An extensive study using a publicly available traffic data benchmark has proved the strength of the GOA approach in comparison to the existing FS methods.

Chapter 8
A privacy-preserving framework for traffic data publishing

As explained in Chapter 7, sharing network traffic data has become a vital requirement in machine-learning (ML) algorithms when building an efficient and accurate network traffic classification and intrusion detection system (IDS). However, inappropriate sharing and usage of network traffic data could threaten the privacy of companies and prevent sharing of such data. This chapter presents a privacy-preserving strategy-based permutation framework, called PrivTra, in which data privacy, statistical properties, and data-mining utilities can be controlled at the same time. In particular, PrivTra involves the followings: (i) vertically partitioning the original dataset to improve the performance of perturbation; (ii) developing a framework to deal with various types of network traffic data, including numerical, categorical, and hierarchical attributes; (iii) grouping the portioned sets into a number of clusters based on the proposed framework; and (iv) accomplishing the perturbation process by altering the original attribute value with a new value (cluster centroid). The effectiveness of PrivTra is shown through several experiments, such as real network traffic, intrusion detection, and simulated network datasets. Through the experimental analysis, this chapter shows that PrivTra deals effectively with multivariate traffic attributes, produces compatible results as the original data, improves the performance of the five supervised approaches, and provides a high level of privacy protection.

8.1 Introduction

As discussed in Chapter 7, sharing traffic data between spatial-domain networks is highly desirable to create an accurate and global predictive traffic-classification model. However, such collaborative spatial-domain classifiers are deficient in privacy protections. In particular, ISPs and websites are extremely reluctant to share their operational data among them. The reason being they are competitors in business, and they are worried that their customers' privacy could be affected if they share data. Moreover, many customers are reluctant to install software from web analytics services, such as Alexa [316]. They are worried that this kind of software will keep track of all websites the customers visit and report all the sites they visited. Tragically, even good intentions do not certainly turn to good security and privacy protections. This can be confirmed by the notion that large-scale data breaches have become more frequent [317]. Eventually, we trust the fact that many distributed data-analysis applications will be gaining good grip only if privacy is guaranteed.

Nevertheless, to counter the emergence of new applications and patterns, a number of network classifiers and IDSs based on ML methods [4,20,242,318–322] have been proposed to assist network experts to analyze the security risks and detect attacks against their systems. However, a key problem in the research and development of such efficient and accurate network traffic classification and IDSs (based on ML) is the lack of sufficient traffic data, especially for industrial network (e.g., SCADA—supervisory control and data acquisition) systems [25,26]. Unfortunately, such data are not so easy to obtain because organizations do not want to reveal their private traffic data for various privacy, security, and legal reasons [25,27,28]. For instance, organizations do not want to admit that they have been attacked and therefore are unwilling to divulge any information about this. Thus, it has been widely recognized today that traffic data confidentiality and privacy are increasingly becoming an important aspect of data sharing and integration [28,323,324].

This chapter describes a new privacy-preserving data framework to facilitate the publishing of network traffic data, while ensuring that private data will not be disclosed. Figure 8.1 depicts a typical scenario for the data-collection phase and publishing phase. In the former phase, a data publisher collects the data from the record owner (network traffic companies/organizations). In the latter phase, the data publisher releases the transformed data to a data miner or to the public, called a data recipient, who will then conduct data mining on the published data.

The main important points of this chapter can be summarized as follows:

• A privacy-preserving framework (PrivTra) based on a permutation method is described to deal with network traffic data. Although the vast majority of existing approaches, e.g., [29–31] to privacy-preserving computation have been active in other domains, including marketing data and biomedical data, such studied schemes are not readily applicable to private data in traditional and industrial networks. This is because their design assumes that the data being protected have

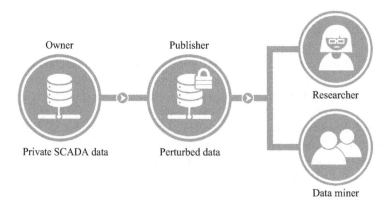

Figure 8.1   Data collection and data publishing

to be numeric. A key challenge with network traffic data is the need to deal with various types of attributes: numerical attributes with real values, categorical attributes with unranked nominal values, and attributes with a hierarchical structure. For example, byte counts are numerical, protocols are categorical, and IP addresses have a hierarchical structure [81]. Consequently, the PrivTra framework is presented to satisfy the privacy requirements, while maintaining sufficient data utility. First, the traffic mixed dataset is subdivided into the attributes of flow record, creating fragments, including the *pure* categorical dataset, the *pure* numerical dataset, and the *pure* hierarchical dataset. Next, well-established similarity measures to deal with various types of attributes are proposed to help produce more meaningful clusters. Last, the clustering results on the numerical, categorical, and hierarchical datasets are combined as a categorical dataset, on which the ML classifiers are employed to obtain the final output. In particular, the objective of such a framework is to enforce privacy-preserving paradigms, such as k-anonymity and l-diversity, while minimizing the information loss incurred during the anatomizing process.

- The PrivTra framework is evaluated on both synthetic and real-life datasets. In particular, the effectiveness of PrivTra is compared against a new class of privacy-preserving data-mining methods, namely, PCA-DR [30], scaling data perturbation (SDP) [29], and rotation data perturbation (RDP) [29]. A general observation indicates that the proposed framework outperforms the existing approaches with respect to a comprehensive set of criteria, including *dealing with multivariate data, efficiency, scalability, data quality*, and *privacy level* (see Section 8.4 for details).

The rest of the chapter is organized as follows: Section 8.2 introduces PrivTra as a new method for privacy-preserving data publishing. Section 8.3 describes a proposed SCADA platform as a case study for generating industrial traffic data, its main components, and data processing. Section 8.4 evaluates the performance of PrivTra in anatomizing the traditional and industrial network traffic datasets.

8.2   Privacy preserving framework for network traffic data

A number of studies in many domains, including marketing data and biomedical data, have been proposed to prevent privacy leakage, while still presenting a maximal utility to data analysts. In particular, as encrypted data (using the traditional RSA and AES methods) cannot be used for data analysis [325], various privacy-preserving methods [29–33] for different data-publishing scenarios have been proposed over the past few years. These methods have been divided roughly into three categories, namely, data generalization methods, e.g., [31], data transformation methods, e.g., [29,30], and data micro-aggregation methods, e.g., [32,33]. For data generalization methods, the process is done by mapping sensitive attributes to more generalized values. For the transformation methods, the privacy of the data is preserved by transforming the original data into new values based on random multiplication or by projecting the original data into lower dimensional random space. For data micro-aggregation methods, the original data are partitioned into a small-sized group, and then replace the private values in each group are replaced with the group average.

Although privacy-preserving in data publishing has been studied extensively [29–31], most of the existing studies focus on data with numerical and continuous attributes. However, network traffic flows contain data with various types of attributes (e.g., IP address and port numbers). Consequently, there is a need to address the challenge of how to preserve the privacy of such data, while maintaining the quality of the data since they degrade. To address this problem, the following subsections describe the requirements of a well-developed privacy-preserving framework.

8.2.1   Desired requirements

As a countermeasure and to mitigate the potential threats in the publishing of network traffic data, a well-developed privacy-preserving framework should include the following properties:

- *Dealing with multivariate data*: The privacy framework should have the ability to deal with various types of attributes: numerical attributes with real values, categorical attributes with unranked nominal values, and attributes with a hierarchical structure.
- *Efficiency*: The assessment of the resources used by a privacy-preserving data-mining algorithm depends on its efficiency, which represents the ability of the algorithm to execute with good performance in terms of the transformation process and improve the performance of ML methods. Therefore, the privacy framework should consider these resources.
- *Data quality*: Traffic data are mainly utilized by ML methods to drive certain patterns, such as the type of flow (attacks or normal). Therefore, data quality should be at an acceptable level according to the intended data usage. If data quality is too degraded, the released dataset is useless for the purpose of knowledge extraction. Therefore, the privacy framework needs to be designed in an effective way to preserve the quality of the original data.
- *Privacy level*: A privacy-preserving mining method should incorporate a privacy-protection mechanism in a careful manner, in order to prevent the discovery of sensitive information that is contained in published data.

Based on this comprehensive set of criteria, we have assessed the proposed framework and other baseline methods in Section 8.4 to determine which approach meets specific requirements.

8.2.2   An overview of PrivTra

This section describes the PrivTra privacy-preserving framework for traffic data publishing. In particular, PrivTra is based on the previous requirements and attempts to preserve the privacy of network traffic data by modifying values of sensitive attributes, based on clustering transformation. The corresponding architecture of the PrivTra

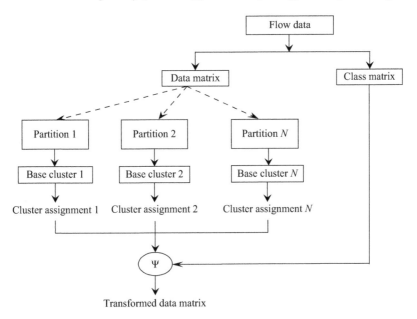

Figure 8.2   A schematic representation of the privacy-preserving architecture for traffic data

framework is shown in Figure 8.2, where the first level involves the partitioning of the original data.

The primary reason for such a step, as mentioned before, is that network traffic data have various types of attributes: numerical attributes with real values, categorical attributes with unranked nominal values, and attributes with a hierarchical structure. The partitioned data are then clustered based on similarity distance. The cluster assignment values produced by the different base clusters and the original class values are merged to form the input for various ML methods (e.g., classifiers). The different steps of the proposed framework are detailed in the following subsections.

8.2.3   Partitioning

Network flows are usually represented as vectors in a multidimensional space. Each dimension represents a distinct attribute describing the flow. Thus, flows are represented as an $m \times n$ matrix D, where there are m rows, one for each flow, and n columns, one for each attribute. This matrix contains categorical, numerical, and hierarchical attributes. For example, byte counts are numerical, protocols are categorical, and IP addresses have a hierarchical structure. A key issue for this scheme is how to deal with such various types of attributes, since the framework relies on distance-based clustering to ensure the privacy of the original data. To resolve this challenging problem, the domain knowledge is exploited to intelligently split the original data for the individual records into N partition sets according to certain flow attributes (e.g., IP address and port numbers). Consequently, the original mixed datasets are vertically partitioned into three sub-datasets: a *pure* categorical dataset, a *pure* numerical dataset, and a *pure* hierarchical dataset.

8.2.4   Clustering to enable privacy preserving

The PrivTra framework takes the clustering concept to find similar flows and replaces it with cluster assignments. However, a key problem with existing clustering algorithms [219,326,327] for multivariate traffic data is the calculation of distance for different types of traffic attributes to accurately group similar patterns together. Thus, such challenges are addressed by presenting a framework that takes into consideration three types of attributes: numerical, categorical, and hierarchical. This section addresses this issue and presents Algorithm 1 that highlights the general steps, which are performed on the traffic data to preserve the privacy of multivariate attributes.

Given the traffic dataset $[x_{ij}] = [d_{ij}] \cdot [class_i]$ where $1 \leq i \leq N_{instances}$ and $1 \leq j \leq N_{attributes}$, the process starts by partitioning the traffic data into multiple traffic data types (as discussed in the previous subsection). Then the partitioned data is passed to the clustering algorithm. The purpose of the clustering algorithm is to group the similar dataset into a number of $N_{cluster}$ clusters. Clustering is performed separately on the corresponding data types (e.g., $[Nij]$, $[Cij]$ and $[Hij]$). At the completion of each clustering, each row of $[dij]$ is replaced with clustering IDSs. The assignment

---

Algorithm 1: Privacy-preserving framework for network traffic data

---

Input :
1 $Data \longleftarrow \{f_1, f_2, \ldots, f_{n-1}\};$
2 $Sim \longleftarrow \{Sim_{NM}, Sim_{HR}, Sim_{CT}\};$
   Output:
3 $[y_{ij}] = [MD_{ij}] \cdot [class_i];$ // modified dataset
4 ;

5 $[Nij, Cij, Hij] \longleftarrow PartitionData(Data);$

6 **if** *Data is Partitioned* **then**
7 $\quad$ **switch** *Attribute Type* **do**
8 $\quad\quad$ **case** *Numerical* **do**
9 $\quad\quad\quad \lfloor \; [NM_{ij}] \longleftarrow \text{NumericalCls}(Sim_{NM}, [Nij]);$
10 $\quad\quad$ **case** *Categorical* **do**
11 $\quad\quad\quad \lfloor \; [CT_{ij}] \longleftarrow \text{CategoricalCls}(Sim_{CT}, [Cij]);$
12 $\quad\quad$ **case** *Hierarchical* **do**
13 $\quad\quad\quad \lfloor \; [HR_{ij}] \longleftarrow \text{hierarchicalCls}(Sim_{HR}, [Hij]);$

14 $[MD_{ij}] \longleftarrow \text{CombModData}([NM_{ij}], [CT_{ij}], [HR_{ij}]);$

IDSs produced by base clusters (including $[NM_{ij}]$, $[CT_{ij}]$, and $[HR_{ij}]$) that are combined to form the final modified data $[y_{ij}] = [MD_{ij}] \cdot [class_i]$. In general, the output of the clustering algorithm depends on the attribute types, the clustering *types*, and the similarity measurements. The following subsections focus on the similarity measurement that is developed for each type of attribute and also discuss the corresponding clustering.

(A) Numerical attributes

Choosing an appropriate similarity measure is crucial for transforming the network traffic data into a new value, based on the clustering concept. Therefore, before transforming numerical attributes, we now formally define a distance/similarity for the numerical types. In general, there is a wide variety of distance/similarity measures for numerical data available in the literature [328]; however, many of them are only good for linear dependence and not for nonlinear ones. Therefore, we have chosen the *Euclidean* distance to measure the distance between numerical attributes due to its ability to deal with nonlinear dependence. Nevertheless, it has been shown that no metric can outperform *Euclidean* distance for ratio-based measurements [329]. The process of calculating the distance between two numerical attributes is formulated as follows:

$$d_n^i = (x_1, x_2) = \|x_1 - x_2\| = [(x_1 - x_2)]^{1/2} \tag{8.1}$$

where the centroid of numerical attributes i in cluster C having N points is given by

$$\bar{c}[i] = \frac{1}{N} \sum_{j=1}^{N} x_j[i]. \tag{8.2}$$

The described approach to transform the numerical attributes of the original data into new values builds on the standard K-means clustering algorithm [326]. This clustering algorithm is chosen as a suitable means of grouping numerical data for the following reasons: (i) it is a data-driven method with relatively few assumptions on the distributions of the underlying data, and (ii) the greedy search strategy of K-means guarantees at least a local minimum of the criterion function, thereby accelerating the convergence. In this work, the K-means clustering algorithm is performed on numerical data instances using each feature column separately. Each K-means [326] cluster represents a region of similar instances, which is "similar" in terms of Euclidean distances between the instances and their cluster centroids. Algorithm 2 summarizes the transformation mechanism used for the numerical attributes.

For each column in the numerical matrix $([N_{ij}])$, the process starts by initializing the center of cluster j. Then the membership of each data item d_i is assigned (based on (8.1)) to the cluster whose center is closest to d_i. After that, cluster centers are updated as in (8.2), in which the center of cluster C_j is set to be equal to the mean of all data items in cluster j, $\{\forall_j : 1 \leq j \leq k\}$. The process is repeated until the centroid does not change. Then, if the cluster centers do not change then the original attribute values are replaced with the cluster assignment.

Algorithm 2: Transformation of numerical attributes

---

1 **Input:**

2 $[N_{ij}]$;
3 *Parameter#* of clusters K;
4 **Output:**

5 $[NM_{ij}]$;
    `// the corresponding centroid`
6 **foreach** *columns in [N_{ij}]* **do**
7   **foreach** $C_k \in [1, K]$ **do**
        `// Initialize cluster` C_k `center` I_k
8         $C_k \longleftarrow$ initialize (I_k);
9   **for** $d_i \in columns_j$ **do**
10         $d_i^c \longleftarrow$ DetermineMember (d_i, C_k);
        `// Assign` d_i `to the cluster` C_k `whose center is close`
        `to` d_i
11         $I_k \longleftarrow$ UpdateCenter (C_k);
        `// Update cluster centers` I_k
12   **if** I_k *not changed* **then**
13             $d_i \longleftarrow K$;
            `// Replace` d_i `with cluster centroid` I_k
14   **else**
15   go to step (9);
16         $col_j \longleftarrow col_j \cup d_i$;
17     $NM \longleftarrow NM \cup col_j$;

The time complexity of the transformation mechanism of the numerical attributes is $O(nkl)$ where $n = |D|$, k is the number of clusters, and l is the number of iterations. However, in practice, the l is considered a constant. Thus, the time complexity of the numerical transformation mechanism is $O(nk)$. The space complexity of K-means is $O(n)$.

(B) Categorical attributes

Measuring the notion of similarity or distance for categorical attributes is not as straightforward as for numerical attributes; this is due to the fact that there is no explicit notion of ordering between categorical values. Categorical attributes (also known as nominal or qualitative multistate attributes) have been studied for a long time in various contexts [330], leading to several categorical measures [331–333]. More recently, however, the *overlap* [334] measure has become the most commonly used similarity measure for categorical data. The popularity of this measure is due to its simplicity and ease of use. Essentially, in determining the similarity between categorical attributes, an $N \times N$ similarity matrix is constructed for each attribute member, denoted as $S_m, m = \{1 \cdots M\}$. Matrix entries represent the similarity between two categorical attributes, x_i and x_j (see (8.3)), and the matrices are effectively merged to form the co-association ($CO(x_i, x_j)$) matrix (see (8.3)):

$$S_m(x_i, x_j) = \begin{cases} 1 & \text{if } x_i = x_j \\ 0 & \text{otherwise} \end{cases}$$

$$CO(x_i, x_j) = \sum_{k=1}^{d} w_k S_k(x_i, x_j) \tag{8.3}$$

where $S_k(x_i, x_j)$ is the per-attribute similarity between two values for the categorical attribute A_k, and $w_k = 1/d$ quantify the weight assigned to the attribute A_K. Having obtained the $CO(x_i, x_j)$ matrix, the cluster centroids are then produced by applying the single-link (SL) method [327] on the resultant matrix, where the original values of attributes are then replaced with the corresponding centroid. Note, the SL method has been chosen due to its simplicity of implementation for massive data.

Algorithm 3 summarizes the transformation mechanism done for the categorical attributes. The cost complexity of categorical attributes transformation is tied to the pairwise similarity between the categorical attributes $O(N^2)$, and also to the time complexity of SL clustering which is $O(N^2)$.

Algorithm 3: Transformation of Categorical Attributes

---

1 **Input:**

2 $[C_{ij}]$;
3 *Parameter*# of clusters K;
4 **Output:**

5 $CT[i,j]$;
   `// the corresponding centroids`
6 $Sim[i,j] \longleftarrow$ null, $CO[i,j] \longleftarrow$ null;
7 **for** $x_i, x_j \in C_{ij}$ **do**
8 $\quad Sim[x_i, x_j] \longleftarrow$ ComputeSimilarity(x_i, x_j);
   $\quad$ `// Compute the similarity between each pair as (8.3)`
9 $\quad CO[x_i, x_j] \longleftarrow$ UpdateMatrix($Sim[x_i, x_j]$);
   $\quad$ `// For each pair update the co-association matrix as`
   $\quad$ `(8.3).`

10 IDs$\longleftarrow$ ComputeDendrogram($CO[i,j]$);
   `// Compute the Single-linkage of the co-association matrix.`
11 $CT[i,j] \longleftarrow$ ReplaceOriginal(*IDs*);

(C) Hierarchical attributes

The traffic data of both traditional and industrial networks include hierarchical attributes (e.g., SrcIP and DstIP). Thus, one of the key challenges is how to calculate the distance between IP addresses. In general, a global IP address is unique and allocated by a central body (IANA), which tries to assign groups of contiguous IP addresses to organizations or geographic regions. This helps in keeping routing tables small and also in managing multicast routing information. IP addresses can be grouped into subnetworks based on the hierarchical structure of an IP address. If a set of IP addresses belongs to the same subnetwork, then they are more likely to exhibit similar behavior than two random IP addresses. Exploring hierarchical structure of IP address has been highlighted in several studies of network traffic analysis and intrusion detection [81,335]. In particular, Mahmood *et al.* [81] have successfully introduced a new hierarchical similarity measure to cluster sources that have similar network traffic behavior. Following the general approach of ECHIDNA [81], the IP address spaces a 32-level binary prefix tree corresponding to the 32 bits in an IP address, covering all 2^{32} possible IP addresses. Using this L-level generalization hierarchy, the hierarchical similarity measure can be defined as

$$S_{HSM} = \frac{|path(root, n_1) - path(root, n_2)|}{L} \tag{8.4}$$

where the numerator determines the length of the common segment between n_1 and n_2, and L is the maximum depth of generalization hierarchy. For example, the distance between 128.0.0.252/32 and 128.0.0.254/31 is $(32-30)/24=0.083$.

Algorithm 4 summarizes the transformation mechanism for the hierarchical attributes. The steps for the hierarchical transformation are as follows:

- Calculate the relationship between any pair of IP addresses using (8.4), leading to a new similarity matrix $n \times m$ between IP addresses. In particular, the IP addresses are mapped to a co-association matrix, where entries can be interpreted as votes ratios on the pairwise co-occurrences of IP addresses and are computed as the number of times each pair of IP addresses has a common and the most significant bit-group in their IP address.
- Convert the values of the corresponding $n \times m$ similarity matrix to distance values and change the format from square to vector.
- Apply the Single-linked method to the corresponding $n \times m$ similarity matrix. The underlying assumption is that IP addresses that have similar traffic behavior are very likely to be colocated in the same cluster.
- Replace the original attributes of IP addresses with the corresponding clustering results.

The hierarchical attributes transformation has complexity of $O(2^N)$ for computing similarity of N IP addresses and $O(N^2)$ for computational complexity of Single-linked method. The overall of the computational complexity of the hierarchical attributes transformation is $O(2^N + N^2)$.

Algorithm 4: Transformation of hierarchical attributes

---

1 **Input:**

2 $[H_{ij}]$;

3 *Parameter#* of clusters K;

4 **Output:**

5 $[HR_{ij}]$;
   // the corresponding centroid

6 $Sim[i,j] \longleftarrow$ null, $HSM[i,j] \longleftarrow$ null;

7 **for** $ip_i \in [H_{ij}]$ **do**

8      $Sim[ip_i, ip_j] \longleftarrow$ ComputeSimilarity (ip_i, ip_j, HSM);
        // Compute the similarity between each pair as (8.4)

9      $HSM[i,j] \longleftarrow$ UpdateMatrix $(HSM[i,j], Sim[ip_i, ip_j])$;
        // For each pair update the *HSM* as (8.4).

10 IDs $\longleftarrow$ ComputeDendrogram $(HSM[i,j])$;
   // Compute the Single-linkage of the hierarchical
        similarity matrix, *HSM*

11 $HR[i,j] \longleftarrow$ ReplaceOriginal(IDs)

8.3 Case study: SCADA platform and processing

The security of industrial control systems (SCADA) has been a topic of scrutiny and research for several years, and many security issues are well known. However, a key challenge in the research and development of security solutions for SCADA systems is the lack of proper modeling tools due to the fact that it is impractical to conduct security experiments on a real system because of the scale and cost of implementing stand-alone systems. The second contribution of this chapter is the development of a SCADA platform to provide a modular SCADA modeling tool that allows real-time communication with external devices using SCADA protocols. Such a platform is important not only (i) to evaluate the PrivTra privacy-preserving framework but also (ii) to enable additional benefits of testing real attacks and trying different security solutions for such systems. This section first presents the water platform and then describes data processing.

8.3.1 Water platform

The success of penetrations and attacks on industrial networks (e.g., SCADA systems) are hardly and rarely reported, and this is due to the sensitive nature of such systems [336]. As a consequence, network traffic and logged data are not publicly-available for security experts to mine normal/abnormal patterns. Therefore, a robust privacy-preserving data-mining algorithms for SCADA systems are an optimal way to address this issue. However, up-to-date, data collection of SCADA systems is not publicly available to enable us to evaluate the PrivTra framework. Thus, we show a virtual SCADA Lab we built to simulate a water-distribution system (WDS) as the supervised infrastructure. In particular, visualization features are used to represent the key parts of a SCADA system. For example, the field devices (e.g., PLC and RTU) and control devices (e.g., MTU and HMI) are represented by a number of virtual machines (VMs) after installing the library [337] of the widely used Modbus protocol [338]. The virtualized network is used as the communication infrastructure at all SCADA network levels (e.g., field and control levels).

To simulate a supervised infrastructure, the library of the well-known and free hydraulic and water quality model is used, called EPANET [339], to develop a WDS server to act as a surrogate for a real WDS. The EPANET model involves three modules, namely, hydraulic, water quality, and water consumption modules. The consumption module is fed with a specific model (e.g., 2010 City of Melbourne water consumption, Australia [340]) so as to simulate the realistic behavior of a WDS. One VM is assigned to the WDS server. This server feeds the simulated data to virtualized field devices and receives the Modbus/TCP control messages via a proxy. This proxy is used as an interface between virtualized field devices and the WDS server. For realistic simulation, the WDS server reads and controls process parameters, such as water flow, pressure, and valve status, in response to message commands from field devices. The manipulated process parameters in the WDS server include

- Water flow, pressure, demand, and level
- Valve status and setting
- Pump status and speed

8.3.2 A water distribution system (WDS) scenario

Figure 8.3 depicts an example of a simple WDS for a small town. This type of town could be divided into three areas (i.e., A, B, and C). Each area has an elevated tank to supply it with water at a satisfactory pressure level. The supplied water is pumped out by three pumps from the treatment system into $Tank_1$. The water is also delivered to $Tank_2$ by two pumps. $Tank_3$ is supplied through gravity because of the elevation of $Tank_2$, which is higher than $Tank_3$. $Tank_1$ is twice as big as $Tank_2$ and $Tank_3$ because it is considered to be the main water source for areas B and C.

The water network is monitored and controlled by the SCADA system. In this scenario, some of the *PLCs*, namely, $PLC_1,\ldots,PLC_4$, depend on each others' readings to control their end devices. Therefore, the MUT server plays a key role in coordinating and exchanging the data readings among these devices, in addition to storing the acquired data in the Historian. The *PLCs* are logically programmed as follows:

- PLC_4 controls the operation of pumps P_1, P_2, and P_3 according to the water level reading of $Tank_1$, which is exchanged between PLC_4 and PLC_3 by the *MUT* server.
- PLC_3 controls pumps P_4 and P_5, which pump out the water from $Tank_1$ into $Tank_2$, according to the water level reading of $Tank_2$. It reads the water level of $Tank_1$ and regulates the valve V_2 to maintain a satisfactory pressure level at the area A. As the highest water level is in $Tank_1$, the greatest water pressure is in area

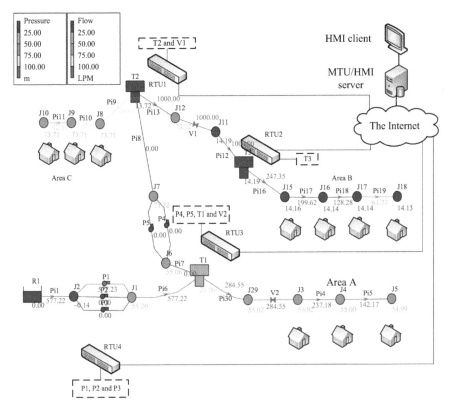

Figure 8.3 Simulation of a water distribution system

A; therefore, PLC_3 adjusts the valve V_2 according to the water level reading of $Tank_1$.

- PLC_1 opens and closes the valve V_1 according to the water level reading of $Tank_3$ and reads the water level reading of $Tank_2$.
- PLC_2 reads the water level reading of $Tank_3$ in order to be sent to PLC_1 by the MUT server.

8.3.3 A scenario of attacks

The purpose of this scenario is to affect the normal behavior of the WDS. The public network (e.g., Internet) is used to interconnect all WDS's components through Ethernet modules. The Modbus/TCP application protocol is setup as a communication protocol. However, all TCP vulnerabilities are inherited and therefore the system is susceptible to external attacks, such as DoS (denial of service) attacks and spoofing.

High-level control attacks are simulated here, as they are difficult to detect because they do not fully stop the service (as is the case with DoS attacks), but they drastically reduce the performance of the SCADA system. These types of attacks require prior knowledge of the target system, and this can be obtained by the specifications, or by correlation analysis for the network traffic of that system. As mentioned from the specifications of the simulation system, PLC_4 controls the pumps P_1, P_2, and P_3 in accordance with the water level reading of $Tank_1$. This can be read by the MUT server from PLC_3 and sent from the MUT server to PLC_4. We launch a man-in-the-middle attack to intercept the message sent from the MUT server to PLC_4. This is done by acting as a proxy between these devices.

The intercepted messages are modified to send false readings of the water levels. Two false readings of the water level of $Tank_1$ are sent to PLC_4: (i) when the water level of $Tank_1$ reaches the level at which PLC_4 should turn on the three pumps, a false reading is sent to inform PLC_4 that the water level is above 98%. This type of attack will be performed repetitively until the water goes down to the lowest level. (ii) When PLC_4 should turn on the two pumps, a false reading is sent to let PLC_4 know that the water level is between 70% and 80%. This type of false reading will be sent till the water level becomes lower than 70%. These types of attacks can be launched in a number of ways, and they are hard to detect because: (i) the false message is still legitimate in terms of the Modbus/TCP protocol specifications; and (ii) the attack cannot be detected by any individual process parameter (such as water level readings) unless the statuses of the three pumps are taken into account.

8.4   Evaluation

The objective of this section is to study the performance of the PrivTra framework on data quality in terms of accuracy and discernability cost. Specifically, the followings are presented: (i) a brief description of the datasets, and (ii) an introduction to the experimental setup; then seek answers to the following questions:

- How well are the well-known classifiers able to distinguish between normal and attack flows based on the transformed data?
- How does the proposed scheme affect the runtime of classification methods?
- What is the runtime performance of the proposed scheme in compared with existing methods?
- How closely can the original value of an attribute be estimated from the transformed datasets?

8.4.1   Datasets

To assess the advantages of the PrivTra framework, eight simulated datasets are used in the experiments. We experimented also with two other publicly available datasets, namely, DARPA and Internet traffic data. These two datasets have become a benchmark for many studies since the work of Andrew *et al.* [17]. They have different types of attributes: continuous, categorical, and hierarchical. Table 8.1 summarizes the proportion of normal and anomaly flows, the number of attributes, and the number of classes for each dataset.

Table 8.1 Datasets used in the experiments

Data	No. of instances	No. of attributes	No. of classes
MHIRD	699	10	2
MHORD	2,500	3	2
SPFDS	1,000	15	2
DOSDS	4,000	15	2
SPDOS	2,500	15	3
SHIRD	1,800	4	2
SHORD	400	4	2
ITD	21,000	149	12
WTP	512	39	2
DARPA	10,000	42	5

The characteristics of the ten datasets used are described later:

- *Internet traffic data (ITD)*: The traffic datasets collected by the high-performance network monitor [245] are some of the largest publicly available network traffic traces that are used in our experiment. These datasets are based on traces captured using its loss-limited, full-payload capture to disk, where timestamps with a resolution of better than 35 nanoseconds are provided. The data were taken for several different periods in time from one site on the Internet. This site is a research facility, which hosts up to 1,000 users connected to the Internet via a full-duplex Gigabyte Ethernet link. Full-duplex traffic on this connection was monitored for each traffic set. The site hosts several biology-related facilities, collectively referred to Genome Campus (Cambridge Lab). There are three institutions on-site that employ about 1,000 researchers, administrators, and technical staff. This campus is connected to the Internet via a full-duplex Gigabyte Ethernet link. It was on this connection to the Internet that the monitor was placed. Each traffic set consists of a full 24-hour, week-day period in both link directions. Refer to Chapters 6 and 7, for more details about this dataset.
- *DARPA Data*: Since 1999, the DARPA'99 dataset has been the most widely used dataset for the IDS evaluations that use ML methods. This dataset was prepared by Stolfo *et al.* [244] and is built based on the data captured in the DARPA'99 IDS evaluation program [341]. This dataset contains raw traffic flow records with an associated label to indicate whether the record was labeled as either normal or an attack. In particular, the simulated attacks fall in one of the most common types of attacks, including *DoS attack*, *User to Root attack*, *Remote to Local attack*, and *Probing Attack*. The original DARPA dataset is about 4 gigabytes of compressed raw (binary) tcpdump data of 7 weeks of network traffic, which can be processed into about 5 million connection records, each with about 100 bytes. To validate our work, a sample of the original DARPA dataset is selected (the size of the dataset is ultimately limited by the amount of memory, since transformation methods need to load the entire training data into the memory).

This sample dataset consists of approximately 10,000 single connection vectors, each of which contains 41 attributes.

- *Water treatment plant*: This dataset was collected from the daily measures of sensors in an urban waste water treatment plant (WTP). The objective is to classify the operational state of the plant in order to identify abnormality through the state variables of the plant at each of the stages of the treatment process. As shown in Table 8.1, this dataset consists of 527 instances and each instance contains 38 attributes and is labeled either normal or abnormal.

- *Labeled wireless sensor network data*: The labeled wireless sensor network provides four datasets: multi-hop outdoor real data (MHORD), multi-hop indoor real data (MHIRD), single-hop outdoor real data (SHORD), and single-hop indoor real data (SHIRD). These datasets were collected from a simple single-hop and a multi-hop wireless sensor network deployment using TelosB motes. Each dataset consists of correlated process parameters (e.g., humidity and temperature) collected during a 6-hour period at intervals of 5 s. The single-hop data was collected on May 9, 2010 and the multi-hop data was collected on July10, 2010.

- *Simulated SCADA system data*: There are so many types of attacks targeting SCADA systems with some researchers listing more than 50 different types of attacks targeting DNP3 [336] and Modbus [342]. However, for the sake of simplicity, we used our SCADA simulator (described in Section 8.3) to simulate two attacks commands. The first attack is *spoofing*, where an intruder connects to the local filed network to send fake messages to the PLCs as they were coming from a real MTU. The second attack is *DoS*, where the attackers launch flood attacks against the WDS. In order to construct the sets of SCADA flows, the simulated traces are splinted into three datasets. The first dataset (detonated as SPFDS) contains *normal/spoofing* traffic. The second dataset (donated as DOSDS) contains *normal/DoS* traffic. The third dataset (detonated as SPDOS) is a combination of the *spoofing*, *DoS*, and *normal* traffic, which are useful to show how the different high-level control attacks can mislead the proposed privacy framework.

8.4.2 Baseline methods

PrivTra is benchmarked with the most current and relevant privacy-preserving methods as follows:

- *The principle component analysis-based transformation (PCA-DR)* [30]: This method preserves the privacy of a confidential attribute by replacing the original attributes of a dataset with a smaller number of uncorrelated variables called the principle components. The transformed matrix then shifted by multiplying it with an arbitrarily selected shifting factor to enhance security.

- *The SDP method* [29]: This method perturbed the confidential attributes by using a multiplicative noise perturbation. In particular, the used noise could be either positive or negative, and the set of operations takes only the value multiplied corresponding to a multiplicative noise applied to each confidential attribute.

- *The RDP Method* [29]: This method is similar to SDP. However, the operation set used of this method takes only the value rotation (instead of multiply value) to identify a common rotation angle between the confidential attributes. Unlike the previous method, RDP can be applied more than once to some confidential attributes.

8.4.3 Quality evaluation using benchmarking ML methods

To evaluate the quality of the datasets that are optimized by the PrivTra framework and to ensure that the output of the PrivTra does not convolve with specific ML methods (e.g., classifiers), both original and transformed data are evaluated and trained on various ML classifiers (discussed in details in Chapter 7). These ML methods include: K-nearest neighbors (KNN) [39], Naive Bayes (NB) [311], decision tree (J48) [312], support vector machine (SVM) [315], and multilayer perceptron (MLP) [343]. The reasons for choosing these ML methods are (i) as reported in [298], these ML algorithms can achieve superior performance and are the top five out of ten evaluated ML algorithms, (ii) previous studies show the capability of such methods to handle high-dimensional data, and (iii) these five ML algorithms work differently and represent an ideal cross section of ML algorithms to use for testing learning bias.

8.4.4 Experiment setup

Algorithm 5 shows the experimental procedures to evaluate the impact of the framework and the baseline methods on the classification quality. In particular, a cross-validation strategy is used to make the best use of the traffic data and to obtain stable result. For each dataset, all instances are randomized and divided into two subsets as training and testing sets. Consequently, we evaluate the effect of the PrivTra framework and the baseline methods by building a classifier on a training set and measuring the classification accuracy on the testing set. Since the previously presented five ML methods can exhibit an order effect, the result of each classifier is averaged over ten runs on each transformation method.

Note, the categorical and hierarchical attributes are removed from the datasets when the baseline methods are applied. This is because the baseline methods deal only with numerical data. However, PrivTra applies to all traffic datasets regardless of the types of attributes in these datasets.

8.4.5 Experiment results

This section tests the effectiveness of the output of PrivTra on different supervised ML methods and compares it with the output of the baseline methods. The purpose of this investigation is also to see if PrivTra can significantly improve the performance of the chosen classifiers. Four types of external evaluation metrics are used to verify the performance of the PrivTra framework. In particular, *recall*, *precision*, and *overall accuracy* metrics (see Chapter 7) are used, as well as F-measure, which is defined as follows. F-measure is the equally weighted (harmonic) mean of precision and recall:

$$\text{F-measure} = \frac{\text{Recall} \times \text{Precision}}{\text{Recall} + \text{Precision}} \tag{8.5}$$

Algorithm 5: Experimental procedure

---

1 **Input:**

2 Parameter $N = 10$; $M = 10$;

3 Transformations(T)=$\{PrivTra, SDP, RDP, PCA - RD\}$;

4 DATA= $\{DARPA, WTP, \cdots, D_n\}$;

5 Classifiers=$\{K - NN, NB, J48, SVM, MLP\}$;

6 **Output:**

7 PerfoMetrics=$\{$Accuracy, F-measure, Recall, Precision$\}$;

8 **foreach** $Transformations_i \in [1, T]$ **do**

9   **foreach** $D_i \in DATA$ **do**

10        $TransData = $ apply $Transformations_i$ to $(Test'_{Data})$;

11        $TransData = Transformations_i^t(D_i)$;

12   **foreach** $times \in [1, M]$ **do**

13           $randomize$ instance-order for $TransData$;

14   generate N bins from the randomized $TransData$;

15   **foreach** $fold \in [1, N]$ **do**

16              $Test_{Data} = bin[fold]$;

17              $Train_{Data} = TransData - Test_{Data}$;

18              $Train'_{Data} = $ select Subset from $Train_{Data}$;

19              $Test'_{Data} = $ select Subset from $Test_{Data}$;

20   **foreach** $Classifier_i \in Classifiers$ **do**

21                 $Classifier_i = learner(Train'_{Data})$;

22                 $Results_i = $ apply $Classifier_i$ to $(Test'_{Data})$;

23           $OverallResult = OverallResult \cup Results_i$;

24        $PerfoMetrics = $ average $(OverallResult)$;

(A) Experiment results

We reinforce our earlier motivation, which was stated in Section 8.2 by measuring the data quality on the classifiers before and after transformation. We expect the transformed data to maintain a reasonable degree of accuracy. The classification results, including *overall accuracy, precision, recall*, and *F*-measure, over the original data and transformed datasets are given in the following sections.

Metric 1: Accuracy

Table 8.2 shows the overall accuracy derived without transformation methods and the accuracy that was of the closest magnitude after the application of each of the transformation methods. In general, it can be observed from Table 8.2 that all the transformation methods are always effective in improving the performance of the five classifiers in comparison to the original data, except on the transformed data of the PCA-DR method (the accuracy values in bold indicate better performance). This is

Table 8.2   Comparison of the overall accuracy of different classifiers using different transformation methods

ML tech	Methods	MHIRD	MHORD	SPFDS	DOSDS	SPDOS	SHIRD	SHORD	ITD	WTP	DARPA
MLP	**Original**	96.93	98.43	**98.55**	97.61	98.31	97.25	98.30	91.19	**97.98**	98.55
	PCA-DR	**98.47**	97.96	98.15	**98.21**	97.70	98.22	98.63	90.36	96.96	77.94
	RDP	97.18	97.85	97.83	97.20	**98.78**	97.70	98.57	91.11	97.41	98.63
	PrivTra	97.71	**98.76**	98.50	97.03	97.19	**98.95**	98.15	**97.50**	97.94	**98.78**
	SDP	98.14	97.63	98.42	97.39	97.24	98.04	**98.74**	91.22	96.74	97.22
J48	**Original**	**98.16**	97.71	**98.82**	96.81	97.72	97.49	97.64	96.62	96.41	**97.80**
	PCA-DR	97.15	**98.60**	98.03	**96.95**	96.84	97.44	97.26	92.60	96.01	77.06
	RDP	97.54	97.14	98.69	96.12	**98.52**	**98.69**	**98.29**	95.91	96.42	97.57
	PrivTra	94.93	96.51	98.44	96.83	97.65	98.49	97.44	**97.11**	94.85	**97.80**
	SDP	97.91	97.51	98.12	95.98	98.42	98.38	97.62	96.69	96.69	97.33
NB	**Original**	97.38	97.07	97.21	97.70	97.62	97.70	**98.64**	87.70	95.67	96.95
	PCA-DR	98.00	**98.16**	**98.44**	97.40	**97.64**	97.05	97.66	74.07	96.11	76.73
	RDP	**98.88**	97.33	96.85	**97.89**	97.42	**98.55**	97.98	88.06	96.11	97.73
	PrivTra	98.65	97.79	98.42	97.49	97.57	97.58	98.08	**98.07**	**97.84**	**98.56**
	SDP	97.50	97.63	97.15	96.76	97.35	98.50	97.55	85.57	96.49	97.50
7KNN	**Original**	97.07	97.50	97.91	98.48	**98.16**	97.03	97.83	92.33	96.17	96.98
	PCA-DR	98.18	97.85	97.48	98.52	97.29	98.50	97.82	91.44	95.86	77.90
	RDP	98.18	97.51	97.96	**98.56**	97.63	**98.69**	97.15	92.75	**97.25**	97.99
	PrivTra	98.76	**97.91**	96.97	97.06	97.30	97.61	98.03	**98.18**	96.30	97.37
	SDP	**96.93**	97.49	**98.56**	97.79	97.02	98.78	**98.09**	93.49	96.85	**98.49**
SVM	**Original**	97.72	97.02	98.15	96.09	97.38	96.82	**98.52**	72.59	96.40	**97.97**
	PCA-DR	97.14	96.98	98.38	97.09	97.73	96.16	97.13	53.88	95.52	77.16
	RDP	**97.88**	97.50	**98.61**	96.33	**98.46**	96.57	96.87	73.19	97.41	97.79
	PrivTra	97.53	**98.96**	97.36	97.90	97.42	**97.33**	97.97	**97.81**	**97.93**	97.31
	SDP	97.81	97.73	98.14	96.25	96.99	95.91	97.08	72.07	97.87	97.46

likely due to the fact that this method could weaken the dependence among different attributes. Nevertheless, it was evident from Table 8.2 that the proposed PrivTra framework achieves improvements as good as the baseline methods on all ten datasets. This similarity in accuracy values shows that the positive benefits of transformation methods can be achieved without significant negative effect on classification accuracy. However, it is notable from Table 8.2 that the J48 classifier performs poorly on the three datasets (namely, MHIRD, DOSDS, and WTP) using the PrivTra framework. As the output of the PrivTra framework contains binary data, the J48 classifier suffers from such data type.

Metric #2: Precision and recall

Figures 8.4 and 8.5 compare the *precision* and *recall* values acquired by the classifiers based on the transformed data of the framework and other baseline methods. This is an important task as it gives a more informative picture of classifiers' performance as these classifiers tend to be affected by skewed classes (i.e., attack and normal) distributions. A general observation is that most of the datasets transformed with PrivTra framework have the best precision compare to other baseline methods. This is mainly because PrivTra provides a true representation of original data. However, the transformed data of PrivTra framework often leads to dramatic degradation on $7K$NN performance. This can possibly explained by the fact that $7K$NN applies Euclidean distance, which is not adapted to binary data. According to the calculated F-measures, all of the transformation methods improved the performance of most classification methods, though in many cases performance did not vary considerably between untransformed (i.e., original) and transformed data or between the varied transformations and classification methods that were applied to the various datasets. There are certain notable exceptions, in particular datasets, for which specific classification systems seemed wholly unsuited regardless of any transformation method applied, and also a few cases in which a transformation method greatly improved the performance of a classification method. The DOSDS and the DARPA datasets both resulted in lower overall performance across transformation and classification methods, yet there is a substantial spread in the performance of transformation and classification methods. For the DOSDS dataset, the MLP classification system was the strongest performer overall, and performance was significantly improved for several classification systems through the use of the PrivTra transformation method. In the case of the SVM classification method, performance was almost doubled following this transformation. The PrivTra transformation method generally had the greatest positive impact on performance across datasets and transformation methods, although it actually greatly reduced performance when the $7K$NN classification method was applied to the DOSDS dataset. Performance on the DAPRA set was somewhat higher on average than the DOSDS dataset, although the MLP classification method showed especially poor performance with this dataset.

Overall, when performance was already relatively high for a dataset (and this tended to be relatively consistent across classification methods), the transformation methods did not show tremendous variance, though in certain cases of difficult

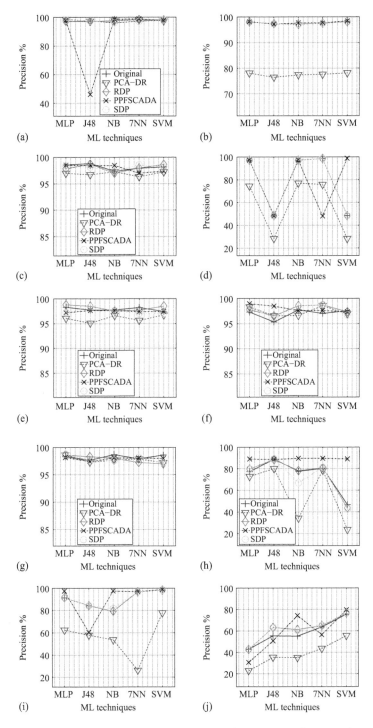

Figure 8.4 *Comparison of the precision values of the PrivTra framework against the baseline transformation methods: (a) MHIRD data, (b) MHORD data, (c) SPFDS data, (d) DOSDS data, (e) SPDOS data, (f) SHIRD data, (g) SHORD data, (h) ITD data, (i) WTP data, and (j) DARPAP data*

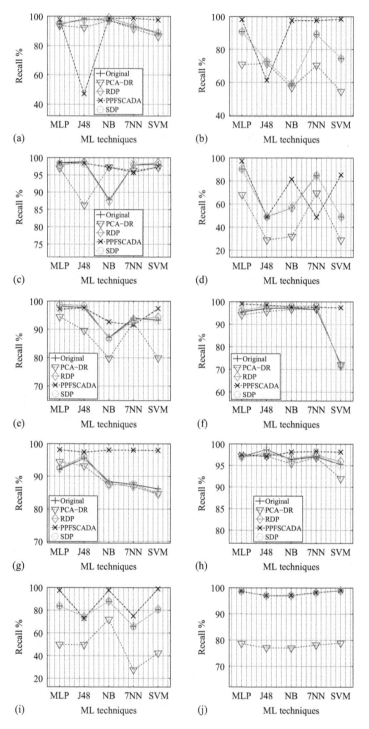

Figure 8.5   *Comparison of the recall values of the PrivTra framework against the baseline transformation methods: (a) MHIRD data, (b) MHORD data, (c) SPFDS data, (d) DOSDS data, (e) SPDOS data, (f) SHIRD data, (g) SHORD data, (h) ITD data, (i) WTP data, and (j) DARPA data*

datasets particular transformation methods did have significant impacts on the performance of specific classification methods. Performance was increased by the PrivTra transformation method to the greatest degree, and the MLP classification method was similarly the highest performer across a greater number of datasets than other classification methods, although not to as significant a degree as PrivTra outperformed other transformation methods, on average. Given these results, it is necessary to question the benefits of conducting additional transformation processing on datasets that show high performance without any transformation being performed; depending on the resource and time intensity of the additional transformation, the benefit achieved by such a transformation might not be worthwhile and, in many cases, might not be significant enough to affect the outcome of other measures and analyses. On the other hand, poor performance in pre-transformation analysis can be greatly improved through transformation in some cases, and multiple transformations might be necessary to achieve the best results.

Metric 3: F-measure

On an extremely imbalanced dataset, the accuracy rates cannot provide information on minority class (e.g., attack). Therefore, the purpose of this section is to compare the PrivTra framework and the baseline methods according to the so popular F-measure, which equally weights precision and recall. Table 8.3 shows the performance of the five classifiers on the transformed datasets. Again, it can be found that the transformed methods help the classifiers to achieve better performance than the original datasets, which is consistent with the previous observation. To focus on key trends, it can be seen from Table 8.3 that the degree of performance improvement of other transformed methods depends on the type of the classifiers. For instance, as shown in Table 8.3, the F-measure values for all datasets of the proposed PrivTra perform the best for SVM, NB, and MLP classifiers. However, the only case result in a significant reduction in performance is with $7K$NN and J48 classifier due to the presence of irrelevant attributes and the binary data. Nevertheless, it is notable that the baseline methods achieve superior performance with the MLP, $7K$NN, and J48. The only case where there is a significant difference is the F-measure values of NB and SVM suggesting that these algorithms suffer from the presence of continuous-valued attributes that are generated by the baseline methods.

(B) Computational efficiency

Here, some results of the experiments are presented to analyze the efficiency PrivTra and the baseline methods. In particular, two series of experimental tests are carried out. First, we focused on assessing the time requirement to perform the transformation for different datasets, and then compare the performance of classifiers before and after applying the transformation methods on the original datasets. The computational efficiency test is conducted in MATLAB® v12 on a PC with 3.16 GHz CPU and 3.49 GB memory. For each set of experiments, ten trials were executed and the average value has been computed.

Table 8.3 *Comparing F-measure values of different classifiers using different transformation methods*

ML tech	Method	MHIRD	MHORD	SPFDS	DOSDS	SPDOS	SHIRD	SHORD	ITD	WTP	DARPA
MLP	**Original**	95.74	94.79	**98.55**	94.20	98.31	96.36	95.13	86.01	88.92	**58.24**
	PCA-DR	96.07	94.31	96.99	92.43	95.26	96.20	96.54	83.27	77.10	33.71
	RDP	96.00	94.21	97.83	93.78	**98.78**	96.81	95.40	87.47	88.35	58.02
	PrivTra	**97.71**	**98.76**	98.50	**97.03**	97.19	**98.95**	**98.15**	**93.06**	**97.94**	44.95
	SDP	96.95	93.99	98.42	93.97	97.24	97.15	95.57	87.58	87.68	58.02
J48	**Original**	**97.87**	83.91	**98.82**	47.66	97.72	96.21	96.61	93.57	79.73	70.65
	PCA-DR	94.74	**94.97**	91.18	47.80	92.25	96.11	95.17	87.78	74.37	48.63
	RDP	97.25	83.33	98.69	**46.96**	98.52	97.41	97.25	92.91	79.74	**76.63**
	PrivTra	46.52	74.88	98.44	47.68	97.65	**98.49**	**97.44**	92.69	66.06	66.74
	SDP	97.62	83.71	98.12	46.83	98.42	97.10	96.59	**93.69**	**80.01**	76.63
NB	**Original**	**96.80**	73.93	92.32	72.69	92.11	97.48	93.24	85.92	83.22	71.99
	PCA-DR	97.42	86.94	97.27	68.75	87.41	96.61	92.26	50.26	82.78	50.02
	RDP	98.30	74.21	91.96	72.90	91.91	**98.33**	92.57	86.36	83.66	76.81
	PrivTra	98.65	**97.79**	**97.84**	**89.11**	**95.11**	97.58	**98.08**	**93.69**	**97.84**	**85.78**
	SDP	96.93	74.52	92.26	73.43	91.84	98.28	92.15	78.76	85.21	76.23
7KNN	**Original**	94.98	93.31	97.91	91.40	**96.11**	96.81	92.42	87.80	78.56	76.14
	PCA-DR	94.84	94.21	96.32	**92.74**	94.01	97.62	92.41	86.71	47.81	54.89
	RDP	96.08	93.32	97.96	91.48	95.59	**98.47**	91.75	88.20	79.68	**76.98**
	PrivTra	**98.76**	**97.91**	96.39	47.91	94.41	97.61	**98.03**	**93.77**	**84.40**	70.55
	SDP	94.84	93.30	**98.56**	90.71	94.98	98.56	92.69	88.95	79.27	76.98
SVM	**Original**	93.10	83.86	98.15	46.94	95.33	83.11	91.96	62.58	87.13	84.47
	PCA-DR	91.55	83.82	97.22	47.93	87.51	82.73	90.56	37.63	74.78	63.99
	RDP	93.27	84.36	**98.61**	47.18	96.41	82.56	90.31	60.01	88.15	85.07
	PrivTra	**97.53**	**98.96**	97.36	90.81	**97.42**	**97.33**	**97.97**	**93.37**	**97.93**	**86.94**
	SDP	93.20	84.58	98.14	47.10	94.95	81.88	90.52	58.73	88.61	85.07

Table 8.4   Comparison of runtime performances taken for transformation (ms)

Data	PCA-DR	PrivTra	SDP	RDP
MHIRD	4.90	3.67	1.70	1.97
MHORD	4.72	3.54	1.69	2.73
SPFDS	5.23	3.85	1.59	2.28
DOSDS	6.95	5.90	2.07	2.96
SPDOS	12.07	10.08	3.64	3.91
SHIRD	4.44	3.32	1.60	2.63
SHORD	5.13	4.85	2.10	3.03
ITD	1,100.98	1,020.06	258.96	364.29
WTP	2.80	3.10	1.71	2.67
DARPA	105.80	98.05	31.75	33.57

(B1) Efficiency of transformation methods

The objective of this test is to evaluate the runtime taken for transformation of the original data. The time requirements (of PrivTra and baseline methods shown in Table 8.4) have been evaluated in terms of CPU time. In the testing phase, the same working load of the system was ensured and the transformation process is measured in terms of CPU time (in milliseconds).

Table 8.4 shows the time that was required to perform the transformation. Lower values indicate better performance and are shown in bold. From Table 8.4, we observe that SDP and RDP efficiently transform the original data faster than transformed data in comparison to the PCA-DR method and PrivTra framework. On the other hand, it can be seen that the PrivTra framework often performs the transformation process better than the PCA-DR method on most of the datasets except on two, these being WTP and ITD datasets. This can be explained by the fact that the dimensionality of these two datasets is higher than the other datasets. For instance, the dimensionalities of WTP and ITD are 39 and 249, respectively. An improvement of such criteria would be a valuable contribution in future work.

(B2) Efficiency of transformed data on classifiers

The aim of this test is to evaluate the runtime of the classifiers using the transformed data of the framework and the baseline methods. This is an important task, since the supervised methods (discussed in Section 8.4.3) consist of two stages: a model-building stage and a classification step. The former stage uses the training data to build the classifier model, while the latter step uses the testing data to evaluate the generated model. This chapter focused on the model-building stage due to its extremely time-consuming computations, and an accurate model needs to be retrained frequently.

Table 8.5 collects the results obtained for the classifiers' performance over the transformed data by the proposed framework and the baseline methods. Lower values indicate better performance and are shown in bold. The table clearly shows that the

Table 8.5 Comparison of the performance of different classifiers based on transformed data

ML tech	Method	MHIRD	MHORD	DOSDS	SPFDS	SPDOS	SHIRD	SHORD	ITD	WTP	DARPA
MLP	**Original**	2.37	1.99	2.04	1.78	3.06	1.90	2.22	15.42	2.69	1,040.49
	PCA-DR	**1.88**	**1.88**	**1.52**	**1.23**	**2.21**	**1.81**	**2.01**	**14.10**	**1.34**	1,038.32
	RDP	1.98	1.98	1.97	1.63	3.10	1.85	2.04	15.49	2.52	386.26
	PrivTra	1.92	1.94	2.00	1.62	3.04	1.82	2.05	15.30	2.54	**383.42**
	SDP	1.95	1.93	2.23	1.76	3.06	1.92	2.09	15.43	2.53	386.94
J48	**Original**	1.40	1.34	1.17	1.06	1.53	1.32	1.41	3.02	0.80	24.14
	PCA-DR	1.31	1.32	1.09	0.98	1.49	1.28	1.38	**2.69**	0.76	23.51
	RDP	1.32	**1.31**	1.07	0.97	1.46	**1.25**	**1.35**	2.74	**0.78**	24.40
	PrivTra	1.30	**1.31**	**1.08**	**0.95**	**1.44**	1.29	1.36	3.46	0.80	**22.82**
	SDP	**1.29**	1.40	**1.08**	0.96	**1.44**	1.28	1.42	2.74	0.88	23.76
NB	**Original**	1.49	1.37	1.15	1.10	1.54	1.31	1.41	3.22	0.79	**40.49**
	PCA-DR	1.35	1.32	1.11	0.99	1.49	1.30	1.37	3.08	0.74	41.23
	RDP	1.36	1.34	**1.09**	1.00	**1.47**	**1.25**	1.37	3.19	**0.72**	41.92
	PrivTra	**1.34**	**1.31**	1.16	**0.98**	1.50	1.28	**1.35**	3.28	0.73	43.32
	SDP	1.30	1.34	1.19	1.03	1.48	1.26	**1.35**	**3.05**	0.71	42.26
7KNN	**Original**	2.38	2.25	1.85	1.42	3.29	2.18	2.51	7.96	0.86	**989.21**
	PCA-DR	**1.91**	**1.88**	**1.40**	**1.18**	**2.25**	**1.80**	**2.04**	**5.69**	**0.74**	1,005.80
	RDP	2.31	2.29	1.71	1.37	3.36	2.16	2.52	15.23	0.77	1,112.28
	PrivTra	3.05	2.68	1.90	1.47	4.00	2.87	2.84	7.19	0.78	1,767.42
	SDP	2.29	2.26	1.69	1.35	3.24	2.11	2.46	14.85	0.78	1,117.52
SVM	**Original**	1.38	1.37	1.17	1.04	1.50	1.37	1.53	3.58	0.77	26.27
	PCA-DR	1.31	1.32	1.34	1.05	1.46	1.33	1.48	**3.15**	**0.74**	27.20
	RDP	**1.30**	1.32	1.15	0.99	1.46	1.28	**1.38**	3.64	0.69	**24.33**
	PrivTra	1.42	1.34	**1.10**	**0.96**	**1.45**	**1.27**	1.41	3.49	**0.74**	24.94
	SDP	1.34	**1.31**	1.11	0.98	1.49	**1.27**	1.42	3.18	0.77	24.36

transformed data improve the runtime of the classifiers compared with the original data. It can be observed in Table 8.5 that the outcomes of PCA-DR often outperform other methods on the classifier's speed as well as on the independent dataset. This can be explained by the fact that PCA-DR often produces transformed data with less dimensionality than the original data. Note also that PrivTra often proves to be the second best performing transformed method compared to SDP and RDP. Nevertheless, according to Table 8.5, it can be seen that the output of PrivTra helps the NB method to perform better than PCA-DR; this is because NB tends to be more efficient with discretized attributes.

(B3) Scalability test

To test the scalability of the framework in comparison to PCA-DR, SDP, and RDP methods, each method is applied to samples of traffic of increasing size from the DARPA traces using all the flows' attributes (41 attributes). The execution time measures the time taken by PrivTra, PCA-DR, SDP, and RDP to transform the traffic samples on a time-shared dual 3.16 GHz CPU with 3.49 GB memory, running on Windows HP.

Figure 8.6 illustrates the performance of PrivTra, PCA-DR, SDP, and the RDP methods with traffic samples varying from approximately 10×10^3 to 60×10^3 traffic instances. The test averaged over ten trials for each sample to give more accurate average execution times. For all datasets, the k value for the PrivTra was set to 2 (normal and attack), except for the Internet traffic dataset (ITD), where the value of k was set to 10. This is due to the large number of applications is presented in such dataset. Figure 8.6a shows that the SDP and the RDP methods have better performance than the PrivTra and PCA-DR. This is due to the simplicity of these two methods. Furthermore, PrivTra shows significant reduction of computational time in comparison to PCA-DR.

The running time of the PrivTra framework did not depend only upon the number of instances but also upon the dimensionality of the data. Consequently, we need

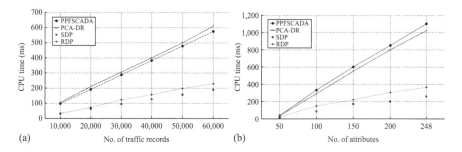

Figure 8.6 *Comparison of the scalability of the four transformation methods. (a) Scalability based on number of records, (b) Scalability based on number of attributes*

to measure the scalability of our framework with an increasing number of attributes and compare it with existing ones. This is particularly important when the number of attributes is large. To do so, we run our experiments on the (ITD) dataset, since this data have the largest number of attributes. In general, we applied each method to samples of traffic with the number of attributes varying from approximately 5 to 249 attributes. We then measure the execution time of each method. The execution time on each sample is repeated 10 times. Figure 8.6(b) shows again that the time taken by SDP and the RDP methods to transform the data is much less than PCA-DR and PrivTra. However, we observe from Figure 8.6 that the two enhancements that can further improve the speed-up factor of PrivTra without changing the way the data transform should include the usage of graphics processing units (GPU) and parallel computing.

(C) Quantifying privacy

Quantifying the privacy of the proposed framework is a key motivation to satisfy the requirements presented in Section 8.2. In particular, the quantity used to measure privacy should indicate how closely the original value of an attribute can be estimated from transformed datasets. This section presents a comparison of the proposed framework with some existing ones, RDP, SDP [344], and PCA-DR [30], in terms of quantifying the privacy. The data security index measures the privacy-preservation level with respect to the variance of data before and after perturbation as follows:

$$S = \frac{Var(X - Y)}{Var(X)} \tag{8.6}$$

where X and Y represent the original and the transformed data respectively. $Var(X)$ is the variance of X. In particular, the previous measures the level of privacy preservation; thus, the larger the index value, the better the protection level.

Table 8.6 compares the level of privacy (%) of the proposed PrivTra framework with the results of baseline methods. The privacy level is computed as (8.6).

Table 8.6   Quantifying privacy of geometric data transformation

Data	PCA-DR	PrivTra	RDP	SDP
MHIRD	1.311	1.630	0.426	0.655
MHORD	0.997	1.334	0.324	0.498
SPFDS	1.786	2.144	0.581	0.893
DOSDS	0.391	1.524	0.127	0.196
SPDOS	0.428	2.539	0.139	0.214
SHIRD	0.376	9.486	0.122	0.188
SHORD	0.955	2.277	0.310	0.477
ITD	1.799	3.798	0.585	0.900
WTP	1.080	2.645	0.351	0.540
DARPA	3.659	8.476	0.214	0.330

The previous table shows that the PrivTra framework outperforms all other methods in terms of a high privacy level on all datasets. RDP and SDP obtain a similar percentage of privacy level, which is lower than that of PCA-DR. Apart from the problem of the low level of privacy, these methods (RDP and SDP) are invertible. Thus, one may be able to estimate the real value of data easily.

To further explore the privacy level of the PrivTra framework against the baseline methods, we performed a Friedman test [345] followed by Nemenyi posthoc test [346]. The former test compares the framework and the baseline methods over N datasets by ranking each method on each dataset separately. In particular, the transformation method with the best performance is ranked 1, the second best ranks 2, and so on. In the case of ties, average ranks are assigned, then the average ranks of all methods on all datasets are calculated and compared. The latter test compares the privacy level in a pairwise manner. In particular, this test determines which method performs statistically different if the average ranks exceed the critical difference $CD_\alpha = q_\alpha \sqrt{k(k+1)/6N}$, where the q_α is calculated based on the *studentized range statistic* [347] divided by $\sqrt{2}$.

Figure 8.7 shows that the privacy level of the PrivTra framework (based on Friedman test) has average ranks significantly different from both RDP and SDP methods. However, the privacy level of PrivTra framework outperforms the PCA-DR method in practice, we reject the hypothesis that there is a significant difference. This is due to the 95% confidence interval for the difference between these methods (under the P-value of 0.05) is $[-.052, 2.52]$ which contains zero.

Figure 8.8 shows the result of a posthoc Nemenyi test with $\alpha = 0.1$ on the ten datasets. The result indicates that privacy level of the PrivTra framework is statistically better than those of RDP and SDP. There is no clear evidence to indicate statistical privacy differences between PrivTra framework and PCA-DR method. This is because the average rank of the PCA-DR method does not exceed the critical difference CD_α.

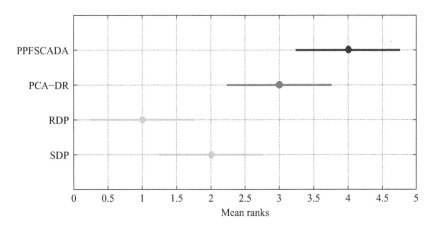

Figure 8.7   *Comparison of privacy level for the four preserving privacy methods based on Friedman test*

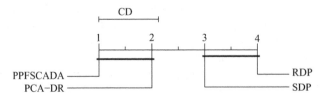

Figure 8.8   Privacy level comparison of all preserving privacy methods against each other based on Nemenyi test

Table 8.7   Compliance of the proposed PrivTra framework and the related methods to desirable requirements

Approach	Dealing with multivariate data	Efficiency problem	Improve data quality	Privacy level
PrivTra	Yes	Suffer from	Yes	High
PCA-DR	No	Partially address	Yes	High
SDP	No	Yes	Yes	Low
RDP	No	Yes	Yes	Low

Note, we perform the posthoc Nemenyi test with ($\alpha = 0.1$, 0.05, and 0.01) and the calculated statistical significance of the privacy level gives almost the same critical difference value. In general, the observations from Figures 8.7 and 8.8 are consistent with the original findings in Table 8.6.

8.4.6   Discussion and summary

As shown in Table 8.7, the PrivTra framework and the baseline methods are validated against the desired requirements (see Section 8.2) that need to be met by any privacy-preserving method. These requirements include four properties: the ability to deal with multivariate data, the capability to improve data utility, the need for efficiency, and the capability of enhancing privacy level. Table 8.7 shows that the proposed PrivTra framework has advantages over the related baseline methods.

First, PrivTra can deal with various types of attributes, while the other related methods can deal only with numerical attributes. Second, extensive experiments show that the PrivTra framework also improves the quality of data. However, the PrivTra framework is significantly better than the baseline methods, but it suffers from the computational time problem. Therefore, a promising future research direction would be to reduce the execution time of the PrivTra framework by using parallel computing, such as multicore CPU or GPU.

8.5 Conclusion

Sharing traffic data is significantly desirable to create accurate and global collaborative classifiers between spatial-domain networks. However, due to various privacy, security, and legal reasons, collaborators avoid to reveal and publish their private traffic data publicly. This chapter described a privacy-preserving framework that ensures the utility of published data and also satisfies the privacy requirements of traffic data. The key contribution of our scheme is the development of a privacy framework (namely, PrivTra) that allows automated permutation to be made to multivariate network traffic data and attributes, including numerical attributes with real values, categorical attributes with unranked nominal values, and attributes with a hierarchical structure. Through experiments, we showed that the PrivTra framework can effectively and efficiently render a balance between data utility and data privacy in comparison to baseline approaches.

Chapter 9

A semi-supervised approach for network traffic labeling

As discussed in the previous two chapters, the recent promising studies for network classification have relied on the analysis of the statistics of traffic flows and the use of machine learning (ML) methods. However, due to the high cost of manual labeling, it is hard to obtain sufficient, reliable, and up-to-date labeled data for effective IP traffic classification. This chapter discusses a novel semi-supervised approach, called Sem-Tra, which automatically alleviates the shortage of labeled flows for ML by exploiting the advantages of both supervised and unsupervised models. In particular, SemTra involves the followings: (i) generating multi-view representations of the original data based on dimensionality reduction methods to have strong discrimination ability; (ii) incorporating the generated representations into the ensemble clustering model to provide a combined clustering output with better quality and stability; (iii) adapting the concept of self-training to iteratively utilize the few labeled data along with unlabeled within local and global viewpoints; and (iv) obtaining the final class decision by combining the decisions of mapping strategy of clusters, the local self-training and global self-training approaches. Extensive experiments were carried out to compare the effectiveness of SemTra over representative semi-supervised methods using 16 network traffic datasets. The results clearly show that SemTra is able to yield noticeable improvement in accuracy (as high as 94.96%) and stability (as high as 95.04%) in the labeling process.

9.1 Introduction

The LOA and GOA methods described in Chapters 6 and 7 are supervised learning methods that require the traffic flows to be labeled in advance to improve the quality of transport layer statistics (TLS), and to identify the optimal and stable feature set from the TLS data. Nevertheless, the traditional setting of supervised methods also required a large amount of training traffic flows to be available in advance to construct a classifier model with a good generalization ability. It is noteworthy that these training flows should be labeled. That means the labels of such training flows should be known in advance. However, in practice, only a limited amount of labeled data is available because obtaining the labels for network flows requires payload data and human efforts. For example, a common practice for labeling network flows requires the payload data and therefore it is time-consuming as well as expensive to manually label the data. Nevertheless, due to privacy concerns, it is hard to release any pay-load data, thereby making it difficult to have *efficient* supervised methods for traffic classification. Thus, the lack of labeled data has motivated the use of unsupervised *clustering* algorithms for traffic classification. The key idea is to discover the structure in traffic data by automatically grouping a set of unlabeled instances to construct application-oriented traffic classifiers using the clustering results. However, traffic classifiers based on the concept of clustering algorithms suffer from a number of limitations, such as (i) setting an optimal number of clusters, (ii) obtaining high-purity traffic clusters, and (iii) mapping a large number of traffic clusters, to a small number of real applications without prior knowledge (class label).

Recently, with the availability of unlabeled data and the difficulty of obtaining labeled ones, a limited number of semi-supervised learning approaches for network traffic classification were proposed, e.g., [34,35]. Unfortunately, these suffer from force assignments problem (as unlabeled flows must belong to fixed traffic classes), scalability, and *novel class* detection problems. This chapter overcomes such limitations with an alternative semi-supervised approach for traffic flow labeling, termed as SemTra, which is based on incorporating the predictions of multiple unsuper-vised and supervised models for better predictions. In particular, the prediction information for unlabeled instances is derived from diversified and heterogeneous models. The strength of one usually complements the weakness of the other, and thus maximizing the agreement among them can boost the performance of the labeling process.

The important points made in this chapter can be summarized as follows:

- A multi-view approach, which creates multiple representations of the original traffic data (termed as single-view data), is presented here. This is particularly important since many interesting patterns cannot be extracted from a single view and also each representation may reveal different view of the data. Also we incor-porated two different distance metrics (including *Euclidean distance* and *point symmetry distance*) in a clustering algorithm to reveal the underlying data space structure from multiple data representations by considering both spherical and arbitrary shapes.
- Explore the concept of evidence accumulation clustering (EAC) [348] to combine the results of each clustering output on different representations. In particular, the EAC would not directly generate a class label prediction for unlabeled instances, but it would provide useful constraints on the joint prediction for such unlabeled instances.
- Describe a novel mapping strategy based on both the internal-structure of the cluster, as well as a probability function to improve the mapping process from a cluster to a class label. A local self-training approach is described to address the overlapping issue within a cluster and to iteratively predict the class label for unlabeled data from the local viewpoint.
- Describe a meta-level learning approach that combines the output of the initial clustering process on the multiple representations and the original attributes to

form a global view. The resultant global view is subsequently fed to a global self-training method to iteratively predict the class label from the global viewpoint. Cascading the decision of the clustering process enables local and global self-training to make better class label predictions.

The performance of SemTra is evaluated on 16 traffic datasets, which included binary classes (e.g., normal/attack) and multi-classes (e.g., WWW, FTP, and peer-to-peer (P2P)). The performance of SemTra is also compared with a few well-known semi-supervised methods, namely, *SemiBoost* [349], *probabilistic graphical model (PGM)* [35], *bipartite graph-based consensus maximization (BGCM)* [350], and *offline/real-time semi-supervised classification (ORTSC)* [34], using various metrics including accuracy, F-measure, stability, and runtime performance. Experimental results show that SemTra is, in most cases, more effective than the benchmarked semi-supervised methods, with an average accuracy of 94.96% on the binary-class dataset and 93.84% on the multi-class datasets. The rest of the chapter is organized as follows. SemTra is discussed in detail in Section 9.2, and the performance of SemTra is evaluated on different network traffic datasets in Section 9.3.

9.2   The semi-supervised traffic flow labeling

A more recent class of network traffic classification approaches developed using ML methods, e.g., [12,34,35,351,352], have become popular because of their high detection accuracy and efficiency. However, accurate ground truth creation is mandatory for proper training and evaluation. To produce accurate results, a huge and accurately labeled dataset is necessary, involving a tremendous workload and cost. SemTra is a new semi-supervised labeling approach to produce such amount of data without involving tedious labeling processes and achieve that goal at reasonable cost.

Figure 9.1 provides an overview of SemTra, consisting the following modules: (1) representation extraction, (2) initial clustering analysis, (3) ensemble clustering analysis, (4.1) label propagation, (4.2) local self-training, (5) global self-training and (6) function agreement. In the representation extraction module, to achieve diversity among traffic data, different representations are extracted by transforming raw traffic data to feature vectors of fixed dimensionality. In the initial clustering analysis module, a clustering algorithm is applied to different representations received from the representation extraction module. As a result, a different partition for a given dataset is generated based on each representation and different distance measurements. In the ensemble clustering analysis, all partitions previously obtained by applying the clustering analysis on different representations using different distances measurements are fed to the clustering ensemble module for the reconciliation to a final partition. The label propagation module infers each cluster's class label by making full use of both labeled traffic data and internal structure information in each cluster. In the local self-training, the labeled data in each cluster are iteratively utilized along with unlabeled data to predict the class label. In the global self-training step, an adapted classifier-based method has been developed to iteratively manipulate the whole dataset along

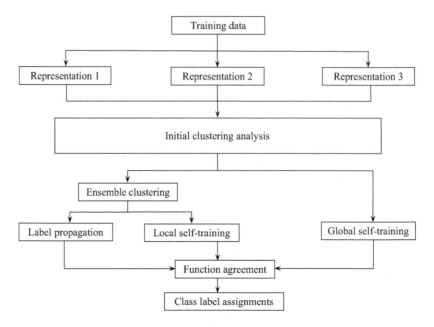

Figure 9.1   Overview of the proposed SemTra approach

with the cluster-association matrix (which summarizes the results of the initial clustering analysis) to predict the class label from a global perspective. In the agreement function, the decisions of the label propagation and the local and global self-training steps are combined to generate the final class label for the unlabeled data.

9.2.1   The multi-view layer

Multi-view learning is a proven approach to improve classification performance [353,354]. However, this approach is not applicable to the process of traffic labeling. This is due to the fact that traffic data are represented just by a single view, also meaning that the data are represented by only one set of attributes (and therefore not properly separated into several distinct sets of attributes). To improve the performance of the labeling process, a multi-view layer that provides multiple representations of the original data is proposed in this chapter. This is based on the assumption that many interesting patterns cannot be extracted from a single view, and also each representation may reveal different structures of the data.

In the proposed multi-view layer, traffic data are processed with different heuristics for dimensionality reduction to act as representation methods. Employing dimensionality reduction to the labeling process for traffic data can also bring several advantages: (i) it reduces noise and correlation within the data, (ii) it obtains 2D/3D visualization for exploratory data analysis, (iii) it reduces the space and time-computational complexity of the classifier and clustering methods, and (iv) it alleviates the problem of over-fitting by constructing combinations of the variables. Dimensionality reduction methods fall into two categories, namely, *global* and *local* [355]. The former derive embeddings in which all points satisfy a given criterion, whereas the latter methods construct embeddings in which only local neighborhoods are required to meet a given criterion. Consequently, the global methods tend to give a more "faithful" representation of the data's global structure, and their metrics-preserving properties are better theoretically understood. Thus, we have chosen the three common global methods as suitable candidates for the proposed multi-view layer. These methods include the followings: Isomap [356], random projections (RP) [357], and kernel principle component analysis (KPCA) [358].

- **Isomap:** This approach is a well-known manifold method that guarantees a globally optimal solution. It preserves the intrinsic geometry of the nonlinear data by utilizing the geodesic manifold distances between data points. In particular, the process of creating a new view of traffic data is briefly summarized as follows:
  - Construct a neighborhood graph. In particular, two flows are considered to be neighbors if they satisfy a predefined condition, which states that either their distance in the original datasets is shorter than a constant, or one of the flows belongs to the k-nearest neighbors of the other flows. Based on this neighborhood information, a weighted graph containing all flows in the datasets is built.
  - Compute the shortest path distances in the neighborhood graph using Dijkstra's algorithm [359]. The output of calculating the shortest path is a matrix expressing the geodesic distances of each pair of flows.
  - Apply a classical multidimensional scaling (MDS) to the output matrix (obtained in the previous step) to construct an embedding of the data that best preserves the manifold's estimated intrinsic geometry.
- **RP:** This approach is one of the most powerful dimension reduction methods, which uses RP matrices to project the data into lower dimensional spaces. In the following, we formally describe the steps of using the RP approach to create a new view of the traffic data.
  - Transform the instances of flows in the datasets $X \in \mathbb{R}^p$ into a lower dimensional space $S \in \mathbb{R}^q$, where $q \ll p$, via

  $$S = RX \tag{9.1}$$

  The output is a matrix G of size $q \times N$, where q is the new dimensionality of the flows and N is the size of the traffic dataset.

  $$G = (x_1 \,|x_2| \cdots |x_N) \tag{9.2}$$

  - Generate j random matrices $\{R_i\}_{i=1}^{j}$, where j is the number of desirable views. The two common ways of generating the random entries are as follows:
    - The vectors are uniformly distributed over the q dimensional unit sphere.
    - The elements of vectors are chosen from a Bernoulli $+1/-1$ distribution and the vectors are normalized.
  - Normalize the columns so that their l_2 norm will be 1.
  - Obtain $\{T_i\}_{i=1}^{j}$ views by projecting the matrix G onto the random matrices $\{R_i\}_{i=1}^{j}$, i.e., $T_i = R_i \cdot G$, where $i = 1, \ldots, j$.

- **KPCA:** This approach is a generalization of principle component analysis (PCA), which is one of the primary statistical methods for feature extraction and data modeling. This method utilizes the *kernel trick* to model the nonlinear structures that exist in network traffic data. In particular, to perform KPCA on the network traffic data, the following steps have to be carried out:
  - Choose a kernel mapping $K(x_m, x_n)$ (e.g., Gaussian, Sigmoid, and Polynomial).
  - Obtain a matrix of $N \times N$ kernel elements (referred to as **K**) from the original traffic data.
  - Get the eigenvectors $a_i = \left[a_1^{(i)}, \ldots, a_N^{(i)} \right]^T$, and the eigenvalues λ_i of the covariance matrix in the feature space by solving the eigenvalue problem of **K**.
  - Obtain the principal components of each given instance X in the feature space as follows:

$$(f(x) \cdot \phi_i) = \sum_{n=1}^{N} a_n^{(i)} k(x, x_n) \tag{9.3}$$

  - Keep only a small number of principal components corresponding to the largest eigenvalues without losing much information by applying a regular PCA.

However, from the discussion on the design idea of the multi-view layer, the dimensionality reduction methods which could be used to create multiple representations (of the original traffic data) should not be limited to what we discussed.

The process of creating a multi-view of the original traffic data is summarized in Algorithm 1. Let $N_{ij} = \{(x_1, y_1), (x_2, y_2), (x_n, y_n)\}$ be a set of n flow instances.

Algorithm 1: Processing of generating multi-view layer

   Input :
1   $Data(N_{ij}) \longleftarrow \{f_1, f_2, \ldots, f_{n-1}\}$;
2   $ViewType \longleftarrow \{Iso, RP, KPCA\}$;
   Output:
3   $View_{ij}$ // multi-view data
4   **if** *Label is Removed* **then**
5 | **switch** *View Type* **do**
6 | **case** *Isomap* **do**
7 | $\lfloor [NM_{Iso}] \longleftarrow IsomapView([N_{ij}])$;
8 | **case** *RP* **do**
9 | $\lfloor [NM_{PR}] \longleftarrow RPView([N_{ij}])$;
10 | **case** *KPCA* **do**
11 | $\lfloor [NM_{KPCA}] \longleftarrow KPCAView([N_{ij}])$;

12   $[View_{ij}] \longleftarrow ([NM_{Iso}], [NM_{PR}], [NM_{KPCA}])$;

Each $x_i = \{x_{ij} | 1 \leq j \leq m\}$, where m is the number of features and x_{ij} is the value of the jth feature for the ith flow instance. The process starts by discarding the label class from the original data before passing on to view type which is based on dimensionality reduction methods. Then, project the original data into lower dimensional spaces ($\mathbb{R}^q$ where $q \ll n$) based on each method. Their output is a set of column vectors in the lower dimensional space.

Figure 9.2 illustrates how the proposed multi-view layer produces very distinct representations of the original DOSDS dataset [360]. A single representation simply

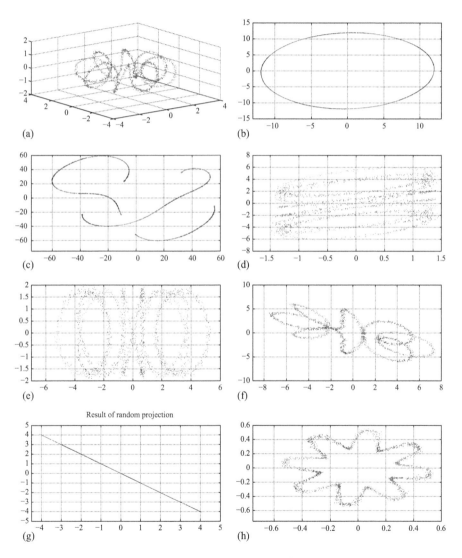

Figure 9.2 *Different views of the traffic data using the multi-view layer: (a) original view, (b) Isomap view, (c)–(g) random projection view, and (h) KPCA view*

captures partial structural information and thus, the joint use of the different representation is more likely to capture the intrinsic structure of the given traffic data. An open issue for research is how to discover a consensus partition of all representations that is superior to any single representation. To address this problem, our multi-view layer exploits the complementary information in different views of network data, as discussed in Section 9.2.3.

9.2.2   Initial clustering analysis

To achieve a better class separation, we opted to bring in clustering to partitioned traffic data into multiple clusters. Clustering is the process of partitioning a dataset into multiple groups, where each group contains data patterns that are very similar in terms of specific distance measurements. Based on the different data representations with lower dimensionality, any existing algorithm is applicable to efficiently cluster the data. Among the various clustering algorithms, K-means [361] has been chosen for the following reasons: (i) it is a data-driven method with relatively a few assumptions on the distribution of the underlying data, and (ii) it guarantees a local minimum of the criterion function, thereby accelerating the convergence of clusters on large datasets. The major limitation, however, is its inability to identify clusters with arbitrary shapes, ultimately imposing hyperspherical-shaped clusters on the data.

In the first stage, K-means is performed on the training instances to obtain k disjoint clusters. In an ideal situation, each K-means cluster represents a region of similar instances, which "similar" in terms of distances between the instances and their centroid. This basic K-means cluster works well when the flows (applications) conform to the assumptions and the procedure of K-means . The assumptions are that the flows are generated by a mixture model, and that there is a correspondence between mixture components and classes. However, these assumptions are often violated in practice and can result in poor performance due to high similarity between different patterns. Since these assumptions hold in traffic data, our approach achieves diversity among patterns by exploiting both different distance metrics as well as different number of clusters k. In particular, the *Euclidean distance* [362] and *point symmetry distance* [362] are considered. The Euclidean distance is one of the most common forms of the general Minkowski distance metrics, which measures dissimilarity, and helps the conventional K-means algorithm to detect hyperspherical-shaped clusters. Given N patterns $x_i = (x_{i_1}, \ldots, x_{i_n})^T$, where $i=\{1, \ldots, N\}$, the Euclidean distance metric for measuring the dissimilarity between the jth and kth patterns is defined by:

$$d(j, k) = \left(\sum_{i=1}^{n} |x_{ji} - x_{ki}|^2 \right)^{(1/2)} \tag{9.4}$$

noteworthy that the smaller value of $d(j, k)$ is, the greater the similarity will be. By using Euclidean distance as a measure of similarity, hyperspherical-shaped clusters of equal size are usually detected [363].

On the other hand, to take care of clusters with arbitrary shapes and size, and for situations where there is no a priori information about the geometric characteristics of a traffic dataset, it is necessary to consider another more flexible measure. A nonmetric distance based on the concept of "point symmetry" is applied to the K-means algorithm. The point symmetry distance is defined as follows: given N patterns $\underline{x}_j, i = \{1, \ldots, N\}$, and reference vector $\underline{c}$ (e.g., a cluster centroid), the *point symmetry distance* between a pattern $\underline{x}_j$ and the reference vector $\underline{c}$ is defined as:

$$d_s(x_j, c) = \min \frac{\left\| (\underline{x}_j - \underline{c}) + (\underline{x}_i - \underline{c}) \right\|}{\left\| (\underline{x}_j - \underline{c}) + (\underline{x}_i - \underline{c}) \right\|} \tag{9.5}$$

The denominator normalizes the point symmetry distance and makes it insensitive to Euclidean distances. In particular, $d_s(\underline{x}_j, c)$ is minimized when the pattern $x_i = 2\underline{c} - \underline{x}_j$ exists in the dataset (i.e., $d_s(\underline{x}_j; \underline{c}) = 0$).

In general, by using different distance metrics, the vicinities identified for a given flow can be different, even when the same k is used; whereas by using different k values, the predictions for a given flow also can be different, even when the same distance metric is used. Thus, K-means may be able to somewhat diversify the network flows by partitioning them with different distance metrics and/or different k values. Such a setting can also bring another advantage, that is, since it is usually difficult to decide which distance metric and k value are better for the labeling task. Inspired by the work in sensor fusion and classifier combination [267,350,364], the functions of such distance metrics can be combined to explore distinct views of flow relationships. Therefore, the K-means clustering algorithm takes each data representation X as input and organizes the n flows into k clusters according to different distance metrics and may produce different partitions for the same dataset, either in terms of cluster membership and/or the number of clusters produced.

An open issue for research is to find the final consensus partition (from the different K-means runs on different representations) in a computationally efficient manner. To address this problem, the use of a consensus function in Section 9.2.3 is considered.

9.2.3   Ensemble clustering

In the area of ML, combining several self-contained predicting algorithms (into an ensemble to yield better performance in terms of accuracy than any of the base predictors) is backed by a sound theoretical background [365–367]. Thus, with the aim of achieving accurate results superior to that of any individual clustering, in this section, a cluster ensemble approach is described to combine the partitions of different clustering algorithms based on each representation to produce a consensus partition.

Figure 9.3 shows a general picture of the cluster ensemble framework. Essentially, all segment representations received from the representation extracting module (see Section 9.2.1) are fed to the ensemble clustering-based module. As a result, multiple partitions for a given dataset are generated based on each representation as well as on the various clustering settings. Then, producing the final solution can simply be

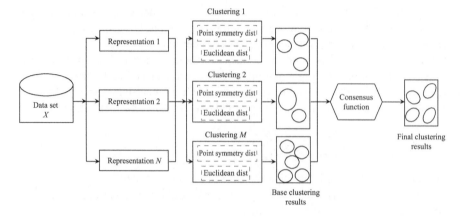

Figure 9.3   The basic process of cluster ensemble

achieved by aggregating all partitions of the base clustering according to a *consensus function*. In the following subsections, the various steps of the framework of the cluster ensemble are discussed in detail.

Consensus function of clustering

The consensus function is concerned with finding a consensus partition that improves the performance of *weak* clustering algorithms. Although there is a wide variety of consensus functions in the literature [368,369], we explored the EAC [348] method as the optimal consensus function to extract the final partition by combining the results of the different data representations and multiple-distance metrics. This method combines the results of multiple-distance metrics, which are obtained from the initial clustering step, into a single data partition by viewing each distance metric result as independent evidence of data organization. In particular, each result of K-means clustering is mapped to co-occurrences, where entries can be interpreted as votes on the pairwise co-occurrences of flows and are computed as the number of times each pair of flows co-occurs in the same cluster. The underlying assumption is that flows belonging to a "natural" cluster are very likely to be allocated to the same cluster regardless of what data representation or distance measure is used. Formally, the value of each co-occurrence matrix entry can be calculated as follows:

$$C(x_i, x_j) = \frac{1}{m} \sum_{t=1}^{m} \delta(P_t(x_i), P_t(x_j)) \tag{9.6}$$

$$\delta(P_t(x_i), P_t(x_j)) = \begin{cases} 1 & \text{if } P(x_i)= P(x_j) \\ 0 & \text{otherwise} \end{cases} \tag{9.7}$$

where $C(x_i, x_j)$ donates the number of times the pairs of flows (x_i, x_j) appear in the same cluster among m partitions, and $\delta(P_t(x_i), P_t(x_j)) = 1$ if $x_i = x_j$, and 0 otherwise.

The final consensus clustering is extracted by applying the graph-based *METIS* algorithm [370] on the co-association matrix. The main principle of this algorithm is to minimize the edge cutting by making the weight of vertex distributed evenly among different regions. Thus, it is expected that obtaining the final partition in such a way will better explain the natural grouping of the traffic data.

Cluster mapping process

The final step of our ensemble clustering approach is the mapping phase. The aim is to map descriptive labels to clusters that reflect their contents. This step is very important to determine the label associated with each flow in the final partition. Unfortunately, estimating the labeling confidence in ensemble clustering is not as straightforward as in classification. This is because the labeling confidence for classification can be estimated directly by checking the probability of the unlabeled flows being labeled to a finite number of classes, whereas the process of ensemble clustering tends to group highly correlated traffic flows to geometrically remain very close. Consequently, the underlying challenge is to classify such flows, especially when patterns from multiple classes overlap within a cluster.

A mapping mechanism to estimate the genuine class label of unlabeled flows is described here. In general, the performance of the proposed mapping process depends on the content of the cluster. If all the flows in a cluster belong to the same class, then the mapping is unique and is simply mapped to the correspondent class. We refer to these clusters as *atomic* clusters [267]. *Nonatomic* clusters, however, are comprised of different classes, and these are labeled according to the proposed mapping strategy, which depends on the internal structure of cluster and the probabilistic value of the labeled flows in the cluster.

In particular, for the internal structure of a cluster, we assume an important property of each class: that instances belonging to the same class should be closer to each other (referred to as *cohesion*) and also should be apart from the instances that belong to other classes (*referred to as separation*) [371]. This assumption is generalized by introducing the concept of cohesion of cluster.

Definition 9.1 (Cohesion of cluster). *Instances within class y_i are said to be cohesive if they have minimum mean distance $\overline{D}_{i_{\min}}$ among all $\overline{D}_i$. The mean distance $\overline{D}_i$ is defined as*

$$\overline{D}_i = \frac{1}{\left|\Omega_{l_{y_i}}^{C_k}\right|} \sum_{l=1}^{\left|\Omega_{l_{y_i}}^{C_k}\right|} \sum_{u=1}^{|\Gamma_u^{C_k}|} D(x_l, x_u) \tag{9.8}$$

where $\Omega_{l_{y_i}}^{k}$ is a set of label instances of class y_i in cluster k, and $\Gamma_u^{C_k}$ is a set of unlabeled instances in cluster k. $D(x_l, x_u)$ is the distance between the labeled instance x_l and unlabeled instance x_u in some appropriate metric. For a fair comparison between cohesion of different classes with unlabeled instances within a cluster, all cohesion factors should have the same scale. To do so, its weighted factor is defined.

Definition 9.2 (weighted cohesion factor—WCF). *The WCF of class y_i in cluster C^k is defined as*

$$WCF = 1 - \frac{\overline{D}_i}{\sum_{l=1}^{q} \overline{D}_l} \tag{9.9}$$

It is obvious that the value of *WCF* close to 1 implies a high level of cohesion between instances labeled with class y_i and unlabeled instances Γ_u^k, and a value close to 0 implies a low level of cohesion. However, knowing the WCF value does not necessarily reflect the actual class of a cluster. Therefore, we need to utilize a probabilistic measurement $P(\omega_{lk})$ to find a mapping from a cluster to an actual class label.

Let $\Omega_{l_{y_i}}^k$ be the subset of labeled instances representing all labeled instances that appear in cluster C_k:

$$\Omega_{l_{y_i}}^k = \left\{ y | y \in \Omega_{l_{y_i}}^k, F_{y_i} > 0 \right\} = \bigcup_{i=1}^{n} y_i^k, \ \Omega_{l_{y_i}}^k \neq 0 \tag{9.10}$$

where F_{y_i} is the number of assurances (frequency) of class y_i in cluster C^k. Let N denote the total number of observed labeled instances in cluster C^k:

$$N = \sum_{y \in \Omega_{l_{y_i}}^k} F_y = \sum_{i=1}^{n} |y_i^k|, \quad N \in \mathbb{IN}, N \geq n. \tag{9.11}$$

Definition 9.3 (probability measurement). *The probability of the labeled instances for a given class y_i in cluster k is defined as*

$$P(\omega_{1k}) = \frac{F_{y_i}}{N} \tag{9.12}$$

Finally, the decision function for assigning a class label to a cluster is based on the maximum decision function of both the *WCF* and the probabilistic value $P\omega_{1k}$. This is particularly important since reliance on any single measurement may lead to misleading conclusions. The decision function for assigning class label to a cluster is defined as follows:

$$C_i^k = \arg\max \left(P(\omega_{1k}) \times \left[1 - \frac{\overline{D}_i}{\sum_{l=1}^{|k|} \overline{D}_l} \right] \right) \tag{9.13}$$

WCF penalizes the probability of instances Ω_l labeled to a particular class y_i in cluster s with its mean distance from the unlabeled instances Γ_u, i.e., a high value of $\overline{D}_i$ yields a low MP_i score and vice versa.

To this end, if a cluster C^k is given a class label with respect to the decision function defined in (9.13), each of its unlabeled instances can automatically inherit the same class label. To complete the mapping, clusters that do not have any labeled instances assigned to them should have a different class label from any of the existing classes and be named *novel class*.

Figure 9.4 illustrates the type and the proportion of the clusters with respect to the number of clusters on both binary and multi-class traffic datasets. A general

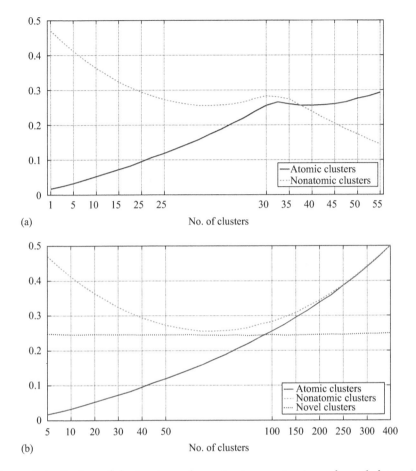

Figure 9.4   *Portion of clusters types (e.g., atomic, nonatomic, and novel clusters) based on the number of clusters: (a) variation of number# of clusters on the multi-class dataset (IT1) and (b) variation of number# of clusters on the binary-class dataset (DOSDS)*

observation from Figure 9.4, indicates that even though setting the number of cluster to a large k can increase the portion of high-purity traffic clusters (referred to as atomic clusters), there is still a large proportion of nonatomic and novel clusters requiring further investigation.

9.2.4   Local self-training

In the previous phase, the proposed mapping strategy ensures that each training flow is associated with only one cluster. However, the traffic datasets may contain overlapping patterns from different classes, resulting in subgroups or overlap within clusters.

However, identifying the class boundaries between overlapping class patterns within clusters is a difficult problem. To handle such a challenge, the second phase of Sem-Tra refines the decision boundaries for each class by utilizing the available labeled and unlabeled flows in each cluster. In particular, the proposed approach learns the accurate decision boundaries and iteratively improves the labeling process. At each iteration, the labeled flows in each cluster are selected to train the given classification learning algorithm. The trained classification model will produce k scores, indicating the likelihood that the unlabeled flow belongs to each of the k traffic classes. Unlabeled flow then must be assigned to the traffic class with the highest score. The assigned labels are hereafter referred to as pseudo-labels. The labeled flows along with the selected pseudo-label flows are utilized in the next iteration to retrain the classifier, and the process is repeated.

Choice of supervised learning algorithms

To strike a good balance between accuracy and scalability, the described approach finds a discriminative decision boundary in the *nonatomic* clusters [267] (that builds on the idea of the support vector machine (SVM) algorithm [315]). The SVM algorithm is chosen as a suitable candidate for the following reasons:

- It is scalable to very large date sets.
- It is highly accurate, owing to its ability to model complex nonlinear decision boundaries, which can be generalized to overlapping and fuzzy patterns.
- It has a small number of user-tunable parameters.

In practice, the SVM algorithm transforms training data into a higher dimension. Within this new dimension, it then searches for the linear optimal decision boundary (which is referred to as a *hyperplane*). The SVM uses both the *support vector* and the *margin* to find a hyperplane that separates objects of one class from objects of other classes at the maximal margin. To this end, the SVM finds the maximum marginal hyperplane using the following objective function:

$$\min_{w,b,\xi} = C \sum_{i=1}^{n} \xi_i + \frac{1}{2} \|w\|^2 \tag{9.14}$$

$$s.t \ y_i(w^T x_i + b) \geq 1 - \xi_i$$

$$\xi_i \geq 0, \quad i = 1, \ldots, N$$

where x_i belongs to the training instances D_l, ξ_i is a slack variable for labeled data, and C is a constant parameter used as a trade-off between the two goals of learning minimization of error and maximization of margin. Note that the SVM algorithm is used for classification and prediction, which means that the training flows need to be labeled first. Consequently, we need to incorporate pseudo-labels flows with the labeled flows. To do so, we modify the objective functions of SVM algorithm as follows:

$$\min_{w,b,\xi} = C\left(\sum_{i=1}^{n}\xi_i + \lambda_1\sum_{j=1}^{m}\xi_j\right) + \frac{1}{2}\|w\|^2 \tag{9.15}$$

$$s.t\ y_i(w\cdot x_i + b) \geq 1 - \xi_i \quad \text{(labeled data)}$$

$$\lambda_1 y_j(w\cdot x_j + b) \geq 1 - \xi_j \quad \text{(labeled data)}$$

$$\xi_i \geq 0, \quad i = 1,\ldots,n,\ \xi_j \geq 0, \quad j = 1,\ldots,m$$

where x_j belongs to the pseudo-label flows $D_{p2}\ D_{p2}\ (D_{p2} \subset D_u)$; ξ_j is a slack variable for pseudo-labels flows, and $\lambda_1 \in [0, 1]$ is a weighting parameter to regulate the impact of labeled flows and pseudo-labels flows. Hence, the modified objective functions are still convex, avoiding the problem of local maxima (minima).

However, to efficiently solve the optimization problem of the modified objective function, we used the Gauss–Seidel/smo method introduced in [372] to calculate its dual. In particular, the iterative process of the self-training utilized the modified objective function to gradually increase the amount of pseudo-label flows, which is expected to play an important role in the labeling of new data. Therefore, we do not re-weight the labeled and pseudo-label data in the objective functions. Furthermore, we define a hybrid objective function to estimate the optimum values of λ_1 during local self-training.

The following steps are taken by SemTra in the second phase to assign class labels to unlabeled flows in each *nonatomic* cluster. Let $X = (x_1,\ldots,X_n) \in \mathbb{R}^{n\times d}$ denote the entire dataset, which consists of n flow instances in d-dimensional space. The dataset includes both the labeled data $X_l = (x_l, y_l)_{l=1}^{L} \in X \times Y$, (where $y_i \in 0, 1$, representing a binary classification decision of "0" to indicate *normal* and "1" to indicate *anomaly* class assignments) and unlabeled data $X_u = (x_u)_{u=L+1}^{L+U} \in X$.

- **Step 1.** Train the standard SVM algorithm using X_l, and perform prediction on X_u. The output of this step would be the predicted labels of the unlabeled flows being labeled to different classes $\left[y^{(1)}(1),\ldots,y^{(1)}(l_n)\right]$
- **Step 2.** Estimate the initial labeling confidence by consulting the probabilities of the predicted labels, obtained in the previous step. For example, suppose the probability of the flow **a** being classified to class l_1 and l_2 is 0.95 and 0.05, respectively, whereas that of the flow **b** is 0.60 and 0.40, respectively. Then, the flow **a** is more likely to be labeled to class l_1. The assigned labels are hereafter referred to as the pseudo-labels and denoted as X_s.
- **Step 3.** Utilize the labeled flows along with pseudo-labels flows to produce a new augmented training data $X_l^k = X_l + X_s$, and remove the pseudo-labels from the unlabeled set $X_u^k = X_u - X_s$.
- **Step 4.** Use the augmented training data $X_l^k = X_l + X_s$ for training the SVM in the next iteration (k), resulting in a new classier model which can be used to perform prediction on $X_u^k = X_u - X_s$.

- **Step 5.** Calculate the modified objective function value in (9.16) after using the augmented training data X_l^k as follows:

$$f(w^{(k)}, \xi^{(k)}) = C \left(\sum_{i=1}^{n} \xi_i^{(k)} + \lambda_1 \sum_{j=1}^{m} \xi_j^{(k)} \right) + \frac{1}{2} \| w^{(k)} \|^2 \qquad (9.16)$$

- **Step 6.** Repeat the steps 2–5 until the stopping criterion determines when the process should stop. Here, a predefined stopping criterion δ_0 terminates the process if the value of the objective function in the current iteration k is worse than the value of the objective function in the previous iteration $k - 1$; otherwise, the algorithm continues to expand the labeled data at the next iteration. Consequently, at the end of the $(k+1)$ iteration, the output would be the predicted labeled $\left[y^{(k+1)}(1), \ldots, y^{(k+1)}(l_n) \right]$.

From the local point of view, data instances in the same cluster can be very similar. However, due to the overlapping issue existing within a cluster, unlabeled instances may have different class labels with respect to the global point of view (whole datasets). Thus, this issue will be addressed in the following section.

9.2.5　Global self-training on meta-level features

In the previous section, it was explained how the local self-training phase can predict the class label based on the local information in each cluster. However, this phase might not fully exploit the distribution of unlabeled instances in the context of the whole dataset (i.e., by building the classification model only from instances in each cluster, while ignoring instances in other clusters). With the aim of improving the labeling process, this section proposes new extended meta-level features to represent the global information as well as global self-training to learn at the meta level. The extended meta-level features are comprised of two parts: the first part represents the original features, whereas the second part represents the output of each cluster on each representation that is subsequently considered a new attribute. Consequently, the labeled instances in the extended meta-level set would be represented as follows:

$$\Gamma_l = \{ [F_1(X_l), \ldots, F_N(X_l), C_1(X_l), \ldots, C_M(X_l), Y_l] \}_{i=1}^{L} \qquad (9.17)$$

where L stands for the number of instances, $F_1(X_l), \ldots, F_N$ represents the original features of labeled instances X_l, and $C_1(X_l), \ldots, C_M(X_l)$ is the output of each cluster on different data representations of labeled instances X_l.

The unlabeled instances would be represented as follows:

$$\Gamma_u = \{ [F_1(X_u), \ldots, F_N(X_u), C_1(X_u), \ldots, C_M(X_u)] \}_{u=L+1}^{L+U} \qquad (9.18)$$

where $L + U$ stands for the number of unlabeled instances, $F_1(X_u), \ldots, F_N(X_u)$ represents original features of unlabeled instances X_u, and $C_1(X_u), \ldots, C_M(X_u)$ is the output of each cluster on different data representations of unlabeled instances X_u.

The extended meta-level features are applied as a training set for the global self-training process. Given that the global self-training step tries to use unlabeled instances in the meta level to adjust the decision boundary learned from the small number of labeled instances, such that it goes through the less dense region while keeping the labeled data correctly classified. In particular, the global self-training initially initiates an SVM using labeled instances and assigns potential labels to unlabeled instances. Then, it iteratively maximizes the margin for both labeled and unlabeled instances with their potential labels by flipping the labels of the unlabeled instances on different sides of the decision boundary. An optimal prediction is reached when the decision boundary not only classifies the labeled instances as accurately as possible, but also avoids going through the high-density region.

9.2.6 Function agreement and labeling

Algorithm 2 sketches the labeling process of SemTra. During this process, the unlabeled flows must be assigned labels following two main criteria: (i) unlabeled flows

---

Algorithm 2: Function of agreement and labeling

    Input   :

1 $D_L = \{(x_1, y_1), \ldots, (x_l, y_l)\}$, $D_{UL} = \{x_{l+1}, \ldots, x_n\}$;

2 $Iter = 50, \beta = 2, \vartheta = Iter - 1$;

    Output :

3 $[D_L] = [x_{ij}] \cdot [class_i]$; // Augmented labeled data

4 **foreach** $i \in [1, Iter]$ **do**

5      $MP \longleftarrow$ ApplyMP(D_{UL}); // mapping function

6   **if** $D_{UL} \in$ *atomic* **then**

7          $D_L \longleftarrow D_L \cup atomic(X)$;

8          $D_{UL} \longleftarrow D_{UL} \setminus atomic(X)$;

9   **if** $D_{UL} \in$ *Novel* **then**

10         $D_L \longleftarrow D_L \cup Novel(X)$;

11         $D_{UL} \longleftarrow D_{UL} \setminus Novel(X)$;

12      $LST \longleftarrow$ ApplyLST(D_{UL});// Local self-training

13      $GST \longleftarrow$ ApplyLST(D_{UL});// Global self-training

14   **for** $x \in D_{UL}$ **do**

15   majority-voting $\longleftarrow$ ComputeVote (MP, LST, GST, x) ;

16   **if** *majority-voting* $\geq \beta$ **then**

17           $D_L \longleftarrow D_L \cup x$;

18   **else**

19   *tempList* $\longleftarrow$ *tempList* $\cup x$;

20   *tempCount* $\longleftarrow$ Count(*tempList*);

21   **if** *tempCount(x)* $\geq \vartheta$ **then**

22   *outlierList* $\longleftarrow$ *outlierList* $\cup x$;

                // Add to outlier List

23   *tempList* $\longleftarrow$ *tempList* $\setminus$ *outlierList*;

24      $D_{UL} \longleftarrow$ *tempList*;

---

with high similarity must share the same label, and (ii) those unlabeled flows which are highly similar to a labeled flow must share its label. Thus, to follow these two criteria, we assume that all the unlabeled instances (in atomic clusters) belong to the same class, so the algorithm (see lines 5–11) immediately assigns the class label of instances with its corresponding cluster's label and then updates the labeled and unlabeled instances (D_L, D_{UL}). Lines 9–11 of Algorithm 2 check whether clusters have only unlabeled instances and do not have any labeled instances assigned to them. If so, the algorithm defines these unlabeled instances in such clusters as *novel class* and then updates the labeled and unlabeled instances (D_L, D_{UL}).

However, the remaining unlabeled instances do not necessarily match any of previously mentioned criteria. This implies that we may need additional guidance to improve the labeling process by combining the decision of the first phase (cluster mapping process) along with the second phase (local self-training) and the third phase (global self-training) to give a final decision on the class membership of unlabeled flows. Since the prediction of these three phases is derived from diversified and heterogeneous sources, the consensus combination can significantly boost the performance by producing more accurate results. In lines 12–24 of Algorithm 2, a class label is assigned to an unlabeled instance by taking majority votes among the three different phases. Otherwise, if all phases did not have agreement on the predicted class, Algorithm 2 would consider such instances as outliers and remove them from the dataset.

9.3   Experimental evaluation

This section demonstrates the effectiveness of the proposed SemTra approach by conducting extensive experiments on a number of benchmark datasets covering traditional computer network traffic datasets and industrial network (SCADA) datasets. In particular, the objective of this section is to investigate the effectiveness of the proposed SemTra in generating accurate and stable class labels for unlabeled flows on both binary-class and multi-class datasets.

9.3.1   Datasets used in experiments

To illustrate the broad applicability of the proposed SemTra approach, 16 traffic datasets are used in the experiments, including: multi-hop outdoor real data (MHORD) [240], multi-hop indoor real data (MHIRD) [240], single-hop outdoor real data (SHORD) [240], single-hop indoor real data (SHIRD) [240], simulated *spoofing* attack for SCADA system (detonated as SPFDS) [360], simulated denial of service attack *DOS* for SCADA system (detonated as DOSDS) [360], simulated both *spoofing* and attacks for SCADA system (detonated as SPDOS) [360], and the operational state of a *water treatment plant* (WTP). We experimented also with two other publicly available datasets, namely DARPA [244] and *internet traffic data* (ITD) [245]. For ITD datasets, a different number of datasets have been collected from different periods of time and from different networks, and thus we refer to them

Table 9.1   Summary of datasets used in the experiments

Data	No. of instances	No. of attributes	No. of classes
MHIRD	699	10	2
MHORD	2,500	3	2
SPFDS	1,000	15	2
DOSDS	4,000	15	2
SPDOS	2,500	15	3
SHIRD	1,800	4	2
SHORD	400	4	2
WTP	512	39	2
ITD 1	21,000	149	13
ITD 2	23,000	149	11
ITD 3	22,000	149	12
ITD 4	23,000	149	12
ITD 5	21,500	149	10
ITD 6	20,500	149	11
ITD 7	21,000	149	10
DARPA	60,000	42	5

as ITD1, ITD2, etc. Table 9.1 summarizes the proportion of normal and anomalous flows, the number of attributes and the number of classes for each dataset. This chapter does not collect the descriptions of the datasets due to space restrictions. Thus, for more complete details, we recommend that readers should consult the original references [240,360].

9.3.2   The baseline methods

To understand the common advantages/disadvantages of using semi-supervised learning to label network flows, the performance of SemTra is evaluated against four of the most current and relevant semi-supervised approaches.

- **PGM** [35]: This approach uses a self-training algorithm, and PGMs are proposed to assign a label to unlabeled flows. This approach extends Naive Bayes to learn from both labeled and unlabeled data. The first stage employs Naive Bayes to define a probability distribution over all known and unknown variables in labeled flows. In the second stage, this approach specifies a rule which states how the probability distribution relates to their decision rule. In particular, it introduces two algorithms, called *hard assignment* and *soft assignment*, to approximate the traffic labels.
- **ORTSC** [34]: This is a flexible mathematical approach that leverages both labeled and unlabeled flows. This approach involves two steps. First, it employs a *K*-means clustering algorithm to partition a training dataset that consists of scarce labeled flows combined with abundant unlabeled flows. Second, the available labeled flows are used to obtain a mapping from the clusters to the different known

q classes (Y) based on a probabilistic assignment. To estimate these probabilities, the authors use the set of flows in the training data that are labeled to map clusters to different applications. This approach is fast and can handle both previously unseen applications and changed behavior of existing applications.

- **BGCM** [350]: This approach combines the outputs of multiple supervised and unsupervised models. In particular, it is assumed that each model partitions a given dataset into groups so that the instances in the same group share either the same predicted class label or the same cluster label. Thus, the outputs of models are summarized by a bipartite graph with connections only between group and instance nodes. A group node and an instance node are connected if the instance is assigned to the group. To obtain the final consensus labeling, the authors introduced the BGCM algorithm, which is essentially a block coordinate descent-based algorithm that performs an iterative propagation of probability estimates among neighboring nodes.

- **Boosting for semi-supervised learning (SemiBoost)** [349]: This approach is similar to the most boosting algorithms. SemiBoost improves the accuracy of classification iteratively. At each iteration, a number of unlabeled instances will be selected and used to train a new classification model. In particular, the authors used a pairwise similarity measurements to guide the selection of unlabeled instances at each iteration, and to assign class labels to them.

9.3.3   The experimental setup

Algorithm 3 shows the process details of the experiment. For each dataset, each semi-supervised method ($M=5 \in N=10$) cross-validation strategy is used. The 10-fold cross-validation is repeated $M=5$ times, with the order of the instances of the dataset being randomized each time. This is because many of the algorithms are biased by the data order; that is, certain orderings dramatically improve or degrade performance. For each semi-supervised approach, its corresponding runtime, overall accuracy, F-measure value and stability value are obtained for each dataset.

9.3.4   Performance metrics

We adopt the overall accuracy and F-measure as the evaluation metrics for the performance of SemTra, as well as the baseline approaches outlined in the previous section. F-measure is defined as the harmonic mean of recall and precision as follows:

$$\text{F-measure} = \frac{(1 + \beta)^2 \cdot \text{Recall} \cdot \text{Precision}}{(\beta)^2 \cdot \text{Recall} + \text{Precision}} \tag{9.19}$$

where a coefficient, β, is set to 1 to adjust the relative importance of precision versus recall. In particular, recall is defined as the number of traffic flows that are correctly classified divided by the actual number of flows in each class. Precision is defined as the number of flows that are correctly classified divided by the number of all the flows predicted as the same class. Since different semi-supervised methods may produce different class labels for specific instances for the different runs, therefore, the stability of the results across different runs is considered to be important for assessing the

---

Algorithm 3: Experimental procedure

---

1 **Input:**

2 $M = 5$;
3 SemiTech(ST)=$\{PGM, ORTSC, BGCM, SemiBoost, SemTra\}$;
4 DATA= $\{DARPA, WTP, \ldots, D_n\}$;
5 **Output:**

6 PerfoMetrics=$\{$Accuracy, F-measure, Stability, Runtime$\}$;
7 **foreach** $SemiTech_i \in [1, ST]$ **do**
8   **foreach** $D_i \in DATA$ **do**
9   **foreach** $times \in [1, M]$ **do**
10   *randomise instance-order for D_i*;
11   *generate N bins from the randomised D_i*;
12   **foreach** *fold* $\in [1, N]$ **do**
13                 $Labeled_{Data} = bin[fold]$;
14                 $Unlabeled_{Data} = D_i - Labeled_{Data}$;
15                 $Train'_{Data} = Labeled_{Data} + Subset\ from\ Unlabeled_{Data}$;
16                 $Test'_{Data} = Unlabeled_{Data} - Train'_{Data}$;
17   **foreach** $ST_i \in SemiTech$ **do**
18                     $ST^i_{Model} = learning(Train'_{Data}, ST_i)$;
19                     $Results_i = testing(Test'_{Data}, ST^i_{Model})$;

20   *OverallResult= OverallResult $\cup$ Results$_i$*;
21   *PerfoMetrics=average (OverallResult)*;

---

semi-supervised methods. This chapter carries out an experimental study to examine the stability of the semi-supervised methods. In doing so, we consider a pairwise approach to measuring the stability of the semi-supervised methods. In particular, the match between each of the $n(n-1)/2$ runs of each semi-supervised method is calculated and the stability index is obtained as the averaged degree of match across different runs. Let $S_r(R_i, R_j)$ be the degree of match between runs R_i and R_j. The semi-supervised pairwise stability index S_k is

$$S_k = \frac{2}{n(n-1)} \sum_{i=1}^{n-1} \sum_{j=i+1}^{n} S_r(R_i, R_j). \tag{9.20}$$

where

$$S_r(R_i, R_j) = \begin{cases} 1 & \text{if } R_i(x_i) = R_j(x_j) \\ 0 & \text{otherwise} \end{cases} \tag{9.21}$$

Clearly, it can be seen that S_k is the average stability measure for the final predicted class labels across different runs. It takes values from $[0, 1]$, with 0 indicating the results between predicted class labels of R_i and R_j are totally different, and 1 indicating that the results of predicted class labels across different runs are identical.

9.3.5   Analysis of the experimental results

This section provides a summary of the experimental results relating to the *accuracy*, *performance* and *stability* of the SemTra approach as well as the baseline methods. Also, following the approach of García *et al.* [373] to compare algorithms on multiple datasets, we performed a nonparametric *Friedman* test followed by a *Nemenyi posthoc* test to further explore the statistical significance of the experimental results.

To further explore the accuracy and F-measure of SemTra against the baseline methods, we performed a Friedman test [345] followed by a Nemenyi posthoc test [346]. The former test compares the proposed framework and the baseline methods over N datasets by ranking each method on each dataset separately. In particular, the transformation method with the best performance is given rank 1, the second best is given rank 2, and so on. In the case of ties, average ranks are assigned, then the average ranks of all methods for all datasets are calculated and compared. The latter test compares the performance of the semi-supervised methods in a pairwise manner. In particular, this test determines which method performs statistically differently if the average rank exceeds the critical difference $CD_\alpha = q_\alpha \sqrt{k(k+1)/6N}$, where q_α is calculated based on the *studentized range statistic* [347] divided by $\sqrt{2}$.

Results on the two-classes problem

Here, the binary-class dataset is first to demonstrate the role that different semi-supervised methods play in terms of the accuracy and F-measure values. Table 9.2 is dedicated to the two-class problem, and it shows the 10-fold cross-validation results of the five different semi-supervised methods: SemiBoost, SemTra, PGM, BGCM, and ORTSC. The two main dimensions of this table are overall accuracy (value 1) and F-measure (value 2). The means and standard deviations of the results are obtained by five different methods. By looking at the results of the five methods, we observe the following:

- Generally, all five semi-supervised methods achieve significant accuracy scores on the binary-class traffic datasets. In particular, SemiBoost obtains the best mean accuracy values, with more than one value being above 95%. SemTra has the second highest accuracy, with an average of 94.96% that has a tiny margin of 2% to the SemiBoost method. PGM ranks 3 with average accuracy of 93.32%. BGCM and ORTSC rank 4 and 5, respectively, with average accuracies of 93.33% and 93.02%.
- As for standard deviations, SemiBoost ranges from 0 to 2 on the SD range, while SemTra does much the same thing except for a few values above 2. PGM method ranges from 2 to 5 as does BGCM with the largest BGCM value being a slightly over 5 standard deviations. ORTSC method ranges from 3 to 6 standard deviations.
- On an extremely imbalanced dataset, the accuracy rates cannot provide information about a minority class (e.g., attack). Therefore, in this section, we also compare the performance of SemTra with the baseline methods according to the very popular F-measure that equally weights precision and recall. SemiBoost and

Table 9.2 Comparing overall accuracy and F-measure values of semi-supervised methods on eight binary-class traffic datasets

Dataset	SemiBoost				SemTra				PGM				BGCM				ORTSC			
	Accuracy		F-measure		Accuracy		F-measure		Accuracy		F-measure		Accuracy		F-measure		Accuracy		F-measure	
	Mean	S.Dv	Mean	S.Dv	Mean	S.Dv	Mean	S.Dv	Mean	S.Dv	Mean	S.Dv	Mean	S.Dv	Mean	S.Dv	Mean	S.Dv	Mean	S.Dv
MHIRD	96.78	2.00	93.92	2.56	95.53	0.88	92.54	2.65	93.10	3.46	90.06	4.45	93.65	2.77	89.69	5.04	92.52	4.01	87.67	5.16
MHORD	97.08	0.34	93.65	1.56	95.80	0.25	90.27	2.09	93.24	3.37	90.11	3.53	93.19	3.61	89.62	4.45	93.88	2.55	89.26	5.40
SPFDS	96.74	1.42	94.62	1.89	94.59	1.92	91.95	1.29	94.59	3.60	90.43	3.60	93.52	2.21	91.69	3.27	92.32	3.24	90.29	3.07
DOSDS	98.48	1.94	93.49	0.50	94.64	1.33	92.38	1.02	94.71	2.30	89.51	4.73	93.72	2.78	89.62	4.51	92.54	4.42	88.88	4.45
SPDOS	96.96	1.21	94.30	2.05	93.84	2.22	90.41	1.90	94.21	3.80	89.76	4.86	93.57	2.12	88.47	4.19	93.08	3.53	90.83	4.16
SHIRD	95.86	0.29	94.98	2.08	94.69	1.15	91.34	1.02	93.92	2.34	92.53	4.56	92.71	3.78	90.51	4.26	93.79	2.42	89.76	3.71
SHORD	97.33	0.91	92.51	2.57	95.82	0.25	91.27	1.42	94.56	2.41	92.12	2.33	93.55	2.17	90.34	3.43	93.16	3.40	90.99	5.41
WTR	96.43	1.04	94.63	1.96	94.79	1.64	91.00	2.08	93.04	2.71	90.91	3.04	92.69	3.47	88.91	4.36	92.90	2.84	90.62	3.36

SemTra produce the best results among the five semi-supervised methods. The average F-measure scores of Semi-Boost and SemTra are always higher than the PGM, BGCM, and ORTSC methods by about 0.72%–4.23% on all binary-class datasets.

To further explore whether the overall accuracy on binary-class datasets is significantly different, we performed a Friedman test, followed by a Nemenyi posthoc test. The result of the Friedman test (at $\alpha = 0.1$) is $p = 0$, which indicates that the overall accuracy of all semi-supervised methods is equivalent.

Thus, to further explore semi-supervised methods whose overall accuracy is statistically significant difference, we performed a Nemenyi test. Figure 9.5 shows the results with $\alpha = 0.1$ on the binary datasets. These indicate that overall accuracy of SemiBoost had the highest value compared to the PGCM, PGM, and ORTSC methods. However, there is no consistent evidence to indicate statistical differences between the SemiBoost and SemTra approaches.

The null hypothesis of the Friedman test is that all the semi-supervised methods are equivalent.

To further explore whether the F-measure on binary-class datasets is significantly different, we performed a Friedman test, followed by a Nemenyi posthoc test. The result of the Friedman test (at $\alpha = 0.1$) is $p = 0$, and this result indicates that the overall accuracy of all semi-supervised methods is equivalent. Thus, to further explore semi-supervised methods whose F-measure had statistically significant differences, we performed a Nemenyi test. Figure 9.6 shows the results with $\alpha = 0.1$ on the binary datasets, and the results indicate that overall accuracy of SemiBoost had the highest value compared to the PGCM, PGM, and ORTSC.

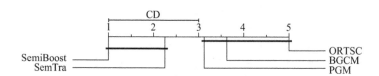

Figure 9.5   Overall accuracy comparison of all semi-supervised methods with each other on the binary-class datasets

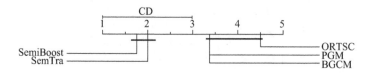

Figure 9.6   F-measure comparison of all semi-supervised methods with each other on the binary-class traffic datasets

However, there is no consistent evidence to indicate statistical differences between SemiBoost and SemTra methods. From these results, we can conclude that the SemTra performs as well as SemiBoost in binary-class traffic datasets.

Results on multi-classes problem

This section provides the performance evaluation of *SemTra* against the baseline methods over eight multi-class traffic datasets. We consider the cases where the traffic dataset contains different types of traffic applications (e.g., WWW, FTP, P2P, and MAIL) rather than only normal and attack classes.

The overall performance is evaluated in terms of overall accuracy, and we also compare *SemTra* and the baseline methods according to the very popular F-measure. This is because on an extremely imbalanced dataset, the overall accuracy rate cannot provide information over imbalanced data. Thus, we need to consider such cases where the number of *WWW* flow instances is much greater than the number of instances in any other class. Table 9.3 shows the overall accuracy of the five semi-supervised methods on eight multi-class traffic datasets.

First, a general observation is that the proposed SemTra approach significantly outperforms all of the baseline methods. Its average overall accuracy of 93.84% is 9.23% higher than the second best (PGM) and 52.48% better than the worst (Semi-Boost's 41.36%). This is because SemTra can combine the decision of multiple labeling processes to obtain accurate labels and discard unsupported ones. Surprisingly, SemiBoost performs poorly on all eight datasets, as it is designed to work well only with binary-class datasets.

Second, in terms of F-measure, SemTra is the best among the four semi-supervised baseline methods, with an average of 90.02%. The average F-measure score of SemTra is always higher than other baseline methods by approximately 23.03%–52.60%. It can be seen also that the average F-measure score of PGM is ranked 2, with an average F-measure score of 66.99%. We note that there is a large gap between the scores of PGM with respect to overall accuracy and F-measure. This is because the PGM method was biased toward the majority class (e.g., WWW and P2P).

To further explore whether the overall accuracy and F-measure of semi-supervised methods on multi-classes datasets are significantly different, we performed a Friedman test, followed by a Nemenyi posthoc test. The results of the Friedman test indicate that the overall accuracy and F-measure of all semi-supervised methods are equivalent. Thus, to further explore semi-supervised methods, whose F-measures have statistically significant differences, we performed a Nemenyi test. Figure 9.7 shows the overall accuracy results with $\alpha = 0.1$ on multi-class datasets. The results indicate that overall accuracy of SemTra is scored the highest value compared to the PGM, PGCM, SemiBoost, and ORTSC.

Figure 9.8 shows the Nemenyi test of F-measure for all semi-supervised methods; the results indicate that the SemTra method is statistically better than those of BGCM, SemiBoost, and ORTSC, and there is clear evidence of a statistical difference between SemTra and PGM in terms of the F-measure.

Table 9.3 Comparing overall accuracy and F-measure values of semi-supervised methods on eight multi-class traffic datasets

Dataset	SemiBoost				SemTra				PGM				BGCM				ORTSC			
	Accuracy		F-measure		Accuracy		F-measure		Accuracy		F-measure		Accuracy		F-measure		Accuracy		F-measure	
	Mean	S.Dv	Mean	S. Dv	Mean	S. Dv	Mean	S. Dv	Mean	S. Dv	Mean	S. Dv	Mean	S. Dv	Mean	S. Dv	Mean	S. Dv	Mean	S. Dv
ITD 1	39.85	1.79	35.92	3.21	93.80	1.52	89.84	1.56	85.26	2.70	69.65	3.48	53.61	5.30	51.27	6.36	46.01	6.86	39.65	7.94
ITD 2	42.27	2.56	35.96	3.06	93.76	1.89	90.11	2.61	83.14	4.02	70.11	4.51	54.77	5.99	49.76	6.42	45.89	7.31	41.87	7.15
ITD 3	41.84	2.37	38.73	4.58	93.36	1.70	90.39	2.34	84.69	3.63	66.88	6.16	54.06	5.40	51.85	5.65	46.04	6.45	42.00	7.90
ITD 4	41.54	1.58	41.00	4.65	93.90	1.34	89.69	2.36	83.80	3.58	63.05	5.13	55.77	4.67	50.36	5.30	46.02	7.86	39.72	7.84
ITD 5	40.70	2.58	37.66	3.92	93.64	1.90	89.70	2.65	85.31	2.67	67.11	2.42	53.66	3.42	49.23	5.48	46.06	6.71	41.40	7.02
ITD 6	42.79	1.92	35.22	2.60	93.76	1.91	90.38	1.14	85.04	3.65	67.52	3.85	56.44	5.32	51.37	6.62	46.04	6.33	39.89	7.34
ITD 7	41.50	1.79	38.85	2.23	94.07	1.27	90.10	2.08	85.12	5.33	66.24	3.71	55.62	6.08	50.83	6.34	45.99	6.82	41.11	7.91
DARPA	40.40	2.44	36.03	3.23	94.42	1.07	89.95	1.97	84.53	3.49	65.33	4.31	55.27	4.87	52.34	5.91	45.85	6.97	40.84	8.31

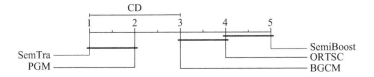

Figure 9.7   Overall accuracy comparison of all semi-supervised methods with each other on the multi-class traffic datasets

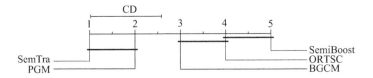

Figure 9.8   F-measure comparison of all semi-supervised methods on the multi-class traffic datasets

Table 9.4   Comparison of runtime performances taken for labeling

Dataset	ORTSC	PGM	BGCM	SemiBoost	SemTra
MHIRD	0.39	1.24	1.87	64.85	79.75
MHORD	0.39	1.25	1.90	64.11	78.85
SPFDS	0.28	0.86	1.77	30.48	37.49
DOSDS	0.21	0.67	1.26	54.79	67.38
SPDOS	0.50	1.53	3.08	91.41	112.41
SHIRD	0.40	1.20	1.83	57.56	70.79
SHORD	0.51	1.36	2.28	73.67	90.60
WTP	0.08	0.16	1.98	2.17	2.67
ITD 1	1.17	3.19	220.89	892.13	1,097.12
ITD 2	1.28	3.49	222.88	977.09	1,201.61
ITD 3	1.23	3.34	221.89	934.61	1,149.36
ITD 4	1.29	3.50	222.98	978.55	1,203.39
ITD 5	1.20	3.26	221.39	913.37	1,123.24
ITD 6	1.14	3.11	220.39	870.89	1,071.00
ITD 7	1.17	3.19	220.89	892.13	1,097.12
DARPA	13.75	37.4	786.57	1,559.7	1,795.10

Running times and scalability

Table 9.4 shows the runtime of the five semi-supervised methods. It can be observed that the individual semi-supervised methods of ORTSC, PGM, and BGCM are much faster than SemiBoost and SemTra, respectively. ORTSC is consistently faster than all other semi-supervised methods. Several observations can be made from Table 9.4.

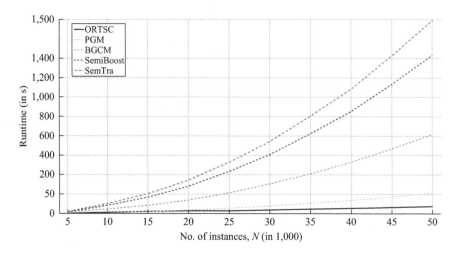

Figure 9.9   Scalability of semi-supervised methods on DARPA dataset

First, it can be seen that the runtime of ORTSC is only 36.35% of the runtime of PGM, 1.06% of the runtime of BGCM, 0.30% of the runtime of SemiBoost and 0.24% of the runtime of SemTra. Second, it can be seen that both SemTra and SemiBoost have the worst runtime in comparison with other three semi-supervised methods (see Figure 9.9). Thus, future work should be devoted to reducing the computational time of the SemTra approach.

In order to further explore whether the runtime of the five semi-supervised methods is significantly different, we performed a Friedman test. The null hypothesis of the Friedman test indicates that all semi-supervised methods are equivalent in terms of runtime. The result of the test is $p = 0$, which means that, at $a=0.1$; hence, there is evidence to reject the null hypothesis and all the five semi-supervised methods are different in terms of runtime. Thus, we have conducted a posthoc Nemenyi test. Figure 9.10 shows the results with $a=0.1$ on the 16 datasets. The results indicate that the runtime of ORTSC method is statically better than those of BGCM, SemiBoost, and SemTra, respectively, and there is no consistent evidence to indicate a statistical runtime difference between ORTSC and PGM methods.

Figure 9.10 shows the scalability of SemTra method and the other five semi-supervised methods with a varying number of instances in the dataset. Considering the page limitations, we use only the DARPA dataset. We vary the number of flows from 1,000 to 50,000 and plot them on the graph. It is clear from the trend that all semi-supervised methods scale linearly with respect to the number of instances.

Stability

The aim here is to evaluate the stability of the proposed SemTra approach and the baselines methods in generating accurate class labels for unlabeled flows across different

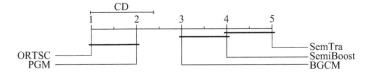

Figure 9.10   Runtime comparison of all semi-supervised methods with the Nemenyi test

Table 9.5   Comparison of the stability of the SemTra approach and the baseline methods

Dataset	SemTra	SemiBoost	PGM	BGCM	ORTSC
MHIRD	97.35	97.44	94.05	90.96	90.84
MHORD	97.91	98.44	94.97	91.55	90.60
SPFDS	98.71	98.11	94.90	92.73	92.93
DOSDS	98.98	99.50	93.77	91.49	91.55
SPDOS	98.10	97.95	93.64	91.81	91.84
SHIRD	98.98	97.92	93.94	91.74	92.29
SHORD	98.58	97.43	96.17	92.57	90.59
WTR	96.42	93.04	91.96	85.64	85.64
ITD 1	95.99	92.86	90.35	84.53	76.80
ITD 2	96.94	91.79	91.52	83.64	77.06
ITD 3	95.89	91.94	90.49	83.58	77.85
ITD 4	96.16	90.42	88.84	84.35	77.10
ITD 5	96.14	90.35	89.87	84.70	77.16
ITD 6	95.85	91.08	92.58	84.52	77.98
ITD 7	97.36	92.40	91.15	83.38	77.66
DARPA	97.92	97.77	95.29	88.66	85.09

runs. An important property of a semi-supervised process is the ability to indicate randomness in assigning class labels.

Table 9.5 shows the stability indices for all semi-supervised methods on the 16 datasets. Equation (9.20) is used to measure the stability. The following setup was used in the experiment to evaluate the stability. The number of trials was set to $n = 100$. From each dataset, 30% of data in each class was reserved for testing, and thus were excluded from the training dataset. In each trial, 90% of the remaining data were randomly sampled to form a trial local dataset. Note, the stability indices have been computed from the training dataset only.

It can be seen from Table 9.5 that SemTra ranks 1 not only on the binary-class dataset but also on the multi-class datasets, with margin of 2.38% over the second most stable semi-supervised method (SemiBoost) and 12.3% over the least stable method (ORTSC). This is explained by the fact that SemTra is designed to assign an accurate class label based on a fusion of multiple decisions. The SemiBoost method achieves good stability results on all binary-class datasets, but it performs badly on

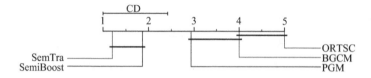

Figure 9.11   Stability comparison of all semi-supervised methods with the Nemenyi test

Table 9.6   Compliance summary of the semi-supervised performance based on empirical evaluation metrics

Semi. methods	Binary-class	Multi-class	Novel class detection	Outlier detection	Stability	Efficiency problem
SemTra	Yes	Yes	Yes	Partially	High	Suffer from
SemiBoost	Yes	No	No	No	High/Low	Suffer from
PGM	Yes	Partially	No	No	High/Mid	Partially
BGCM	Yes	No	No	No	Low	Suffer from
ORTSC	Yes	No	Partially	No	Low	No

the multi-class datasets. This is because it was designed to deal with only binary-class datasets. Notably, smaller differences in terms of stability indices can be observed among SemiBoost and PGM methods with a margin of 2.17%. It can be seen from Table 9.5 that the ORTSC method has the lowest stability indices on both binary and multi-class traffic data. This is because ORTSC method is based on only K-means clustering algorithm, which is considered to be sensitive to random initialization. The second worse stability result was produced by the BGCM method, especially on multi-class traffic data.

To further explore whether the stability indices of SemTra with the four semi-supervised are significantly different, we perform two tests, including Friedman tests and posthoc Nemenyi test. The result of the former test is $p = 0$ which means that $a = 0.1$, this result indicates that the stability indices for all five semi-supervised methods are not equivalent. Thus, posthoc Nemenyi tests were conducted to explore further difference in such methods. Figure 9.11 shows that *SemiTra* is statistically better than PGM, BGCM, and ORTSC methods. However, there is no consistent evidence to indicate a significant different between *SemiTra* and SemiBoost.

Discussion and summary

As shown in Table 9.6, SemTra and the baseline methods are validated against the desired requirements for the labeling process. These requirements include five properties to deal with (i) binary-class and multi-class datasets, (ii) detection of novel classes, (iii) detection of outliers, (iv) prediction of stable class assignments, and (v) coping with efficiency.

Table 9.6 shows that SemTra has advantages over the related baseline methods. First, SemTra can deal with various types of classes, while the related methods can deal only with binary-class (except for PGM, which can deal partially with multi-class). Second, extensive experiments show that SemTra is also capable of detecting novel classes as well as partially detecting outliers, while the other related methods are not able to detect either novel classes or outliers (except ORTSC, which can partially deal with detection of novel classes and these are termed "known class"). Regarding the stability value, it can be seen that SemTra assigns a stable class to the same instances. The baseline methods have high stability on binary-class datasets and low stability on multi-class datasets. However, SemTra performs significantly better than the baseline methods on number of metrics, although it has the highest computational time. A possible solution is to rely on specific technology high-performance computing (HPC) to enable such algorithms to be executed more efficiently.

9.4 Conclusion

The capability of accurate traffic classification ML-based is very important for the management, monitoring, and provision of networks. This chapter investigated the problem of lacking labeled traffic data to achieve an improvement in network traffic classification task, and a novel semi-supervised method for automatically labeling traffic data with a minimum human effort was proposed. In particular, the proposed SemTra approach incorporates the advantages of the complementary predictive powers of supervised and unsupervised algorithms over multiple representations of the original traffic dataset.

An extensive study using a publicly available traffic data benchmark has proved the strength of the proposed SemTra approach in achieving an improvement in the network traffic classification task in comparison to the state-of-art semi-supervised learning approaches.

Chapter 10

A hybrid clustering-classification for accurate and efficient network classification

The traffic classification is the foundation for many network activities, such as quality of service (QoS), security monitoring, lawful interception, and intrusion detection system (IDS). A recent statistics-based method to address the unsatisfactory results of traditional port-based and payload-based methods has attracted attention. However, the presence of non-informative attributes and noise instances degrade the performance of this method. Thus, to address this problem, in this chapter, a hybrid clustering-classification method (called *CluClas*) is described to improve the accuracy and efficiency of network traffic classification by selecting informative attributes and representative instances. An extensive empirical study on four traffic data sets shows the effectiveness of the CluClas method.

10.1 Introduction

The process of classifying network traffic into a set of categories according to the applications that generate them is known as traffic classification. Traffic classification methods are essential tools for improving the QoS and enhancing system security, which have been widely studied in recent years. Traditional network classification methods [8,374], including port-based methods that directly identify applications by the port number, the packet headers, and deep packet inspection methods, have shown a number of drawbacks, especially with the rapid evolution of new traffic applications. For example, new applications and encrypted traffic can easily evade detection by using a method such as dynamic port assignment. To address this limitation, a new method based on statistical characteristics of IP flows [10,65,375] (e.g., mean and variance of packet size and inter-packet time in traffic flows) and machine learning (ML) algorithms shows promising results.

The classification process for statistics-based classifiers can be divided into two phases, including training and testing [10,65,375]. The former phase feeds the training data to learning algorithms to build classifier models, while the latter phase is used to predict the application types based on the generated model obtained from the training phase. Two types of learning methods can be used for both training and testing phases, depending on whether the class labels are available or not. For example, supervised learning algorithms are used with labeled data; on the other hand, unsupervised learning is used with unlabeled data.

To the best of the knowledge, there are a limited number of studies that combine the advantages of both supervised and unsupervised learning algorithms to improve the performance of network classifiers. Thus, in this chapter, we describe a novel hybrid clustering-classification method (namely, CluClas) to eliminate noise attributes and instances for better network classification. In particular, the Clus-Clas method first preprocesses the traffic data and removes redundant and irrelevant attributes from the global perspective. Second, the K-means clustering algorithm [47] is applied on the training set to discard noise instances and select the centroid of each cluster as representative training instances. This step is important for some learning algorithms that may be noise-fragile, and also to reduce the amount of computation for such learning algorithms. Finally, using a hidden Markov model (HMM) [376], a network classifier is built on the representative training instances, which can be used for evaluating new traffic in real time.

Four publicly available traffic data sets [178,243,244,291] are used to evaluate the CluClas method. The experimental results show that the method achieved better results in comparison to individual methods, including K-means and HMM.

The rest of the chapter is organized as follows. Section 10.2 presents related work in the area of network classification and ML. Section 10.3 describes the hybrid clustering-classification method. Experimental evaluation and discussion of the results are presented in Section 10.4, and Section 10.5 concludes this chapter.

10.2   Existing solutions

Classification methods based on ML are divided into two categories: *supervised* and *unsupervised*. An extensive study of ML and traffic classification can be found in the survey of Nguyen *et al.* [66]. For supervised algorithms [65,244,375], the class of each traffic flow must be known before the learning stage. A classification model is built using a training set of example instances that represents each class. The model is then able to predict class membership for new instances by examining the feature values of unknown flows.

Supervised learning creates knowledge structures that support the task of classifying new instances into predefined classes [377]. A group of sample instances, pre-classified into classes, are being provided to the learning machine. A classification model is the output of the learning process. A classification model is constructed by analyzing and generalizing from the provided instances. As a result, supervised learning's main focus is on modeling the input and output relationships. Its main goal is to find a mapping from input features to an output class. The knowledge learnt can be presented as classification rules, a decision tree, a flowchart, etc. This knowledge will be used later to classify a new instance. There are two major steps in supervised learning: *training* and *testing*. Training is a learning phase that analyzes the provided data, which is called the training data set, and builds a classification model. Testing is also known as classifying. In this phase, the model that has been built in the training phase is used to classify previously unseen instances.

Unlike classification methods in supervised ML, clustering methods [378,379] do not use any predefined training instances; instead, they find natural clusters in the data using internalized heuristics [380]. McGregor *et al.* in [379] is one of the earliest works to use unsupervised ML methods to group network traffic flows using transport layer attributes with expectation maximization (EM) method. Even though the authors do not evaluate the accuracy of the classification as well as which traffic flow attributes produce the best results, this method clusters traffic with similar observable properties into different application types. In [381], Zander *et al.* extend this work by using another EM algorithm called AutoClass and analyze the best set of attributes to use. Both [379] and [381] with Bayesian clustering methods were implemented by an EM algorithm that is guaranteed to converge to a local maximum. To find the global maximum, AutoClass repeats EM searches starting from pseudorandom points in the parameter space; thus, it performs much better than the original EM method. Both the early works in [163] and [381] have shown that cluster analysis has the ability to group Internet traffic using only transport layer characteristics. Erman *et al.* in [34] proposed to use K-means and DBSCAN clustering methods to evaluate the predicating performance. They also demonstrated that both K-means and DBSCAN perform better and work more quickly than the clustering method of AutoClass used in [381]. However, these unsupervised methods are not as good as supervised methods. Thus, this chapter will exploit the advantages of both supervised and unsupervised methods for a better accuracy of network classifiers.

10.3   CluClas—a hybrid clustering and classification method

The CluClas method is described here to improve the accuracy and the efficiency of network traffic classification. CluClas is based on combining the advantages of clustering and classification algorithms. Figure 10.1 illustrates the overall view of the CluClas method. In particular, this method comprises three phases: (i) the pre-processing of the data to discard and remove irrelevant and redundant attributes of the original data from a global perspective, (ii) identifying the most representative instances with the aim of improving the efficiency of the learning process as well as the overall prediction accuracy by partitioning the samples belong to a single class only and extracting the centroid of each cluster to act as a representative instance of that application class, and (iii) building a network traffic classification model based on the HMM.

The following subsections illustrate the process and details of the CluClas method.

10.3.1   Discarding irrelevant and redundant attributes

The quality of the data always affects the accuracy and execution of the ML algorithm during the training phase [20,37]. This is due to the presence of irrelevant and redundant attributes in the data. Thus, to discard these non-informative attributes, feature selection (FS) methods are used. FS methods can be divided into two

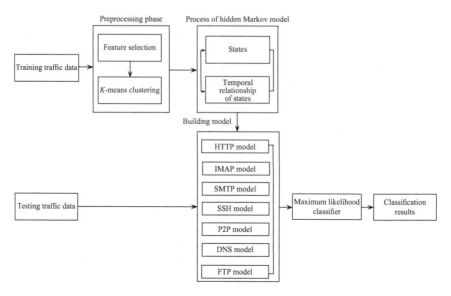

Figure 10.1   Overview of the CluClas method

Table 10.1   Summary of data sets used in the experiments

Data sets	Features	Classes	Training instances	Testing instances
ITD	149	12	15,750	5,250
DARPA	41	2	7,500	2,500
wide	20	6	10,030	3,100
isp	20	14	10,500	3,500

main categories: the wrapper method and the filter method [265,382]. The former method [265] employs an existing ML method [383] as a classifier and uses the classifier's accuracy as the evaluation measure to select the best possible attributes. Such a method tends to be not only computationally expensive but also inherits a *bias* toward the predetermined learning algorithm. The latter method [265] relies on the natural characteristics of the data (e.g., correlation) and does not require a pre-determined mining algorithm to select feature subsets. As a result, this method does not inherit the *bias* of any mining algorithm, and it is also computationally effective. However, the filter methods eliminate both irrelevant and redundant attributes from a local perspective, and thus it can be tricked in a situation where the dependence between a pair of attributes is weak, but the total intercorrelation of one attribute to the others is strong. Thus, in this chapter, we introduce a new FS method to select informative attributes from a global perspective [15,40]. The process of discarding irrelevant and redundant attributes from a global perspective and only keeping the optimal attributes is presented in Table 10.1.

Algorithm 1 shows the procedure of discarding the irrelevant and redundant attributes in two parts. In the first part, the algorithm eliminates irrelevant

---

Algorithm 1: The process of selecting optimal attributes globally

---

Input:
Given the input data set D
Specify the number of optimal features K.

Remove irrelevant attributes
1. Compute the mutual information for each attribute, x_i.

1.a $SU(x_i, Y) = 2.0 \times \left[\frac{gain}{H(Y)+H(x_i)} \right]$.

2. Rank the attributes in descending order based on the value of $SU(Y|x_i)$.
3. Select x_i whose relevant score is greater than 0.

3.a If $SU(x_i, Y) > 0$ then $X_{rr} = X_{rr} \cup \{x_i\}$.

4. Compute the mean of relevant scores.

4.a $\mu_{rv} = \frac{\sum_{i=0}^{|X_{rr}|} SU(x_i, Y)}{|X_{rr}|}$.

Remove redundant attributes
5. For each $x_j \in X_{rr}$.

1

5.a Compute the intercorrelation between attributes, as

$SU(x_i, x_j) = 2.0 \times \left[\frac{gain}{H(x_i)+H(x_j)} \right]$.

6. Compute the mean of the redundant scores as

6.a $\mu_{rd} = \frac{\sum_{i=0}^{|X_{rr}|} SU(x_i, x_j)}{|X_{rr}|}$.

7. Compute the weight value based on both the relevant and redundant scores.

7.a $w = \frac{\mu_{rd}}{\mu_{rr}}$.

8. For each $x_j \in X_{rr}$.

8.a Use the weight value to calculate the importance of attributes from a global prospective.

$S(x_i) = w \cdot x_{rv}^i - x_{rd}^i$.

8.b Select the optimal attributes $S_{optimal}$.

If $S(x_i) > 0$ then $S_{optimal} = S_{optimal} \cup x_i$.

9. Return the final set of optimal attributes, $S_{optimal}$.

---

attributes by applying the *symmetrical uncertainty* correlation measure. In particular, the *symmetrical uncertainty* correlation evaluates the reliability of each individual attribute for predicting the accurate class label as follows:

$$H = (Y) = - \sum_{y \in Y} p(y) \log_2 p(y), \tag{10.1}$$

$$H(Y|X) = -\sum_{x \in X} p(x) \sum_{y \in Y} p(y|x) \log_2(y|x), \tag{10.2}$$

$$
\begin{aligned}
gain &= H(Y) - H(Y|X) \\
&= H(X) - H(X|Y) \\
&= H(Y) + H(X) - H(X,Y)
\end{aligned}
\tag{10.3}
$$

Information gain is considered to be a bias in attributes with more values. Thus the correlation value in (10.1) should be normalized to the range [0, 1] as follows:

$$SU(X,Y) = 2.0 \times \left[\frac{gain}{H(Y) + H(X)} \right] \tag{10.4}$$

Note that attributes whose *symmetrical uncertainty* value is zero are removed, which means that attributes do not have the power to distinguish between traffic classes. The remaining attributes are then ranked in descending order according to their value of symmetrical uncertainty, and the mean of these attributes is calculated, μ_{rv}. In the second part, the intercorrelation between attributes is computed and the total values of the symmetrical uncertainty related to that attribute are added. The weight factor w is computed (as in line 5.a) to be used for selecting optimal attributes from a global perspective. Finally, attributes greater than 0 are selected, which means that they not only can accurately predict the class but also have a low correlation to other attributes.

10.3.2   Identifying representative instances in CluClas

An original training data set may contain noise instances that can affect noise-fragile learning algorithms. Thus, an instance selection step is important to discard as many instances as possible without significant degradation of reduced data set for learning processes. To do so, a clustering algorithm is applied on the training set and selects only the centroid of each cluster, which can act as a representative instance. As a result of selecting only representative instances, we can not only reduce the amount of computation but also improve the accuracy of an ML algorithm such as the k-nearest neighbors, Naive Bayes, and so on. To cluster the training data, there are a large number of clustering algorithms [219]. However, in this study, the proposed CluClas method to finding representative instances is based particularly on a K-means clustering algorithm [47]. In particular, the K-means algorithm is chosen for a number of reasons, including (i) it is simple to implement, (ii) it does not need to recompute the centroid, (iii) it has a limited number of parameter settings, (iv) it can generate tighter clusters in a comparison to hierarchical clustering, and (v) it is computationally faster than EM and hierarchical clustering algorithms, especially with a large number of variables. The K-means clustering algorithm partitions the traffic flows into k disjoint clusters (where k is a predefined parameter). Each cluster represents a region of similar instances based on the Euclidean distance between the instances and their centroids.

Algorithm 2: The process of selecting the most representative instances

---

   Input:
      Given the input data set D to be clustered.
      specify the number of clusters k.
   Building Cluster:
      1. Select k random instances from the training set as an initial centroid.
      2. For each training instance $X \in D$, do the following.
         a. Compute the Euclidean distance as

$$\arg\min \sum_{i=1}^{k} \sum_{x_j \in C_i} \left\| \mathbf{x_j} - \mathbf{m_i} \right\|.$$

         b. Find and assign X to the closest cluster C.

$$C_i^t = \left\{ x_j : \left\| x_j - m_i^t \right\| \leq \left\| x_j - m_l^t \right\| \text{ for all } l = 1, \dots, k \right\}.$$

         c. Update the centroid of C.

$$m_i^{t+1} = \frac{1}{|C_i^t|} \sum_{x_j \in C_i^t} x_j.$$

      3. Repeat step 2 until the centroids of clusters stabilize based on the mean square error.
      4. Return the centroid of each cluster as a representative instance.

Algorithm 2 illustrates the process of selecting the most representative instances based on the concept of the K-means clustering algorithm. Particularly, in this chapter, since a traffic data set can contain patterns from different classes, the concept of *homogeneous clustering* is adapted to partition and identify the instances belonging to each class separately.

At the completion of the K-means cluster, the centroid of each cluster is selected to represent all of the data in the corresponding cluster. Consequently, the number of training sets becomes much smaller than the original instances.

10.3.3   The CluClas learning process

At the completion of the clustering process, the centroid of each cluster is utilized to build a representative training data set to generate the classification model. A classification model is chosen here instead of clustering as it has a better accuracy [163]. The method to building a traffic classifier is based on the concept of the HMM [376]. This is due to its powerful modeling; it is far more powerful than many statistical methods. HMM is one of the most popular statistical methods widely applied in pattern recognition [384,385]. This is due to its good capability to grasp temporal statistical properties of stochastic processes. The basic idea of the HMM process is to construct an optimal model that can explain in a time sequence the occurrence of observations, which can be then used to identify other observation sequences. In particular, for modeling the data distribution, the method is based on a finite mixture model for the probability of the cluster labels. The main assumption is that the traffic applications

y_i are modeled as random variables drawn from a probability distribution described as a HMM:

$$p(x) = \sum_{i=1}^{M} p(x|\theta_i)p_i \qquad (10.5)$$

where x denotes the observation, p_i denotes the weight of the ith model, and $p(x|\theta_i)$ is the density function for the observation x given the component model p_i with the parameters θ_i. Here we assume that the models $p(x|\theta_i)$ are HMMs; thus, the observation density parameters θ_i for the ith component are the transition matrices. $p(x|\theta_i)$ can be computed via the forward part of the forward backward procedure. By applying the HMM on the representative training sets, it would create a set of hidden states Q and a state transition probability matrix A that includes the probability of moving from one hidden state to another. In general, there are at most M^2 transitions among the hidden states, where M denotes the number of states.

10.3.4   Classification/Prediction process in CluClas method

Figure 10.1 also illustrates the process of classification phase. Given a new statistical flow instance of TCP, the log-likelihood for this observation is calculated based on all generated Markov models M^k, with $\prod^k = (\pi_1^k, \ldots, \pi_n^k)$ and $A^K = \left\{ a_{\sigma_i,\sigma_j}^k \right\}$ as

$$\log Pr(O|M^{(k)}) = \log \left(\pi_k^{o_1} + \sum_{i=1}^{n} \log a_{o_i,o_i+1}^k \right) \qquad (10.6)$$

Hence, each flow will be assigned to its application type for which the log-likelihood is the largest.

10.4   Experimental evaluation

The aim of this section is to comprehensively evaluate the CluClas method by performing a large number of experiments. This section presents the carried out experimental evaluation in four parts. Section 10.4.1 discusses the experimental setting. In Section 10.4.2, four traffic data sets are described. In Section 10.4.3, the evaluation metric is presented. Section 10.4.4 summarizes the results of the CluClas method and compares it to individual K-means and HMM classification.

10.4.1   Experimental setting

To get robust results, the experiments are repeated ten times with the same set of parameters. For these experiments, the value of k for K-means clustering algorithm is set to 400, since the large value of k can result in better performance. For the CluClas method, the K-means clustering is used to partition instances of flow from the same class into k clusters and the centroid of each cluster was then selected as training instances for HMM to build an accurate classification model. For the traditional

HMM method, each model individual application type is built and then used the built model to classify the testing traffic data.

To test the effectiveness of each method, the data set was divided into two sets. In particular, 75% of the data was selected randomly as training set, and the remaining data was considered as testing set. All experiments were performed on a 64-bit Windows-based system with 4-duo and Core(i7), 3.30 GHz Intel CPU with 8-GB of memory. For the implementation, Java is used and integrated it with Weka software [64].

10.4.2   Traffic data sets

To evaluate the performance of the CluClas method, several experiments were conducted using four publicly available traffic data sets. In what follows, the characteristics of the four traffic data sets are discussed.

- *Internet traffic data* (ITD): The traffic data sets collected by the high-performance network monitor (described in [244]) are some of the largest publicly available network traffic traces used in the experiments. These data sets are based on traces captured using its loss-limited, full-payload capture to disk, where timestamps with a resolution of better than 35 ns are provided. The data were taken for several different time periods from one site on the Internet. This site is a research-facility that hosts up to 1,000 users connected to the Internet via a full-duplex gigabyte Ethernet link.
- *DARPA* data sets: Since 1999, the DARPA99 data have been the most widely used data set for evaluations that use ML methods. This data set was prepared by Stolfo *et al.* [244] and is built based on the data captured in the *DARPA* cup99 IDS evaluation program. This data set contains raw traffic flow records, each with an associated label to indicate whether the record was labeled as either normal or an attack. In particular, the simulated attacks fall in one of the most common types of attacks, including denial of service attack, user to root attack, remote to local attack, and a probing attack.
- *wide* data set [291]: This is a real network traffic data set randomly selected from 182 *wide traces*. This data set is annotated by using a deep packet inspection tool and manual inspection to assist researchers in evaluating their IDS models. In particular, the flows in this data set are categorized into six type of traffic applications, including HTTP (dominate application), P2P, DNS, FTP, CHAT, and MAIL.
- *isp* data set [178]: This annotated data set is obtained from *isp* traces. The *isp* traces is a full payload traffic data set collected from a medium-sized Australian *isp* network that hosts few hundred users and internal servers for web, mail, and name services. The *isp* data set consists of 30k flows randomly sampled from 14 types of traffic applications, including BT, DNS, eBuddy, FTP, HTTP, IMAP, MSN, POP3, RSP, SMTP, SSH, SSL, XMPP, and YahooMsg.

The focused of this study is on TCP flows (as did most of the previous works [20,375]). This is due to the clear start-end information for TCP flows.

Table 10.1 summarizes the number of features, the number of classes in the four data sets, and the proportion of training and testing instances.

10.4.3 Evaluation metrics

This section investigates the performance of the CluClas method using well-known confusion metrics. These metrics include classification accuracy (CA), precision, recall, and F-measure. Each metrics is explained in the following:

- *Overall accuracy*: It is the percentage of all normal and anomaly instances that are correctly classified, which is defined as follows in terms of the metrics defined in Table 10.2: CA is defined as

$$CA = \frac{TP + TN}{|\Omega|} \qquad (10.7)$$

where Ω is the total number of instances in the data set.
- *Recall*: It is the percentage of anomaly instances correctly detected, which is defined as follows in terms of the metrics defined in Table 10.2:

$$Recall = \frac{TP}{TP + FN} \qquad (10.8)$$

- *Precision*: It is the percentage of correctly detected anomaly instances over all the detected anomaly instances, which is defined as follows in terms of the metrics defined in Table 10.2:

$$Precision = \frac{TP}{TP + FP} \qquad (10.9)$$

- *F-measure* is the equally weighted (harmonic) mean of precision and recall, which is defined as follows:

$$F\text{-}measure = 2 \cdot \frac{Recall \times Precision}{Recall + Precision} \qquad (10.10)$$

For the theoretical basis of F-measure, please refer to [386] for details.

Table 10.2 Standard confusion metrics for evaluation of attack classification

Actual label of flows	Predicted label of flows	
	Normal	Attack
Normal	True negative (TN)	False positive (FP)
Attack	False negative (FN)	True positive (TP)

10.4.4 Results and discussion

In the following subsection, the results of the CluClas method are presented and compared against each individual method.

Accuracy performance

The accuracy of the K-means, HMM, and CluClas methods on *DARPA, isp, wide,* and *ITD* data sets is discussed in this section. Since the evaluation process of clustering algorithms is totally different from classification algorithms, we adapted the evaluation concept of the classification to evaluate the clustering outputs. To do so, we labeled the cluster based on the dominant application in each cluster. In particular, the labeling function (LF) assigns a class label to each cluster as

$$LF = \arg\max_{A_i \in A} \sum_{x_j \in C} \Psi(\theta(x_j), A_i) \tag{10.11}$$

where A and C denote the actual application class label and the cluster, respectively. $\Psi(\theta(x_j), A_i)$ returns the actual class label of a flow instance x, and it can be defined as follows:

$$\Psi(\theta(x_j), A_i) = \begin{cases} 1 & \text{if } \theta(x_j) = A_i \\ 0 & \text{otherwise} \end{cases} \tag{10.12}$$

After labeling the cluster, we can use the standard confusion metrics to evaluate the quality of K-means clustering.

Figure 10.2(a)–(d) illustrates the accuracy value obtained by each individual method. For the K-means and CluClas, the k value was set to 400 (Figure 10.3 justifies the setting of the k value). In general, we can observe that CluClas has better performance than the K-means and HMM methods in terms of TPR, FPR, precision, accuracy, and F-measure on all data sets. In particular, the average F-measure scores of CluClas are always higher than K-means and HMM by about 3.47%–12.21% on all four traffic data sets, and the overall accuracy is always higher than K-means and HMM by about 7.19%–17.48% on all four traffic data sets. This can be explained by the fact that the CluClas method discards the irrelevant and redundant attributes, chooses informative sample flows which can represent the whole data fairly well, and combines the advantages of both K-means and HMM to efficiently build the classification model. It can be seen from Figure 10.2(a)–(d) that the performance of the HMM method outperforms the K-means on all four data sets by about 2.01%–6.45% and 2.17%–7.06% with respect to the overall accuracy and F-measure values.

Figure 10.3(a)–(d) shows the overall accuracy of K-means and CluClas methods with respect to the number of clusters, k. It can be seen that the performance of both K-means and CluClas keeps improving as the number of clusters increased on all four data sets. For example, on the *isp* data set, it can be seen as the number of clusters gradually increased from 5 to 400, the average accuracy of CluClas also keeps improving from 70.011% to 97.016% and from 51.12% to 85.01% for K-means clustering. This can be explained by the fact that setting the number of clusters to a

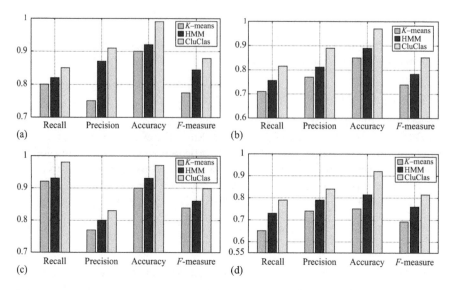

Figure 10.2   *The accuracy performance of K-means, HMM, CluClas methods on four different traffic data sets: (a) comparing the accuracy performance of K-means, HMM, and CluClas methods on DARPA data set; (b) comparing the accuracy performance of K-means, HMM, and CluClas methods on isp data set; (c) comparing the accuracy performance of K-means, HMM, and CluClas methods on wide data set; and (d) comparing the accuracy performance of K-means, HMM, and CluClas methods on ITD data set*

low value would underestimate the natural grouping within the traffic data and thus force samples from different applications to be a part of the same cluster.

Runtime performance

Another key motivation of the CluClas method is to improve the runtime performance of network classification. Thus, in this section, the runtime performance of the CluClas method is compared against each individual method. For each method, the test was repeated ten times to give the average execution time and to have greater confidence in the obtained results.

Figure 10.4(a) shows the normalized training time for the K-means, CluClas, and HMM methods on all four data sets. This is particularly important because the model building phase is computationally time consuming. Note that the value of 1 represents the slowest training time. It can be seen from Figure 10.4(b) that K-means has the fastest training time in comparison to both the CluClas and HMM methods. In particular, the average building time for the K-means method is only 30.12% of the building time of CluClas and 8.34% of the runtime of HMM. Also, it can be seen from Figure 10.4(b) that the CluClas method achieved the second fastest training time

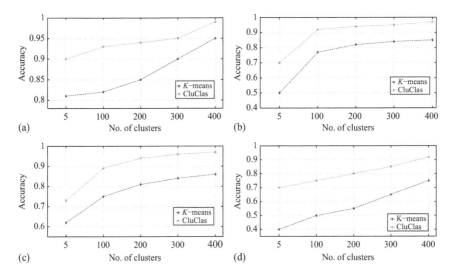

Figure 10.3 The influence of k value variation on accuracy of K-means, HMM,
CluClas methods on four different traffic data sets: (a) the influence of
k value variation on accuracy of K-means and CluClas methods on
DARPA *data set; (b) the influence of* k *value variation on accuracy of*
K-means and CluClas methods on isp *data set; (c) the influence of* k
value variation on accuracy of K-means and CluClas methods on
wide *data set; and (d) the influence of* k *value variation on accuracy*
of K-means and CluClas methods on ITD *data set*

in comparison to HMM, with an average of 27.65%. A promising future research
direction would be to reduce the execution time of these three methods by using
parallel computing, such as multicore CPUs or graphics processing units (GPU).

Figure 10.4(b) compares the normalized classification time of the *K*-means,
CluClas, and HMM methods on all four data sets. This is particularly important
when considering real-time classification of potentially thousands of simultaneous
network flows. Note that the value of 1 represents the slowest classification time. From
Figure 10.4(b), it can be seen that the *K*-means algorithm has the best classification
time, while HMM has the worst classification time. Generally, we observed marginal
differences between these three methods in terms of classification time. To make the
result more precise, the average classification time of *K*-means was about 85.46%
of CluClas and 76.23% of HMM. On the other hand, it is notable that the average
classification time of CluClas was only 89.19% of HMM.

Figure 10.4(c) analyzes the runtime behavior of CluClas and the *K*-means methods when the *k* value was varied. Note that the number of clusters, *k*, varies from 5 to
400. Not surprisingly, it can be observed from Figure 10.4(c) that the computational
time of both methods is affected as the *k* value increases. However, the runtime of
K-means generally is better than CluClas as the value of *k* increases.

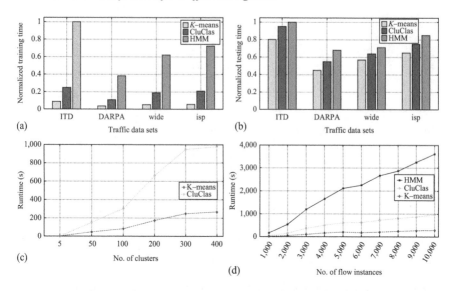

Figure 10.4   *The runtime and scalability performance of K-means, HMM, CluClas methods on four different traffic data sets: (a) comparing the building model time of K-means, HMM, and CluClas methods on all traffic data sets; (b) comparing the classification time of K-means, HMM, and CluClas methods on all traffic data sets; (c) runtime performance of K-means and CluClas methods with respect to the different K value on* wide *data set; and (d) comparing the scalability of K-means, HMM, and CluClas methods on* wide *data set*

This section also examined the scalability of the CluClas method against individual methods, including K-means and HMM. With ever-looming page limitations, it was felt sufficient to evaluate the scalability of the CluClas and the other two methods only on the *wide* data set. For the scalability analysis, the performance of each method was evaluated with traffic samples varying from approximately 1,000 to 10,000 traffic samples (the size of the samples in the training data set is limited by the amount of memory since these methods need to load the entire training data into memory before building the model). As can be seen from Figure 10.4d, K-means scales better than CluClas and HMM, respectively. On the other hand, CluClas obtains better scalability results than HMM; this can be explained by the fact that the CluClas worked only on small representative samples, while the traditional HMM was required to process all of the instances.

10.5   Conclusion

This chapter described the CluClas method for network traffic classification. First, the traffic data was preprocessed by applying a new FS method on the training data to identify informative attributes and remove irrelevant and redundant attributes. Second, representative instances from the training data set are selected to improve the accuracy and efficiency of the learning capability. In particular, we select these representative instances by applying a K-means clustering algorithm to partition the training instances into k disjoint clusters and then select only the centroid of each cluster. Third, the HMM is built on the representative training data to improve overall CA. We compared the method with the individual K-means and HMM in terms of CA and runtime performance over four traffic data sets. The experimental results show that the CluClas method achieved higher CA compared to K-means and HMM. On the other hand, while the CluClas method has improved the accuracy and runtime of network classification, future work could be devoted to improving the scalability of ClaClus method by using (i) the GPU environment and/or (ii) parallel computing.

Chapter 11
Conclusion

Network traffic classification has the potential to resolve key issues for network operators, including network management problems, quality of service provisioning, Internet accounting and charging, and lawful interception [1]. The traditional network classification techniques that rely mostly on well-known port numbers have been used to identify Internet traffic. Such an approach was successful because traditional applications used fixed port numbers; however [9,10] show that the current generations of peer-to-peer (P2P) applications try to hide their traffic by using dynamic port numbers. Consequently, applications whose port numbers are unknown cannot be identified in advance.

Another approach relies on the inspection of packet contents and analyses the packets' payload content to check if they contain signatures of well-known or anomalous applications. Features are extracted from the traffic data and later compared to well-known signatures of applications provided by human experts. This works well for Internet traffic; however, several studies [9,12,171] have shown that this approach has a number of drawbacks and limitations. First, it cannot identify a new or unknown attack for which signatures are not available, so there is a need to maintain an up-to-date list of signatures. This is a problem because new applications and attacks emerge every day; hence, it is not practical and sometimes impossible to keep up with the latest signatures. Second, deep packet inspection is a difficult task as this requires significant processing time and memory. Finally, if the application uses encryption, this approach no longer works. Significant recent research has attracted some attention based on TLS (transport layer statistics) data and efficient data mining algorithms. This assumes that applications typically send data in some sort of pattern, which can be used as a means of classification of connections by different traffic classes. To extract such patterns, only TCP/IP headers are needed to observe flow statistics such as mean packet size, flow length, and total number of packets.

In this book, we investigated several key issues related to the problem of accurate and effective network traffic classification. We were particularly motivated by the specific problems associated with network traffic classification based on Machine Learning (ML) and TLS. Most past research has applied different categories of ML, including supervised learning and unsupervised learning algorithms, on the TLS of the traffic data to address the problem of network traffic analysis.

Significant recent research has revealed that TLS data allows the ML classification-based techniques to rely on sufficient information. In light of these findings, we focused our efforts on the modeling and improvement of network traffic classification based on the concept of ML and TLS data.

The first research question surveyed the most significant recent clustering algorithms. The next two research questions focused on devising more effective pre-processing approaches to improve the quality of selected features to train network classifiers by discarding the irrelevant and redundant features from the original features of the TLS. We then considered a framework to preserve the privacy of network traffic data to help network collaborators to publish their traffic data and make them publicly available for the common good. In particular, such a framework dealt with the unique characteristics of network traffic data to preserve the data privacy and improve their utility for building an accurate traffic classifiers.

Finally, a semi-supervised approach was presented to construct a traffic classification model with a good generalization ability and to evaluate the generated traffic classification. The semi-supervised approach allowed us to discover the emergence of a new class and eliminate outlier instances. Specifically, the following research questions have been addressed in this book:

1. *How to optimize various feature-selection methods and improve the quality of TLS data for accurate and effective network traffic classification?*
2. *How to identify the optimal and stable feature set in the temporal-domain and the spatial-domain for accurate and effective network traffic classification?*
3. *How to preserve the privacy of traffic data publishing for accurate intrusion detection systems and network traffic classification?*
4. *How to "automatically" label raw traffic data for evaluating and building an accurate network traffic classification?*

11.1   Contribution

Here is the outline of the innovations and advantages of the work conducted in this book:

1. *Improve the quality of TLS data for accurate and effective network traffic classification.* TLS was specifically introduced to address the problems caused by traditional classification techniques which use port number and payload. However, the presence of irrelevant and redundant features in the TLS data can affect the accuracy and efficiency of network traffic classification. To achieve better overall classification performance, several feature selection techniques can be used to filter out such irrelevant and redundant features from the original features of the TLS. A key issue with these feature selection techniques is that they are designed with different evaluation criteria (e.g., information-based measure, dependence-based measure, consistency-based measure, and distance-based measure). Therefore, it is a challenge to choose a suitable one for identifying the best features (that minimize redundancy and maximize relevance) for network traffic classification. To address this issue, new metrics were presented, allowing us to extensively evaluate and compare such techniques from

different perspectives including *goodness*, *stability*, and *similarity*. Several issues associated with each feature selection technique were recorded. Consequently, we continue our efforts toward developing an integrated FS technique that is built on the key strengths of existing FS techniques. In particular, a local optimization approach (LOA) is proposed to identify efficiently and accurately select the "best" features by first combining the results of some well-known FS techniques to find consistent features and then use the proposed concept of *support* to select a smallest set of features and cover data optimality. The empirical study over number of high-dimensional network traffic datasets demonstrates significant gain in accuracy and improved runtime performance of a network classifier compared to individual results produced by some well-known FS techniques.

2. *Identify the optimal and stable feature in the temporal-domain and the spatial-domain for accurate network traffic classification.* Obtaining an optimal and stable feature set across the temporal-domain and the spatial-domain is crucial in enhancing the confidence of network operators. This is because an optimal feature selection set does not necessarily imply high stability and vice versa. Thus, with the aim of discovering more-valuable features for the description of traffic flows with respect to both stability and optimality criteria, a global optimization approach (GOA) was proposed. In particular, to avoid a situation where the dependence between a pair of features is weak, but the total intercorrelation of one attribute to the others is strong, the proposed GOA first selects informative features for each feature selection technique from a global perspective. Second, the outputs of multiple well-known FS techniques are combined to obtain a possible optimal feature subsets across different traffic datasets. Third, an adaptive threshold based on entropy is proposed to extract the stable features. Finally, a new *goodness* measure is proposed within a random Forest framework to estimate the final optimum feature subset. Experimental studies on network traffic data in spatial and temporal domains showed that the proposed GOA outperforms the commonly used feature selection techniques in identifying both optimal and stable features for traffic classification. Nevertheless, to enhance the performance of the GOA, an efficient discretization method is used to significantly improve the accuracy of different ML algorithms which suffer from the presence of continuous-valued features in the temporal-domain and the spatial-domain traffic data.

3. *Preserve the privacy for traffic data publishing for accurate network traffic classification.* Sharing traffic data between multiple organizations/sites has become vital requirements for such organizations to create a collaborative anomaly detection, an accurate and a global predictive traffic classification model. However, inappropriate sharing and usage of traffic data could threaten the privacy and security of the data providers resulting in preventing the sharing of data. Consequently, a privacy-preserving framework was proposed to enhance the trust between data providers for publishing network traffic data by maintaining provable privacy of the original traffic data and providing masked data equivalent to the original ones. In particular, our proposed privacy-preserving framework involves (i) vertically partitioning the original dataset to improve the performance

of perturbation; (ii) developing a framework to deal with various types of network traffic data including numerical, categorical, and hierarchical attributes; (iii) grouping the portioned sets into a number of clusters based on the proposed framework; and (iv) the perturbation process is accomplished by the alteration of the original attribute value by a new value (clusters centroid). Extensive experimental analysis on a number of traffic datasets showed that the proposed privacy framework can effectively deal with multivariate traffic attributes, produces compatible results as the original data, improves the performances of the five supervised approaches, and provides high level of privacy protection compared to the traditional privacy-preserving approaches that are still frequently used in many real-world applications.

4. *Automatically label raw traffic data for accurate network traffic classification.* To maintain good traffic classification performance, sufficient, reliable, and up-to-date labeled data is needed. However, due to the high cost and time of manual labeling, it is hard or impossible to obtain such labeled data. As such, a new a novel semi-supervised approach, called *SemTra*, was proposed to automatically alleviate the shortage of labeled flows for ML by exploiting the advantages of both supervised and unsupervised models. In particular, *SemTra* involves the following: (i) generating multi-view representations of the original data based on dimensionality reduction methods to have strong discrimination ability; (ii) incorporating the generated representations into the ensemble clustering model to provide a combined clustering output with better quality and stability; (iii) adapting the concept of self-training to iteratively utilize the few labeled data along with unlabeled within local and global viewpoints; and (iv) obtaining the final class decision by combining the decisions of mapping strategy of clusters, the local self-training, and global self-training approaches. Extensive experimental analysis on a large number of traffic datasets showed that the *SemTra* approach addressed several limitations of the existing semi-supervised approaches, including accurate prediction information for unlabeled instances on multiclass traffic data (e.g., WWW, FTP, P2P, and MAIL) rather than only on normal and attack classes, high stability in predicting actual classes, better novel class detection in the presence of concept-drift, and efficient elimination of outlier instances.

11.2   Future work

This book has proposed a set of innovative approaches to improve the effectiveness and accuracy of network traffic classification. However, as highlighted in the various chapters, there is still room for improvement to these approaches, and also to address other relevant issues in the area of network traffic classification which have not been covered in the book. Based on our current analysis, in this section, we highlight some of these key areas and issues for future exploration.

- Chapter 6 described the LOA to identify the "best" features in the TLS by utilizing the label information. In particular, the LOA approach is designed for *supervised learning* which requires the traffic flows to be labeled in advance to eliminate these features from the TLS data. However, unlabeled traffic data with extremely high dimensionality faces the serious challenge of defining the concept of irrelevant and redundant features in such data. Therefore, it would be valuable to extend the LOA approach to make it applicable for *unsupervised learning*. Also, reducing the computational time and enabling the LOA approach to process large-scale problems efficiently would be a significant achievement by adopting high-performance distributed computing frameworks and protocols, such as MapReduce and MPI.

- Chapter 7 provided details of the GOA to identify both an optimal and stable feature set for network classification. GOA has achieved significant results in accurately classifying traffic from temporal and spatial domains compared to existing feature selection algorithms. However, the generation of the candidate feature set by this approach depends on a multi-criterion fusion which is computationally expensive. Future work would be devoted to enhance the performance of the GOA and to reduce its preprocessing time by using parallel computing such as multicore CPUs or graphics processing units. Nevertheless, theoretical justification is significantly important and should be considered to explain why and how the GOA in fact has found the trade-off between stability and accuracy.

- Chapter 8 described the *PrivTra* framework that aims to preserving privacy in traffic data publishing and to enhancing data mining utility. In particular, we considered different supervised techniques to evaluate the data utility of this privacy framework. However, evaluating the effectiveness of transformed data of such a framework on unsupervised learning points to an interesting direction for future work. Nevertheless, the proposed framework could be used in the area of distributed network classification. Therefore, it is potentially useful to consider the communication cost and amount of data when exchanging the knowledge (based on the processed data) between collaborative learning for effective detection of new patterns and attacks. Furthermore, an investigation into ways of providing probabilistic privacy and accuracy guarantees by using the proposed framework would be extremely useful.

- Chapter 9 provided details of the *SemTra* semi-supervised approach for automatically labeling traffic flow. However, we would like to explore whether any theoretical performance guarantees can be offered by this approach. Although the proposed semi-supervised approach has shown promising results, there is a need to minimize the size of the labeled and unlabeled data by selecting only the most-representative instances of each class rather than the whole traffic dataset to improve the quality and computational time of the labeling process. Furthermore, distinguishing among multiple novel classes is important. Nevertheless, enabling a dynamic number of cluster settings rather than a manual setting to provide a better drift detection mechanism is significantly important and should be considered in the future. Also, within the scope of our current and future work, we would extend the proposed semi-supervised approach to handle class imbalance and to maintain high accuracy (recall) on minority classes without sacrificing the performance of majority classes.

References

[1]   T. T. Nguyen, A novel approach for practical, real-time, machine learn-ing based IP traffic classification, Ph.D. thesis, Swinburne University of Technology Melbourne, Australia (2009).

[2]   L. Burgstahler, K. Dolzer, C. Hauser, *et al.*, Beyond technology: The miss-ing pieces for QoS success, in: Proc. of the ACM SIGCOMM Workshop on Revisiting IP QoS: What have we learned, why do we care? 2003, pp. 121–130.

[3]   M. Miller, and J. Slay, Lessons learned from the Maroochy water breach, in: Proc. of the IFIP International Federation for Information Processing, Vol. 253, 2010.

[4]   K. Poulsen, Slammer worm crashed Ohio nuke plant network, The Reg-ister, http://www.theregister.co.uk/2003/08/20/slammer_worm_crashed_ ohio_nuke/ (August 20, 2003).

[5]   N. Falliere, L. Murchu, and E. Chien, W32. Stuxnet Dossier, White Paper, Symantec Corp, Security Response (2011).

[6]   T. Thomas, Al qaeda and the internet: The danger of 'cyberplanning', Tech. rep., DTIC Document (2003).

[7]   C. Estan, S. Savage, and G. Varghese, Automatically inferring patterns of resource consumption in network traffic, Computer Communication Review 33 (4) (2003) 137–150.

[8]   T. Karagiannis, K. Papagiannaki, and M. Faloutsos, BLINC: multilevel traffic classification in the dark, in: ACM SIGCOMM Computer Communication Review, Vol. 35, 2005, pp. 229–240.

[9]   A. Moore, and K. Papagiannaki, Toward the accurate identification of net-work applications, in: Proc. of International Workshop on Passive and Active Network Measurement (PAM), 2005, pp. 41–54.

[10] T. Karagiannis, A. Broido, M. Faloutsos, *et al.*, Transport layer identification of P2P traffic, in: Proc. of the 4th ACM SIGCOMM Conference on Internet Measurement, ACM, 2004, pp. 121–134.

[11] P. Haffner, S. Sen, O. Spatscheck, and D. Wang, ACAS: automated construc-tion of application signatures, in: Proc. of the ACM SIGCOMM Workshop on Mining Network Data, 2005, pp. 197–202.

[12] T. Auld, A. W. Moore, and S. F. Gull, Bayesian neural networks for internet traffic classification, IEEE Transactions on Neural Networks 18 (1) (2007) 223–239.

[13]   J. Erman, A. Mahanti, M. Arlitt, and C. Williamson, Identifying and dis-
       criminating between web and peer-to-peer traffic in the network core, in:
       Proc. of the 16th ACM International Conference on World Wide Web, 2007,
       pp. 883–892.

[14]   H. Kim, K. Claffy, M. Fomenkov, D. Barman, M. Faloutsos, and K. Lee, Inter-
       net traffic classification demystified: myths, caveats, and the best practices,
       in: Proc. of the ACM CoNEXT Conference, 2008, pp. 11–23.

[15]   T. Chou, K. Yen, and J. Luo, Network intrusion detection design using
       feature selection of soft computing paradigms, International Journal of
       Computational Intelligence 4 (3) (2008) 196–208.

[16]   I. Guyon, and A. Elisseeff, An introduction to variable and feature selection,
       The Journal of Machine Learning Research 3 (2003) 1157–1182.

[17]   A. W. Moore, and D. Zuev, Internet traffic classification using Bayesian anal-
       ysis techniques, in: ACM SIGMETRICS Performance Evaluation Review,
       Vol. 33, 2005, pp. 50–60.

[18]   S. Lee, H. Kim, D. Barman, *et al.*, NetraMark: a network traffic classifica-
       tion benchmark, ACM SIGCOMM Computer Communication Review 41 (1)
       (2011) 22–30.

[19]   W. Li, M. Canini, A. W. Moore, and R. Bolla, Efficient application identifi-
       cation and the temporal and spatial stability of classification schema, Journal
       of Computer Networks 53 (6) (2009) 790–809.

[20]   A. Fahad, Z. Tari, I. Khalil, I. Habib, and H. Alnuweiri, Toward an efficient and
       scalable feature selection approach for internet traffic classification, Journal
       of Computer Networks 57 (9) (2013) 2040–2057.

[21]   M. Hall, Correlation-based feature selection for discrete and numeric class
       machine learning, Ph.D. thesis (2000).

[22]   H. Liu, and H. Motoda, Feature Selection for Knowledge Discovery and Data
       Mining, Boston, MA, USA: Kluwer Academic, Springer, 1998.

[23]   M. Soysal, and E. G. Schmidt, Machine learning algorithms for accurate flow-
       based network traffic classification: evaluation and comparison, Journal of
       Performance Evaluation 67 (6) (2010) 451–467.

[24]   M. Govindarajan, A hybrid RBF-SVM ensemble approach for data mining
       applications, International Journal of Intelligent Systems and Applications
       (IJISA) 6 (3) (2014) 84–95.

[25]   A. Mahmood, C. Leckie, J. Hu, Z. Tari, and M. Atiquzzaman, Network traffic
       analysis and SCADA security, Handbook of Information and Communication
       Security, Springer, 2010, pp. 383–405.

[26]   K. Chan, T. Dillon, and C. Kwong, Modeling of a liquid epoxy molding
       process using a particle swarm optimization-based fuzzy regression approach,
       IEEE Transactions on Industrial Informatics 7 (1) (2011) 148–158.

[27]   J. Liu, Y. Xiao, S. Li, W. Liang, and C. Chen, Cyber security and privacy issues
       in smart grids, IEEE Communications Surveys & Tutorials (99) (2010) 1–17.

[28]   A. Khelil, D. Germanus, and N. Suri, Protection of SCADA communication
       channels, in: J. Lopez, R. Setola, S.D. Wolthusen (eds), Critical Infrastructure
       Protection (2012) 177–196.

[29] S. Oliveira, and O. Zaiane, Privacy preserving clustering by data transformation, Journal of Information and Data Management 1 (1) (2010) 37–51.

[30] R. Vidya Banu, and N. Nagaveni, Evaluation of a perturbation-based technique for privacy preservation in a multi-party clustering scenario, Journal of Information Sciences 232 (2013) 437–448.

[31] G. Ghinita, P. Kalnis, and Y. Tao, Anonymous publication of sensitive transactional data, IEEE Transactions on Knowledge and Data Engineering 23 (2) (2011) 161–174.

[32] A. N. Mahmood, M. E. Kabir, and A. K. Mustafa, New multi-dimensional sorting based k-anonymity microaggregation for statistical disclosure control, in: Proc. of the 8th International Conference on Security and Privacy in Communication Systems (SecureComm), 2013, pp. 256–272.

[33] J. Domingo-Ferrer, A. Martínez-Ballesté, J. M. Mateo-Sanz, and F. Sebé, Efficient multivariate data-oriented microaggregation, The VLDB Journal 15 (4) (2006) 355–369.

[34] J. Erman, A. Mahanti, M. Arlitt, I. Cohen, and C. Williamson, Offline/realtime traffic classification using semi-supervised learning, Journal of Performance Evaluation 64 (9) (2007) 1194–1213.

[35] C. Rotsos, J. Van Gael, A. W. Moore, and Z. Ghahramani, Probabilistic graphical models for semi-supervised traffic classification, in: Proc. of the 6th ACM International Wireless Communications and Mobile Computing Conference, 2010, pp. 752–757.

[36] R. Yuan, Z. Li, X. Guan, and L. Xu, An SVM-based machine learning method for accurate internet traffic classification, Journal of Information Systems Frontiers 12 (2) (2010) 149–156.

[37] N. Williams, S. Zander, and G. Armitage, A preliminary performance comparison of five machine learning algorithms for practical IP traffic flow classification, ACM SIGCOMM Computer Communication Review 36 (5) (2006) 5–16.

[38] H. Almuallim, and T. Dietterich, Learning Boolean concepts in the presence of many irrelevant features, Journal of Artificial Intelligence 69 (1–2) (1994) 279–305.

[39] R. Duda, and P. Hart, Pattern Classification and Scene Analysis, Wiley, 1996.

[40] A. Fahad, Z. Tari, I. Khalil, A. Almalawi, and A. Y. Zomaya, An optimal and stable feature selection approach for traffic classification based on multi-criterion fusion, Future Generation Computer Systems (FGCS) 36 (2014) 156–169.

[41] A. Fahad, Z. Tari, A. Almalawi, A. Goscinski, I. Khalil, and A. Mahmood, PPF-SCADA: privacy preserving framework for SCADA data publishing, Journal of Future Generation Computer Systems (FGCS) 37 (2014) 496–511.

[42] C. Lian, S. Ruan, and T. Denœux, An evidential classifier based on feature selection and two-step classification strategy, Pattern Recognition 48 (7) (2015) 2318–2327.

[43]   Y. Hong, S. Kwong, Y. Chang, and Q. Ren, Unsupervised feature selection using clustering ensembles and population based incremental learning algorithm, Pattern Recognition 41 (9) (2008) 2742–2756.

[44]   E. De la Hoz, E. de la Hoz, A. Ortiz, J. Ortega, and A. Martínez-Álvarez, Feature selection by multi-objective optimisation: application to network anomaly detection by hierarchical self-organising maps, Knowledge-Based Systems 71 (2014) 322–338.

[45]   Y. Hong, S. Kwong, Y. Chang, and Q. Ren, Consensus unsupervised feature ranking from multiple views, Pattern Recognition Letters 29 (5) (2008) 595–602.

[46]   L. Boratto, and S. Carta, Using collaborative filtering to overcome the curse of dimensionality when clustering users in a group recommender system, in: Proc. of the 16th International Conference on Enterprise Information Systems (ICEIS), 2014, pp. 564–572.

[47]   H. Liu, and H. Motoda, Computational Methods of Feature Selection, CRC Press, 2007.

[48]   J. Dai, W. Wang, H. Tian, and L. Liu, Attribute selection based on a new conditional entropy for incomplete decision systems, Knowledge-Based Systems 39 (2013) 207–213.

[49]   B. Xue, L. Cervante, L. Shang, W. N. Browne, and M. Zhang, A multi-objective particle swarm optimisation for filter-based feature selection in classification problems, Connection Science 24 (2–3) (2012) 91–116.

[50]   V. Singh, and S. Pathak, Feature selection using classifier in high dimensional data, arXiv preprint arXiv:1401.0898.

[51]   R. Ruiz, J. C. Riquelme, J. S. Aguilar-Ruiz, and M. García-Torres, Fast feature selection aimed at high-dimensional data via hybrid-sequential-ranked searches, Expert Systems with Applications 39 (12) (2012) 11094–11102.

[52]   M. S. Srivastava, M. N. Joshi, and M. Gaur, A review paper on feature selection methodologies and their applications, International Journal of Computer Science and Network Security (IJCSNS) 14 (5) (2014) 78.

[53]   H. Banati, and M. Bajaj, Fire fly based feature selection approach, International Journal of Computer Science Issues (IJCSI) 8 (4) (2011) 473.

[54]   W. Zhu, G. Si, Y. Zhang, and J. Wang, Neighborhood effective information ratio for hybrid feature subset evaluation and selection, Journal of Neurocomputing 99 (2013) 25–37.

[55]   R. Wald, T. M. Khoshgoftaar, and A. Napolitano, How the choice of wrapper learner and performance metric affects subset evaluation, in: Proc. of the 25th IEEE International Conference on Tools with Artificial Intelligence (ICTAI), 2013, pp. 426–432.

[56]   G. Nandi, An enhanced approach to Las Vegas filter (LVF) feature selection algorithm, in: Proc. of the 2nd National Conference on Emerging Trends and Applications in Computer Science (NCETACS), 2011, pp. 1–3.

[57]   N. R. Suri, M. N. Murty, and G. Athithan, Unsupervised feature selection for outlier detection in categorical data using mutual information, in: 12th

IEEE International Conference on Hybrid Intelligent Systems (HIS), 2012, pp. 253–258.

[58] S. Jiang, and L. Wang, Unsupervised feature selection based on clustering, in: Proc. of the 5th IEEE International Conference on Bio-Inspired Computing: Theories and Applications (BIC-TA), 2010, pp. 263–270.

[59] C.-N. Hsu, H.-J. Huang, and S. Dietrich, The ANNIGMA-wrapper approach to fast feature selection for neural nets, IEEE Transactions on Systems, Man, and Cybernetics, Part B (Cybernetics) 32 (2) (2002) 207–212.

[60] H. Zhou, J. Wu, Y. Wang, and M. Tian, Wrapper approach for feature subset selection using GA, in: Proc. of the IEEE International Symposium on Intelligent Signal Processing and Communication Systems (ISPACS), 2007, pp. 188–191.

[61] C. Freeman, D. Kulić, and O. Basir, An evaluation of classifier-specific filter measure performance for feature selection, Journal of Pattern Recognition 48 (5) (2015) 1812–1826.

[62] H. Liu, and L. Yu, Toward integrating feature selection algorithms for classification and clustering, IEEE Transactions on Knowledge and Data Engineering (TKDE) 17 (4) (2005) 491–502.

[63] F. Azmandian, A. Yilmazer, J. G. Dy, J. A. Aslam, and D. R. Kaeli, Harnessing the power of GPUs to speed up feature selection for outlier detection, Springer Journal of Computer Science and Technology 29 (3) (2014) 408.

[64] I. H. Witten, E. Frank, L. E. Trigg, M. A. Hall, G. Holmes, and S. J. Cunningham, Weka: practical machine learning tools and techniques with java implementations, Working paper 99/11, University of Waikato, Department of Computer Science, Hamilton, New Zealand.

[65] Y. Wang, Y. Xiang, J. Zhang, W. Zhou, G. Wei, and L. T. Yang, Internet traffic classification using constrained clustering, IEEE Transactions on Parallel and Distributed Systems (TPDS) 25 (11) (2014) 2932–2943.

[66] T. T. Nguyen, and G. Armitage, A survey of techniques for internet traffic classification using machine learning, IEEE Communications Surveys & Tutorials 10 (4) (2008) 56–76.

[67] D. Cai, C. Zhang, and X. He, Unsupervised feature selection for multi-cluster data, in: Proc. of the 16th ACM International Conference on Knowledge Discovery and Data Mining, 2010, pp. 333–342.

[68] H. Elghazel, and A. Aussem, Feature selection for unsupervised learning using random cluster ensembles, in: Proc. of the 10th IEEE International Conference on Data Mining (ICDM), 2010, pp. 168–175.

[69] T. F. Covões, E. R. Hruschka, L. N. de Castro, and Á. M. Santos, A cluster-based feature selection approach, Journal of Hybrid Artificial Intelligence Systems (2009) 169–176.

[70] V. A. Bolón-Canedo, N. Sánchez-Maroño, and A. Alonso-Betanzos, Feature selection for high-dimensional data, Progress in Artificial Intelligence 5 (2) (2016) 65–75.

[71] J. Han, J. Pei, and M. Kamber, Data Mining: Concepts and Techniques, Elsevier, 2011.

[72]   X. Wu, K. Yu, W. Ding, H. Wang, and X. Zhu, Online feature selection with streaming features, IEEE Transactions on Pattern Analysis and Machine Intelligence (PAMMI) 35 (5) (2013) 1178–1192.

[73]   M. S. Kankanhalli, J. Wang, and R. Jain, Experiential sampling in multimedia systems, IEEE Transactions on Multimedia 8 (5) (2006) 937–946.

[74]   Yogita, and D. Toshniwal, A framework for outlier detection in evolving data streams by weighting attributes in clustering, Procedia Technology 6 (2012) 214–222.

[75]   C. Zhang, J. Ruan, and Y. Tan, An incremental feature subset selection algorithm based on Boolean matrix in decision system, Convergence Information Technology 12 (2011) 16–23.

[76]   S. Alelyani, J. Tang, and H. Liu, Feature selection for clustering: a review, Data Clustering: Algorithms and Applications 29 (2013) 110–121.

[77]   M. E. Celebi, H. A. Kingravi, and P. A. Vela, A comparative study of efficient initialization methods for the k-means clustering algorithm, Expert Systems with Applications 40 (1) (2013) 200–210.

[78]   R. T. Ng, and J. Han, Clarans: A method for clustering objects for spatial data mining, IEEE Transactions on Knowledge and Data Engineering (TKDE) 14 (5) (2002) 1003–1016.

[79]   S.-J. Horng, M.-Y. Su, Y.-H. Chen, *et al.*, A novel intrusion detection system based on hierarchical clustering and support vector machines, Expert Systems with Applications 38 (1) (2011) 306–313.

[80]   D. G. O. Saunders, J. Win, L. M. Cano, L. J. Szabo, S. Kamoun, and S. Raffaele, Using hierarchical clustering of secreted protein families to classify and rank candidate effectors of rust fungi, PLoS One 7 (1) (2012) 1–14.

[81]   A. N. Mahmood, C. Leckie, and P. Udaya, An efficient clustering scheme to exploit hierarchical data in network traffic analysis, IEEE Transactions on Knowledge and Data Engineering (TKDE) 20 (6) (2008) 752–767.

[82]   G. Karypis, E.-H. Han, and V. Kumar, Chameleon: hierarchical clustering using dynamic modeling, IEEE Journal of Computer 32 (8) (1999) 68–75.

[83]   M. Ester, H.-P. Kriegel, J. Sander, and X. Xu, A density-based algorithm for discovering clusters in large spatial databases with noise, in: KDD, Vol. 96, 1996, pp. 226–231.

[84]   A. Hinneburg, and D. A. Keim, An efficient approach to clustering in large multimedia databases with noise, in: KDD, Vol. 98, 1998, pp. 58–65.

[85]   M. Ankerst, M. M. Breunig, H.-P. Kriegel, and J. Sander, Optics: ordering points to identify the clustering structure, ACM SIGMOD Record 28 (2) (1999) 49–60.

[86]   K. Leung, and C. Leckie, Unsupervised anomaly detection in network intrusion detection using clusters, in: Proc. of the Twenty-eighth Australasian Conference on Computer Science, 2005, pp. 333–342.

[87]   A. Hinneburg, D. A. Keim, *et al.*, Optimal grid-clustering: towards breaking the curse of dimensionality in high-dimensional clustering, in: Proc. International Conference on Very Large Data Bases (VLDB), Vol. 99, 1999, pp. 506–517.

[88] W. Wang, J. Yang, and R. Muntz, Sting: a statistical information grid approach to spatial data mining, in: Proc. International Conference on Very Large Data Bases (VLDB), Vol. 97, 1997, pp. 186–195.

[89] K. H. Law, and L. F. Kwok, IDS false alarm filtering using KNN classifier, in: Proc. of the Springer International Workshop on Information Security Applications, 2004, pp. 114–121.

[90] A. Patcha, and J.-M. Park, An overview of anomaly detection techniques: existing solutions and latest technological trends, Journal of Computer Networks 51 (12) (2007) 3448–3470.

[91] H. Debiao, C. Jianhua, and H. Jin, An id-based proxy signature schemes without bilinear pairings, Annals of Telecommunications – Annales des Télécommunications 66 (11) (2011) 657– 662.

[92] X. Fan, and G. Gong, Accelerating signature-based broadcast authentication for wireless sensor networks, Journal of Ad Hoc Networks 10 (4) (2012) 723–736.

[93] M. Xie, J. Hu, S. Han, and H.-H. Chen, Scalable hypergrid k-NN-based online anomaly detection in wireless sensor networks, IEEE Transactions on Parallel and Distributed Systems (TPDS) 24 (8) (2013) 1661–1670.

[94] D. Damopoulos, G. Kambourakis, and G. Portokalidis, The best of both worlds: a framework for the synergistic operation of host and cloud anomaly-based IDS for smartphones, in: Proc. of the 7th ACM European Workshop on System Security, 2014, p. 6.

[95] F. Angiulli, S. Basta, S. Lodi, and C. Sartori, Distributed strategies for mining outliers in large data sets, IEEE Transactions on Knowledge and Data Engineering (DKE) 25 (7) (2013) 1520–1532.

[96] H. Moradi Koupaie, S. Ibrahim, and J. Hosseinkhani, Outlier detection in stream data by clustering method, International Journal of Advanced Computer Science and Information Technology (IJACSIT) 2 (3) (2013) 24–25.

[97] E. Eskin, A. Arnold, M. Prerau, L. Portnoy, and S. J. Stolfo, Methods of unsupervised anomaly detection using a geometric framework, US Patent 9,306,966 (2016).

[98] N. Görnitz, M. Kloft, K. Rieck, and U. Brefeld, Toward supervised anomaly detection, Journal of Artificial Intelligence Research 46 (2013) 235–262.

[99] M. Kuusela, T. Vatanen, E. Malmi, T. Raiko, T. Aaltonen, and Y. Nagai, Semi-supervised anomaly detection – towards model-independent searches of new physics, Journal of Physics: Conference Series 368 (2012) 012032.

[100] D. Wulsin, J. Gupta, R. Mani, J. Blanco, and B. Litt, Modeling electroen-cephalography waveforms with semi-supervised deep belief nets: fast classification and anomaly measurement, Journal of Neural Engineering 8 (3) (2011) 036015.

[101] S. J. Skudlarek, and H. Yamamoto, Unsupervised anomaly detection within non-numerical sequence data by average index difference, with application to masquerade detection, Applied Stochastic Models in Business and Industry 30 (5) (2014) 632–656.

[102]   A. Tang, S. Sethumadhavan, and S. J. Stolfo, Unsupervised anomaly-based malware detection using hardware features, in: Proc. of the Springer International Workshop on Recent Advances in Intrusion Detection, 2014, pp. 109–129.

[103]   V. Chandola, A. Banerjee, and V. Kumar, Anomaly detection: a survey, ACM Computing Surveys 41 (3) (2009) 15.

[104]   S. Sadik, and L. Gruenwald, Research issues in outlier detection for data streams, ACM SIGKDD Explorations Newsletter 15 (1) (2014) 33–40.

[105]   L. Portnoy, Intrusion detection with unlabeled data using clustering, Ph.D. thesis, Columbia University (2000).

[106]   J. Dukart, K. Mueller, H. Barthel, *et al.*, Meta-analysis based SVM classification enables accurate detection of Alzheimer's disease across different clinical centers using FDG-PET and MRI, Journal of Psychiatry Research: Neuroimaging 212 (3) (2013) 230–236.

[107]   L. Choi, Z. Liu, C. E. Matthews, and M. S. Buchowski, Validation of accelerometer wear and nonwear time classification algorithm, Medicine and Science in Sports and Exercise 43 (2) (2011) 357.

[108]   V. Saligrama, and Z. Chen, Video anomaly detection based on local statistical aggregates, in: IEEE Conference on Computer Vision and Pattern Recognition (CVPR), 2012, pp. 2112–2119.

[109]   F. Simmross-Wattenberg, J. I. Asensio-Perez, P. Casaseca-de-la Higuera, M. Martin-Fernandez, I. A. Dimitriadis, and C. Alberola-Lopez, Anomaly detection in network traffic based on statistical inference and \alpha-stable modeling, IEEE Transactions on Dependable and Secure Computing 8 (4) (2011) 494–509.

[110]   J. Yu, A nonlinear kernel Gaussian mixture model based inferential monitoring approach for fault detection and diagnosis of chemical processes, Journal of Chemical Engineering Science 68 (1) (2012) 506–519.

[111]   J. Ceberio, E. Irurozki, A. Mendiburu, and J. A. Lozano, A distance-based ranking model estimation of distribution algorithm for the flowshop scheduling problem, IEEE Transactions on Evolutionary Computation 18 (2) (2014) 286–300.

[112]   R. T. Aldahdooh, and W. Ashour, DIMK-means distance-based initialization method for k-means clustering algorithm, International Journal of Intelligent Systems and Applications 5 (2) (2013) 41.

[113]   M. Parimala, D. Lopez, and N. Senthilkumar, A survey on density based clustering algorithms for mining large spatial databases, International Journal of Advanced Science and Technology 31 (1) (2011) 59–66.

[114]   X.-y. Zhang, Q. Shen, H.-y. Gao, Z. Zhao, and S. Ci, A density-based method for initializing the k-means clustering algorithm, in: Proc. of International Conference on Network and Computational Intelligence (ICNCI), Vol. 46, 2012, pp. 46–53.

[115]   X. Wang, A fast exact k-nearest neighbors algorithm for high dimensional search using k-means clustering and triangle inequality, in: Proc. of the IEEE International Joint Conference on Neural Networks (IJCNN), 2011, pp. 1293–1299.

[116]   Y. Ma, B. Ma, and T. Jiang, Applying improved clustering algorithm into EC environment data mining, Applied Mechanics & Materials 596 (2014) 951–959.

[117]   S. Dua, and X. Du, Data Mining and Machine Learning in Cybersecurity, 1st Edition, Auerbach Publications, 2011.

[118]   Y. Yang, Z. Liu, and Z. Xing, A review of uncertain data stream clustering algorithms, in: Proc. of the 8th International Conference on Internet Computing for Science and Engineering (ICICSE), 2015, pp. 111–116.

[119]   M. Yeh, B. Dai, and M. Chen, Clustering over multiple evolving streams by events and correlations, IEEE Transactions on Knowledge and Data Engineering (TKDE) 19 (10) (2007) 1349–1362.

[120]   N. Y. Almusallam, Z. Tari, P. Bertok, and A. Y. Zomaya, Dimensionality reduction for intrusion detection systems in multi-data streams – a review and proposal of unsupervised feature selection scheme, in: Emergent Computation, Springer, 2017, pp. 467–487.

[121]   L. Golab, and M. T. Özsu, Issues in data stream management, ACM SIGMOD Record 32 (2) (2003) 5–14.

[122]   J. Leskovec, A. Rajaraman, and J. D. Ullman, Mining of Massive Datasets, 2nd Edition, Cambridge University Press, New York, NY, USA, 2014.

[123]   A. Bifet, G. Holmes, R. Kirkby, and B. Pfahringer, MOA: massive online analysis, Journal of Machine Learning Research 11 (2010) 1601–1604. http://dl.acm.org/citation.cfm?id=1756006.1859903

[124]   W. Zang, P. Zhang, C. Zhou, and L. Guo, Comparative study between incremental and ensemble learning on data streams: case study, Journal of Big Data 1 (1) (2014) 5. doi:10.1186/2196-1115-1-5.

[125]   I. Mierswa, M. Wurst, R. Klinkenberg, M. Scholz, and T. Euler, Yale: Rapid prototyping for complex data mining tasks, in: Proc. of the 12th ACM SIGKDD International Conference on Knowledge Discovery and Data Mining, 2006, pp. 935–940.

[126]   L. Feng, S. Liu, Y. Xiao, e.-J. Wang, *et al.*, Subspace detection on concept drifting data stream, in: Springer Conference on Adaptation, Learning and Optimization, 2015, pp. 51–59.

[127]   M. Elahi, K. Li, W. Nisar, X. Lv, and H. Wang, Detection of local outlier over dynamic data streams using efficient partitioning method, in: WRI World Congress on Computer Science and Information Engineering, Vol. 4, 2009, pp. 76–81.

[128]   A. Bifet, and G. D. F. Morales, Big data stream learning with SAMOA, in: IEEE International Conference on Data Mining Workshop, 2014, pp. 1199–1202.

[129]   M. Elahi, K. Li, W. Nisar, X. Lv, and H. Wang, Efficient clustering-based outlier detection algorithm for dynamic data stream, in: Proc. of the International Conference on Fuzzy Systems and Knowledge Discovery, Vol. 5, 2008, pp. 298–304.

[130]   J. Ren, Q. Wu, J. Zhang, and C. Hu, Efficient outlier detection algorithm for heterogeneous data streams, in: Proc. of the 6th International Conference on Fuzzy Systems and Knowledge Discovery, Vol. 5, 2009, pp. 259–264.

[131]   Z. Chen, A. Delis, and P. Wei, Identification and management of sessions generated by instant messaging and peer-to-peer systems, International Journal of Cooperative Information Systems 17 (01) (2008) 1–51.

[132]   M. Cotton, L. Eggert, J. Touch, M. Westerlund, and S. Cheshire, Internet assigned numbers authority (IANA) procedures for the management of the service name and transport protocol port number registry (2011), http://www.iana.org/assignments/port-numbers; [Date last accessed: 2014, 22 February].

[133]   C. Fraleigh, S. Moon, B. Lyles, *et al.*, Packet-level traffic measurements from the sprint IP backbone, IEEE Network 17 (6) (2003) 6–16.

[134]   D. Moore, K. Keys, R. Koga, E. Lagache, and K. C. Claffy, The CoralReef software suite as a tool for system and network administrators, in: Proc. of the 15th USENIX Conference on System Administration, USENIX Association, 2001, pp. 133–144.

[135]   R. Keralapura, A. Nucci, and C.-N. Chuah, A novel self-learning architecture for P2P traffic classification in high speed networks, Journal of Computer Networks 54 (7) (2010) 1055–1068.

[136]   Z. Chen, P. Wei, and A. Delis, Catching remote administration Trojans (RATs), Software: Practice and Experience 38 (7) (2008) 667–703.

[137]   S. Sen, O. Spatscheck, and D. Wang, Accurate, scalable in-network identification of P2P traffic using application signatures, in: Proc. of the 13th ACM International Conference on World Wide Web, 2004, pp. 512–521.

[138]   H. Dreger, A. Feldmann, M. Mai, V. Paxson, and R. Sommer, Dynamic application-layer protocol analysis for network intrusion detection, in: USENIX Security Symposium, 2006, pp. 257–272.

[139]   J. Ma, K. Levchenko, C. Kreibich, S. Savage, and G. M. Voelker, Unexpected means of protocol inference, in: Proc. of the 6th ACM SIGCOMM Conference on Internet Measurement, 2006, pp. 313–326.

[140]   A. Spognardi, A. Lucarelli, and R. Di Pietro, A methodology for P2P file-sharing traffic detection, in: Proc. of the 2nd IEEE International Workshop on Hot Topics in Peer-to-Peer Systems (HOT-P2P), 2005, pp. 52–61.

[141]   C. Dewes, A. Wichmann, and A. Feldmann, An analysis of internet chat systems, in: Proc. of the 3rd ACM SIGCOMM Conference on Internet Measurement, 2003, pp. 51–64.

[142]   M. Iliofotou, P. Pappu, M. Faloutsos, M. Mitzenmacher, S. Singh, and G. Varghese, Network monitoring using traffic dispersion graphs (TDGS), in: Proc. of the 7th ACM SIGCOMM Conference on Internet Measurement, 2007, pp. 315–320.

[143]   F. Risso, M. Baldi, O. Morandi, A. Baldini, and P. Monclus, Lightweight, payload-based traffic classification: an experimental evaluation, in: Proc. of the IEEE International Conference on Communications (ICC), 2008, pp. 5869–5875.

[144]   M. Roughan, S. Sen, O. Spatscheck, and N. Duffield, Class-of-service mapping for QoS: a statistical signature-based approach to IP traffic classification, in: Proc. of the 4th ACM SIGCOMM Conference on Internet Measurement, 2004, pp. 135–148.

[145] D. Bonfiglio, M. Mellia, M. Meo, D. Rossi, and P. Tofanelli, Revealing Skype traffic: when randomness plays with you, in: Proc. of the ACM SIGCOMM Computer Communication Review, Vol. 37, 2007, pp. 37–48.

[146] M. Crotti, M. Dusi, F. Gringoli, and L. Salgarelli, Traffic classification through simple statistical fingerprinting, Proc. of the ACM SIGCOMM Computer Communication Review 37 (1) (2007) 5–16.

[147] D. Zuev, and A. Moore, Traffic classification using a statistical approach, in: Proc. of the 6th International Workshop on Passive and Active Network Measurement (PAM), 2005, pp. 321–324.

[148] A. Moore, D. Zuev, and M. Crogan, Discriminators for Use in Flow-based Classification, Queen Mary and Westfield College, Department of Computer Science, 2005.

[149] F. Tan, Improving Feature Selection Techniques for Machine Learning, Vol. 68, Georgia State University, 2007.

[150] N. V. Chawla, L. O. Hall, and A. Joshi, Wrapper-based computation and evaluation of sampling methods for imbalanced datasets, in: Proc. of the 1st ACM International Workshop on Utility-based Data Mining, 2005, pp. 24–33.

[151] R. Kohavi, and G. H. John, Wrappers for feature subset selection, Journal of Artificial Intelligence 97 (1) (1997) 273–324.

[152] P. Van Der Putten, and M. Van Someren, A bias-variance analysis of a real world learning problem: the coil challenge 2000, Journal of Machine Learning 57 (1–2) (2004) 177–195.

[153] S. Zander, T. Nguyen, and G. Armitage, Automated traffic classification and application identification using machine learning, in: Proc. of the 30th IEEE Local Computer Networks Conference (LCN), 2005, pp. 250–257.

[154] D. Lei, Y. Xiaochun, and X. Jun, Optimizing traffic classification using hybrid feature selection, in: Proc. of the 9th IEEE International Conference on Web-Age Information Management (WAIM), 2008, pp. 520–525.

[155] S. Valenti, and D. Rossi, Identifying key features for P2P traffic classification, in: Proc. of IEEE International Conference on Communications (ICC), 2011, pp. 1–6.

[156] J.-j. Zhao, X.-h. Huang, Q. Sun, and Y. Ma, Real-time feature selection in traffic classification, The Journal of China Universities of Posts and Telecommunications 15 (2008) 68–72.

[157] H. A. Jamil, A. Mohammed, A. Hamza, S. M. Nor, and M. N. Marsono, Selection of on-line features for peer-to-peer network traffic classification, in: Recent Advances in Intelligent Informatics, Springer, 2014, pp. 379–390.

[158] H. A. Jamil, R. Zarei, N. O. Fadlelssied, M. Aliyu, S. M. Nor, and M. N. Marsono, Analysis of features selection for P2P traffic detection using support vector machine, in: Proc. of the IEEE International Conference of Information and Communication Technology (ICoICT), 2013, pp. 116–121.

[159] L. Zhen, and L. Qiong, Balanced feature selection method for internet traffic classification, IET Networks 1 (2) (2012) 74–83.

[160] H. Zhang, G. Lu, M. T. Qassrawi, Y. Zhang, and X. Yu, Feature selection for optimizing traffic classification, Journal of Computer Communications 35 (12) (2012) 1457–1471.

[161] Z. Chen, M. Roussopoulos, Z. Liang, Y. Zhang, Z. Chen, and A. Delis, Malware characteristics and threats on the internet ecosystem, Journal of Systems and Software 85 (7) (2012) 1650–1672.

[162] L. Bernaille, R. Teixeira, I. Akodkenou, A. Soule, and K. Salamatian, Traffic classification on the fly, ACM SIGCOMM Computer Communication Review 36 (2) (2006) 23–26.

[163] J. Erman, M. Arlitt, and A. Mahanti, Traffic classification using clustering algorithms, in: Proc. of the ACM SIGCOMM Workshop on Mining Network Data, 2006, pp. 281–286.

[164] A. McGregor, M. Hall, P. Lorier, and J. Brunskill, Flow clustering using machine learning techniques, in: Proc. of the 5th International Workshop on Passive and Active Network Measurement (PAM), 2004, pp. 205–214.

[165] J. P. Early, C. E. Brodley, and C. Rosenberg, Behavioral authentication of server flows, in: Proc. of the 19th IEEE Computer Security Applications Conference, 2003, pp. 46–55.

[166] Y.-s. Lim, H.-c. Kim, J. Jeong, C.-k. Kim, T. T. Kwon, and Y. Choi, Internet traffic classification demystified: on the sources of the discriminative power, in: Proc. of the 6th ACM International Conference Co-NEXT, 2010, pp. 9–21.

[167] G. Xie, M. Iliofotou, R. Keralapura, M. Faloutsos, and A. Nucci, Subflow: Towards practical flow-level traffic classification, in: Proc. of the 31st IEEE International Conference on Computer Communications (INFOCOM), 2012, pp. 2541–2545.

[168] J. Zhang, Y. Xiang, Y. Wang, W. Zhou, Y. Xiang, and Y. Guan, Network traffic classification using correlation information, IEEE Transactions on Parallel and Distributed Systems (TPDS) 24 (1) (2013) 104–117.

[169] J. Erman, A. Mahanti, and M. Arlitt, Qrp05-4: Internet traffic identification using machine learning, in: Proc. of the IEEE Global Telecommunications Conference (GLOBECOM), 2006, pp. 1–6.

[170] D. H. Fisher Jr, M. J. Pazzani, and P. Langley, Concept Formation Knowledge and Experience in Unsupervised Learning, Morgan Kaufmann Publishers Inc., 1991.

[171] J. Yuan, Z. Li, and R. Yuan, Information entropy based clustering method for unsupervised internet traffic classification, in: Proc. of the IEEE International Conference on Communications (ICC), 2008, pp. 1588–1592.

[172] M. Iliofotou, H.-c. Kim, M. Faloutsos, M. Mitzenmacher, P. Pappu, and G. Varghese, Graph-based P2P traffic classification at the internet backbone, in: Proc. of the IEEE INFOCOM Workshop, 2009, pp. 1–6.

[173] J. Zhang, C. Chen, Y. Xiang, W. Zhou, and A. V. Vasilakos, An effective network traffic classification method with unknown flow detection, IEEE Transactions on Network and Service Management 10 (2) (2013) 133–147.

[174] Y. Wang, Y. Xiang, and J. Zhang, Network traffic clustering using random forest proximities, in: Proc. of the IEEE International Conference on Communications (ICC), 2013, pp. 2058–2062.

[175] G.-z. Lin, Y. Xin, X.-x. Niu, and H.-b. Jiang, Network traffic classification based on semi-supervised clustering, The Journal of China Universities of Posts and Telecommunications 17 (2010) 84–88.

[176] F. Qian, G.-m. Hu, and X.-m. Yao, Semi-supervised internet network traffic classification using a Gaussian mixture model, AEU-International Journal of Electronics and Communications 62 (7) (2008) 557–564.

[177] Y. Wang, Y. Xiang, J. Zhang, and S. Yu, A novel semi-supervised approach for network traffic clustering, in: Proc. of the 5th IEEE International Conference on Network and System Security (NSS), 2011, pp. 169–175.

[178] P. Li, Y. Wang, and X. Tao, A semi-supervised network traffic classification method based on incremental learning, in: Proc. of the Springer International Conference on Information Technology and Software Engineering, 2013, pp. 955–964.

[179] R. S. Wong, T.-S. Moh, and M. Moh, Efficient semi-supervised learning bitTorrent traffic detection-an extended summary, Distributed Computing and Networking, Springer, 2012, pp. 540–543.

[180] A. Shrivastav, and A. Tiwari, Network traffic classification using semi-supervised approach, in: Proc. of the 2nd IEEE International Conference on Machine Learning and Computing (ICMLC), 2010, pp. 345–349.

[181] F. Gargiulo, C. Mazzariello, and C. Sansone, Automatically building datasets of labeled IP traffic traces: a self-training approach, Journal of Applied Soft Computing 12 (6) (2012) 1640–1649.

[182] P. Casas, J. Mazel, and P. Owezarski, MINETRAC: mining flows for unsupervised analysis & semi-supervised classification, in: Proc. of the 23rd International Teletraffic Congress, International Teletraffic Congress, 2011, pp. 87–94.

[183] J. Zhang, X. Chen, Y. Xiang, W. Zhou, and J. Wu, Robust network traffic classification, IEEE/ACM Transactions on Networking (TON) 23 (4) (2015) 1257–1270.

[184] J. Yan, X. Yun, Z. Wu, H. Luo, and S. Zhang, A novel weighted combination technique for traffic classification, in: Proc. of the 2nd IEEE International Conference on Cloud Computing and Intelligent Systems (CCIS), Vol. 2, 2012, pp. 757–761.

[185] J. M. Reddy, and C. Hota, P2P traffic classification using ensemble learning, in: Proc. of the 5th IBM ACM Collaborative Academia Research Exchange Workshop, 2013, pp. 14–18.

[186] H. He, C. Che, F. Ma, J. Zhang, and X. Luo, Traffic classification using ensemble learning and co-training, in: Proc. of the 8th Conference on Applied Informatics and Communications, World Scientific and Engineering Academy and Society (WSEAS), 2008, pp. 458–463.

[187] H. He, X. Luo, F. Ma, C. Che, and J. Wang, Network traffic classification based on ensemble learning and co-training, Science in China Series F: Information Sciences 52 (2) (2009) 338–346.

[188] M. S. Aliakbarian, and A. Fanian, Internet traffic classification using MOEA and online refinement in voting on ensemble methods, in: Proc. of the 21st IEEE Iranian Conference on Electrical Engineering (ICEE), 2013, pp. 1–6.

[189] K. Xu, Z.-L. Zhang, and S. Bhattacharyya, Profiling internet backbone traffic: behavior models and applications, ACM SIGCOMM Computer Communication Review 35 (2005) 169–180.

[190] E. Cohen, N. Duffield, H. Kaplan, C. Lund, and M. Thorup, Algorithms and estimators for accurate summarization of internet traffic, in: Proc. of the 7th ACM SIGCOMM Conference on Internet Measurement, 2007, pp. 265–278.

[191] A. Mahmood, C. Leckie, R. Islam, and Z. Tari, Hierarchical summarization techniques for network traffic, in: Proc. of the 6th IEEE Conference on Industrial Electronics and Applications (ICIEA), 2011, pp. 2474–2479.

[192] D. Hoplaros, Z. Tari, and I. Khalil, Data summarization for network traffic monitoring, Journal of Network and Computer Applications 37 (2014) 194–205.

[193] V. Chandola, and V. Kumar, Summarization – compressing data into an informative representation, Journal of Knowledge and Information Systems 12 (3) (2007) 355–378.

[194] C. C. Aggarwal, J. Han, J. Wang, and S. Y. Philip, On high dimensional projected clustering of data streams, Journal of Data Mining and Knowledge Discovery 10 (3) (2005) 251–273.

[195] P. Guarda, and N. Zannone, Towards the development of privacy-aware systems, Journal of Information and Software Technology 51 (2) (2009) 337–350.

[196] S. D. Warren, and L. D. Brandeis, The right to privacy, Harvard Law Review 4 (5) (1890) 193–220.

[197] J. Park Yong, Provision of internet privacy and market conditions: an empirical analysis, Journal of Telecommunications Policy 35 (7) (2011) 650–662.

[198] G. D. Bissias, M. Liberatore, D. Jensen, and B. N. Levine, Privacy vulnerabilities in encrypted http streams, in: Proc. of Privacy Enhancing Technologies, Springer, 2006, pp. 1–11.

[199] A. Iacovazzi, and A. Baiocchi, Internet traffic privacy enhancement with masking: optimization and tradeoffs, IEEE Transactions on Parallel and Distributed Systems (TPDS) 25 (2) (2014) 353–362.

[200] S. Mazumder, T. Sharma, R. Mitra, N. Sengupta, and J. Sil, Generation of sufficient cut points to discretize network traffic data sets, Swarm, Evolutionary, and Memetic Computing, Springer, 2012, pp. 528–539.

[201] Y. Liu, Z. Li, S. Guo, and T. Feng, Efficient, accurate internet traffic classification using discretization in naive Bayes, in: Proc. of the IEEE International Conference on Networking, Sensing and Control (ICNSC), 2008, pp. 1589–1592.

[202] C. Benoit, Cisco systems netFlow services export version 9, RFC 3954, Internet Engineering Task Force, 2004

[203] R. R. Kompella, and C. Estan, The power of slicing in internet flow measurement, in: Proc. of the 5th ACM SIGCOMM Conference on Internet Measurement, 2005, pp. 106–118.

[204] N. Hohn, and D. Veitch, Inverting sampled traffic, in: Proc. of the 3rd ACM SIGCOMM Conference on Internet Measurement, 2003, pp. 222–233.

[205] A. Kumar, and J. Xu, Sketch guided sampling-using on-line estimates of flow size for adaptive data collection, in: Proc. of the 25th IEEE International Conference on Computer Communications (INFOCOM), 2006, pp. 1–12.

[206] A. Ramachandran, S. Seetharaman, N. Feamster, and V. Vazirani, Fast monitoring of traffic subpopulations, in: Proc. of the 8th ACM SIGCOMM Conference on Internet Measurement, 2008, pp. 257–270.

[207] M. Saxena, and R. R. Kompella, CLAMP: efficient class-based sampling for flexible flow monitoring, Journal of Computer Networks 54 (14) (2010) 2345–2356.

[208] G. He, and J. C. Hou, On sampling self-similar internet traffic, Journal of Computer Networks 50 (16) (2006) 2919–2936.

[209] H. He, and E. A. Garcia, Learning from imbalanced data, IEEE Transactions on Knowledge and Data Engineering 21 (9) (2009) 1263–1284.

[210] L. Zhen, and L. Qiong, Studying cost-sensitive learning for multi-class imbalance in internet traffic classification, Journal of China Universities of Posts and Telecommunications 19 (6) (2012) 63–72.

[211] L. Yang, and G. Michailidis, Sampled based estimation of network traffic flow characteristics, in: Proc. of the 26th IEEE International Conference on Computer Communications (INFOCOM), 2007, pp. 1775–1783.

[212] S. Fernandes, C. Kamienski, J. Kelner, D. Mariz, and D. Sadok, A stratified traffic sampling methodology for seeing the big picture, Journal of Computer Networks 52 (14) (2008) 2677–2689.

[213] S. Zander, T. Nguyen, and G. Armitage, Sub-flow packet sampling for scalable ML classification of interactive traffic, in: Proc. of the 37th IEEE Conference on Local Computer Networks (LCN), 2012, pp. 68–75.

[214] F. Gringoli, L. Salgarelli, M. Dusi, N. Cascarano, F. Risso, *et al.*, GT: picking up the truth from the ground for internet traffic, ACM SIGCOMM Computer Communication Review 39 (5) (2009) 12–18.

[215] M. Dusi, F. Gringoli, and L. Salgarelli, Quantifying the accuracy of the ground truth associated with internet traffic traces, Journal of Computer Networks 55 (5) (2011) 1158–1167.

[216] J.-q. Lu, X. Tian, X.-h. Huang, Y.-j. Wu, Y. Ma, and Z.-s. Su, Flowsing: a multi-agent based offline ground-truth generator, Journal of China Universities of Posts and Telecommunications 18 (2011) 106–111.

[217] C. C. Aggarwal, and C. Zhai, A survey of text clustering algorithms, Mining Text Data, Springer, 2012, pp. 77–128.

[218] A. A. Abbasi, and M. Younis, A survey on clustering algorithms for wireless sensor networks, Journal of Computer Communications 30 (14) (2007) 2826–2841.

[219] R. Xu, and D. Wunsch, Survey of clustering algorithms, IEEE Transactions on Neural Networks 16 (3) (2005) 645–678.

[220]   R. Yuan, Z. Li, X. Guan, and L. Xu, An SVM-based machine learning method for accurate internet traffic classification, Journal of Information Systems Frontiers 12 (2) (2010) 149–156.

[221]   J. C. Bezdek, R. Ehrlich, and W. Full, FCM: The fuzzy c-means clustering algorithm, Journal of Computers & Geosciences 10 (2) (1984) 191–203.

[222]   T. Zhang, R. Ramakrishnan, and M. Livny, Birch: an efficient data clustering method for very large databases, in: ACM SIGMOD Record, Vol. 25, 1996, pp. 103–114.

[223]   A. P. Dempster, N. M. Laird, and D. B. Rubin, Maximum likelihood from incomplete data via the EM algorithm, Journal of the Royal Statistical Society. Series B (Methodological) 39 (1) (1977) 1–22.

[224]   J. MacQueen, Some methods for classification and analysis of multivariate observations, in: Proc. of the 5th Berkeley Symposium on Mathematical Statistics and Probability, Vol. 1, 1967, pp. 281–297.

[225]   Z. Huang, A fast clustering algorithm to cluster very large categorical data sets in data mining, in: Proc. of the SIGMOD Workshop on Research Issues on Data Mining and Knowledge Discovery, 1997, pp. 1–8.

[226]   H.-S. Park, and C.-H. Jun, A simple and fast algorithm for k-medoids clustering, Journal on Expert Systems with Applications 36 (2) (2009) 3336–3341.

[227]   R. T. Ng, and J. Han, Efficient and effective clustering methods for spatial data mining, in: Proc. International Conference on Very Large Data Bases (VLDB), 1994, pp. 144–155.

[228]   L. Kaufman, and P. J. Rousseeuw, Finding groups in data: an introduction to cluster analysis, Vol. 344, John Wiley & Sons, 2009.

[229]   S. Guha, R. Rastogi, and K. Shim, Cure: an efficient clustering algorithm for large databases, in: ACM SIGMOD Record, Vol. 27, 1998, pp. 73–84.

[230]   S. Guha, R. Rastogi, and K. Shim, Rock: a robust clustering algorithm for categorical attributes, Journal of Information systems 25 (5) (2000) 345–366.

[231]   A. Mahmood, C. Leckie, and P. Udaya, An efficient clustering scheme to exploit hierarchical data in network traffic analysis, IEEE Transactions on Knowledge and Data Engineering (TKDE) 20 (6) (2008) 752–767.

[232]   X. Xu, M. Ester, H.-P. Kriegel, and J. Sander, A distribution-based clustering algorithm for mining in large spatial databases, in: Proc. of 14th IEEE International Conference on Data Engineering (ICDE), 1998, pp. 324–331.

[233]   G. Sheikholeslami, S. Chatterjee, and A. Zhang, Wavecluster: a multi-resolution clustering approach for very large spatial databases, in: Proc. International Conference on Very Large Data Bases (VLDB), Vol. 98, 1998, pp. 428–439.

[234]   A. K. Jain, and R. C. Dubes, Algorithms for Clustering Data, Prentice-Hall, Inc., 1988.

[235]   D. H. Fisher, Knowledge acquisition via incremental conceptual clustering, Springer Journal of Machine Learning 2 (2) (1987) 139–172.

[236]   J. H. Gennari, P. Langley, and D. Fisher, Models of incremental concept formation, Journal of Artificial intelligence 40 (1) (1989) 11–61.

[237] T. Kohonen, The self-organizing map, Journal of Neurocomputing 21 (1) (1998) 1–6.

[238] J. Han, M. Kamber, and J. Pei, Data mining: concepts and techniques, Morgan Kaufmann Publishers Inc., 2011.

[239] M. Meilă, and D. Heckerman, An experimental comparison of several clustering and initialization methods, in: Proc. of the 14th Conference on Uncertainty in Artificial Intelligence, Morgan Kaufmann Publishers Inc., 1998, pp. 386–395.

[240] S. Suthaharan, M. Alzahrani, S. Rajasegarar, C. Leckie, and M. Palaniswami, Labelled data collection for anomaly detection in wireless sensor networks, in: Proc. of the 6th IEEE International Conference on Intelligent Sensors, Sensor Networks and Information Processing (ISSNIP), 2010, pp. 269–274.

[241] A. Almalawi, Z. Tari, A. Fahad, and I. Khalil, A framework for improving the accuracy of unsupervised intrusion detection for SCADA systems, in: Proc. of the 12th IEEE International Conference on Trust, Security and Privacy in Computing and Communications (TrustCom), 2013, pp. 292–301.

[242] A. Almalawi, Z. Tari, I. Khalil, and A. Fahad, SCADAVT-A framework for SCADA security testbed based on virtualization technology, in: Proc. of the 38th International Conference on Local Computer Networks (LCN), 2013, pp. 639–646.

[243] S. Stolfo, W. Fan, W. Lee, A. Prodromidis, and P. Chan, Cost-based modeling for fraud and intrusion detection: results from the jam project, in: Proc. of the DARPA IEEE Information Survivability Conference and Exposition (DISCEX), Vol. 2, 2000, pp. 130–144.

[244] A. Moore, J. Hall, C. Kreibich, E. Harris, and I. Pratt, Architecture of a network monitor, in: Passive & Active Measurement Workshop (PAM), 2003.

[245] A. Moore, and D. Zuev, Internet traffic classification using Bayesian analysis techniques, in: Proc. of the ACM International Conference on Measurement and Modeling of Computer Systems (SIGMETRICS), 2005, pp. 50–60.

[246] L. Hubert, and P. Arabie, Comparing partitions, Journal of Classification 2 (1) (1985) 193–218.

[247] A. N. Mahmood, C. Leckie, and P. Udaya, Echidna: efficient clustering of hierarchical data for network traffic analysis, in: Proc. of the International Conference on Performance of Computer and Communication Networks; Mobile and Wireless Communications Systems (NETWORKING), Springer, 2006, pp. 1092–1098.

[248] S. G. Eick, M. C. Nelson, and J. D. Schmidt, Graphical analysis of computer log files, Communications of the ACM (CACM) 37 (12) (1994) 50–56.

[249] H. Liu, and R. Setiono, Chi2: Feature selection and discretization of numeric attributes, in: Proc. of the 7th International Conference on Tools with Artificial Intelligence, 1995, pp. 388–391.

[250] P. Mitra, C. Murthy, and S. K. Pal, Unsupervised feature selection using feature similarity, IEEE Transactions on Pattern Analysis and Machine Intelligence (PAMMI) 24 (3) (2002) 301–312.

[251]   Z. Zhao, and H. Liu, Spectral feature selection for supervised and unsu-
        pervised learning, in: Proc. of the 24th ACM International Conference on
        Machine Learning, 2007, pp. 1151–1157.

[252]   J. He, S. Kumar, and S.-F. Chang, On the difficulty of nearest neighbor
        search, arXiv preprint arXiv:1206.6411.

[253]   D. Xu, and Y. Tian, A comprehensive survey of clustering algorithms, Annals
        of Data Science 2 (2) (2015) 165–193.

[254]   Q. Gu, Z. Li, and J. Han, Generalized fisher score for feature selection, arXiv
        preprint arXiv:1202.3725.

[255]   C. Su, and J. Hsu, An extended Chi2 algorithm for discretization of real
        value attributes, IEEE Transactions on Knowledge and Data Engineering
        (TKDE) 17 (3) (2005) 437–441.

[256]   X. He, D. Cai, and P. Niyogi, Laplacian score for feature selection, in:
        Advances in Neural Information Processing Systems, 2006, pp. 507–514.

[257]   A. J. Onwuegbuzie, L. Daniel, and N. L. Leech, Pearson product-moment
        correlation coefficient, Encyclopedia of Measurement and Statistics (2007)
        751–756.

[258]   C. R. Rao, Linear Statistical Inference and Its Applications, Vol. 22, John
        Wiley & Sons, 2009.

[259]   M. S. Sainin, and R. Alfred, A genetic based wrapper feature selection
        approach using nearest neighbour distance matrix, in: Proc. of the 3rd IEEE
        Conference on Data Mining and Optimization (DMO), 2011, pp. 237–242.

[260]   T. Kanungo, D. M. Mount, N. S. Netanyahu, C. D. Piatko, R. Silverman,
        and A. Y. Wu, An efficient k-means clustering algorithm: analysis and
        implementation, IEEE Transactions on Pattern Analysis and Machine
        Intelligence (PAMMI) 24 (7) (2002) 881–892.

[261]   G. H. John, and P. Langley, Estimating continuous distributions in Bayesian
        classifiers, in: Proc. of the Eleventh Conference on Uncertainty in Artificial
        Intelligence, Morgan Kaufmann Publishers Inc., 1995, pp. 338–345.

[262]   J. Quinlan, C4. 5: Programs for Machine Learning, Morgan Kaufmann, 1993.

[263]   D. W. Aha, D. Kibler, and M. K. Albert, Instance-based learning algorithms,
        Machine Learning 6 (1) (1991) 37–66.

[264]   H.-L. Chen, B. Yang, J. Liu, and D.-Y. Liu, A support vector machine
        classifier with rough set-based feature selection for breast cancer diagnosis,
        Expert Systems with Applications 38 (7) (2011) 9014–9022.

[265]   A. Blum, and P. Langley, Selection of relevant features and examples in
        machine learning, Journal of Artificial Intelligence 97 (1–2) (1997) 245–271.

[266]   J. Zhang, C. Chen, Y. Xiang, and W. Zhou, Internet traffic classification
        by aggregating correlated naive Bayes predictions, IEEE Transactions on
        Information Forensics and Security 8 (1) (2013) 5–15.

[267]   B. Verma, and A. Rahman, Cluster-oriented ensemble classifier: impact
        of multicluster characterization on ensemble classifier learning, IEEE
        Transactions on Knowledge and Data Engineering (TKDE) 24 (4) (2012)
        605–618.

[268] J. Kittler, M. Hatef, R. Duin, and J. Matas, On combining classifiers, IEEE Transactions on Pattern Analysis and Machine Intelligence (PAMMI) 20 (3) (1998) 226–239.

[269] J. Kodovsky, J. Fridrich, and V. Holub, Ensemble classifiers for steganalysis of digital media, IEEE Transactions on Information Forensics and Security (TIFS) 7 (2) (2012) 432–444.

[270] Y. Yang, and K. Chen, Temporal data clustering via weighted clustering ensemble with different representations, IEEE Transactions on Knowledge and Data Engineering (TKDE) 23 (2) (2011) 307–320.

[271] W. Zhuang, Y. Ye, Y. Chen, and T. Li, Ensemble clustering for internet security applications, IEEE Transactions on Systems, Man, and Cybernetics, Part C: Applications and Reviews 42 (6) (2012) 1784–1796.

[272] T. Cover, J. Thomas, J. Wiley, *et al.*, Elements of Information Theory, Vol. 6, Wiley Online Library, 1991.

[273] J. Han, and M. Kamber, Data Mining: Concepts and Techniques, Morgan Kaufmann, 2006.

[274] I. Jolliffe, Principal Component Analysis, New York, NY, USA: Springer, 1986.

[275] L. Yu, and H. Liu, Feature selection for high-dimensional data: a fast correlation-based filter solution, in: Proc. of the International Workshop Then Conference Machine Learning, Vol. 20, 2003, pp. 856–863.

[276] M. Dash, and H. Liu, Consistency-based search in feature selection, Journal of Artificial Intelligence 151 (1–2) (2003) 155–176.

[277] M. Dash, and H. Liu, Feature selection for classification, Intelligent Data Analysis 1 (3) (1997) 131–156.

[278] Y. Wang, F. Makedon, J. Ford, and J. Pearlman, HykGene: a hybrid approach for selecting marker genes for phenotype classification using microarray gene expression data, Bioinformatics 21 (8) (2005) 1530.

[279] Y. Yang, and J. Pedersen, A comparative study on feature selection in text categorization, in: Proc. of the International Workshop Then Conference Machine Learning, 1997, pp. 412–420.

[280] P. Belhumeur, J. Hespanha, and D. Kriegman, Eigenfaces vs. Fisherfaces: recognition using class specific linear projection, IEEE Transactions on Pattern Analysis and Machine Intelligence (PAMMI) 19 (7) (1997) 711–720.

[281] S. Yan, D. Xu, Q. Yang, L. Zhang, X. Tang, and H. Zhang, Multilinear discriminant analysis for face recognition, IEEE Transactions on Image Processing (TIP) 16 (1) (2007) 212–220.

[282] W. Zhang, Z. Lin, and X. Tang, Learning semi-riemannian metrics for semi-supervised feature extraction, IEEE Transactions on Knowledge and Data Engineering (TKDE) 23 (4) (2010) 600–611.

[283] U. Fayyad, and K. Irani, Multi-interval discretization of continuous-valued attributes for classification learning, in: Proc. of the 13th International Joint Conference on Artificial Intelligence (IJCAI), 1993, pp. 1022–1027.

[284] P. Fung, F. Morstatter, and H. Liu, Feature selection strategy in text classi-
       fication, in: Proc. of the Pacific Asia Conference on Knowledge Discovery
       and Data Mining (PAKDD), 2011, pp. 24–27.

[285] I. H. Witten, and E. Frank, Data Mining: Practical Machine Learning Tools
       and Techniques, Morgan Kaufmann, 2005.

[286] P. Somol, and J. Novovicova, Evaluating stability and comparing output of
       feature selectors that optimize feature subset cardinality, IEEE Transactions
       on Pattern Analysis and Machine Intelligence (PAMMI) 32 (11) (2010)
       1921–1939.

[287] M. Mahoney, and P. Chan, An analysis of the 1999 DARPA/Lincoln
       laboratory evaluation data for network anomaly detection, Recent Advances
       in Intrusion Detection, Springer, 2003, pp. 220–237.

[288] F. Silveira, C. Diot, N. Taft, and R. Govindan, ASTUTE: detecting a different
       class of traffic anomalies, ACM SIGCOMM Computer Communication
       Review 40 (4) (2010) 267–278.

[289] R. Kohavi, A study of cross-validation and bootstrap for accuracy estimation
       and model selection, in: Proc. of International Joint Conference on Artificial
       Intelligence, Vol. 14, 1995, pp. 1137–1145.

[290] M. Hall, E. Frank, G. Holmes, B. Pfahringer, P. Reutemann, and I. Witten,
       The WEKA data mining software: an update, ACM SIGKDD Explorations
       Newsletter 11 (1) (2009) 10–18.

[291] MAWI working group traffic archive, [ONLINE]   http://mawi.wide.ad.jp/
       mawi/.

[292] MIT Lincoln Laboratory, 1998 DARPA intrusion detection evaluation data
       set (1999), http://www.ll.mit.edu/IST/ideval/data/1998/.

[293] T.-h. Kim, D. Bhattacharyya, and S. K. Bandyopadhyay, Supervised chro-
       mosome clustering and image classification, Journal of Future Generation
       Computer Systems (FGCS) 27 (4) (2011) 372–376.

[294] E. Xing, M. Jordan, R. Karp, *et al.*, Feature selection for high-dimensional
       genomic microarray data, in: Proc. of the International Workshop Then
       Conference Machine Learning, 2001, pp. 601–608.

[295] G. Qu, S. Hariri, and M. Yousif, A new dependency and correlation analysis
       for features, IEEE Transactions on Knowledge and Data Engineering 17 (9)
       (2005) 1199–1207.

[296] A. J. Ferreira, and M. A. Figueiredo, An unsupervised approach to feature
       discretization and selection, Journal of Pattern Recognition 45 (9) (2012)
       3048–3060.

[297] I. Csiszár, Maxent, mathematics, and information theory, Maximum Entropy
       and Bayesian Methods, Springer, 1996, pp. 35–50.

[298] X. Wu, V. Kumar, J. Ross Quinlan, *et al.*, Top 10 algorithms in data mining,
       Journal of Knowledge and Information Systems 14 (1) (2008) 1–37.

[299] H. Liu, F. Hussain, C. Tan, and M. Dash, Discretization: an enabling
       technique, Journal of Data Mining and Knowledge Discovery 6 (4) (2002)
       393–423.

[300]   J. Dougherty, R. Kohavi, M. Sahami, *et al.*, Supervised and unsupervised discretization of continuous features, in: Proc. of the International Workshop Then Conference Machine Learning, 1995, pp. 194–202.

[301]   D. Fisher, L. Xu, and N. Zard, Ordering effects in clustering, in: Proc. of the 9th International Workshop on Machine Learning, 1992, pp. 163–168.

[302]   M. Hall, and G. Holmes, Benchmarking attribute selection techniques for discrete class data mining, IEEE Transactions on Knowledge and Data Engineering (TKDE) 15 (6) (2003) 1437–1447.

[303]   K. Kira, and L. Rendell, The feature selection problem: traditional methods and a new algorithm, in: Proc. of the National Conference on Artificial Intelligence, John Wiley & Sons Ltd, 1992, pp. 129–129.

[304]   M. Robnik-Šikonja, and I. Kononenko, An adaptation of relief for attribute estimation in regression, in: Proc. of the 14th International Conference Machine Learning (ICML'97), 1997, pp. 296–304.

[305]   R. Rosenfeld, Adaptive statistical language modeling: a maximum entropy approach, Ph.D. thesis, IBM (2005).

[306]   A. Ratnaparkhi, A maximum entropy model for part-of-speech tagging, in: Proc. of the Conference on Empirical Methods in Natural Language Processing, Vol. 1, 1996, pp. 133–142.

[307]   G. Fumera, F. Roli, and A. Serrau, A theoretical analysis of bagging as a linear combination of classifiers, IEEE Transactions on Pattern Analysis and Machine Intelligence (PAMMI) 30 (7) (2008) 1293–1299.

[308]   L. Breiman, Random forests, Machine Learning 45 (1) (2001) 5–32.

[309]   D. Schuschel, and C. Hsu, A weight analysis-based wrapper approach to neural nets feature subset selection, in: Proc. of the 10th IEEE International Conference on Tools with Artificial Intelligence, 2002, pp. 89–96.

[310]   A. Jain, and D. Zongker, Feature selection: evaluation, application, and small sample performance, IEEE Transactions on Pattern Analysis and Machine Intelligence (PAMMI) 19 (2) (1997) 153–158.

[311]   G. John, and P. Langley, Estimating continuous distributions in Bayesian classifiers, in: Proc. of the 11th Conference on Uncertainty in Artificial Intelligence, Vol. 1, 1995, pp. 338–345.

[312]   J. Quinlan, Induction of decision trees, Journal on Machine Learning 1 (1) (1986) 81–106.

[313]   B. Boser, I. Guyon, and V. Vapnik, A training algorithm for optimal margin classifiers, in: Proc. of the 5th ACM Annual Workshop on Computational Learning Theory, 1992, pp. 144–152.

[314]   C. Cortes, and V. Vapnik, Support-vector networks, Journal on Machine learning 20 (3) (1995) 273–297.

[315]   V. Vapnik, The Nature of Statistical Learning Theory, Springer Verlag, 2000.

[316]   B. Kahle, and B. Gilliat, Alexa the web information company, http://www.alexa.com/. (January 2009).

[317]   P. R. Clearinghouse, A chronology of data breaches, http://www.privacyrights.org/ar/ChronDataBreaches.htm. (January 2009).

[318]   Y. Zhang, L. Wang, W. Sun, R. Green, and M. Alam, Distributed intrusion detection system in a multi-layer network architecture of smart grids, IEEE Transactions on Smart Grid 2 (4) (2011) 796–808.

[319]   O. Linda, T. Vollmer, and M. Manic, Neural network based intrusion detection system for critical infrastructures, in: Proc. of the International Joint Conference on Neural Networks (IJCNN), 2009, pp. 1827–1834.

[320]   C.-H. Tsang, and S. Kwong, Multi-agent intrusion detection system in industrial network using ant colony clustering approach and unsupervised feature extraction, in: IEEE International Conference on Industrial Technology, 2005, pp. 51–56.

[321]   K. Kim, G. Parthasarathy, O. Uluyol, W. Foslien, S. Sheng, and P. Fleming, Use of SCADA Data for Failure Detection in Wind Turbines, National Renewable Energy Laboratory, 2011.

[322]   H. Tze-Haw, S. Xingxing, and H. M. Lin, Optimized data acquisition by time series clustering in OPC in: Proc. of the 6th IEEE Conference on Industrial Electronics and Applications (ICIEA), 2011, pp. 2486–2492.

[323]   C. Alcaraz, G. Fernandez, and F. Carvajal, Security aspects of SCADA and DCS environments, in: J. Lopez, R. Setola, S.D. Wolthusen (eds), Critical Infrastructure Protection (2012) 120–149.

[324]   M. Lisovich, D. Mulligan, and S. Wicker, Inferring personal information from demand-response systems, IEEE Security & Privacy 8 (1) (2010) 11–20.

[325]   J. Zhong, V. Mirchandani, P. Bertok, and J. Harland, μ-fractal based data perturbation algorithm for privacy protection, in: Proc. of the Pacific Asia Conference on Information Systems, 2012.

[326]   M. Anderberg, Cluster analysis for applications, Tech. rep., DTIC Document (1973).

[327]   J. Gower, and G. Ross, Minimum spanning trees and single linkage cluster analysis, Applied Statistics 78 (9) (1969) 54–64.

[328]   P. Sneath, and R. Sokal, Numerical Taxonomy. the Principles and Practice of Numerical Classification, W. H. Freeman and Co., 1973.

[329]   G. Stegmayer, D. Milone, L. Kamenetzky, M. López, and F. Carrari, A biologically inspired validity measure for comparison of clustering methods over metabolic data sets, IEEE/ACM Transactions on Computational Biology and Bioinformatics 9 (3) (2012) 706–716.

[330]   S. Boriah, V. Chandola, and V. Kumar, Similarity measures for categorical data: a comparative evaluation, in: Proc. of the 8th SIAM International Conference on Data Mining, 2010, pp. 243–254.

[331]   H. Cramér, The Elements of Probability Theory and Some of Its Applications, John Wiley and Sons, 1955.

[332]   K. Maung, Measurement of association in a contingency table with special reference to the pigmentation of hair and eye colours of Scottish school children, Annals of Human Genetics 11 (1) (1941) 189–223.

[333]   K. Pearson, On the general theory of multiple contingency with special reference to partial contingency, Biometrika 11 (3) (1916) 145–158.

[334]   C. Stanfill, and D. Waltz, Toward memory-based reasoning, Communications of the ACM 29 (12) (1986) 1213–1228.

[335]   J. Wang, D. Miller, and G. Kesidis, Efficient mining of the multidimensional traffic cluster hierarchy for digesting, visualization, and anomaly identification, IEEE Journal of Selected Areas in Communications (JSAC) 24 (10) (2006) 1929–1941.

[336]   S. East, J. Butts, M. Papa, and S. Shenoi, A taxonomy of attacks on the DNP3 protocol, in: Proc. of 3rd Annual IFIP International Conference on Critical Infrastructure Protection, (2009), pp. 67–81.

[337]   Witte Software, ModBus/TCP simulator, http://www.modbustools. com;[Date last accessed: 15.08.2013] (2011).

[338]   Modbus-IDA, Modbus messaging on TCP/IP implementation guide v1.0a. http://www.modbus.org/specs.php; 2013 [Date last accessed: 15.03.2013].

[339]   A. Lewis, The EPANET programmers' toolkit for analysis of water distribution systems, http://www.epa.gov/nrmrl/wswrd/dw/epanet.html (1999).

[340]   Melbourne Water, Daily residential water use for Melbourne, http://www.melbournewater.com.au (July 2012).

[341]   R. Lippmann, D. Fried, I. Graf, *et al.*, Evaluating intrusion detection systems: the 1998 DARPA off-line intrusion detection evaluation, in: Proc. of the DARPA IEEE Information Survivability Conference and Exposition, Vol. 2, 2000, pp. 12–26.

[342]   P. Huitsing, R. Chandia, M. Papa, and S. Shenoi, Attack taxonomies for the Modbus protocols, Journal of Critical Infrastructure Protection 1 (2008) 37–44.

[343]   S. Pal, and S. Mitra, Multilayer perceptron, fuzzy sets, and classification, IEEE Transactions on Neural Networks 3 (5) (1992) 683–697.

[344]   S. Oliveira, and O. Zaiane, Privacy preserving clustering by data transformation, in: Proc. of the 18th Brazilian Symposium on Databases, 2003, pp. 304–318.

[345]   M. Friedman, A comparison of alternative tests of significance for the problem of m rankings, The Annals of Mathematical Statistics 11 (1) (1940) 86–92.

[346]   M. Hollander, D. A. Wolfe, and E. Chicken, Nonparametric Statistical Methods, Vol. 751, John Wiley & Sons, 2013.

[347]   D. Newman, The distribution of range in samples from a normal population, expressed in terms of an independent estimate of standard deviation, Biometrika 31 (1–2) (1939) 20–30.

[348]   A. L. Fred, and A. K. Jain, Combining multiple clusterings using evidence accumulation, IEEE Transactions on Pattern Analysis and Machine Intelligence (PAMMI) 27 (6) (2005) 835–850.

[349]   P. K. Mallapragada, R. Jin, A. K. Jain, and Y. Liu, SemiBoost: boosting for semi-supervised learning, IEEE Transactions on Pattern Analysis and Machine Intelligence (PAMMI) 31 (11) (2009) 2000–2014.

[350]   J. Gao, F. Liang, W. Fan, Y. Sun, and J. Han, A graph-based consensus maximization approach for combining multiple supervised and unsupervised

models, IEEE Transactions on Knowledge and Data Engineering (TKDE) 25 (1) (2013) 15–28.

[351] J. L. Rrushi, C. Bellettini, and E. Damiani, Composite intrusion detection in process control networks, Ph.D. thesis, University of Milano (April 2009).

[352] L. Portnoy, E. Eskin, and S. Stolfo, Intrusion detection with unlabeled data using clustering, in: Proc. of the ACM CSS Workshop on Data Mining Applied to Security (DMSA), 2001, pp. 5–8.

[353] Z. Wang, and S. Chen, Multi-view kernel machine on single-view data, Journal on Neurocomputing 72 (10) (2009) 2444–2449.

[354] I. Muslea, S. Minton, and C. A. Knoblock, Active+ semi-supervised learning= robust multi-view learning, in: Proc. of the 19th International Conference on Machine Learning (ICML), Vol. 2, 2002, pp. 435–442.

[355] L. Van der Maaten, E. Postma, and H. Van Den Herik, Dimensionality reduction: a comparative review, Journal of Machine Learning Research 10 (2009) 1–41.

[356] L. Teng, H. Li, X. Fu, W. Chen, and I.-F. Shen, Dimension reduction of microarray data based on local tangent space alignment, in: Proc. of the IEEE 4th Conference on Cognitive Informatics (ICCI), 2005, pp. 154–159.

[357] J. Bourgain, On lipschitz embedding of finite metric spaces in Hilbert space, Journal of Israel Journal of Mathematics 52 (1–2) (1985) 46–52.

[358] J. Shawe-Taylor, and N. Cristianini, Kernel Methods for Pattern Analysis, Cambridge University Press, 2004.

[359] E. W. Dijkstra, A note on two problems in connexion with graphs, Journal of Numerische Mathematik 1 (1) (1959) 269–271.

[360] A. Almalawi, Z. Tari, I. Khalil, and A. Fahad, SCADAVT-A framework for SCADA security testbed based on virtualization technology, in: Proc. of the 38th IEEE Conference on Local Computer Networks (LCN), 2013, pp. 639–646.

[361] J. A. Hartigan, and M. A. Wong, Algorithm as 136: a k-means clustering algorithm, JSTOR Journal of the Royal Statistical Society. Series C (Applied Statistics) 28 (1) (1979) 100–108.

[362] M.-C. Su, and C.-H. Chou, A modified version of the k-means algorithm with a distance based on cluster symmetry, IEEE Transactions on Pattern Analysis and Machine Intelligence (PAMMI) 23 (6) (2001) 674–680.

[363] M.-C. Su, and C.-H. Chou, A k-means algorithm with a novel non-metric distance, in: Proc. of the Joint Conference of Information Science, Association for Intelligent Machinery, Atlantic City, US, 2000, pp. 417–420.

[364] G. Li, K. Chang, and S. Hoi, Multi-view semi-supervised learning with consensus, IEEE Transactions on Knowledge and Data Engineering (TKDE) 24 (11) (2012) 2040–2051.

[365] Z.-H. Zhou, and M. Li, Semi-supervised regression with co-training style algorithms, IEEE Transactions on Knowledge and Data Engineering (TKDE) 19 (11) (2007) 1479–1493.

[366] N. Iam-On, T. Boongeon, S. Garrett, and C. Price, A link-based cluster ensemble approach for categorical data clustering, IEEE Transactions on Knowledge and Data Engineering (TKDE) 24 (3) (2012) 413–425.

[367] A. Strehl, and J. Ghosh, Cluster ensembles—a knowledge reuse framework for combining multiple partitions, The Journal of Machine Learning Research 3 (2003) 583–617.

[368] H. Ayad, and M. Kamel, Cumulative voting consensus method for partitions with variable number of clusters, IEEE Transactions on Pattern Analysis and Machine Intelligence (PAMMI) 30 (1) (2008) 160–173.

[369] S. Vega-Pons, and J. Ruiz-Shulcloper, A survey of clustering ensemble algorithms, International Journal of Pattern Recognition and Artificial Intelligence 25 (03) (2011) 337–372.

[370] G. Karypis, and V. Kumar, Parallel multilevel series k-way partitioning scheme for irregular graphs, SIAM Review 41 (2) (1999) 278–300.

[371] M. M. Masud, Q. Chen, L. Khan, *et al.*, Classification and adaptive novel class detection of feature-evolving data streams, IEEE Transactions on Knowledge and Data Engineering (TKDE) 25 (7) (2013) 1484–1497.

[372] R. Collobert, F. Sinz, J. Weston, and L. Bottou, Large scale transductive SVMs, The Journal of Machine Learning Research 7 (2006) 1687–1712.

[373] S. García, A. Fernández, J. Luengo, and F. Herrera, Advanced nonparametric tests for multiple comparisons in the design of experiments in computational intelligence and data mining: experimental analysis of power, Journal of Information Sciences 180 (10) (2010) 2044–2064.

[374] A. Moore, and K. Papagiannaki, Toward the accurate identification of network applications, Springer Journal of Passive and Active Network Measurement (2005) 41–54.

[375] J. Zhang, C. Chen, Y. Xiang, and W. Zhou, Internet traffic classification by aggregating correlated naive Bayes predictions, IEEE Transactions on Information Forensics and Security 8 (1) (2013) 5–15.

[376] D. R. Miller, T. Leek, and R. M. Schwartz, A hidden Markov model information retrieval system, in: Proc. of the 22nd ACM Conference on Research and Development in Information Retrieval (SIGIR), 1999, pp. 214–221.

[377] S. Li, H. Wu, D. Wan, and J. Zhu, An effective feature selection method for hyperspectral image classification based on genetic algorithm and support vector machine, Journal of Knowledge-based Systems 24 (1) (2011) 40–48.

[378] A. McGregor, M. Hall, P. Lorier, and J. Brunskill, Flow clustering using machine learning techniques, in: Proc. of the 5th International Workshop on Passive and Active Network Measurement (PAM), 2004, pp. 205–214.

[379] A. McGregor, M. Hall, P. Lorier, and J. Brunskill, Flow clustering using machine learning techniques, Passive and Active Network Measurement, Springer, 2004, pp. 205–214.

[380] I. Kononenko, Estimating attributes: analysis and extensions of relief, Machine Learning: ECML-94, Springer, 1994, pp. 171–182.

[381]   S. Zander, T. Nguyen, and G. Armitage, Automated traffic classification and application identification using machine learning, in: Proc. of 30th IEEE Conference on Local Computer Networks (LCN), 2005, pp. 250–257.

[382]   R. Kohavi, and G. John, Wrappers for feature subset selection, Journal of Artificial Intelligence 97 (1–2) (1997) 273–324.

[383]   T. Auld, A. Moore, and S. Gull, Bayesian neural networks for internet traffic classification, IEEE Transactions on Neural Networks 18 (1) (2007) 223–239.

[384]   L. Khan, M. Awad, and B. Thuraisingham, A new intrusion detection system using support vector machines and hierarchical clustering, Journal of Very Large Data Bases (VLDB) 16 (4) (2007) 507–521.

[385]   D. Bouchaffra, Conformation-based hidden Markov models: application to human face identification, IEEE Transactions on Neural Networks 21 (4) (2010) 595–608.

[386]   W. M. Shaw Jr, On the foundation of evaluation, Journal of the American Society for Information Science 37 (5) (1986) 346–348.

[387]   Y. Xu, J.-Y. Yang and J.-F. Lu, An efficient kernel-based nonlinear regression method for two-class classification, in: Proc. of International Conference on Machine Learning and Cybernetics, 2005, vol. 7, pp. 4442–4445.

Index